Succession Law

in

Ireland

*For Sinead, Damian
and Imogen*

Succession Law

in

Ireland

by

James C. Brady

B.C.L., LL.B. (N.U.I.), Ph.D. (Q.U.B.),
Professor of the Law of Property and Equity,
Former Dean of the Faculty of Law, University College Dublin

with a
FOREWORD
by
The Hon. Mr. Justice Thomas A. Finlay
Chief Justice of Ireland

Butterworth (Ireland) Limited
Dublin
1989

Ireland	Butterworth (Ireland) Ltd DUBLIN
Australia	Butterworths Pty Ltd, SYDNEY, MELBOURNE, BRISBANE, ADELAIDE, PERTH, CANBERRA and HOBART
Canada	Butterworths Canada Ltd, TORONTO and VANCOUVER
Malaysia	Malayan Law Journal Sdn Bhd, KUALA LUMPUR
New Zealand	Butterworths of New Zealand Ltd, WELLINGTON and AUCKLAND
Singapore	Butterworth & Co (Asia) Pte Ltd, SINGAPORE
United Kingdom	Butterworth & Co (Publishers) Ltd, 88 Kingsway, LONDON WC2B 6AB and 4, Hill Street, EDINBURGH EH2 3JZ
USA	Butterworths Legal Publishers, ST PAUL, Minnesota, SEATTLE, Washington, BOSTON, Massachusetts, AUSTIN, Texas and D & S Publishers, CLEARWATER, Florida

First Published 1989

A CIP catalogue record for this book is available from the British Library

© Butterworth (Ireland) Ltd

ISBN Hardback 1 85475 100 X

Typeset by Turnergraphic Ltd, Winchester Road, Basingstoke
Printed and bound in Great Britain by Hartnoll, Bodmin, Cornwall

Foreword

One of the most rewarding and encouraging features of the last decade or so in the administration of justice in Ireland has been the very substantial increase in the number of textbooks on Irish law published and made available to both students and practitioners. This increase in numbers has almost exclusively occurred without any fall in quality. It has been the product of the research and scholarship of both practitioners and academic lawyers.

It gives me both a general and a very special pleasure, therefore, to welcome and confidently to recommend this book which has been written by Professor James C. Brady, one of our most distinguished academic lawyers.

A book which related to Irish Law on the making of wills has been for a very considerable period desirable but it became a necessity on the passing of the Succession Act 1965.

The contents of this book, however, demonstrate that it was fortunate and wise to delay for a significant period after its passing a treatise on the Succession Act. This delay has permitted the scholarly and wisely critical consideration contained in this book of the decisions of the Courts on the provisions of the Succession Act 1965 and, in particular, on its relationship to the constitutional position of the family in our law.

I have absolutely no doubt that this book will be welcomed as an intensely useful tool in the hands of lawyers be they practitioners, judges or academic lawyers. The considerations contained in the chapter on the Freedom of Testation would of themselves justify the publication of the book. They are, however, by no means the only, though they may be one of the most valuable important contributions contained in it to our knowledge of the law.

I have no doubt that the book will receive the welcome to which it is entitled and those concerned with the administration of justice and development of law in this country owe a debt to Professor Brady,

Thomas A. Finlay
Chief Justice of Ireland,
Four Courts,
Dublin 7

Preface

This book is essentially about the making of wills and their construction by the courts, and the rules governing the disposition of a deceased person's property when he has failed to make a will and dies intestate. It doesn't purport to be a book on probate practice though it touches on some aspects of that practice. Nor does it deal with the will as an instrument of tax planning or as a tax avoidance mechanism. Such matters are no doubt of considerable importance to the legal practitioner and his client but they merit a detailed and specialist treatment which is outside the ambit of a general book like this on the law of succession.

For approximately 130 years the Wills Act, 1837, which was enacted during a notable period of statutory law reform in England, governed the law relating to wills in Ireland and in England. This coincidence of Irish and English law meant that Irish lawyers were relatively free to consult English textbooks and militated against the development of an indigenous Irish literature on the law of succession. Irish independence was to have little effect on the reliance by Irish lawyers on English textbooks and such remained the case until the nineteen sixties when a period of statutory law reform in Ireland, which was comparable in many respects to that in England in the eighteen thirties, saw Irish law loosened if not altogether detached from its English roots.

One of the most significant measures enacted during that period was the Succession Act, 1965, which sought, *inter alia*, to make the Irish law of succession more consistent with, and reflective of, the mores and aspirations of the Irish people and more particularly those set out in the Constitution of 1937. To that end the Succession Act introduced certain novel features into the law of succession some of which were borrowed from the Civilian systems of mainland Europe. Now that more than twenty years have elapsed since the coming into force of the Succession Act on 1 January 1967, it is time to measure the success of these statutory innovations.

Not the least significant of these statutory changes was the diminution of the principle of freedom of testation, which was perceived as a peculiarly English phenomenon which was inconsistent with the place of the family in Irish life. A possible consequence of the conferring of a legal right share in the deceased's estate on his surviving spouse, and the conferring on children of a right to apply to court to have proper provision made for them out of the deceased's estate, will be that the Irish courts will prove to be more amenable to the substantial compliance doctrine which has seen American courts admit to probate wills which fail to satisfy certain technical requirements of the Wills legislation. It is arguable that the insistence by the Irish and English courts on a strict compliance with the legislation governing the execution of wills owed much to the unspoken belief that the intestacy rules effected a fairer distribution of a deceased's property. The wheel has turned full circle in Ireland and the Irish courts have a measure of discretion in respect of testate succession which is denied to them when a deceased person dies intestate.

Despite these important policy shifts and changes the fact that the Succession Act substantially re-enacts many of the provisions governing the execution of wills which were contained in the Wills Act, 1837 is reflected in the many footnotes and other references to English case law and materials contained in this book. Such references also owe much to the fact that the Wills Act, 1837, is still the dominant legislation in Northern Ireland.

Debts of gratitude are owed to a number of people for their help and encouragement to me in the writing of this book, but responsibility for any errors contained herein is mine alone. Particular thanks are due to my colleague Tony Kerr not least for his many useful case references, and to Tony Eklof of the Law Library at University College Dublin for his willingness to accommodate my constant and occasionally excessive demands for library materials. My thanks are also owed to Mrs Eileen Dawson of University College for her unfailing courtesy to me and her skill in translating pages of holograph material into superb typescript. I am also profoundly grateful to my wife Joan whose constant support and encouragement lightened the labour involved in writing this book and whose faith in the successful outcome of the venture never wavered.

James C. Brady
Professor of Property and Equity
University College Dublin

Contents

Table of Statutes

Table of Statutory Instruments

Table of Cases

[C]

[D]

[G]

[H]

[I]

[J]

[K]

[L]

[M]

[R]

[S]

[T]

[U]

[V]

[W]

[Y]

[Z]

Chapter 1
THE NATURE OF A WILL

1.1 Introduction

1.1.1 The word "will" is used to describe the document or documents, in which a person called the testator or testatrix, according to gender, sets out his or her wishes in relation to certain matters, which are to take effect on his or her death. Throughout this book references are confined, unless the facts of particular cases dictate otherwise, to the making of wills by testators, but this is done in the cause of brevity and has no other significance. References to a testator accordingly apply, *mutatis mutandi*, to a testatrix.

1.1.2 The making of a will is not confined, as we shall see, to the disposition of the testator's property on his death, but this is the most important and common purpose for making a will, and is how the lay person popularly perceives its function.[1] That being so this book is primarily, though not exclusively, concerned with the disposition of a testator's property on death.

1.1.3 It is said that a person may leave only one effective will but this does not mean, as might be popularly assumed, that a testator is limited to the making of a single testamentary document. This is not so, and a will may consist of a number of such documents, provided that each is executed in accordance with the necessary statutory formalities.[2] It is customary however to speak of the primary and principal testamentary document as the testator's will, and subsequent and additional documents as codicils to the

---

[1] The most obvious other function of a will is the appointment of executors to administer the deceased's estate. For other uses of the will see generally Mellows "The Law of Succession" (4th ed. 1983) at p. 6, 7

[2] For these statutory requirements see *post* pp. 30 *et seq.*

will, but, it is the aggregate or net effect of all such testamentary documents which constitutes the testator's will. It was pointed out by the Privy Council in *Douglas-Menzies* v *Umphelby*[3] that, on a man's death it is the court's task to find out which documents constitute his last will. Thus some extant writing might have been revoked, or be inconsistent with some later writing, in which case it will be discarded, but,

> "all that survive this scrutiny forms part of the ultimate will or effective expression of his wishes about his estate. In this sense it is inaccurate to speak of a man leaving two wills; he does leave, and can leave, but one will."[4]

1.1.4 Apart from its dispositive effect, the salient characteristics of a will are (1) that it does not take effect until the death of the testator, and (2) that it is revocable by the testator at any time before his death.

1.1.5 In so far as a will has no effect until the death of the testator it is said to be ambulatory,[5] which term is also used in the sense that a testator may dispose of property in his will which he does not own at the time of its execution, but which he acquires before his death.[6] This ambulatory nature of the will also means that a testator does not lose control over property which he has disposed of in his will but is free to make subsequent *inter vivos* dispositions of such property. We shall see, however, that if a testator has entered into a binding contract with another that he will not revoke his will in which he has left something to that other, or that he *will* leave some specified property in his will to that other, breach of the testator's contractual obligations may give rise to an action for damages against the deceased's estate or, in appropriate circumstances an action for specific performance against his personal representatives.[7]

1.1.6 Contractual ramifications apart, a will is merely declaratory of a testator's intentions until his death,[8] and a beneficiary runs the risk that the testator will dispose of the property which is the subject matter of his gift in the will before the will takes effect. A beneficiary's interest under a will is also at risk to the possibility that on the testator's death his liabilities and

---

[3] [1908] A.C. 224 See Parry and Clark "The Law of Succession" (8th ed. 1983) at p. 4

[4] See *In b. Wafer* [1960] Ir. Jur. Rep. 19 where a testator had executed two wills both of which were admitted to probate as together constituting the last will of the deceased. See also *In b. McCarthy* [1965] Ir. Jur. Rep. 56 and pp. 89 *et seq.*

[5] There is an exception to the general rule that a will is ineffective until the death of the testator in that if a will revokes a former will the revocation may take effect when the later will is executed. See generally *post* p. 89.

[6] See Mellows "The Law of Succession" at p. 8

[7] See *post* p. 5

[8] See *Re Westminsters Deed of Appointment* [1959] Ch. 265, 271

debts will exceed the value of his assets, and the property which is left to the beneficiary might have to be sold by the deceased's personal representatives to pay off his creditors.[9]

1.1.7 Not every document which takes effect on death is a will, but it is the case that such a document, if otherwise executed in conformity with the statutory formalities for wills, may be admitted to probate, although the person making it did not refer to it as a will, or think about it in those terms.[10] Thus Sir James Hannen P. pointed out in *Milnes* v *Foden*[11] that "it is not necessary that the testator should intend to perform or be aware that he has performed a testamentary act". He went on to say, that it is enough if there is proof, either in the document itself, or from clear evidence *dehors* the document, that it was the writer's intention to convey the benefits which would be conveyed by it, if considered as a will, and that death would be the event which would give effect to it. Of course such document would also have had to be properly executed.

1.1.8 Clearly an *inter vivos* disposition by deed, which usually takes effect forthwith, is quite unlike a will which takes effect on death. Such a disposition may, however, be made conditional on the happening of a certain event and, if that certain event is the death of the grantor, the deed, if otherwise properly executed, will be admitted to probate. Such was the outcome in the celebrated English case *In the Goods of Morgan*[12] where the deceased had executed three deeds of gift, by which property was given to trustees to be held for the benefit of his children. Each of the deeds contained a clause that it was not to take effect until the death of the grantor and, having been signed and witnessed in accordance with the formalities necessary for the execution of wills, they were admitted to probate as together representing the will of the deceased.

1.1.9 Since it is an essential characteristic of a will that it is revocable prior to death, a declaration in a will that it is irrevocable does not make it so.[13] Indeed, to permit an action to be brought for breach of contract not to revoke a will, is clearly at odds with the principle of revocability, but the courts have managed to square the circle by admitting to probate the last valid will of the deceased, whether or not it conforms with the deceased's contractual obligations, and by giving effect to those contractual obligations

[9] See *post* p. 279
[10] See *post* p. 32
[11] (1890) 15 P.D. 105
[12] (1866) L.R. 1 P.D. 214
[13] *Vynior's Case* (1609) 8 Co. Rep. 81b *In b. Heys* [1914] P. 192

outside the will. [14] The courts have likewise permitted actions for breach of a contract to make a will, or leave specified property in a will, which contracts sit uneasily with the principle of freedom of testation, for so long a cornerstone of our succession law.[15] Be that as it may, if a deceased testator has entered into a valid contract with another person, that he will make a will in that other's favour, and he fails to do so, that other person may proceed against the deceased's estate.

1.1.10 It is often the case, however, that the promise made by a testator falls short of a binding contract. This may happen in domestic family situations where, for example, a daughter has given up her career to return home and care for an elderly and ailing parent.[16] The daughter may have done this on the implicit ground that she would receive certain testamentary gifts in return for her services, or she may have been led by oral statements, or even the demeanour of the deceased, to expect such gifts. If such gifts do not materialise the equitable doctrine of part performance[17] may be available in such a situation to enable the daughter to have an alleged contract enforced, but, failing that, other recent developments in equity jurisdiction might be called in aid by the daughter.

1.1.11 If such daughter can establish that she was led by the deceased, either explicitly or implicitly, to expect a testamentary gift in return for her services, then she may invoke the burgeoning doctrine of estoppel, and more particularly the doctrine of estoppel by encouragement or acquiescence, in support of her claim.[18] It is now arguably the case, that it will not be necessary for the claimant daughter to show that she has acted to her detriment on the basis of her expectation, and it will suffice if she can show that she has simply altered her position in some way.[19] There is also now the possibility that the court will employ the constructive trust as a long stop in achieving an equitable result in the circumstances of the particular case. There is growing evidence to suggest that the Irish and English courts are prepared to use the constructive trust as a remedial device in the

[14] See Mellows "The Law of Succession" at pp. 13 *et seq* and Lee "Contracts to make wills" (1971) 87 Law Quarterly Review 358

[15] See *Synge* v *Synge* [1894] 1 Q.B. 466 and *Schaefer* v *Schuman* [1972] A.C. 572. On the principle of freedom of testation see post pp. 183 *et seq.*

[16] See *Re Gavin* [1979] Ch. 16 where such a daughter was not allowed to rely on the principle in *Strong* v *Bird* (1874) L.R. 18 Eq. 315 to retain the house in which she had cared for an elderly parent. See post pp. 13 *et seq.*

[17] On the doctrine of part performance see Keane "Equity and the Law of Trusts in the Republic of Ireland" (1988) at pp. 250 *et seq* and Hanbury and Maudsley "Modern Equity" (12th ed. by Jill E. Martin, 1985) at pp. 665 *et seq.*

[18] See Hanbury and Maudsley "Modern Equity" at pp. 855 *et seq* and Snell's "Principles of Equity" (28th ed. 1982) at pp. 558 *et seq.*

[19] See *Greasley* v *Cooke* [1980] 1 W.L.R. 1306

American sense, and this development would also offer some hope of equitable redress to a claimant in the position of our dutiful, albeit legally naive, daughter.[20]

1.2 Mutual Wills

1.2.1 The constructive trust is also employed by the courts in relation to so-called mutual wills, which arise when two people, usually husband and wife, make wills, under each of which, property is left to the survivor of them, with remainders to named beneficiaries, usually their children.[21] Since the essence of a mutual will is that it is made in pursuance of an agreement that it shall not be revoked without the prior consent of the other party, it is at odds with the cardinal principle that wills are always revocable before death.

1.2.2 As with a contract not to revoke a will, which we dealt with earlier,[22] the courts take the view that the will made in consequence of such an agreement remains revocable, but, if the first of the two parties to die does so, having relied on the other party to adhere to the agreement on the making of mutual wills, the courts will impose a trust in favour of the intended beneficiaries of the mutual wills, which will be enforceable against the estate of the survivor.[23]

1.2.3 There is an absolute dearth of Irish case law on the subject of mutual wills.[24] There is no reason however to suppose that the making of mutual wills is uncommon in Ireland, or, that such wills having been agreed, Irish testators are more honourable than their English counterparts. The reason offered by an English textwriter[25] for the relative dearth of English case law on the subject of mutual wills is, no doubt, equally applicable in Ireland. That reason is, that many wills simply contain no mention of the prior agreement to make mutual wills and it "may well be that the comparative dearth of reported cases on mutual wills is due to the fact that in many cases an unrecited agreement has gone unnoticed".[26] Prudence would

---

[20] On the constructive trust of a "new model" (to use Lord Denning's term in *Eves* v *Eves* [1973] 1 W.L.R. 1388) see Hanbury and Maudsley "Modern Equity" at pp. 328 *et seq* and Keane "Equity and the Law of Trusts in the Republic of Ireland" (1988) at pp. 186 *et seq*.

[21] See Mitchell "Some Aspects of Mutual Wills" (1951) M.L.R. 136; Burgess "A Fresh Look at Mutual Wills" (1970) 34 Conv. 230; Youdan "The Mutual Wills Doctrine" (1979) 29 U. of Toronto L.J. 390

[22] See *ante* p. 3

[23] See Hanbury and Maudsley "Modern Equity" at p. 319

[24] See Wylie "Irish Land Law" (2nd ed. 1986) at p. 487

[25] Mellows "The Law of Succession" at p. 25

[26] *Ibid*

therefore dictate that, a prior agreement not to revoke a will unilaterally, should be recited in the will itself.[27]

1.2.4 In the absence of Irish authority we must turn to English case law for guidance on the resolution of problems arising from mutual wills, and, particularly, problems arising from the imposition by the court of a trust, to give effect to an agreement not to revoke such a will unilaterally. No question of a trust arises however, when one party to an agreement to make mutual wills alters his will unilaterally during the lifetime of the other party, who is then released from his obligation under the agreement, and may sue the guilty party for breach of contract.[28] That being so, a trust, in practical terms, will only arise when the first of the parties to an agreement to make mutual wills dies, and the survivor acts in breach of the agreement. Lord Camden said in the leading English case *Dufour* v *Pereira*[29] that, when one party to an agreement to make mutual wills dies, having put his part of the agreement into execution, and the other party then refuses

"he is guilty of a fraud, can never unbind himself, and becomes a trustee of course. For no man shall deceive another to his prejudice. By engaging to do something that is in his power, he is made a trustee for the performance, and transmits that trust to those that claim under him."

1.2.5 Two main questions and one rather academic question arise in relation to the trust which is found by the courts in cases of mutual wills. The main questions are (1) When does the trust arise, and (2) What property is subject to the trust. The other more academic question which arises is what sort of trust is involved in cases of mutual wills? The traditional answer to the latter question is that the trust involved is an implied one which the court imposes, in order to give effect to the intentions of the parties.[30] This is an attractive view since the parties, if they had addressed the possibility of one of them reneging on the agreement would, no doubt, have intended that a trust should attach to the property of the survivor. The more modern view however, is that the trust is more in the nature of a constructive trust which is imposed by the courts to achieve justice in the particular case.[31] Too much can be made of the differences between implied and constructive trusts,[32] and the English

---

[27] See e.g. *Re Hagger* [1930] 2 Ch. 190

[28] There may be a problem in calculating the amount of damages for breach of contract in such a situation. See Mellows "The Law of Succession" at p. 27

[29] (1769), 1 Dick. 419, 420

[30] See Keeton and Sheridan, "Law of Trusts" (11th ed. 1983)

[31] Thus problems posed by mutual wills are dealt with in the context of constructive trusts in Hanbury and Maudsley "Modern Equity" at pp. 319 *et seq.*

[32] The implied trust is said to arise from the implied intention of the parties while a constructive trust has nothing to do with intention but is imposed by the court in the interests of achieving justice *inter partes*

Court of Appeal under Lord Denning's leadership was prepared to run the two together to achieve justice *inter partes* in the particular case.[33]

1.2.6 There are three possible times when the trust may be said to come into being.[34] It could be said to arise when the agreement is entered into, it could be said to arise on the death of the first party, and, thirdly it could be said to arise on the death of the survivor. The first possibility is unlikely, since, as we have seen, a party may revoke a mutual will made in pursuance of an agreement, by giving notice to the other party during their joint lifetimes.[35] It is also said that the death of the survivor cannot be the relevant time, since it has been held that

> "where a beneficiary died between the date of the death of the first to die and the survivor, the estate of that beneficiary was able to claim its share on the ground that the interest was vested and there was no lapse."[36]

A fourth possibility, which has been suggested by some textwriters, is that the trust arises when the survivor receives a benefit under the first will. That date, it is argued, is highly significant if the trust involved is a constructive trust which can be imposed only where the survivor receives a benefit under the first will.[37] It is conceded however that even if the trust arises when the survivor takes a benefit under the first will, the trust may relate back to the death.[38] Common sense and authority combine to confirm that the trust arises on the death of the first party.[39]

1.2.7 The problem then arises as to what property the trust attaches to. In the absence of evidence in the express terms of the will there are a number of possibilities. Firstly, and most obviously, the trust may attach to the property which the survivor receives under the will of the first to die. The trust may also attach to all the property which the survivor owned at the time of the first party's death, or, it may attach to all the property owned by the survivor at the time of his death. The other possibility is that the trust attaches to property which the survivor owned at any time between the time of the first death and his own.

1.2.8 There can be no doubt but that the trust should attach to property which is received by the survivor under the will of the first to die, and this

[33] See e.g. *Hussey* v *Palmer* [1972] 1 W.L.R. 1286

[34] See Mitchell "Some Aspects of Mutual Wills" (1951) 14 Modern Law Review, 136

[35] The giving of notice will preclude the other party from claiming that he acted to his prejudice in making a will in conformity with the agreement which the offending party has broken.

[36] Hanbury and Maudsley "Modern Equity" at pp. 319–20

[37] *Ibid* at p. 320

[38] *Ibid*

[39] See *Re Hagger* [1930] 2 Ch. 190, 195 (per Clauson J.)

indeed provides the rationale for the imposition of a constructive trust on the estate of the survivor. It also seems reasonably clear that the trust should attach to property owned by the survivor at the time of the first party's death, unless there is a contrary intention in the agreement. What is more problematic is whether the trust should attach to all property owned by the survivor at his death, and to all property owned by the survivor at any time between the death of the first party, and his own death.

1.2.9 Again, in the absence of a contrary intention in the agreement, there seems to be no reason in principle why the trust should not attach to all property owned by the survivor at the time of his death. It does, after all, in the absence of a contrary agreement, attach to all property owned by the first party to die at the time of his death, including property acquired by such party between the date of the agreement and his death.[40] The survivor is thus reduced in status to that of a life tenant of his property, being able to enjoy the income thereof but being obliged to leave the capital intact for the ultimate beneficiaries.[41]

1.2.10 The many ramifications which attend the imposition of a trust in cases involving mutual wills, has led certain textwriters to the gloomy conclusion that it "is a clumsy and inadequate way of dealing with a complicated problem".[42] Parties who propose to execute mutual wills are thus well advised to set out clearly, in the agreement relating thereto, the trusts which they wish to govern the property subject to the agreement, and, more particularly, the property which they intend to be so subject. Mere reference in an agreement to the making of mutual wills does not suffice to avoid the many pitfalls which, the case law reveals, lie in wait for the testator who makes his will in a certain way in the expectation that another will do the same.

1.2.11 There is a circumstance in which a will may become irrevocable. Revocation of a will requires, as we shall see, the same degree of mental competency as that required of a testator in the execution of a will and if, after the execution of his will, a testator's mental competency is permanently impaired that will have the effect of making his will irrevocable.[43]

---

[40] The agreement thus acts as a covenant to settle after acquired property. See *Paul* v *Paul* (1882) 20 Ch. D. 742

[41] See *Re Cleaver* [1981] 1 W.L.R. 939 where Nourse J. adopted the somewhat convoluted reasoning in the Australian case *Birmingham* v *Renfrew* (1936) 57 C.L.R. 666

[42] Hanbury and Maudsley "Modern Equity" at p. 322

[43] See *post* p. 93

1.3 Donatio Mortis Causa

1.3.1 A *donatio mortis causa,* which effectively means "a gift in the face of death", lies somewhere between an *inter vivos* gift and a testamentary gift, sharing some of the characteristics of each but also differing from each in important respects. Like an *inter vivos* gift, the subject matter of the gift passes to the donee during the life of the donor, but, unlike an *inter vivos* gift, which usually takes effect forthwith, a *donatio mortis causa* is conditional upon, and takes effect upon, the death of the donor.[44] Thus the subject matter of the gift reverts to the donor if he recovers from the malady which threatened his life at the time of the gift, if the donee predeceases him, or the donor simply decides to revoke the gift before his death. Like a gift under a will, a *donatio mortis causa* takes effect on the death of the donor, but, unlike a testamentary gift, the subject matter of the *donatio,* or control over it, is given to the donee during the donor's life.[45] A *donatio mortis causa* is however, like a testamentary gift, subject to the rules governing satisfaction and ademption.[46]

1.3.2 The *donatio mortis causa* is generally dealt with by textwriters in the context of exceptions to the rule, that equity will not perfect an imperfect gift or assist a volunteer.[47] If the subject-matter of the *donatio* is a chattel the donee's title becomes absolute on the donor's death, without more ado, but, if the subject-matter is a chose in action, the legal title to which, vests in the donor's personal representatives on his death, the donee may call equity to oblige the personal representatives to complete his title.[48]

1.3.3 The three essentials for a valid *donatio mortis causa* were set out by a distinguished Newryman, Lord Russell L.C.J., in *Cain* v *Moon*[49] These are, (a) the gift must have been made in contemplation, though not necessarily in the expectation, of death; (b) the subject-matter of the gift must have been delivered to the donee; (c) the gift must have been made under such circumstances as to show that the property is to revert to the donor if he should recover. Each of these three essentials will be considered in turn.

---

[44] See Keane "Equity and the Law of Trusts in the Republic of Ireland" at pp. 368 *et seq.*; Hanbury and Maudsley "Modern Equity" at pp. 137 *et seq.* and Mellows "The Law of Succession" at pp. 458 *et seq.*

[45] See *post* p. 11

[46] See *Hudson* v *Spencer* [1910] 2 Ch. 285 and Snell's "Principles of Equity" (28th ed.) at p. 382 and generally post pp. 166 *et seq.*

[47] See e.g. Hanbury and Maudsley "Modern Equity" at p. 136, and Snell's "Principles of Equity" (28th ed. 1982) at pp. 377 *et seq.*

[48] *Re Lillingston* [1952] 2 All E.R. 184

[49] [1896] 2 Q.B. 283. See also *Re Mulroy* [1924] 1 I.R. 98

1.3.4 (a) Contemplation of death

It is not enough that the donor was contemplating death in the general sense, that we must all "shake off this mortal coil". The donor must have been contemplating death in a more specific context, and, it is normally the case, that *donationes mortis causa* are made by donors suffering from specific terminal illnesses. A *donatio mortis causa* may also be made when the donor is proposing to embark on a particularly hazardous journey, but there is some Canadian authority to the effect that regular air travel does not qualify as hazardous in this sense.[50]

1.3.5 If a donor makes a *donatio mortis causa* in contemplation of death from a particular illness, and dies from some other ailment, this does not invalidate the *donatio*.[51] A gift made in contemplation of suicide however will not constitute a valid *donatio mortis causa*.

1.3.6 Gavan Duffy P. had to consider the effect of the donor's suicide on the validity of a *donatio mortis causa* in the somewhat unusual fact situation in *Mills v Shields and Kelly*.[53] There one Alfred Mills, while suffering from a neurosis as to the state of his health, and, while contemplating a journey to Dublin for medical treatment, which treatment he believed would involve some danger to his life, deposited, *inter alia*, a parcel of currency notes with a priest. He asked the priest to give the parcel to his brother, Ernest, who was resident in South Africa, should anything happen to him while he was away in Dublin.

1.3.7 Alfred Mills, having set out for Dublin some three weeks later, left the train at a stop en route, and took his own life by hanging. Gavan Duffy P. found, nevertheless, that the deceased had made a valid *donatio mortis causa* of the currency notes. The learned President was able to distinguish *Agnew v Belfast Banking Co.*[54] in holding that the *donatio* was not invalidated by the death of the donor from a cause other than that apparently contemplated by the donor, nor, by the mere possibility that the donor contemplated being overcome by an irresistible impulse to commit suicide.[55]

---

[50] See *Thompson v Mechan* [1958] O.R. 357 cited in Hanbury and Maudsley "Modern Equity" at p. 138 n. 70

[51] See e.g. *Wilkes v Allington* [1931] 2 Ch. 104 where a donor knowing that he suffered from an incurable illness made a *donatio* and died two months later of pneumonia, the *donatio* remained valid.

[52] *Agnew v Belfast Banking Co.* [1896] 2 I.R. 204; *Re Dudman* [1925] 1 Ch. 553

[53] [1948] I.R. 367

[54] [1896] 2 I.R. 204

[55] [1948] I.R. 367, 370

1.3.8 The invalidity of a *donatio mortis causa* made in contemplation of suicide is based on sound policy reasons, and it is interesting to note that English textwriters do not consider that the position has altered now that suicide is no longer a crime in England, since the Suicide Act 1961.[56]

1.3.9 (b) Delivery of subject-matter

Delivery of the subject-matter of the gift must be made to the donee, with the intention that the donor thereby relinquishes dominion over the property. It is not sufficient that property is handed over to the donee merely for safe-keeping, but, the donee may permit retention of the property by the donor after initial delivery, provided that the donor's retention is in the nature of custodianship only.[57]

1.3.10 In the case of chattels, the matter of delivery is relatively straightforward, the donor may either hand over the chattels to the donee, or make a symbolic delivery of them by handing over to the donee a key to a box in which they are kept.[57a] Delivery may also be to an agent of the donee, and, in *Mills* v *Shields and Kelly* Gavan Duffy P. held that the delivery was valid despite being made, not to an agent of the donee, but to the donor's own agent, the latter holding the property on trust for the donee.[58]

1.3.11 The delivery of choses in action, where title does not pass to the donee merely by the handing over of a document, is more problematic. Thus in the case of Alfred Mills, the deceased had also given to the priest a number of certificates of stocks and shares, and the question arose as to whether simple delivery of these choses in action was sufficient. In *Mills* v *Shields and Kelly* (No. 2)[59] Gavan Duffy P. held that certificates of shares of public companies registered in Ireland, and certificates of shares of public companies registered in England, and Post Office Savings certificates, were not documents of such a nature that delivery thereof could constitute a valid *donatio mortis causa*, since such certificates contained insufficient indicia of the terms of the contract under which they were held. Gavan Duffy P. found support for that view in *Delgoffe* v *Fader*[60] and *Duckworth*

[56] See Hanbury and Maudsley "Modern Equity" at p. 138 n. 72 and Snell's "Principles of Equity" at p. 378 n. 12

[57] See *Re Mulroy* [1924] 1 I.R. 98

[57a] *Re Wasserberg* [1915] 1 Ch. 195; *Re Cole* [1964] Ch. 175. It may not suffice however to hand over a key if the donor retains a duplicate key; see *Re Craven's Estate* [1927] Ch. 423 at p. 427

[58] In this respect Gavan Duffy P. followed *Re Korvine's Trust* [1921] 1 Ch. 343

[59] [1950] I.R. 21

[60] [1939] Ch. 922 followed also by Gavan Duffy P. in *Re Foran Decd.* (1950) 84 I.L.T.R. 187

v *Lee*[61]; in the latter, an attempt to affirm delivery of an I.O.U. as a valid *donatio mortis causa* failed on the ground that the document was a mere memorandum, and imperfect at that, since it omitted to mention the interest which the debtor had to pay.

1.3.12 Dicta in *Delgoffe* v *Fader* upon which Gavan Duffy P. had relied in *Mills* v *Shields and Kelly* (No. 2), and similar dicta by Byrne J. in *Re Weston*,[62] were disapproved of in *Birch* v *Treasury Solicitor*[63] where the Court of Appeal held, that it is enough that the donor hand over such documents which constitute the essential indicia or evidence of title, possession of, or production of which, would entitle the possessor to the money or property purported to be given. It is difficult to defend the stricter approach taken by Gavan Duffy P. in the light of recent English developments, and it is interesting that a recent eminent Irish textwriter compares unfavourably Gavan Duffy P.'s approach, with the so-called "necessity of production" text adopted recently by the Australian courts.[64] The same textwriter concludes "that *Mills* v *Shield* (sic) would not necessarily be followed today".[65]

1.3.13 Although, as we have seen, a *donatio mortis causa* is conditional upon the donor's death, until which time it is revocable, and is automatically revoked if the donor recovers from his life-threatening illness, the donor cannot revoke a *donatio* in his will. This is so because the donee's title is complete before the will takes effect.[66]

1.3.14 (c) Gift must be conditional on death

In order to constitute a *donatio mortis causa* the donor must have intended the gift to be conditional on his death, and revocable in the event of his recovery. In the absence of such condition, a gift may still take effect as an ordinary *inter vivos* gift if it otherwise complies with the formalities for such gifts.[67] Although the *donatio mortis causa* is conditional on a future event, viz. the death of the donor, it takes effect immediately in that the subject matter of the *donatio* vests in the donee, whose title is defeasible

---

[61] [1899] 1 I.R. 405

[62] [1902] 1 Ch. 680. Byrne J. was of the opinion that the document in question must contain all the essential terms of the contract.

[63] [1951] Ch. 298

[64] See *Dufficy* v *Mollica* [1968] 3 N.S.W.R. 751 cited by Keane in "Equity and the Law of Trusts in the Republic of Ireland" at p. 371 n. 8

[65] *Ibid* at p. 371

[66] *Jones* v *Selby* (1710) Prec. Ch. 300

[67] See *Edwards* v *Jones* (1836) 1 My. & Cr. 226

should the donor recover. Thus, an intention on the donor's part to make a future gift, will be inconsistent with an intention to make a *donatio mortis causa*.[68]

1.3.15 The condition that the gift is to take effect only on the death of the donor need not be expressly stated, but may be implied from the circumstances of the case.[69]

1.4 Property incapable of being the subject of a donatio mortis causa

1.4.1 Some property is deemed to be incapable of transfer by way of a *donatio mortis causa*. Thus, it has long been the orthodox view that there cannot be a *donatio mortis causa* of land. Some textwriters argue that the matter cannot be regarded as settled,[70] but there is little authority to support that view, other than the oft-cited decision in *Duffield* v *Elwes*[71] where a *donatio mortis causa* of a mortgage of land was upheld.

1.4.2 Not all forms of personalty are capable of passing by way of a *donatio mortis causa*. As we have seen, an I.O.U. does not necessarily so pass,[72] nor does a promissory note signed by the donor[73] or a cheque drawn by the donor on his own account.[74] Of course the *donatio* in such a case would take effect if the cheque was cashed before the death of the donor, had been cashed by the bank before it had received notice of the donor's death, or, the donee had given value for the cheque.[75]

1.5 The Rule in *Strong* v *Bird*

1.5.1 We have seen that an unconditional *inter vivos* gift cannot take effect as a *donatio mortis causa*,[76] but, if title to the subject-matter of such gift does not vest in the donee during the donor's lifetime, the gift may still take effect if title vests in the donee as personal representative of the donor. Such is the effect of the so-called rule in *Strong* v *Bird*.[77]

---

[68] See *Treasury Solicitor* v *Lewis* [1900] 2 Ch. 812
[69] See *Gordon* v *Parker* (1818), 3 Madd. 184; *Re Lillington* [1952] 2 All E.R. 184
[70] See e.g. Pettit "Equity and the Law of Trusts" (5th ed.) at p. 104
[71] (1827) 1 Bli (n.s.) 497
[72] *Duckworth* v *Lee* [1899] 1 I.R. 405; cf. *Hewitt* v *Kaye (1868) L.R. 6 Eq. 198, 200*
[73] *Bouts* v *Ellis* (1853) 4 de G.M. & G. 249; *Re Leaper* [1916] 1 Ch. 579
[74] *Re Beaumont* [1902] 1 Ch. 886
[75] See Hanbury and Maudsley "Modern Equity" at p. 140
[76] See *ante* p. 9
[77] (1874) L.R. 18 Eq. 315. See "A Fresh Look at Strong v Bird" by Gilbert Kodilinye in (1982) Conveyancer, 14

1.5.2 The case from which the rule takes its name involved the narrow question whether, a debt owed to a testatrix was released by the appointment of the debtor as executor of the deceased creditor's estate. The facts were that B had borrowed £1,100 from A his step-mother who lived in B's house, paying him £212.10s a quarter for her board. It had been agreed that B's debt should be paid off by a deduction of £100 from the rent paid by A each quarter. After deductions of this amount for two quarters, A resumed paying the full rent, and continued to do so until her death, some four years later. The residuary legatees under A's will claimed the balance of the debt from B, who had been appointed sole executor of, and proved, A's will. Jessel M.R. held, that the appointment of B as executor of A's will released the debt he owed to A's estate.

1.5.3 The decision in *Strong* v *Bird*, which was handed down almost contemporaneously with the passage of the legislation effecting the union of judicature, was, ironically, brought about by a combination of rules of common law and equity. The rule at common law was that, a debt, being a chose in action, an executor could not sue himself for a debt which he owed to the estate.[78] The executor would still be liable to account for the debt in equity, which would treat the debtor as having paid the debt to the estate, leaving the executor with assets distributable among those beneficially entitled to the estate.[79] Jessel M.R. precluded the residuary legatees proceeding in equity, by holding, that B was not liable to account for the debt since the deceased had shown a continuing intention to forgive the debt. That intention had been perfected at law by B being appointed his stepmother's executor, and there was "no equity against him to take the property away from him".[80]

1.5.4 The rule in *Strong* v *Bird* has been extended beyond the release of a debt, and has been used to validate an imperfect *inter vivos* gift of property made by the deceased during his lifetime. Indeed, this extension has led to the rule being generally treated by textwriters as an exception to the rule that equity will not perfect an imperfect gift or assist a volunteer.[81] Thus in *Re Stewart*[82] Neville J. applied the rule in *Strong* v *Bird* in holding that, an imperfect gift of bearer bonds was completed by the appointment of the donee as executor of the donor's will. Neville J. gave his reasons as follows:

"The reasoning by which the conclusion is reached is of a double

---

[78] See *Bone* v *Commissioner of Stamp Duties* (1974) 132 C.L.R. 38, 53 (per Mason J.)

[79] See Underwhite and Hayton "Law of Trusts and Trustees" (14th ed. 1987) at p. 112

[80] (1874) L.R. 18 Eq. 315, 318

[81] See e.g. Hanbury and Maudsley "Modern Equity" at pp. 136 *et seq.* and Snell's "Principles of Equity" at pp. 125, 126

[82] [1908] 2 Ch. 251

14

character – first, that the vesting of the property in the executor at the testator's death completes the imperfect gift made in the lifetime, and secondly, that the intention of the testator to give the beneficial interest to the executor is sufficient to countervail the equity of beneficiaries under the will, the testator having vested the legal estate in the executor."[83]

1.5.5 Neville J. made it clear however, that the intention to give

"must not be an intention of testamentary benefaction, although the intended donee is the executor; for, in that case, the rule cannot apply, the prescribed formalities for testamentary disposition not having been observed."

This aspect of Neville J.'s judgment was followed by Johnston J. in *Re Wilson*[84] when he refused to apply the rule in *Strong* v *Bird* to certain of the facts in that case. In Johnston J.'s view the plain meaning of the document, which contained a promise by the testator to give a benefit to his son, whom he appointed executor of his will was that

"if the promise is not translated into an effective disposition by a legal transfer in the lifetime of the testator, then the donee must be satisfied with whatever testamentary provision the testator may make for him."[85]

1.5.6 Johnston J. cited *Re Hyslop*[86] as authority for the proposition, that the appointment of a debtor as executor will not in itself be sufficient to release a debt owed by the executor.[87] North J. said, in that case, that in order that the principle established in *Strong* v *Bird* be brought into operation, there must be evidence of some equity in the debtor, apart from his appointment as executor.[88] The evidence in *Re Hyslop* showed that the deceased's intention to cancel the debt was testamentary.

1.5.7 The rule in *Strong* v *Bird* will equally not apply if the evidence shows that the donor's intention was to make a future gift of the property in question. Thus in *Re Freeland*[89] the plaintiff, who had been appointed executrix of the deceased's will, claimed entitlement to a car which she claimed the deceased had given to her, without due legal formality, in the deceased donor's lifetime. The evidence however disclosed that the

---

[83] *Ibid* at p. 254
[84] [1933] I.R. 729
[85] *Ibid* at pp. 748–9
[86] [1894] 3 Ch. 522
[87] [1933] I.R. 729, 741
[88] Johnston J. also considered the decisions in *Re Pink* [1912] 2 Ch. 528 and *Re Innes* [1910] 1 Ch. 188
[89] [1952] Ch. 110

deceased had allowed other people to use the car and that it had not been the donor's intention to give the car immediately to the plaintiff. Accordingly, the rule in *Strong* v *Bird* had no application in that case. The facts in *Re Freeland* also show another reason for the exclusion of the *Strong* v *Bird* principle. The intention to release a debt or make an immediate *inter vivos* disposition must continue until the death of the donor. It follows that any fluctuation or vacillation in that intention will preclude the operation of the principle. It has been argued that, in the vast majority of cases "it has been simply a question of fact as to whether a continuing intent existed, the onus of proof being on the claimant".[89a]

1.5.8 The extension of the rule in *Strong* v *Bird* to the perfection of imperfect gifts has provoked much criticism,[90] but it now seems to be well established and is likely to endure. Johnston J. said of the decision in *Re Stewart:*[91]

> "I do not agree with Mr Lavery's critical attitude towards that case. It was referred to with approval or at any rate, without disapproval by Kennedy L.J. in the Court of Appeal four years later in *Pink* v *Pink,*[92] and has never been doubted in any case of which I am aware."[93]

1.5.9 The further extension of the principle in *Strong* v *Bird* to administrators, has provoked much judicial and academic disapproval. This extension of the rule occurred in *Re James*[94] where Farwell J. held that for the purposes of the rule in *Strong* v *Bird* an administrator is in exactly the same position as an executor. In that case the donor, who had inherited his father's house on the latter's intestacy, purported to give the house to his father's housekeeper, handing over the title deeds to her, but he did not formally convey the house to her. On the donor's death, the housekeeper was appointed as one of two administrices of the donor's estate, and legal title to the house accordingly vested in her jointly with the other administratrix. Farwell J. held, that the rule in *Strong* v *Bird* applied to perfect the imperfect gift made by the donor during his lifetime, since he had a continuing intention to give the house, which she occupied as donee, until his death.

1.5.10 Walton J. was extremely critical of the extension of the rule in

---

[89a] Kodilinye *op. cit.* at p. 28

[90] See e.g. Parry and Clark "The Law of Succession" (8th ed. 1983) at p. 27 where it is described as "an imperfect rule".

[91] [1908] 2 Ch. 251

[92] [1912] 2 Ch. 528

[93] [1933] I.R. 729, 741

[94] [1935] Ch. 449

Strong v *Bird* to administrators when he said in *Re Gonin*[95] that he started

> "from the simple proposition that if the defendant in *Strong* v *Bird* itself had been an administrator instead of an executor the case would have been decided the other way, since it distinctly proceeded upon the basis that at law the appointment of a person as an executor affected a release of any debt due from the executor to the testator, a doctrine which was never applied to an administrator."

Walton J. went on to point out, that the appointment of an administrator, unlike that of an executor, is not the act of the deceased, but of the law, and it is often a matter of pure chance, which, of many persons equally entitled to a grant of letters of administration, finally takes them out. Walton J. continued:

> "Why, then, should any special tenderness be shown to a person so selected by law and not the will of the testator, and often indifferently selected among many with an equal claim? It would seem an astonishing doctrine of equity that if the person who wishes to take the benefit of the rule in *Strong* v *Bird* manages to be the person to obtain a grant then he will be able to do so, but if a person equally entitled manages to obtain a prior grant, then he will not be able to do so."[96]

1.5.11 With respect to Walton J. his criticisms of the extension of the *Strong* v *Bird* principle in *Re James* are adequately met by the argument, that the crux of the principle adumbrated by Jessel M.R. is, that the gift or release of the debt is perfected by the vesting of the legal title in the donee, and it is irrelevant whether the vesting takes place by the operation of law or act of the donor.[97] The other crucial factor is the will of the donor remains paramount in the requirement that he must have manifested an intention to make an *inter vivos* gift up to the time of his death, and in most cases involving the application of the *Strong* v *Bird* principle, the donor will have assumed that the gift was complete before his death. The view, that it matters not how the legal title to the property vests in the donee, also derives support from certain *obiter dicta* of Buckley J. in the rather unusual case *Re Ralli's Will Trusts*.[98] The latter case also shows that the property may vest in an executor or administrator not as donee but as trustee for the donee.[99]

1.5.12 Among the unresolved problems attaching to the rule in *Strong* v *Bird* are, whether, the rule is binding on a deceased's creditors, as well as

[95] [1979]Ch. 16, 34
[96] *Ibid* at p. 35
[97] See Kodilinye *(supra)* at p. 17
[98] [1964] Ch. 288
[99] See generally Underhill and Hayton "Law of Trusts and Trustees" at p. 177

on beneficiaries entitled under his will or on his intestacy? It is suggested that the probable answer is no.[100]

1.6 Secret Trusts

1.6.1 If a person dies testate, and his will is admitted to probate, it is then open to public inspection on payment of a small fee at the Probate Office.[1] This openness to public scrutiny no doubt helps to ensure that the wishes of the deceased testator are not disregarded, but, it may not suit a testator who wishes to provide discreetly and circumspectly for such persons as mistresses and illegitimate children. Equity has long been willing to accommodate such testators by permitting them to use the so-called secret trust, as a way of disposing of property on death, such disposition not being publicly revealed on the death of the disponer.[1a]

1.6.2 Thus, if A devises property to B absolutely on the face of his will, but communicates to B his intention that B is to hold such property in trust for C, then, if the will is otherwise properly executed, and B has accepted the trusteeship, the courts will enforce the trust in favour of C. At first blush, the enforcement of a trust, which is not set out on the face of the will, would seem to be at odds with the statutory requirements governing the execution of wills.[2] However, the courts of equity recognised, that to apply the statutory requirements governing wills automatically, and without regard to the circumstances of the particular case, might allow a legatee to perpetrate a fraud on the testator. Thus, the original basis of the courts' jurisdiction to enforce secret trusts, was the maxim that "equity will not permit a statute to be used as an engine of fraud".[3]

1.6.3 The avoidance of fraud being the essential reason for their enforcement of secret trusts, the courts were able to claim that such enforcement was not inconsistent with the legislation governing wills, since it was wholly independent of, and separate from, such legislation. Thus,

---

[100] See Parry and Clark "The Law of Succession" at p. 27

[1] Section 42(1) of the Succession Act provides that (a) all original wills of which representation is granted in the Probate Office, and (b) copies of all wills, the originals of which are to be preserved in district probate registries, and (c) such other documents as the President of the High Court may direct, shall be deposited and preserved in the Probate Office under the control of the President of the High Court and may be inspected in accordance with his directions.

[1a] See *Thynn* v *Thynn* (1684) 1 Vern. 296; *Sellack* v *Harris* (1708) 5 Vin. Ab. 521, and generally Holdworth "Secret Trusts" 53 Law Quarterly Review, 501.

[2] See *post* pp. 35 *et seq.*

[3] See *Drakeford* v *Wilkes* (1747) 3 Atr. 939; *Cullen* v *Att. Gen. for Ireland* (1866) L.R. 1 H.L. 190 and generally L.A. Sheridan "Fraud in Equity" (1958)

Lord Warrington pointed out in the leading English case, *Blackwell* v *Blackwell*,[4] that, we must bear in mind

> "that what is enforced is not a trust imposed by the will, but one arising from the acceptance by the legatee of a trust, communicated to him by the testator, on the faith of which acceptance the will was made or left unrevoked as the case may be."

1.6.4 Viscount Sumner, who expressed himself in similar terms, was of the opinion that the enforcement of secret trusts was a perfectly normal exercise of equitable jurisdiction.[5] Viscount Sumner explained the jurisdiction thus:

> "A court of conscience finds a man in the position of an absolute legal owner of a sum of money, which has been bequeathed to him under a valid will, and it declares that, on proof of certain facts relating to the motives and actions of the testator, it will not allow the legal owner to exercise his legal right to do what he will with his own."[6]

Equity thus fastens on the conscience of the legatee a trust which otherwise would be inoperative, in other words, it makes him do what the will in itself has nothing to do with, it lets him take what the will gives him, and then makes him apply it as the Court of conscience directs, in order to give effect to the wishes of the testator, which otherwise would be ineffectual.[7]

1.6.5 The necessary elements on which the question of a secret trust turns are, as Viscount Sumner stated in *Blackwell* v *Blackwell* – intention, communication, and acceptance. Each of these will be considered in turn.

1.6.6 (a) Intention.

The testator must have intended that the primary donee, named in the will, should hold the property on trust, for the secret beneficiary or beneficiaries. The point is neatly illustrated by the facts in *McCormick* v *Grogan*[8] where, a testator had left all his property in 1851, in a three line will, to his friend, Mr Grogan. In 1854, the testator was struck down by cholera and, with only a few hours left to live, sent for Grogan and told him that his will and a letter would be found in his desk. The letter which named various intended beneficiaries, and the intended gifts to them, concluded with the words:

> "I do not wish you to act strictly to the foregoing instructions, but leave it entirely to your good judgment to do as you think I would if living, and as the parties are deserving ..."

[4] [1929] A.C. 318, 342
[5] *Ibid* at pp. 334–5
[6] *Ibid*
[7] *Ibid*
[8] (1867) 1 I.R. Eq. 313

1.6.7 An intended beneficiary, whom Grogan saw fit to exclude from the testator's bounty, having sued, Christian L.J. was of the opinion that the real question was, what sanction did the testator intend? Was it to be the authority of a Court of justice, or the conscience of the devisee? In his opinion it was, expressly and exclusively, the latter. Christian L.J. added, that if we could look into the thoughts of the testator as they were when he was writing the will and the accompanying letter he was persuaded,

> "that what we should find there would be a purpose to this effect – to set up after his decease, not an executor or a trustee, but as it were a second self, whom, while he communicates to him confidentially his ideas as to the distribution of his property, he desires to invest him with all his own irresponsibility in carrying them into effect."[9]

1.6.8 The onus of proof required to establish a secret trust would appear, from Christian L.J.'s observations, to be no higher than that required for the establishment of an ordinary trust. However, when *McCormick* v *Grogan* went on appeal to the House of Lords,[10] Lord Westbury said of the jurisdiction, in relation to secret trusts, that it was

> "founded altogether on personal fraud. It is a jurisdiction by which a court of equity, proceeding on the grounds of fraud, converts the party who has committed it into a trustee for the party who is injured by that fraud. Now, being a jurisdiction founded on a personal fraud, it is incumbent on the court to see that a fraud, a *malus animus,* is proved by the clearest and most indisputable evidence."

1.6.9 That the onus of proof of a secret trust may not now weigh so heavily, is evident from certain observations of Megarry V.-C. in *Re Snowden,*[12] where, he said of Lord Westbury's proposition in *McCormick* v *Grogan*:

> "Of that, it is right to say that the law on the subject has not stood still since 1869, and that it is now clear that secret trusts may be established where there is no possibility of fraud. *McCormick* v *Grogan* has to be read in the light both of earlier cases that were not cited, and also of subsequent cases, in particular *Blackwell* v *Blackwell*. It seems to me that fraud comes into the matter in two ways. First, it provides an historical explanation of the doctrine of secret trusts: the doctrine was evolved as a means of preventing fraud. That, however, does not mean that fraud is an essential ingredient for the application of the doctrine: the reason for the rule is not part of the rule itself. Second, there are

---

[9] This passage was cited with approval by Lord Hatherty L.C. at (1869) I.R. 4 H.L. 82, 95. See also Megarry V-C in *Re Snowden* [1979] 2 All E.R. 172, 179

[10] (1869) L.R. 4 H.L. 82

[11] *Ibid* at p. 97

[12] [1979] 2 All E.R. 172

some cases within the doctrine where fraud is indeed involved. There are cases where for the legatee to assert that he is a beneficial owner, free from any trust, would be a fraud on his part."[13]

Megarry V.-C. went on to hold "that in order to establish a secret trust where no question of fraud arises, the standard of proof is the ordinary civil standard of proof that is required to establish an ordinary trust."[14]

1.6.10 That a secret trust can impose an obligation not only to hold property on trust for a beneficiary after the testator's death, but, an obligation to make provision for the intended beneficiary after the legatee's death, can be seen in *Ottaway* v *Norman*.[15]

1.6.11 (b) Communication.

As we have seen, it is the communication of the testator's intention to a legatee that he is not to take absolutely under the will, but to hold in trust for someone else, and the legatee's acceptance of that trusteeship, that gives rise to an enforceable secret trust.[16] If, however, the testator communicates to a legatee the fact that he intends the legatee to hold on trust, but fails to communicate the terms of the trust, the legatee will hold the property given to him by the will on a resulting trust for those otherwise entitled to the testator's estate. The point is neatly illustrated by the decision in *Re Boyes*[17] where a legacy was given to the testator's solicitor, who had undertaken to hold the legacy according to directions which he would receive in a letter from the testator. Such letter having been discovered only after the death of the testator, Kay J. held, that the property contained in the legacy was held on a resulting trust for the testator's next-of-kin.[18]

1.6.12 While the fact of the trust must be communicated to the legatee during the testator's lifetime, it will suffice if there is constructive communication of the terms of the trust. Thus, Kay J. pointed out in *Re Boyes*,[19] that if a devisee or legatee had accepted that he would hold the

[13] *Ibid* at p. 178

[14] *Ibid* at p. 179 Megarry V-C was conscious of the fact that this did not accord with what had been said in *Ottaway* v *Norman* [1972] Ch. 698, 712 but he believed that the point had been taken somewhat shortly in that case where the judge did not seem to have had the advantage of considering the cases cited to Megarry V-C in the instant case.

[15] [1972] Ch. 698

[16] See [1929] A.C. 318, 342 and *ante* p. 19

[17] (1884) 26 Ch. D. 531

[18] See *post* p. 56 *et seq.* for doctrine of incorporation by reference

[19] (1884) 26 Ch. D. 531, 536

property given to him in the will upon a trust, and the terms of such trust were contained in a sealed envelope, given to the devisee or legatee by the testator before his death, then the devisee or legatee would be bound by the trust although he was ignorant of its terms before the testator's death. Lord Wright in *Re Keen*[20] drew an analogy between the latter situation and a ship sailing under sealed orders. Just as the master of a ship may be directed not to open sealed orders until the ship leaves port, a trustee may likewise be directed by the testator not to open a sealed envelope containing details of the trust, until the death of the testator.[21]

1.6.13 While the Irish and English courts are *ad idem* in holding, that the communication of the fact, and terms, of a wholly secret trust, no mention of which appears on the face of the will, can be made at any time before the testator's death, they are at odds with regard to the communication of the terms of a half-secret trust, the fact of which, but not its terms, is revealed in the will. The Irish and English courts agree that the method of communication used by a testator must be consistent with the terms of his will and if, for example, the will indicates future communication of the terms of a half-secret trust, evidence of past communication will be inadmissible.[22]

1.6.14 It is with respect to whether communication of the terms of a half-secret trust is permissible at all after the date of the will, that the Irish and English courts have taken different approaches. The English courts have taken the view that communication of the terms of a half-secret trust made after the date of the will, but before the death of the testator, is not admissible to prove the terms of the trust. The reason for the refusal by the English courts to take cognisance of future communication was given by Viscount Sumner in *Blackwell* v *Blackwell*,[23] where he said that a testator

"cannot reserve to himself a power of making future unwitnessed dispositions by merely naming a trustee and leaving the purposes of the trust to be supplied afterwards, nor can a legatee give testamentary validity to an unexecuted codicil by accepting an indefinite trust, never communicated to him in the testator's lifetime."

1.6.15 While it is generally accepted by textwriters[24] that the Irish courts

---

[20] [1937] Ch. 238, 242

[21] *Ibid* cf *McDonald* v *Moran* (1938) 12 MPR 424 cited in Underhill and Hayton at p. 199 n.3

[22] The primary rule is that one has to consider the terms of the will to determine what form of communication is permissible.

[23] [1929] A.C. 318, 339

[24] See Snell's "Principles of Equity" at p. 112; Hanbury and Maudsley "Modern Equity" at p. 158 and L.A. Sheridan "English and Irish Secret Trusts" (1951) 67 Law Quarterly Review 413

take a different approach to the communication of the terms of a half-secret trust, and equate fully and half-secret trusts, in permitting communication at any time before the death of the testator, this interpretation of the Irish position derives largely from certain *obiter dicta* of Overend J. in *Re Brown*.[25] That case concerned a bequest of property to one W, in reliance upon his carrying out the wishes which the testator had expressed to him and/or might express thereafter. Communication and acceptance was effected for the first time some seven years after the execution of the will, when the testator was on his death-bed. Overend J. held, that the language of the will gave W an absolute interest untramelled by any trust, with the result that there was a validly created fully secret trust outside the will. Overend J. was also of the opinion, however, that even if the language of the will had imposed a trust on W, there was a valid half-secret trust, it being immaterial that the terms of the trust were communicated after the execution of the will, so long as it was accepted by W in the testator's lifetime.[26]

1.6.16 Further support for what might be termed the Overend J. position on communication, is to be found in *Riordan* v *Bannon*[27] where Chatterton V.-C. said:

"The result of cases appears to me to be that a testator cannot by his will reserve to himself the right of disposing subsequently of property by an instrument not executed as required by the statute (of wills), or by parol: but that when, at the time of making his will, he has formed the intention that a legacy thereby given shall be disposed of by the legatee in a particular manner, not thereby disclosed, but communicated to the legatee and assented to by him, at or before the making of the will, or probably, according to *Moss* v *Cooper*,[28] subsequently to the making of it, the court will allow such trust to be proved by admission of the legatee, or other parol evidence, and will, if it be legal, give effect to it."

1.6.17 It has to be conceded by the most ardent supporter of the Irish position on the communication of the terms of a half-secret trust, that all the judicial utterances in support of that position rank as mere *obiter dicta*, with all their attendant vulnerability. The Irish position does, however, derive considerable support from the fact that the bulk of academic

---

[25] [1944] I.R. 90. See also *In re Watters* (1928) 62 I.L.T.R. 61

[26] Overend J. pointed out that this view of the law was long accepted in this country and he referred to the judgement of Monroe J. in *Re King's Estate* (1888) 21 L.R. Ir. 273. In the latter case Monroe J. elicited seven propositions from the case law dealing with secret trusts the fourth of which was that the "rule applies when communication is made subsequently to the execution of the will." ((1888 21 L.R. Ir. 273, 277)

[27] (1875) I.R. 10 Eq. 469, 477

[28] (1861) 1 J. & H. 352

opinion favours it, and, it is the position taken by the courts in most of the American states.[29] The Irish position is referred to approvingly by English textwriters, who are critical of what they perceive to be illogical distinctions between fully secret and half-secret trusts.[30]

1.6.18 Ironically, the English position on communication of the terms of a half-secret trust, is held by some of those critics to be no less secure than the Irish position, since the true *ratio* of *Re Keen*[31] might be that the communication was inconsistent with the terms of the will, and, in *Re Bateman's Will Trusts*[32] which followed *Re Keen*, the rule that the communication could not follow the will, was not challenged. This had led certain textwriters to conclude that the present position is unsatisfactory, and

> "there is no sense in a rule which (in the case of communication between the will and the death) enforces a trust in a bequest 'to X' but disregards the trust in a bequest 'to X upon trust'."[33]

1.6.19 One of the main grounds of criticism of the position taken by the English courts, is that it fails to take cognisance of the fact, that both kinds of secret trust operate dehors the will.[34] Be that as it may, the enforcement of secret trusts, whether fully-secret or half-secret, is essentially a policy issue, and there are compelling policy reasons for not allowing a testator to communicate the terms of a half-secret after the execution of the will. The fact of the half-secret trust is revealed on the face of the will, and it is clearly arguable that the creation of such a trust is a testamentary act, which should be amenable to the statutory provisions governing the execution of wills.[35]

1.6.20 It is also the case that, the avoidance of the legislation governing wills, which the English courts seek to curb, by their position on communication in relation to half-secret trusts, can be done *a fortiori* by the use of a fully secret trust, a fact which has led some commentators to the conclusion "that consistency should be achieved by requiring the communication to be before the will even in the case of a fully secret trust".[36] This, it is hoped, would deter testators who use the secret trust,

---

[29] See the American *Restatement of Trusts* par 55 comments (c) and (h)

[30] See e.g. Hanbury and Maudsley "Modern Equity" at p. 158

[31] [1937] Ch. 236. See generally Burgess "Juridical Nature of Secret Trusts" (1972) 23 N.I.L. Q. 263

[32] [1970] 1 W.L.R. 1463

[33] Hanbury and Maudsley "Modern Equity" at p. 158

[34] See Perrins "Secret Trusts – The Key to the Dehors?" (1985) 49 Conv. (m.s.) 148

[35] See Anne Corrigan's unpublished LL.M. thesis entitled "Secret Trusts" in Ireland in the Law Library of University College Dublin at pp. 184 *et seq.*

[36] Hanbury and Maudsley "Modern Equity" at p. 158

not for the reasons which gave rise to the courts' indulgence of them, but simply because they can't make up their minds.[37]

1.6.21 That attitudes in Ireland might also be hardening in favour of a stricter line on secret trusts can be seen in the observations of a distinguished High Court judge and textwriter, who writes of the criticism levelled at the distinction made by the English courts between fully secret and half-secret trusts:

"There is certainly force in that criticism, but there are also powerful policy reasons for rejecting a totally logical approach in this area: ultimately, the undesirability of allowing the statutory requirements as to the making of wills to be subverted and the public interest in ensuring that they are observed may be decisive considerations in Ireland as in England."[38]

1.6.22 A particular problem arises when property is left absolutely by will to more than one intended trustee, and the trust is communicated to one but not to all. The courts have made distinctions between cases where the intended trustees take as joint tenants and those where they take as tenants in common. Thus Holmes L.J. was able to say in *Geddis* v *Semple*:[39]

"It is, I think, settled that where a gift is given to two persons as joint tenants, a secret trust imparted to one of them will affect the whole gift; but that this arises from the peculiar nature of a joint estate is shown by repeated decisions that this rule does not apply to tenants in common."

1.6.23 Where the intended trustees took as joint tenants a further distinction was made, between cases where communication was made to one prior to the execution of the will, where all would be bound thereby, and cases where communication followed the will, in which case only those who had accepted the trust would be bound by it. Farwell J. said of this distinction in *Re Stead*:[40]

"Personally I am unable to see any difference between a gift made on the faith of an antecedant promise and a gift left unrevoked on the faith of a subsequent promise to carry out the testator's wishes; but apparently a distinction has been made by the various judges who had to consider the question. I am bound, therefore, to decide in accordance with these authorities ..."

1.6.24 The proposition, that only a tenant in common to whom the trust

---

[37] As exemplified by the facts of *Re Snowden* [1979] Ch. 528

[38] Keane "Equity and the Law of Trusts in the Republic of Ireland" at p. 95

[39] [1903] 1 I.R. 73, 76. See Wylie "A Casebook on Equity and Trusts in Ireland" at p. 324 and Brady "Religion and the Law of Charities in Ireland" (n.d.) at pp. 137 *et seq.*

[40] [1900] Ch. 237. See Perrins "Can You Keep Half a Secret?" (1972) 88 L.Q.R. 225

has been communication is bound by it, seems to derive from the decision in *Tee* v *Ferris*.[41] There, three of four tenants in common, who were ignorant of a trust until the death of the testator, were held not to be bound by the trust which had been communicated by the testator to the fourth tenant in common. That case arguably turned on its own facts and is not an authority for the proposition that, an "innocent" tenant in common is never bound by the trust which has been communicated to another tenant in common.[42] Thus, in *Geddis* v *Semple*,[43] Walker L.J. made it clear that it was only because there was no evidence, on the facts of that case, that no inducement had been used by the trustee to whom the trust had been communicated which exonerated the others from the doctrine in *Huginin* v *Basely*.[44]

1.6.25 The law governing secret trusts has become unduly complicated by distinction between tenancies in common and joint tenancies, and fine distinctions in relation to the timing of communication in the latter case. There is much to be said for the view that the same basic principle should apply to both joint tenants and tenants in common, and a tenant of either kind, whether "innocent" or otherwise, should be bound by a trust communicated to his fellow tenants, unless he can show that he received his gift independently of any undertaking given by his co-tenants.[45]

1.6.26 (c) Acceptance

It is the acceptance by a devisee or legatee of a secret trust affecting the devise or legacy which gives rise to the equitable jurisdiction to enforce the trust. Fitzgibbon L.J. said in *Geddis* v *Semple*:[46]

"As regards one of the three, the Reverend Mr Semple, it has been proved that he was party to an arrangement, or understanding with the testator before the will was made, that the property should be so applied; and whether that arrangement or undertaking was indicated by express language, or by silent acquiescence on Mr Semple's part, makes

---

[41] (1856) 2 K. & J. 357

[42] See *Moss* v *Cooper* (1861) 1 J. & H. 352 where Page-Wood V-C held on the evidence that all tenants in common had accepted the secret trust which had been communicated to two of the donees by a third who was held to be the testator's agent.

[43] (1903) 1 I.R. 73,82

[44] (1807) 14 Ves. 273 where Lord Eldon quoted from the speech of Wilmot L. C.J. in *Bridgeton* v *Green* (1757) Wilm. 58 thus: "Let the hand receiving it be ever so chaste, yet, if it comes through a polluted channel the obligation of restitution will follow it." See Miss Corrigan's LL.M. thesis (supra) at p. 90

[45] See Wylie "Irish Land Law" (2nd ed. 1986) at p. 477

[46] [1903] 1 I.R. 73

no difference. His conscience was bound by a secret trust which, in the event which has happened, invalidates the devise to him."

1.6.27 The testator who employs a fully secret trust runs a considerable risk by eschewing the protective formalities of the Succession Act. Clearly, if a proposed trustee refuses to accept the burden of trusteeship, and the testator persists in leaving a gift to him absolutely, the testator must be taken to have accepted that the donee will take absolutely. If a half-secret trust is used, the fact of the trust is revealed in the will, and in no circumstances will the donee take absolutely. The testator may however be loath to reveal the trust in his will, and in those circumstances perhaps the most that he can do to avoid fraud, and preserve secrecy, is to give to the proposed beneficiary a letter signed by himself setting out the proposed trust.

1.6.28 An interesting question arises as to whether, when a secret beneficiary predeceases the testator, the gift will lapse. The general rule under section 91 of the Succession Act is, that a devise or legacy lapses if the beneficiary predeceases the testator and, subject to a contrary intention in the will, falls into the residuary estate. However, in *Re Gardner*[47] the English Court of Appeal held, that the personal representatives of a deceased beneficiary under a secret trust could claim her share, even though she had predeceased the testator. The decision has provoked much academic criticism and the general view is that it was wrongly decided.[48] That decision can only be right if the trust was completely constituted before the death of the testator, and is clearly at odds with the modern view that a secret trust arises from an *inter vivos* declaration of trust, which is completely constituted by the vesting of the property in the trustee on the testator's death.[49]

1.7 Other will substitutes

1.7.1 An American commentator has written that public and professional awareness

"of the delay, expense, inefficiency and occasional corruption in the probate courts has been the dominant factor in bringing about the proliferation of the so-called 'will substitutes' – modes of gratuitous transfer of property by which the death of the donor operates to raise in the donee property interests theretofore enjoyed by the donor, but

---

[47] [1923] 2 Ch. 230

[48] See Nathan and Marshall "Cases and Commentary on the Law of Trusts" (6th ed.) at p. 415; Hanbury and Maudsley "Modern Equity" at p. 265; Cf. Oakley "Constructive Trusts" (1978) at p. 93

[49] See Hanbury and Maudsley "Modern Equity" at pp. 160 *et seq.*

which are exempted by judicial decision or by statute from compliance with the Wills Act."[50]

The same writer goes on to say that it "is the flexibility and comparative informality of the will substitutes which is making the rule of literal compliance with Wills Act formalities ever more incongruous and indefensible."[51]

1.7.2 While Irish lawyers would not share certain of those criticisms of probate practice, notably the charges of impropriety, there is growing evidence that will substitutes are proliferating in Ireland as in the United States. Their comparative informality and flexibility no doubt accounts in some measure for the growing popularity of will substitutes, which is also attributable however to socio-economic changes in society which are presenting new kinds of legal problems to practitioners and courts alike. Thus, for example, the courts have found traditional guidelines inadequate to deal with property disputes in the aftermath of marital and quasi-marital breakdown.[52]

1.7.3 These socio-economic changes, which now see women routinely earning and contributing to family finances, have led to the growing practice of young married couples acquiring the matrimonial home as joint tenants, rather than the more traditional practice of the title deeds being in the name of the husband only. It has to be conceded, however, that title to farmland is held more rarely on a joint tenancy, since for obvious reasons of family inheritance which tend to exclude the female spouse, traditional conveyancing practice still persists in rural Ireland.[53] The effect of a conveyance to a couple as joint tenants has the same dispositive effect as a will in which one spouse leaves the matrimonial home to the other since, under the *jus accresendi,* the property will vest in the surviving spouse who, medical statistics show, is usually the female spouse.

1.7.4 It is also well to remember that a surviving spouse has the power, in any event, to seek the appropriation under section 56 of the Succession Act of the house in which he or she ordinarily resided with the other spouse.[54]

---

[50] Langbein "Substantial Compliance With The Wills Act" (1975) 88 Harvard Law Review 489 at p. 504

[51] *Ibid*

[52] See Brady "Trusts, Law Reform and the Emancipation of Women" (1984) 6 Dublin University Law Journal, 1

[53] It was ignorance of this position to which many political commentators attributed the failure of the Coalition Government in 1986 to have the constitutional referendum on divorce carried.

[54] See *post* p. 191 *et seq.*

1.7.5 Apart from the house in which he or she lives and owns, the most valuable disposable asset of the vast majority of people is the proceeds of one or more life insurance policies. Provision can be made for the disposal of the proceeds of such policies, which arise on the death of the insured, by nominating or designating a beneficiary. Such nomination, like a will, has no effect until the death of the nominator. An American commentator has written, that not only does the nomination of a beneficiary under an insurance contract have precisely the same function as a will, but "constitutes a much more important testament than the will". He goes on to say that, in view of the numbers of people involved,

> "the life insurance beneficiary designation is the principal 'last will and testament' of our legal system ... A properly designated beneficiary will receive the proceeds of the insurance without regard to compliance with the formalities required in the law of wills."[55]

1.7.6 Although it is comparatively easier to nominate a beneficiary under a contract of life insurance than it is to execute a will, there are formal requirements, such as the attested signature of the nominator, which fill the same cautionary and evidentiary role as the formal requirements for the execution of a will.[56] Indeed, as we shall see, in *Re Griffith*[57] a nomination, which failed to satisfy the terms of a contract of life insurance, was admitted to probate as being validly executed as a testamentary instrument.

---

[55] Kimball *The Functions of Designations of Beneficiaries in Modern Life Insurance: U.S.A.*, in "Life Insurance in International Perspective" 74, 76 (J. Kellner & G. Nord eds. 1969) quoted in: angbein, *supra*, at p. 508

[56] See *post* pp. 34 *et seq.*

[57] [1940] Ir. Jur. Rep. 69. See *post* p. 33

Chapter 2
THE MAKING OF A WILL

2.1 Introduction: The statutory formalities

2.1.1 The Statute of Wills 1634,[1] which reproduced in Ireland, the English legislation of a century earlier, required wills of realty to be in writing, but there was no need for a signature or witnesses. The latter two requirements were added by the Statute of Frauds 1695[2] which, like the English Statute of 1677,[3] provided that all devises and bequests of land or tenements had to be in writing, and signed by the person devising or bequeathing the same, and attested in his presence by at least three credible witnesses. The right to make a nuncupative, that is an oral will, continued with regard to personalty, but stringent requirements were attached to such wills if the personalty was worth more than £30, and it became the practice for wills of personalty to be made in writing.[4] The quickening pace of statutory law reform in the 1830s saw the enactment of the Wills Act 1837,[5] which laid down a uniform code for the execution of wills of both realty and personalty.

2.1.2 Section 9 of the 1837 Act is substantially reproduced in section 78 of the Succession Act 1965[6] which provides, that to be valid a will shall be in writing and shall be executed in accordance with the following rules. 1. It shall be signed at the foot or end thereof by the testator, or by some person in his presence and by his direction. 2. Such signature shall be made or

---

[1] 10 Car. 1 sess. 2 c. 2
[2] 7 Will. 3 c. 12
[3] 29 Car. 2 c. 3
[4] Megarry and Wade "The Law of Real Property" (4th ed. 1975), 476
[5] 7 Will 4 & 1 Vict. c. 26
[6] No. 27 of 1965

acknowledged by the testator in the presence of each of two or more witnesses present at the same time, and each witness shall attest by his signature the signature of the testator, in the presence of the testator, but no form of attestation shall be necessary nor shall it be necessary for the witnesses to sign in the presence of each other.

2.1.3 We will consider each of the requirements of writing, signature and attestation in turn.

2.2 Writing

2.2.1 The requirement of writing has been liberally interpreted by the courts with regard to the form of writing, the language employed by the testator, and the material upon which the writing is inscribed. Thus, a will need not be in the testator's handwriting, but may be handwritten, typed, lithographed, or be in any combination of these, all of which satisfy the essential requirement of providing permanent evidence of the testator's intention and the terms of his will.[7] An English textwriter has observed that "probably any permanent form of visual representation will suffice".[8]

2.2.2 While a will may be written in either pencil or ink, or in a combination of these, the court may, in the latter case, treat that part of the will written in pencil as deliberative only, and not conclusive of the testator's final intentions. So the court found in *In b Adams,*[9] where the deceased had filled in the blanks in a printed will form in her own handwriting, partly in ink and partly in pencil. Some portion of the writing in ink extended over that in pencil, some of which had been rubbed out and obliterated, but the words in ink were sensible as read with the printed part of the will. Lord Penzance held that the words in pencil were deliberative only, and probate was granted without them. The decision in *In b. Adams* clearly turned on the facts of that case and if, for example, a testator's pen ran dry before his will was fully written out and he completed it in pencil such a will would be admitted to probate in its entirety, if the court was satisfied that it represented the testator's final testamentary intention.

2.2.3 The material upon which a will may be written must satisfy the requirement of permanency, but otherwise there is no reason in principle why any restriction should be placed on such material. The liberality of the

---

[7] Most home-made wills involve the filling in of blanks in printed will forms. On the requirement of writing see generally Langbein "Substantial Compliance with the Wills Act" (1975) 88 Harvard Law Review 489 at pp. 492 *et seq.*

[8] Mellows "The Law of Succession" (4th ed. 1983), 53

[9] (1872) L.R. 2 P. & D. 367

[10] *In the Goods of Barnes* (1926) 43 T.L.R. 71

courts in this area is illustrated by the admission to probate of a will written on an empty egg shell.[10] Such a will would of course pose problems for Probate Registry practice, but it is arguable that any such problem should not be conclusive of the question of due execution.[11]

2.2.4 The requirement of writing has also been liberally interpreted by the courts with regard to the language employed by the testator, provided the language is intelligible on the face of the will, or can be made so by extrinsic evidence.[12] Thus, a will may be written in a local dialect, a foreign language, or even in a code peculiar to the profession of which the testator was a member.[13]

2.2.5 While a testator need not use any particular form of words, and neither the informality of a document,[14] or its brevity,[15] is a bar to its being admitted to probate, the document being propounded as a will must disclose the necessary *animus testandi* that is that the deceased intended it to be his last will. Hanna J. was able to find such an intention in *In b. Brennan*[16] the facts of which case were, that the deceased, when about to leave her solicitor's office after giving him instructions for the making of a new will, suggested, that as a matter of precaution, and in case of accident, she should sign the instructions. This she did in the presence of her solicitor and his typist, who then signed as witnesses, in conformity with the Statute of Wills. The deceased never returned to her solicitor's office and died two years later. Hanna J. who admitted to probate the document containing the instructions for the new will, referred to *In the Estate of Bryan decd*[17] as authority for the proposition, that parol evidence of the surrounding circumstances, and of statements of the deceased prior to execution, was admissible and, Hanna J. pointed out, in considering such evidence, the principle to be applied by the court had been stated by Ball L.C. in *O'Leary v Douglas*.[18]

---

[11] Mellows posits the case of a testator who, seeking to emulate the Elgin Marbles, chips out his will in the form of a strip cartoon over 176 blocks of marble (The Law of Succession (4th ed. 1983) at pp. 53)

[12] Application of the so-called armchair principle may reveal that the testator used language in a particular way and evidence may be introduced to show the usage of the class of persons to which the testator belonged or to explain local dialect or custom. See *post* pp. 113 *et seq.*

[13] See e.g. *Kell v Charmer* (1856) 23 Beav. 195 in which the testator used a jeweller's code to indicate the size of his sons' shares.

[14] See *In b. Brennan* [1932] I.R. 633, 636

[15] The oft cited example is the will in *Thorn v Dickens* (1906) W.N. 54 which said simply "All is for mother." Extrinsic evidence was admitted which showed that the testator intended his wife to take.

[16] [1932] I.R. 633

[17] [1907] P. 125

[18] 3 L.R. Ir. 323, 330

2.2.6 The nomenclature of the document claimed to be a will, will not be conclusive of its admissibility to probate. Thus in *In re Margaret Greville*[19] the deceased, who had given instructions for the drafting of a document, the effect of which was testamentary, directed, after perusing the draft, that the words "will and testament" be changed to "settlement" and that the word "executor" be deleted, and that a certain named person be directed "to see this settlement carried out". The deceased had made these alterations apparently because of her mistaken belief that only a solicitor could draft a will. Maguire P. applied the tests laid down in Williams on *Executors*,[20] and adopted by Hanna J. in *In the Goods of Slevin*,[21] and held that, despite its form, the document was testamentary in character, and leave was given to apply for a grant of probate. The form of the document was also no bar to its admission to probate in *In re Griffith*,[22] in which case, a person insured under a contract of life assurance had nominated, as beneficiary under the policy, a person who subsequently predeceased him. The assured on the day before his own death executed an instrument purporting to nominate another beneficiary but he failed to comply with certain requirements of the contract with respect to substituting beneficiaries. The said instrument however was signed and witnessed in the manner prescribed for testamentary instruments by the Wills Act, and the assured had not executed any other testamentary instrument. In these circumstances Hanna J. held, that the irrevocable nature of the instrument did not affect its efficacy as a testamentary instrument, and, since no executor had been appointed, liberty should be given to apply for and obtain letters of administration with the said instrument annexed. There are limits to the court's benevolence however, and in *In re Patrick Lynch*[23] a document which was expressed in the form of a deed, but was otherwise executed in conformity with the Wills Act, was not admitted to probate. What distinguished this document from others in cases like *Griffith* was the fact that a clause, which postponed the effect of the gifts until the death of the settlor, followed his signature. It is ironic that the physical location of a clause, which otherwise tended to confirm the testamentary nature of the document, apparently precluded its admission to probate. The cases are not consistent however, and the most that one can say of these "borderline" documents is that their testamentary status will largely depend on the judge's subjective view of them.

---

[19] [1942] Ir. Jur. Rep. 1. See also *In re Anderson* [1940] Ir. Jur. Rep. 71
[20] 11th ed. Vol. 1, p. 80
[21] [1938] I.R. 285
[22] [1940] Ir. Jur. Rep. 69. In admitting the document as a testamentary document Hanna J. said that he was guided by the fact that Gorell Barnes J. had found such a document to be of a testamentary nature in *In re Joseph Baxter* [1903] P.12
[23] [1942] Ir. Jur. Rep. 2

2.3 Signature by the testator

2.3.1 The statutory requirement that a testator sign his will has obvious significance for subsequent proof of genuineness, but it may well surprise the lay person to learn that testator need not sign in his own name or in his own handwriting. This requirement has been widely interpreted by the courts and a testator's initials,[24] an assumed name,[25] a former name,[26] a signature made by means of a stamp,[27] a seal,[28] and a descriptive phrase,[29] have all been held to constitute valid signatures.

2.3.2 It has also long been accepted that a person incapable of writing, whether because of illiteracy or physical infirmity, may sign his will by means of a mark, and it is not a prerequisite to the making of a mark that the testator is incapable of writing.[30] The mark traditionally used was one in the shape of a cross, but it is now established that a mark in any shape will suffice, if it is intended as a signature.[31] Thus, a testator may attempt to sign his will, but because of physical infirmity may be unable to complete the signature, or write legibly, but what he manages to do by way of writing may be accepted as a valid mark. The testator in *In the goods of Kieran*,[32] who was gravely ill at the time of execution of his will, attempted to write his signature but was unable to complete more than two unintelligible hieroglyphics which were claimed to be his initials, and before which his solicitor, who was present at the execution of the will, wrote the word "his" and after which the word "mark". Hanna J. held, that the marks made by the pen of the testator were made by him *animo testandi* and whether they formed a signature by initials or a mark they complied with the Wills Act. That the position is less clear where a testator intends to sign his full name but is prevented from doing so in the required manner by a reason other

---

[24] *In the Goods of Savory* (1851) 15 Jur. 1042; *Hindmarsh v Charlton* (1861) 8 H.L.C. 160; *In the Goods of Emerson* (1882) 9 L.R. Ir. 443; *In the Goods of Kieran* [1933] I.R. 222, 227

[25] *In the Goods of Redding* (1850) 2 Rob. Eccl. 339

[26] *In the Goods of Glover* (1847) 11 Jur. 1022 (a woman signed a will using the name of her first husband)

[27] *Re Jenkins* (1863) 3 Snr. & Jr. 93

[28] *In the Goods of Emerson* (1882) 9 L.R. Ir. 443

[29] The court in *In the Estate of Cook* [1960] 1 W.L.R. 353 admitted to probate a will signed with the words "your loving mother" being satisfied that the testatrix meant these words to represent her name.

[30] *In the Goods of Bryce* 2 Curt. 325. See generally Hanna J.'s review of the law regarding the sufficiency of a mark in *In the Goods of Kieran* [1933] I.R. 222, 226–7

[31] *Baker v Dening* (1838), 8 Ad. & El. 94; *In the Estate of Holtam* (1913) 108 L.T. 732 ("a sort of broken line") *In the Goods of Gannn* (1931) 65 I.L.T.R. 113 (a dot on the I of the testator's Christian name); *Re Finn* (1935) 10 L.J.P. 36 (a blot on the will made by the inked finger of an illiterate testator).

[32] [1933] I.R. 222

than physical infirmity is illustrated by the decision in the English case *Re Colling*.[33] There a testator who was a patient in hospital had started to sign his name in the presence of a fellow patient and a ward sister who had agreed to act as witness. Before the testator had completed his signature the sister was called away to tend another patient, and the signature was completed in her absence. Since the testator had intended to sign his full name, and had not done so in the presence of both witnesses, the execution was held to be invalid. Of course there is always the possibility in circumstances like those in *Re Colling* that the testator may subsequently acknowledge his signature in the presence of both witnesses.[34]

2.3.3 The testator in *In the Goods of Kieran* was able to make the two scrawls in his will unaided, but it would have been no bar to its validity if his hand had been guided in making the mark. The authorities establish that a testator may be helped to make his signature by name or mark, but, as Lord MacDermott L.C.J. pointed out in *Fulton* v *Kee*[35] the

"testator must do some physical act in connection with the signing: the sufficiency of the act is not a matter of efficiency or degree, and in itself the act may be quite inadequate to accomplish the signing: but, considered in relation to the surrounding circumstances, it must suffice to indicate, on the part of the testator, an intention to execute his will".

That the question of the necessary degree of physical participation on the part of a testator who is being assisted in making his signature, is one of great nicety is underlined by the facts in *Fulton* v *Kee*. The testator, who at the time of execution was in the late stages of a crippling disease of the central nervous system, was incapable of any movement, and the evidence of the witness who assisted him in making his mark was to the effect, that the pen was "backed against" the inert fingers of the testator when the mark was made. Indeed, the witness said, in evidence, that he had made the mark. The trial judge had told the jury that if they accepted the evidence of the attesting witnesses, they were entitled to hold that the will had been duly executed. The Court of Appeal found however that there must be some positive physical contribution on the part of the testator, which is sufficient to indicate an intention to execute his will personally, and since the jury was not so instructed a new trial was ordered.[36]

[33] [1972] I.W.L.R. 1440

[34] The problem in *Re Colling* arose from the fact that during the absence of the ward sister the testator had completed his signature and the other witness had signed the will. The will therefore had not been signed by the testator, or his signature acknowledged, before both witnesses had signed. The effect of *Re Colling* is now modified in England by the Administration of Justice Act 1982 (C. 53) which provides that an acknowledgement by a witness of his previous signature has the same effect as the actual making of his signature.

[35] [1961] N.I. 1, 13

[36] See Curran L.J.'s dissenting opinion at [1961] N.I. 1 23

2.3.4 Since it is also the case that a will may be signed by an agent of the testator, it may be difficult in the circumstances of a particular case, to distinguish between an assisted signature and one made by an agent on the direction of the testator. Lord MacDermott pointed out in *Fulton* v *Kee*[37] that one must have regard to all the circumstances, but, speaking generally, he thought that conduct on the part of a testator which would not justify a finding that he had executed his will personally, might well be capable of implying a direction to someone else to sign on his behalf. Lord MacDermott instanced the example of a testator who is completely powerless in his limbs, and who says to his solicitor, who has drawn up the will according to his instructions "now put my hand on yours", and the solicitor then writes the testator's name with the testator's limp fingers upon his. While that would not amount to a personal execution by the testator, Lord MacDermott opined, that in the absence of something to indicate the contrary, he did not see why it should not be regarded as a signing by direction. The trial judge in *Fulton* v *Kee* however, had not explained to the jury the distinction between an assisted signature and one made by an agent on the direction of the testator.

2.3.5 Whatever mode a testator uses to sign his will, the special requirement in each case is, that he intends his initials, mark, stamp or seal to be his signature to the will. Thus in *In the Goods of Emerson*[38] a testator, in the presence of two subscribing witnesses, had affixed a seal stamped with his initials to his will with the words "This is my hand and seal." Warren J. said:

> "It is settled that a seal, qua seal, is not sufficient ... but it is also settled that a mark is a sufficient signature if it be intended to represent a signature. The question is whether the testator intended this seal to be a signature as well as a seal. He said, touching the seal – the initials as well as as the wax – 'This is my hand and seal.' What did he mean by 'my hand'? Obviously his signature. I am of opinion therefore, that this will was signed by the testator."[39]

A testator's intention that his seal is to serve as his signature could of course be evidenced by actions less formal than those in the *Emerson* case.

2.3.6 While the courts have exercised considerable leniency with regard to the requirement of signature, it is necessary that some mark be made of the will by the testator, or by some person in his presence and by his direction. In *Kevil* v *Lynch*[40] the testator held a pen in his hand and put it to the name

[37] *Ibid* at pp. 14, 15
[38] (1882) 9 L.R. Ir. 443
[39] *Ibid*
[40] (1874) 9 I.R. Eq. 249

"Patrick Kevil" which was subscribed to the will, and adopted that name as his signature. No proof could be given that there was any ink in the pen, or any visible trace made, when the testator placed the pen on the will. The Probate Court considered that there was no evidence in the statement of facts, to justify the presumption that a mark had been made by the testator himself, or by some person in his presence and by his direction and, as the case then stood, there was insufficient proof of due execution. The case was remitted to the Quarter Sessions and, in a new statement of facts, it emerged that there had been ink in the pen when the testator placed it on the mark, from which fact the Chairman drew the inference that the ink had stained the paper and the will had been duly executed.[41] Although the fact that there was ink in the pen was crucial to the outcome in *Kevil* v *Lynch* it is arguable that the passing of a dry pen by the testator over a signature already on the will could amount to an acknowledgement of that signature.[42]

2.4 Location of the signature

2.4.1 The requirement in section 9 of the Wills Act, 1837, that a will should be signed at the foot or end thereof by the testator, or by some person in his presence and by his direction, was based on certain findings in a Report of the Real Property Commissioners, that wills were invariably signed in that way, and that the practice was a desirable one, since it impressed upon a testator the seriousness and finality of what he was doing, and rendered void what were termed "imperfect pages".[43] The location of the testator's signature at the foot or end of the will was thus intended to provide evidence of genuineness, and to preclude fraudulent additions to the will after its execution.

2.4.2 The requirement however was construed strictly by the courts, and probate was refused in cases where, although the testamentary intention was clear and undoubted, the testator's signature was not placed literally at the foot or end of the will. In order to remedy what had become a wholly unsatisfactory state of affairs, the Wills Amendment Act, 1852,[44] otherwise Lord St Leonard's Act, provided, that every will should, so far as regards the position of the signature of the testator, or the person signing for him, be deemed to be valid, if the signature was so placed, that it would be apparent of the face of the will that the testator intended to give effect by

---

[41] *Ibid* at p. 251. The Probate Court before which the case had come again held that no fault could be found with the determination of the Chairman in point of law and the Court had no jurisdiction to review or entertain an appeal from the Chairman's determination of fact.

[42] See Mellows *op. cit.* at p. 57

[43] Fourth Report of the Real Property Commissioners (1833) at p. 16. See Davey "The Making and Revocation of Wills" (1980) Conveyancer 64, 67

[44] 15 & 16 Vict. c. 24

such signature to the writing signed as his will. This provision was followed by an enumeration of circumstances, such as the fact that the signature did not immediately follow the foot or end of the will, or that a blank space intervened between the concluding word of the will and the signature, which would not affect the validity of the will. The Act did however contain express prohibitions as to space and time in relation to the signing of a will, and it was provided that a signature would not give effect to any disposition or direction inserted in a will after the testator had signed it.

2.4.3 These general provisions in the 1852 Act have been reproduced in section 78 of the Succession Act 1965, Rule 3 of which provides, that so far as concerns the position of the signature of the testator, or of any person signing for him, it is sufficient if the signature is so placed at or after, or following, or under, or beside, or opposite to the end of the will that it is apparent on the face of the will, that the testator intended to give effect by the signature to the writing signed as his will. The benign circumstances enumerated in the 1852 Act are also reproduced in Rule 4 of section 75 which provides that no will shall be affected by he circumstances –
(a) that the signature does not follow or is not immediately after the foot or end of the will; or (b) that a blank space intervenes between the concluding word of the will and the signature; or (c) that the signature be placed among the words of the testimonium clause or of the clause of attestation, or follows or is after or under the clause of attestation, either with or without a blank space intervening, or follows or is after or under, or beside the names or one of the names of the attesting witnesses; or (d) that the signature is on a side or page or other portion of the paper or papers containing the will in which no clause or paragraph or disposing part of the will is written above the signature; or (e) that there appears to be sufficient space on or at the bottom of the preceding side or page or other portion of the same paper in which the will is written to contain the signature; and the enumeration of the above circumstances shall not restrict the generality of Rule 1.[45]

2.4.4 The express prohibition in the 1852 Act in relation to the timing of the testator's signature is reproduced in Rule 5 of section 78 which provides, that a signature shall not be operative to give effect to any disposition or direction inserted in a will after the signature is made. While the latitude afforded by Rules 3 and 4 of section 78, in relation to the

---

[45] Which provides that to be valid a will shall be signed at the foot or end thereof by the testator, or by some person in his presence and by his direction.

spatial location of the testator's signature, is defensible on broad policy grounds, the dangers which would attach to the admission to probate of insertions made in a will after it has been signed are so great as to justify the express prohibition in Rule 5. Cases deriving from the 1852 Act may still offer some guidance to Irish courts in this area, although such cases are not always consistent, and while they show that the courts were prepared to take a liberal view of the spatial location of the signature, if it was appended later in time than the writing propounded as the will, the converse was not always true. Thus in *In the Goods of White*[46] a testator had added below his signature and the attestation clause, these words: "I find on reading the above, previous to the execution thereof, that I omitted to name my trustees and executors. I hereby appoint my son and my friend L my executors and trustees." Despite proof that the words below the signature were written prior to the execution of the will, the court held that the added words could not be included in probate of the will. The court distinguished the instant case from those cases[47] in which words written underneath the signature were connected by physical marks with words written above the signature, and thus held to be interlineations in connection with the latter. The decision in *In the Goods of White* was technically correct, but surely falls into that category of cases which has led a distinguished American commentator to categorise the law relating to wills as, "being notorious for its harsh and relentless formalism".[48] It is to be hoped that future Irish courts will exercise more robustly the discretion conferred on them by Rules 3 and 4 of section 78, if the express prohibition in Rule 5 is otherwise satisfied.

2.4.5 The apparent simplicity of successive statutory requirements governing the location of the signature notwithstanding, testators have continued to place their signatures in every conceivable place other than at the foot or end of their wills, and such problems were not altogether resolved by the 1852 Act.[49] Some relief has been afforded to errant testators however by the fact that the words "foot" and "end", in relation to wills, are not tautologous, and the courts have exercised a wide discretion as to what constitutes the foot or end of the will in the intention of the testator. Thus, in a case where there was no room at the foot of the will for the signatures of the testator and the witnesses, and the paper was turned sideways and the signature written in the margin at right angles to the will, with the

---

[46] [1896] 1 I.R. 269

[47] *In the Goods of Birt* (1871) L.R. 2 P. & D. 214; *In the Goods of Greenwood* [1892] P. 7; *In the Goods of White* 6 Jur. (N.S.) 808

[48] Langbein "Substantial Compliance with the Wills Act" (1975) 88 Harvard Law Review, 489

[49] "It was not intended by the legislature that all the honest blunders of testators should be overcome by the Act of 1852." *In the Goods of Martin* [1928] N.I. 138, 143 (per Andrews L.J.)

testator's signature near the top of the will, it was held that the signatures were adequate in the circumstances to give effect to the will.[50] Likewise, where a testator's signature was inserted in an oblong box, which had been specially lined off for that purpose in the margin of the will, it was held that the signature was such as to make it apparent on the face of the will that the testator intended to give effect to the document as his will.[51] That the courts do not invariably accept signatures in the margin however is shown by *In the Goods of Harris, decd*,[52] in which Willmer J. said, of the will before him, that it

> "is not a case where, the page being otherwise full, the testator has turned it sideways and signed in the margin, which might very well be taken, in accordance with the habits of ordinary letter writers to be a continuation from the bottom of the page."

2.4.6 Asterisks and other signs of interpolation or interlineation have been judicially recognised[53] as evidence of a testator's intention, that words physically beneath the signature are intended to be above it, provided of course that there is evidence that such words were written before the execution of the will. The cases are not consistent however as to whether, if there is evidence that the testator's signature was appended later in time or intention, but not in space, to the remainder of the will, the signature will be held to validate the will. This inconsistency has led an English textwriter to conclude somewhat resignedly: "All that can be said is that some wills may be saved if the judge wishes to save them."[54]

2.4.7 While a will may be validly executed if written on several sheets of paper, or on a single sheet folded so as to constitute several pages, and the testator's signature appears on only one sheet, the question whether the testator's signature is at the foot or end of the will is often problematic in such cases. Here again, the cases show a diversity of approach. At the liberal end of the scale is the decision in *In the Goods of Ffrench*,[55] in which case the testatrix had written her will on two of the four pages of a sheet of notepaper. The will was signed at the end of the first page and there attested. The second and third pages were blank and certain legacies were written in the fourth page. The Chief Registrar admitted the first page to probate but refused to admit the fourth page since it was not, in his opinion, apparent on the testamentary document that the testatrix

[50] *In the Estate of Roberts, decd.* [1934] P. 102

[51] *In the Goods of Hornby, decd.* [1946] P. 172

[52] [1952] P. 319, 324

[53] *In the Goods of Birt* (1871) L.R. 2 P. & D. 214; *In the Goods of Martin* [1928] N.I. 138, 144 (per Andrews L.J.); *In the Goods of Elliott* [1931] I.R. 340

[54] Mellows "Law of Succession" (3rd ed. 1977) at p. 76

[55] (1889) 23 L.R. Ir. 433

intended to give effect to the words so written as part of her will. On appeal, Warren J. admitted the entire document to probate, being satisfied by the affidavit evidence of a Dr Harrison, who had read the will to the testatrix, that she had approved of both sides of the paper when she made her mark. Since Warren J. did not address the question of the location of the testatrix's signature it is not altogether surprising that the decision in *In the Goods of Ffrench* has provoked adverse criticism, most notably from the Northern Ireland Court of Appeal in *In the Goods of Martin*,[56] in which Andrews L.J. said, that Warren J. had substituted a test of knowledge and approval of the contents of a will for compliance with the statutory requirements.

2.4.8 The deceased's will in the latter case was written on a printed form consisting of a large sheet of paper folded vertically so as to form four numbered pages. The first page contained the appointment of executors, and certain bequests and desires. The letters "P.T.O." were written at the bottom right hand corner of the page. The second page contained further bequests followed by the testator's signature and the attestation clause, and in the bottom right hand corner were again written the letters "P.T.O." There was not enough room on the second page for a residuary clause and directions as to the payment of charitable legacies; and these were written on the upper half of the third page. The Court of Appeal (Andrews and Best LJJ.) varied the order of Moore L.C.J., who had admitted the entire document to probate, and held, that while the first and second pages should be admitted to probate, the third page must be excluded as that portion of the will followed the signature. Considering the matter in the light of section 1 of Lord St Leonard's Act[57] it seemed to Andrews L.J. impossible to hold that the contents of page three should be admitted to probate unless pages two and three could be treated in reality as one page. The Lord Chief Justice had admitted the entire document to probate apparently on the ground that if the paper in which the will was written was folded across instead of down the middle of pages two and three, then not only was the signature "under" all that was written on so-called page three, but also "followed" it. It seemed to Andrews L.J. that in treating pages two and three as really one page the Lord Chief Justice had made "an artificial division across the middle of them".[58] Although the latter approach might be more consonant with the justice and merits of the instant case, Andrews L.J. felt unable to adopt it since he could not do for the testator something which would "be absolutely at variance with what he or his draftsman did for himself".[59] Andrews L.J. went on to point out

---

[56] [1928] N.I. 138, 146. See also Best L.J. at pp. 149, 150

[57] 15 & 16 Vict. c. 24

[58] [1928] N.I. 138, 142

[59] *Ibid*

that in those cases where words written physically beneath, or after, the testator's signature have been deemed to be above it there was clear internal evidence by way of asterisks or other marks of interlineation that such was the testator's intention.[60] The decision in the *Martin* case shows that internal evidence may have the opposite effect, in that the letters "P.T.O." written at the bottom of each page were a key provided by the testator as to the proper sequence of the different parts of his will, and the court had to take cognisance of this.[61]

2.4.9 Both Andrews L.J. and Best L.J. were of the opinion that *In the Goods of Ffrench*[62] had been wrongly decided. While the only ground offered by Warren J. for his decision in that case is clearly indefensible in the light of the statutory requirement as to the location of the testator's signature, it is arguable that a more defensible option was open to Warren J. When the sheet of paper on which Kate Ffrench's will was written was opened out, the fourth page was to the left of the first page on which the testatrix had made her mark. There was no catchword from page to page, each of which was complete in itself, and a benign court might well have held the pages to be in contextual sequence. This was the ground upon which Hanna J. later admitted an entire document to probate in *In re Mary Jane Boylan*.[63] Owing to the manner in which the paper on which it was executed was folded, a will commenced on the lower half of the page and the continuation, including the testatrix's signature and the attestation clause, were on the upper half of the page. Nevertheless, Hanna J. was satisfied that although the will terminated on the upper half of the page, the page was at the time of execution folded in such a way that the whole will was in contextual sequence, and the lower half was anterior to the signature.[64]

2.4.10 If the will is written on more than one page the court must be satisfied that the separate pages constitute a single testamentary document. In *Sterling & Anor* v *Bruce*[65] the purported will was contained in a sealed envelope, which, when opened, revealed seven pages pinned together. One page was blank, most of the other pages commenced with a new clause, and the quality of the writing varied from page to page. In these circumstances, Jones L.J. found that it was probable that the will was not written out as a continuous whole, and could not therefore be deemed to have been duly executed.

[60] *Ibid* at p. 144

[61] *Ibid* at p. 142

[62] (1889) 23 L.R. Ir. 433

[63] []942] Ir. Jur. Rep. 2

[64] Hanna J. held that the facts in the instant case were sufficiently covered by the decision of Sir F. Jeune in *In the Goods of Gilbert* (1898) 78 L.T. 762

[65] [1973] N.I. 255

2.4.11 The facts of the latter case also raised the question, whether a will could be validly executed if the several sheets constituting the will were not physically joined or otherwise attached at the time of execution. It is obviously desirable for practical reasons that the several pages of a will should be attached in some way which would prevent the accidental loss of a page, but the courts have not insisted on the need for such attachment, and there are some cases which suggest that it is sufficient for the valid execution of a will if the other pages were in the same room as that in which the last page was signed and attested.[66] Some English textwriters do not go this far however, and suggest that it is sufficient if for example the pages are held together by finger and thumb, or are pressed together by the testator at the time of execution.[67] This view was criticised by Jones L.J., who said in the *Sterling* case:

"It seems to me that if a will is complete, although on separate sheets, it would be an unreal distinction to admit the will to probate if the various sheets were physically joined or touching at the time of execution but to say that the execution was defective if, though the other formalities of execution had been duly observed, the different sheets making up the will, though in existence and in the same room as was the testator, were not physically joined or touching."[68]

2.4.12 Among the cases cited by Jones L.J. in support of his preferred view that execution was valid if the sheets comprising the will, other than the sheet bearing the execution, were in existence and in the same room as that in which the execution took place, was *In the Goods of Tiernan.*[69] The latter case involved a holograph will written by the testator on three separate sheets of paper which were not physically attached or numbered, and there was no catchword from page to page. The sheets were enclosed in an envelope which, when opened, showed the sheets to be in their natural order. The last sheet contained only the attestation clause and the signature of the testator and witnesses. The evidence of the attesting witnesses revealed some doubt as to the position of the last sheet in relation to the other sheets at the time of execution, but the court was satisfied that the other sheets were also on the table on which the signatures on the last sheet were written, and as a matter of inference were under the control of the testator. Hanna J. was of the opinion that the authorities establish

"that if a will be written on several separate and disconnected sheets of

[66] See the cases referred to by Jones L.J. at [1973] N.I. 255, 262

[67] Mellows goes further and hopes that the "sensible approach" adopted in *Stirling* v *Bruce* will be followed in England. See Mellows op. cit. at p. 54

[68] [1973] N.I. 255, 263

[69] [1942] I.R. 572

paper and the last only be attested, although no part of the will may have been seen by the witnesses, it should be admitted to probate on the presumption that the whole will was in the room and under the control of the testator at the time of the execution. This presumption may, however, be rebutted by the circumstances of the case or by evidence which would be a question for the court or the jury."[70]

Jones L.J., who did not find it necessary in *Sterling & Anor v Bruce*[71] to go as far as Hanna J. in the *Tiernan* case, since the facts before him were such as to rebut any presumption of the nature contemplated by Hanna J., was far from satisfied that the authorities relied on by Hanna J. supported the wide presumption expressed in the *Tiernan* case. Be that as it may, it is arguable that the presumption is consistent with the principle *omnia praesumuntur rite esse acta* and should normally apply in the absence of evidence such as that afforded by the document itself in the *Sterling* case.

2.5 Acknowledgment of signature

2.5.1 Rule 2 of section 78 of the Succession Act provides, as we have seen, that the signature of the testator shall be made *or acknowledged* by him in the simultaneous presence of each of two or more witnesses. The courts have adopted a liberal approach to what constitutes acknowledgment, and the witnesses need not know that the signature which is being acknowledged is appended to a will. It is acknowledgment of the signature and not the will which is important.[72]

2.5.2 While an express verbal acknowledgment is desirable it is not essential, and a testator may acknowledge his signature by gestures or conduct.[73] The silence or passivity of the testator is no bar to a valid acknowledgment, and in *Cooke v Kenny*[74] Hanna J. said:

"If a silent testator, whose signature is physically visible to himself and the witnesses, has the witnesses brought in, and can see and acquiesce in their action of signing the will as his witnesses, from his point of view that is an acknowledgment that it is his signature."

A valid acknowledgement was also inferred by the court from the circumstances in *Gillic v Smyth*,[75] where the evidence of the surviving attesting witness was to the effect that the testator had called upon him and

---

[70] *Ibid* at p. 580

[71] [1973] N.I. 255, 264

[72] *Clery v Barry* (1889) 21 L.R. Ir. 152, 164 (per Palles C.B.). See also *Dubourdieu v Patterson* (1920) 54 I.L.T.R. 23 and *Re Devlin* [1939] Ir. Jur. Rep. 85

[73] *In the Goods of Davies* (1860) 2 Rob. Eccl. 337; *Lewis v Lewis* [1908] P.I.

[74] [1932] I.R. 574, 579

[75] (1915) 49 I.L.T.R. 36

said that the parish priest wanted him to sign a paper. When he went to the chapel he found in the sacristy the parish priest, the testator, and the other attesting witness. In their presence he signed the paper opposite the word "witnesses" and the other witness did likewise. All the writing on the paper was in the handwriting of the parish priest, and at no time was the paper read over to or by the testator in the presence of the witnesses, nor was the nature of the paper explained to the witnesses. Nevertheless, the court held that there was sufficient evidence to prove that the testator had acknowledged his signature in the presence of the witnesses. Palles C.B. said:

> "The signature must have been on the paper when the testator went to call for the witnesses. The question therefore arose whether there was a sufficient acknowledgment, the signature being on the paper and in a position where the witnesses could see it. The witnesses were asked in the presence of the testator to sign the paper; that clearly meant that they were to sign as witnesses, because the word 'witnesses' appeared opposite to the signatures."[76]

2.5.3 A signature can be acknowledged only if it is already inscribed on the will, but it is not necessary, where a testator produces a paper and gives the witnesses to understand it is his will, to have direct evidence that his name was on the paper when he asked the witnesses to sign it.[77] The court may infer from the circumstances that the signature was there at the time the testator acknowledged the paper as his will.[78] It is also sufficient if the testator's signature might be seen by the attesting witnesses, whether they do see it or not, at the time of acknowledgment.[79] It is otherwise if the signature is concealed, or is not apparent, and the witnesses are unable to see it.[80]

2.5.4 That acknowledgment by the testator of his signature must precede attestation by the witnesses, is underlined by the unusual facts in *Burke* v *Moore*,[81] which also point up a difficulty when the acknowledgment is of a signature made, not by the testator himself, but by someone on his behalf and by his direction. An intending testator's name was, by his direction and in his presence, subscribed for him to a document purported to be his will, and two other persons, who were present when his name was subscribed, but not when the direction was given, acted as attesting witnesses. The

---

[76] *Ibid* at p. 37

[77] See *In the Goods of McDonald, decd.* [1942] I.R. 201, 203 (per Maguire P.)

[78] *Gillic* v *Smyth, supra*

[79] *Kelly* v *Keating* (1871) I.R. 5 Eq. 174, 175; *Daintree* v *Butcher* (1888) 13 P.D. 102, 103

[80] *Hudson* v *Parker* (1844) 1 Rob. Ecc. 14; *In the Goods of Gunstan* (1882) 7 P.D. 102; *Re Groffman* [1969] 1 W.L.R. 733

[81] (1879) I.R. 9 Eq. 609

testator then made a mark immediately above the name so subscribed for him. The court held that, there being no evidence that the subscribed name had been acknowledged as his signature by the intending testator in the presence of the attesting witnesses, and his mark having been made by him after the attestation of the witnesses, the execution was invalid. The mere passive presence of the testator when the will was being signed for him before the attesting witnesses, was thus not deemed to constitute an acknowledgment, and this would seem to impose a more exacting standard of acknowledgment for a signature subscribed on the testator's behalf than for a signature subscribed by the testator himself. Lord MacDermott offered an explanation for this distinction in *Fulton* v *Kee*,[82] where he said:

> "where the agent receives his direction in the absence of the witnesses but signs in their presence it would seem that, to comply with the section (s.9 of the 1837 Act) the testator must subsequently acknowledge the signature in the presence of the witnesses: see *Burke* v *Moore*.[83] That is understandable, for in such a case the witnesses, not having witnessed the direction, would have no certain means of identifying the testator with the signature unless he acknowledged it. But where they witness both signature and direction, an acknowledgment by the testator in addition does not appear to be required by either the scheme or the wording of s. 9."

Lord MacDermott might have added that the difficulty may be compounded for the attesting witnesses by the fact that the person signing the will on behalf of the testator may sign his own name rather than that of the testator.[84] Be that as it may, it is arguable, that the testator's presence, together with that of the attesting witnesses, when the will is signed on his behalf, should normally constitute a sufficient acknowledgment of the testator's signature.

2.5.5 That the courts have not been wholly inflexible with regard to this question of acknowledgment, can be seen from the decision in *In the Goods of Pattison*[85] where a testatrix had signed her will without her signature then being attested. She subsequently signed it again, in the presence of two witnesses, who signed above her later signature but before she had written it. The words "signed again in the presence of etc." appeared before the witnesses signatures, and Dodd J. held that these words were evidence of an intention to acknowledge the previous signature, and admitted the will to probate.

---

[82] [1961] N.I. 1, 10
[83] (1879) I.R. 9 Eq. 609
[84] See *ante* p. 34
[85] [1918] 2 I.R. 90

2.6 Attestation

2.6.1 (a) Presence of the witnesses. The requirement that the testator's signature be made or acknowledged in the presence of two or more witnesses has been interpreted liberally by the courts and, as we have seen, it is not necessary that the witnesses actually see the testator write his signature or see the signature when it is being acknowledged.[86]

2.6.2 It may be a relatively straightforward matter for the court to infer that the testator's signature was made, or acknowledged, in the presence of two or more witnesses when the testator and witnesses were physically proximate at the time of the purported attestation, but it may be less easy for the court to infer a valid attestation in the absence of such physical proximity. There is however some authority to the effect that there is a presumption of valid attestation, in the absence of contrary evidence, if a so-called line of sight exists between the testator and the witnesses at the relevant time.[87] Thus, the testator and the witnesses need not be in the same room if, for example, a connecting door between two rooms was ajar and the witnesses could have seen the testator in the act of signing, had they chosen to do so. The attestation will apparently be invalid however if the witnesses would have needed to move in order to make the necessary observation.

2.6.3 The line of sight test may seem somewhat arbitrary in that it validates an attestation when a witness could have seen the act of signing by the testator by simply raising his eyes, or turning his head, but not where he would have been obliged to take a few steps in order to make the necessary observation. The distinction between these two sets of circumstances is indeed a fine one, but it might be said in defence of the line of sight test that it allows the courts to avoid the difficult and invidious task of measuring the degree of movement and dislocation allowable to an attesting witness, and it is also consistent with the maxim *ut res magis valeat quam pereat*.

2.6.4 (b) Signature of witness. The usual and most desirable method of subscription by a witness is that he sign his own name in his own handwriting, not least because a handwritten signature is more easily authenticated. It is not essential however that the witness sign his name or initials, and a description, or a mark, have all been held to constitute a

---

[86] See *ante* p. 45 and *Woodhouse* v *Balfour* (1887) 13 P.D. 2; *Carter* v *Seaton* (1901) 85 L.T. 76

[87] See *Winchilsea* v *Wauchope* (1827) 3 Russ. 441 and Mellows "The Law of Succession" (4th ed. 1983) at p. 57

[88] *Casson* v *Dade* (1781) 1 Bro. C.C. 99. See Mellows at p. 57

sufficient compliance with the statutory requirement of signature.[89] A will may not be deemed to be validly executed however if the evidence shows that a witness, by writing his christian, or first name only, had not completed his intention to attest. In *McConville* v *McCresh*[90] Warren J. held that in order to establish the validity of an attestation by a christian-name, it must be shown that such name, designation, or mark, was used by the witness to identify himself and with a completed intention of thereby attesting the will. Warren J. explained his finding thus:

> "Suppose an intending witness to write his Christian-name, and then, whether from caprice or an opinion formed on the moment that the testator was insane or unfairly treated, to refuse to write his surname, this would not be due execution; and I think the principle is the same whatever may be the nature of the cause which interferes with the completion of the intention: on this ground I condemn the will."[91]

2.6.5 There are important distinctions to be made between subscription by a testator and subscription by an attesting witness. The first of these is that section 78 of the Succession Act does not provide for the subscription by a third party of the name of an attesting witness. While the hand of the latter may be guided or assisted in making his signature there must be some physical act done by the witness in connection with the transfer of the ink to the paper.[92] Thus in *In the Estate of Bulloch*[93] the Northern Ireland Court of Appeal held that a witness should participate by some physical act in the affixing of his name by means of a stamp. In *In the Goods of Maria Mullins decd*[94] the appending to the will by a third party of the name of one of the attesting witnesses at the request of the witness, and in his presence, and in the presence of the testatrix, was held to be insufficient as an act of attestation, but Maguire P. also held in that case that the subsequent erasure of one of two signatures of original witnesses to a codicil, did not have the effect of undoing what had been done by way of valid execution.[95]

---

[89] See *In the Estate of Bulloch* [1968] N.I. 96, 100 (per Lord MacDermott L.C.J.)

[90] (1879) 3 L.R. Ir. 73

[91] *Ibid* at p. 76

[92] *Bell* v *Hughes* (1880) 5 L.R. Ir. 407, 408 (per Warren J.)

[93] [1968] N.I. 96. Lord MacDermott said (at p. 102) of Warren J.'s judgement in *Bell* v *Hughes* that when applied to a case where a rubber stamp is used "it means that the attesting witness must do some physical act, as, for example, by touching the stamp or holding the hand or arm of the person applying it to the paper, with the intention of attesting."

[94] [1944] Ir. Jur. Rep. 21. The testatrix had executed a codicil to her will in the presence of a number of witnesses, two of whom signed the codicil as attesting witnesses. One of the attesting witnesses was named as a legatee in the codicil and, in the belief that his signature made the codicil invalid it was partly erased and the name of another witness inserted.

[95] *Ibid* at p. 23

2.6.6 Section 78 of the Succession Act, like section 9 of the Wills Act, makes no provision for the acknowledgment by a witness of his signature.[96] The position in this jurisdiction now differs from that in England, which has been altered by the Administration of Justice Act, 1982,[97] which provides that each witness may acknowledge his signature in the presence of the testator but not necessarily in the presence of any other witness.

2.6.7 (c) Location of signatures of witnesses. It does not matter where the witnesses sign the will, provided that they append their signatures with the intention of attesting the testator's signature. Thus in *In the Goods of Ellison*[98] the attesting witnesses signed their names in a blank space left in the body of the will for the names of the executors, the testator having acknowledged his signature in their presence and directed them to sign in the space in which their names appeared. Andrews J., who held the attestation valid, said that he would have had some difficulty in holding that "subscribe", in relation to witnesses, did not mean that they should "write underneath" the signature of the testator were it not that the matter had already been decided.[99]

2.6.8 It is clearly desirable however for the signatures of the witnesses to be located close to, if not actually underneath, that of the testator, if only for the reason that it will then be easier for the court to infer that the witnesses signed with the intention of attesting the testator's signature.[100] If the signatures of the witnesses are on a separate sheet of paper or page not physically connected with the rest of the will, the court may be unable to make the necessary inference. The efficacy of some physical connection in this respect is illustrated by the facts in *In the Goods of Braddock*[101] where the attestation of witnesses to a codicil was held valid, the witnesses having signed on the back of the will to which the codicil was pinned.

2.6.9 (d) Attestation clause. Although section 78 of the Succession Act, like section 9 of the Wills Act, provides that no form of attestation is necessary, there are compelling reasons why a formal attestation clause should be used. The use of such a clause, where the will has been signed by the testator, raises a presumption that the will has been properly

---

[96] See *Bell* v *Hughes* (1880) 5 L.R. Ir. 407, 408 (per Warren J.)

[97] c. 53, Section 17

[98] [1907] 2 I.R. 480

[99] *Ibid* at p. 482

[100] The court must be satisfied that the witness signed *qua* witness. See *Re Parker, decd.* (1905) 39 I.L.T.R. 6 where the executor, who was also a legatee, signed above the two witnesses in the belief that it was necessary for an executor so to sign. See also *In the Goods of Streatley* [1891] P. 172; Cf. *Re Beadle* [1974] 1W.L.R. 417

[101] (1876) 1 P.D. 433

executed.[102] In the absence of such a clause, or where the attestation clause is insufficient, the witnesses may be required to prove by affidavit evidence that the will has been duly executed.[103] Where direct affirmative evidence cannot be given, because of the deaths or forgetfulness of attesting witnesses, a formal attestation clause gives rise to the presumption *omnia praesumuntur rite esse acta.*[104] The benign effect of such a clause is graphically illustrated by the facts in *Kavanagh* v *Fegan*[105] where, the presumption of due execution, which arose from the use of a regular attestation clause, was held not to be rebutted by the evidence of an attesting witness who was unsure, *inter alia,* whether she had signed the will before or after the testatrix had signed. Hanna J. held, that the evidence of this witness was not sufficiently reliable and definite to enable him "with confidence to rebut the presumption of the regular execution of the will which arises from the existence of a perfect attestation clause".[106]

2.6.10 While the absence of an attestation clause may present the court with certain evidential difficulties, it will not necessarily preclude the admission of a will to probate if the court is otherwise satisfied from circumstantial evidence that the will has been duly executed. Ball C. said in *Clarke* v *Clarke:*[107]

> "The Court of Probate is no more restricted to direct proof than are other courts. In all, circumstantial evidence supplies the want of direct; and presumptions are constantly drawn to compensate for the loss of positive testimony occasioned by accident or lapse of time."

Thus in *Scarff* v *Scarff*[108] where the will in dispute contained no attestation clause and the attesting witnesses could not be identified or found, the Supreme Court, affirming the decision of O'Byrne J., held that there was sufficient circumstantial evidence to justify the court in drawing the conclusion that the testator had either signed or acknowledged his signature in the presence of the two persons whose names were annexed to the will.

---

[102] See *In re Rochford* [1943] Ir. Jur. Rep. 71, 72, (per Hanna, J.) and *O'Meagher* v *O'Meagher* (1883) 11 L.R. Ir. 117

[103] The court can compel the attendance of a recalcitrant witness or dispense with the need for an affidavit from such witness. See *Re Owens* [1929] I.R. 451

[104] See generally *Rolleston* v *Sinclair* [1924] 1 I.R. 157

[105] [1932] I.R. 566

[106] *Ibid* at p. 570

[107] (1879) 5 L.R. Ir. 47, 54

[108] [1927] I.R. 13

2.7 Competency of Witnesses

2.7.1 Successive statutes governing the execution of wills have been surprisingly lax with regard to the competency of witnesses. The requirement in the Statute of Frauds[109] that the attesting witnesses be credible meant no more than that an attesting witness should not receive any benefit under the will, the risk of fraud in the latter case being obviously greater. The Wills Act 1837,[110] replacing the Wills Act (Ir.) 1751,[111] obviated this risk by providing, that where a person attested the execution of a will, such person, or the spouse of such person, could not receive any benefit under the will but the attestation remained valid. This is the current position in the Republic of Ireland under the Succession Act 1965.[112]

2.7.2 Apart from this now redundant requirement of credibility, there have been no statutory requirements relating to the age or intellectual capacity of an attesting witness. That illiteracy is no disqualification is illustrated by the decision in *Clarke* v *Clarke*[113] where it was argued, unsuccessfully, by counsel, that if witnesses are dead and their handwriting can be proven there is every presumption in favour of due execution of the will, but no such presumption arises in the case of marksmen. Fitzgibbon L.J. said:

> "When the Wills Act admitted marksmen as witnesses, it recognised and disregarded the danger (of fraud) which has been so much pressed upon us, at least to the extent of leaving it open to be proved by parol whether or not attesting marks were affixed by particular individuals; and it cannot have been intended that the possibility of proving a will attested by marksmen was to depend upon their happening to survive the testator, and being available to prove the due execution of the instrument after his death."[114]

2.7.3 The dictates of common sense however have placed some limits on the courts' benignity with regard to the competence of witnesses. Since the witnesses must either see the testator's signature, or had an opportunity of seeing it, at the time of writing, or subsequent acknowledgment, it follows that an attesting witness cannot be blind and the courts have so held.[115] The blindness of an attesting witness is an obvious disqualification, but it can also be said that the mere physical presence of a purported witness is

[109] 7 Will. 3 c. 12, s. 9
[110] 7 Will 4 & 1 Vict. c. 26
[111] 25 Geo. 2 c. 11
[112] Section 82. See *post* p. 155
[113] (1879) 5 L.R. Ir. 47
[114] *Ibid* at pp. 56–57
[115] See *Re Gibson* [1949] P. 434

not sufficient, if he is otherwise incapable of attesting the signature because for example he was unconscious at the relevant time.[116] One could go on confidently to assert that presence, in relation to witnesses, connotes mental as well as physical presence were it not for section 81 of the Succession Act, which reproduced section 14 of the Wills Act 1837. Section 81 provides, that if a person who attests the execution of a will is, at the time of execution or at any time afterwards, incompetent to be admitted a witness to prove the execution, the will shall not on that account be invalid.

2.7.4 At first blush the language of section 81 seems to relate to the mental capacity of an attesting witness, with the somewhat odd result that the execution of a will is unaffected by the fact that a witness is incapable of understanding the nature of the transaction to which he is a party. A learned English author has said, in favour of this construction of the similar language in section 14 of the Wills Act that the need for an intending testator to satisfy himself of the mental capacity of the witness is obviated.[117] Be that as it may, we have already seen that the witnesses may be called upon to prove the due execution of the will by swearing affidavit evidence, and they must at least be competent to do so. If the will is not on its face duly executed and, for example, the only surviving witness is incapable of swearing the necessary affidavit evidence of due execution, it is difficult to see how section 81 will otherwise save the will.

2.7.5 Moreover, it is difficult to see how someone who does not understand the nature of the act in which he is engaged can be said to have signed the will *qua* witness, and the courts have rightly been insistent that for an attestation to be valid, the witness must sign with the intention of attesting the signature of the testator.[118] Of course the use of a formal attestation clause which raises the presumption *omnia praesumuntur rite esse acta* may obviate the need to establish such intention, but the absence of such a clause may present difficulties which are not obviously covered by section 81.

2.8 Presumption of Due Execution

2.8.1 As a general rule the courts lean in favour of testacy, and frequently invoke the maxim *omnia praesumuntur rite esse acta* when questions arise as to whether or not a will has been executed in accordance with the statutory formalities. Thus, there is a rebuttable presumption of law that a

---

[116] See *Hudson* v *Parker* (1844) 1 Rob. Ecc. 44 and Parry and Clark "The Law of Succession" (8th ed. 1983) at pp. 33–4

[117] Mellows "The Law of Succession" (4th ed. 1983) at p. 58

[118] See *Gillic* v *Smyth supra; Kavanagh* v *Fegan supra* and *Cooke* v *Henry supra*

will, which on its face is made in conformity with those formalities, should be admitted to probate.[119] Palles C.B. said in *Clery* v *Barry:*[120]

"The principle is, that where upon the face of an instrument everything is regular, and there is nothing to awaken suspicion or call for additional inquiry, then if the evidence is defective either by reason of the death of witnesses, or a lapse of time affecting their recollection, or of other circumstances which may affect their honesty, the same presumption arises as is usually acted on in the ordinary affairs of mankind."

2.8.2 The maxim that everything is presumed to have been properly executed has obvious importance when the attesting witnesses are dead, or otherwise unable to give affirmative evidence of due execution, but in *Clery* v *Barry* the court applied the maxim despite the contrary evidence of the attesting witnesses. Palles C.B. who was of the opinion that the court should not attach one feather's weight to the testimony of either of the attesting witnesses treated the case as if the witnesses "were dead, or had lost their reason, or from other cause were unable to assist the court in arriving at the truth of the transaction".[121] It is clear however, that if the evidence of the attesting witness which rebutted the presumption of due execution had otherwise been unimpeachable, the will would not have been admitted to probate. Davitt J. was later to say in *In the Goods of McLean*:[122]

"The issue, whether or not a particular will has or has not been duly executed, is usually a pure question of fact. It seems to me that all these cases, looked at broadly, merely illustrate the principle that this question, like any other question of fact, should be decided on the balance of probability after all the evidence, circumstantial as well as direct, has been duly weighed and all the relevant circumstances have been taken into account."

2.8.3 While the use of an attestation clause will inevitably tilt the balance of probability in favour of due execution, the absence of such a clause will simply be another evidential factor to be considered by the court. Thus in *Scarff* v *Scarff*[123] the will in dispute contained no attestation clause, the identity of neither of the attesting interests was known, and they could not be called at the trial, and no person who saw the will being executed could be examined. Nevertheless, the will was admitted to probate, Fitzgibbon J. pointing out that the court did not justify the inference of due execution by reliance on the maxim *omnia praesumuntur rite esse acta* but by the

---

[119] *Kavanagh* v *Fegan* [1932] I.R. 566, 569 (per Hanna J.)

[120] (1889) 21 L.R. Ir. 152, 167

[121] *Ibid* at p. 175

[122] [1950] I.R. 180, 184

[123] [1927] I.R. 13

evidence of all the circumstances attendant upon the creation of the document.[124]

2.8.4 While the maxim *omnia praesumuntur rite esse acta* reflects the courts preference for testacy, the benignity of the courts is not unlimited and the Supreme Court set limits to the application of the maxim in *Clarke* v *Early*.[125] In the latter case the will in dispute was, on its face, signed by the testator and the names of two witnesses were appended below that of the testator. There was no attestation clause, but the handwriting and signature of one of the witnesses was identified by his widow, who also deposed to the fact that a man by the name of the second witness was known to, and friendly with, the testator. There was however no evidence, other than the fact of his purported signature on the will that the testator had actually signed the will and this was to prove fatal to its admission to probate.

2.8.5 O'Higgins C.J. opined, that in order to apply the maxim *omnia praesumuntur rite esse acta* two conditions must be observed; firstly, an intention to do some formal act must be established, and, secondly, there must be an absence of credible evidence that due formality had not been observed. O'Higgins C.J. believed that while the second condition could be said to be satisfied in the instant case, the absence of any evidence that the document was signed by the deceased meant that there was no evidence of an intention on his part "to enter into the formality of making a will".[126] It is at least arguable however that such an intention could have been inferred, if the court was otherwise satisfied of the signature's authenticity, from its location immediately below the dispositive text of the will and above the signature of the witnesses. It is difficult to imagine any other practical reason for such signature other than that it was intended to give effect to the will.

2.8.6 It is interesting to compare the decision in *Clarke* v *Early* with decisions in cases involving lost wills, not least because O'Higgins C.J. believed that the strongest authority in favour of the applicant was *Harris* v *Knight*.[127] In the latter case, probate was granted of a lost will no copy of which was produced, but satisfactory evidence of the contents of which was before the court. Both attesting witnesses to the disputed will were dead, but there was evidence to identify the signature of one of them. There was

---

[124] Fitzgibbon J. however doubted the propriety of what he described as the "blind application" of the maxim *omnia praesumuntur rite sees acta* in *In the Goods of Peverett* [1902] P. 205 see [1927] I.R. 13, 25

[125] [1980] I.R. 223. See Wylie "A Casebook on Irish Land Law" (2nd ed. 1986) at p. 496

[126] [1980] I.R. 223, 226

[127] (1890) 15 P.D. 170

also an allegation that the signature of the testator was a forgery, but there was evidence, which the trial judge accepted, that the testator's signature was genuine. In *Clarke* v *Early*, unlike *Harris* v *Knight*, the disputed will was before the court and there was evidence to verify the signature of one of the witnesses, and evidence from which the authenticity of the signature of the other witness could be implied. There was also an allegation which O'Higgins C.J. thought of doubtful authenticity, that the signature on the disputed will was not that of the deceased. Nevertheless, O'Higgins C.J. held, that in the absence of any evidence that it was signed by the deceased, there was no evidence "of an intention on his part to enter into the formality of making a will".[128]

2.8.7 O'Higgins C.J. went on to say that however likely it was that the document in question represented what the deceased would have wished to do with his will this was not sufficient to justify the court ignoring the absence of any evidence that it was in fact his will. This approach contrasts with that taken by the courts in lost will cases, where the outcome is invariably the one which the court considers likely to have commended itself to the testator.[129] This latter point is graphically illustrated by the decision in *Re Yelland*[130] where Oliver J. admitted to probate, a will which had been destroyed more than twenty years before the action and no copy or other documentary evidence of which was in existence and the only evidence of the contents of which, was given by the surviving beneficiary who had read the will once for some five minutes. While Oliver J. found it extremely difficult to accept that after such a period of time the witness could possibly have recollected the exact and literal terms of a will she had once read and never recorded, he considered her evidence to be consistent with a will likely to have commended itself to the testatrix and, on the balance of probabilities, represented the testamentary dispositions contained in the will. Oliver J. was also satisfied, on a reasonable balance of probabilities, that the disputed will had been properly executed by the testatrix.

2.8.8 It is difficult to resist the conclusion that the presumption of due execution is applied more liberally when there is no documentary evidence of the disputed will.

---

[128] [1980] I.R. 223, 226
[129] See *post* pp. 93 *et seq.*
[130] (1975) 119 S.J. 562

2.9 Incorporation by reference

2.9.1 It is convenient, and not altogether inappropriate, when dealing with the statutory formalities for the execution of a valid will, to consider the doctrine of incorporation by reference, which permits a testator to incorporate in his will a document which has not been formally executed by him. Since this doctrine is clearly at odds with the rationale of the legislation governing wills, it is not surprising that the courts have imposed stringent conditions on its operation. Thus it has been established (1) that the document to be incorporated must be in existence at the date of the will and (2) the document to be incorporated must be clearly identified in the will.[131]

2.9.2 The first condition prevents a testator reserving to himself the power to make future unwitnessed dispositions of his property, and it follows logically that the will must refer to the document to be incorporated as being in existence when the will is executed. Whether or not such document was in existence at the date of the will is to be determined from the evidence before the Court, and, in *In the Goods of Mitchell*[132] the fact that the date on the document was later than the date on the will was not conclusive of its admission to probate. While admitting the document in that case to probate Kenny J. opined however, that a court should be slow to incorporate documents with a will, and particularly so when the document is dated after the will.

2.9.3 It is undoubtedly the requirement, that the document to be incorporated must be in existence at the date of the will, which has led the English courts to insist that communication of the objects of a half-secret trust must precede or be contemporaneous with the execution of the will.[133] Viscount Sumner observed in *Blackwell* v *Blackwell*:[134]

"A testator cannot reserve to himself a power of making future unwitnessed dispositions by merely naming a trustee and leaving the purposes of the trust to be supplied afterwards, nor can a legatee give testamentary validity to an unexecuted codicil by accepting an indefinite trust, never communicated to him in the testator's lifetime ..."

There is contrary Irish authority to the effect that the objects of a half-secret trust, like those of a fully secret trust, can be communicated to the

[131] See *In b. Conwell* (1896) 30 I.L.T.R. 23; *Re O'Connor* [1937] Ir. Jur. Rep. 67; *Singleton* v *Tomlinson* (1878) 3 App. Cas. 404; *In the Goods of Smart* [1902] P. 238; *In the Estate of Mordon* [1944] P. 109
[132] (1966) 100 I.L.T.R. 185
[133] See *ante* p. 22
[134] [1929] A.C. 318, 339

trustees at any time before the death of the testator.[135] This Irish position is generally defended on the ground that the secret trust operates dehors the will and therefore has nothing to do with the legislation governing wills. While this may be true of the fully secret trust, of which no mention is made on the face of the will, it is less true of the half-secret trust, a point underlined by the fact that the mode of communication of the objects of a half-secret trust must be consistent with that outlined in the will.[136]

2.9.4 The Irish position on half-secret trusts must be re-examined in light of the fact that such trusts are used less nowadays to provide covertly for illegitimate children or mistresses, than because a testator simply cannot make his mind up at the date of the will.[137] The latter is scarcely a compelling reason for allowing testators to circumvent the legislation governing the execution of wills. A tightening of the rules on secret trusts on the other hand will scarcely make them less attractive for testators who wish to keep certain of their benefactions from public scrutiny, which the simple device of incorporation by reference will fail to do, since the incorporated document will invariably be included in the probate of the will and so open to public inspection.

2.9.5 The condition that the document to be incorporated must be referred to in the will so as to enable it to be identified, is illustrated by the decision in *In re Eugene O'Connor*[138] in which case a testator had left property in his will to his executors to be disposed of by them "as directed". No such directions were ever given during the testator's lifetime but, after his death, two documents were found in an envelope endorsed with the words "My will – to be opened by my executors." Gavan Duffy J. refused to admit these documents to probate since neither of them was referred to or identified in the will, and they were "mere unexecuted attempts at the making of a will". The courts have also excluded the doctrine of incorporation where the document sought to be incorporated does not conform precisely with the description of it in the will. Thus in *In the Goods of Conwell*[139] a testator referred in his will to instructions to his executors which had been "written, signed, and sealed" by him. A document purporting to be instructions to his executors, in the testator's handwriting and signed by him, was found after his death but the document was not sealed. Warren J. refused to admit the document to probate since it was not sealed "and cannot be the document referred to in the will". It

[135] *Re Browne* [1944] I.R. 90. See Wylie "A Casebook on Equity and Trusts in Ireland" (1985) at p. 322
[136] See *ante* at p. 22
[137] *Ibid*
[138] [1937] Ir. Jur. Rep. 67
[139] (1896) 30 I.L.T.R. 23

could of course be argued that lay people use the term "written, signed and sealed" simply to indicate the formal nature of a document, and in the circumstances of the *Conwell* case the court might have treated the word "sealed" as a superfluity.

2.9.6 The potentially subversive consequences for legislation governing the execution of wills, which would follow a too liberal application of the doctrine of incorporation, is illustrated by the facts of an English case, *In the Estate of Bercovitz decd*.[140] The will in that case was on a single sheet of paper at the top of which were the words "My last will and testament" followed by an attestation clause and the signature of the testator and those of the two attesting witnesses. The will was also signed by the testator at the bottom, but this signature was unattested and the judge at first instance pronounced against the will as not being properly executed. In the Court of Appeal counsel for the defendants sought, unsuccessfully, to amend the notice of appeal, by arguing that the words "My last will and testament" at the top of the will were intended to identify the directions in the lower part, and the whole of the typescript should be incorporated in the will of the testator. Although the Court of Appeal refused to allow that matter to be argued for lack of cogency, Danckwerts L.J. did point out that there was no identification of the directions below the attested signature unless it could be by the words "My last will and testament", but those directions were not a last will and testament for the requirements of the statutes for a will were not satisfied. His Lordship added: "If the process of incorporation by reference could be applied in the circumstances of the present case, it seems to me that there would be very little left of the statutory requirements."[141]

2.9.7 While the document to be incorporated must be identified in the will, the standard of identification is not an absolute one, and there may be circumstances in which the identification is reasonably clear but parol evidence is necessary to resolve an equivocation or ambiguity.[142]

2.10 Conflicts of Law

2.10.1 A number of admendments to the rules of international private law relating to wills, are contained in Part VIII of the Succession Act. We are told in the Explanatory Memorandum that the purpose of these amendments is to enable Ireland to adhere to the Convention on the Conflicts of

---

[140] [1962] 1 W.L.R. 321

[141] *Ibid* at p. 327

[142] See *In the Estate of Mardon* [1944] P. 109. If the reference in the will is so imprecise as to be incapable of being applied to any document in particular it will not suffice. See *Allen* v *Maddock* (1858) 11 Moo. P.C. 427 and Parry and Clark "The Law of Succession" (8th ed. 1983) at p. 41

Laws relating to the form of Testamentary Dispositions, which was drawn up at the Hague in October 1961, under the auspices of the Hague Conference on International Private Law. Thus the provisions of Part VIII follow as closely as possible the wording of the Convention.[143]

2.10.2 Section 102(1) of the Succession Act accordingly provides, that a testamentary disposition[144] shall be valid as regards form, if its form complies with the internal law
(a) of the place where the testator made it, or
(b) of a nationality possessed by the testator, either at the time when he made the disposition, or at the time of his death, or
(c) of a place in which the testator had his domicile either at the time when he made the disposition, or at the time of his death, or
(d) of the place in which the testator had his habitual residence either at the time when he made the disposition, or at the time of his death, or
(e) so far as immoveables are concerned, of the place where they are situated.
The marginal note to section 102(1) refers to articles 1 and 2 of the Hague Convention.[145]

2.10.3 A testamentary disposition, revoking an earlier testamentary disposition, will, without prejudice to subsection 1, be valid as regards form if it complies with any one of the laws according to the terms of which, under subsection 1, the testamentary disposition that has been revoked, was valid.[146] It is also provided for the purposes of Part VIII that, if a national law consists of a non-unified system, the law to be applied shall be determined by the rules in force in that system and, failing any such rules, by the most real connexion which the testator had with any one of the various laws within that system.[147] An example of a non-unified system of law, in this context, would be that in the United States, where the law governing the execution of wills varies from state to state.[148] In the usual case, the law of the state in which a testator was habitually resident or domiciled will determine the validity of his will. The determination of whether or not a testator had his domicile in a particular place will be governed by the law of that place.[149]

---

[143] Explanatory Memorandum at pages 8 and 9
[144] "Testamentary disposition" in Part VIII means any will or other testamentary instrument or act. See s. 101 (1)
[145] The previous law was contained in (c. 114) ss. 1, 2 the Wills Act 1861 (Lord Kingsdown's Act)
[146] s. 102 (2)
[147] s. 102 (3)
[148] See generally Langbein (1975) 88 Harvard Law Review 489
[149] s. 102 (4)

2.10.4 Again, without prejudice to section 102(1), a testamentary dispostion made on board a vessel or aircraft will be valid as regards form, if its form complies with the internal law of the place with which having regard to its registration, if any, and any other relevant circumstances, the vessel or aircraft may be taken to have had the most real connexion.[150]

2.10.5 Articles 4 and 5 of the Hague Convention are given effect to respectively in sections 105 and 106 of the Succession Act. Thus Part VIII applies to the form of testamentary dispositions made by two or more persons in one document.[151] For the purposes of Part VIII, any provision of law which limits the permitted forms of testamentary dispositions by reference to the age, nationality or other personal conditions of the testator, shall be deemed to pertain to matters of form.[152] The same rule applies to the qualifications that must be possessed by witnesses required for the validity of a testamentary disposition, and to the provisions of section 82.[153]

2.10.6 The validity of a foreign will, in respect of which a grant of probate or administration is being sought in Ireland, must be formally proved by evidence, which may consist of a certified copy of a grant from the appropriate court in the jurisdiction concerned, or an affidavit from a practising lawyer in that jurisdiction.[154]

2.10.7 The construction of foreign wills is considered elsewhere in this book.[155]

2.11 The Mental Aspect

2.11.1 In addition to complying with the statutory requirements as to form, the aspirant testator must also satisfy certain mental criteria governing the execution of a valid will. Clearly the testator must have an *animum testandi* which does not mean, as we have seen, that he intends to make a will; it is sufficient that he intends to make a disposition of his property which is to take effect on his death, and such disposition is contained in a document which otherwise conforms with the formal requirements for the execution of a valid will.[1] Thus in *In re Anderson*[2] a document which was duly

---

[150] s. 103
[151] s. 105
[152] s. 106 (1)
[153] s. 106 (2)
[154] See Mongey "Probate Practice in a Nutshell" (1980) at p. 15
[155] See *post* pp. 144 *et seq.*
[1] See *ante* p. 33
[2] [1940] Ir. Jur. Rep. 71

executed as a will commenced with the words "In the event of my death occurring without having made a will" and proceeded to make a number of testamentary dispositions. Hanna J. thought that this document was analagous either to a document prepared with a view to the execution of a subsequent will, or to instructions which a solicitor might take and have executed prior to the execution of a more formal will. He held that, the document being duly executed, but no executor having been appointed, application might be made by issue for letters of administration with the said will annexed.[3]

2.11.2 While a document not expressed as a will may thus be admitted to probate if otherwise duly executed, the converse is not invariably true. Although there is a presumption that a duly executed document which appears on its face to be a will was intended as a will, there may be circumstances attending its execution which negative testamentary intent. It was said in a leading English case that

"if the fact is plainly and conclusively made out, that the paper which appears to be the record of a testamentary act, was in reality never seriously intended as a disposition of property, it is not reasonable that the court should turn it into an effective instrument."[4]

The court in that case was prepared to admit parol evidence to the effect that a will was not intended, despite what it recognised as the momentous consequence that such evidence places all wills "at the mercy of a parol story that the testator did not mean what he said".[5] It is scarcely surprising in the light of that consequence, that a heavy burden of proof rests on those who so seek to contest a duly executed will, and much will depend upon the circumstances of the particular case.[6]

2.12 Capacity

2.12.1 Whether the testator had an *animus testandi* involves more than the issue of intention and is, as we shall see, interwoven with and dependent upon, the question whether he had the capacity to make a valid will. The statutory requirements governing capacity are contained in section 77(1) of the Succession Act which provides, that to be valid, a will shall be made by a person who (a) has attained the age of eighteen years or is or has been

---

[3] Hanna J. referred to *In re Slevin* [1938] I.R. 285

[4] *Lister* v *Smith* (1863) 3 Sur. & Tr. 282, 288. The court there held that a purported will or codicil which is intended as a joke or contrivance to effect some collateral act lacks the necessary *animus testandi*

[5] *Ibid* at p.288

[6] See Langbein "Substantial Compliance with the Wills Act" (1975) 88 Harvard Law Review, 489, 514-5

married, and (b) is of sound disposing mind.[7] The requirement as to age or marital status is a straightforward provision which incorporates a policy judgment, which is beyond the purview of the courts, and must be applied by them regardless of the testator's intention. That the testator must be of sound disposing mind, on the other hand, is less clearcut and has many strands which have greatly exercised the courts.

2.12.2 It is for the court to determine in each particular case whether the will was made by a capable testator, a point which is underlined implicitly in *In the Goods of Michael and Mary Mitten decd*[8] in which case the court had to determine the capacity of a person who was a deaf mute, to make an affidavit verifying the handwriting and due execution of two wills. Hanna J. referred to the settled rule that *prima facie* the will of a person who is a deaf mute is the will of an insane person unless satisfactory evidence to the contrary is forthcoming. The learned judge thought that the same rule should apply to the affidavit of such a person, and he was satisfied by the evidence before the court in the instant case, that the deponent was fully aware of the various matters contained in the affidavit, and that his general intelligence made him a fit person to make such an affidavit. Hanna J.'s assessment of the deponent's capacity was based on the fact that the deponent had been trained for many years in an institute for deaf and dumb patients and had also worked capably and satisfactorily as a tailor.

2.12.3 The test of mental capacity is not satisfied merely by proof that the testator was aware of the act in which he was engaged, that is, the making of a disposition of his property which is to take effect on his death, but also requires that the testator made his will with understanding and reason.[9] The testator must, accordingly, be free of mental disorders which impair his capacity to make such a will. A classic statement of the law in this area is to be found in the judgement of Cockburn C.J. in *Banks* v Goodfellow:[10]

> "If the human instincts and affections, or the moral sense, become perverted by mental desease; if insane suspicion, or aversion, take the place of natural affection; if reason and judgment are lost, and the mind becomes a prey to insane delusions calculated to interfere with and disturb its functions and to lead to a testamentary disposition, due only to their baneful influence – in such a case it is obvious that the condition

[7] It is provided in s. 77(2) that a person who is entitled to appoint a guardian of an infant may make the appointment by will notwithstanding that he has not attained the age of eighteen years or is or had been married.

[8] (1934) 68 I.L.T.R. 38

[9] See generally Davey "The Making and Revocation of Wills" (1980) Conveyancer, 64 at pp.65 *et seq.*

[10] (1870) L.R. 5 Q.B. 549, 565

of the testamentary power fails and that a will made under such circumstances ought not to stand."

2.12.4 If a testator suffers from a delusion, which has been judicially defined as a belief which no rational person could hold and which is impervious to reasoned argument, he may be unable to execute a valid will.[11] That it is for the courts to decide in each case whether the delusion in question robs the testator of testamentary capacity is underlined by the facts of *Banks* v *Goodfellow* where the testator had been deluded that he was being pursued by a man already dead and by evil spirits, which were visible to him. Despite this bizarre evidence of the testator's mental state at the time of execution, the court held that he had testamentary capacity, since it was satisfied that these delusions were not capable of influencing the provisions in his will.

2.12.5 There is some English authority to the effect that if a delusion impairs testamentary capacity in relation to part only of a will the unaffected part of the will may be admitted to probate.[12] This has been achieved by drawing an analogy with the courts' practice of excluding from probate matters not within the knowledge and approval of the testator.[13]

2.12.6 The crucial time in relation to the determination of the testator's capacity is the date of execution of the will, and it follows that a testator who suffers from a mental disorder may make a valid will during a lucid interval.[14] There is, however, a presumption that a person who suffered from an incapacitating mental illness continued to lack testamentary capacity at the time of execution, and a heavy burden of proof lies on the person who seeks to propound such a will.[15] The advice offered by Budd J. in *In the Goods of Corboy*[16] in relation to a physically handicapped testator would apply *a fortiori* to a testator enjoying a period of remission from a mental illness. Budd J. said: "It would seem to me that nothing less than firm medical evidence by a doctor in a position to assess the testator's mental capacity could suffice to discharge the onus of proving him to have been a capable testator."[17]

[11] *Dew* v *Clark* (1826) 3 Add. 79; *In b. Farrell* [1954] 88 I.L.T.R. 57; See Mellows "The Law of Succession" (4th ed. 1983) at pp.36 *et seq.*

[12] *In the Estate of Bohrmann* [1938] 1 All E.R. 271

[13] This analogy has been the subject of critical comment. See Parry and Clark "The Law of Succession" (8th ed. 1983) at p.46

[14] *Cartwright* v *Cartwright* (1793) 1 Phill. 90; *Chambers and Yatman* v *Queen's Proctor* (1840) 2 Curt. 415; *In the Estate of Walker* (1912) 28 T.L.R. 466 and see generally Mellows at pp.35 *et seq.*

[15] *Barry* v *Butlin* (1838) 2 Moo. P.C. 480; *Cleare* v *Cleare* (1869) L.R. 1 P. & D. 655

[16] [1969] I.R. 148

[17] *Ibid* at p.167

2.12.7 The question, whether the testator made his will with understanding and reason, is much wider than a medical appraisal of his mental alertness at the time of execution and includes *inter alia*, his consideration of, and provision for, those with moral claims on his bounty.[18]

2.12.8 It is sometimes the case that a testator has developed an aversion to his spouse or one or more of his children for whom no provision is made in his will. The aversion in question might be so irrational as to throw serious doubt on the testator's capacity to make a valid will, but often the courts had to draw a fine distinction between such an aversion and one based on mere caprice or eccentricity, which is allowable under the principle of freedom of testation, for long a cornerstone of our law on succession. Wigram V.C. put it bluntly in *Bird* v *Luckie*[19]:

> "No man is bound to make a will in such a manner as to deserve approbation from the prudent, the wise or the good. A testator is permitted to be capricious and improvident, and is moreover at liberty to conceal the circumstances and the motives by which he has been actuated in his disposition."

2.12.9 It is now arguably the case that the Irish courts are spared the need to draw such fine distinctions in family situations since Part IX of the Succession Act gives to the surviving spouse a legal right share in the testator's estate, and gives to the children of the testator the right to make application to the court, on the ground that the testator failed to make proper provision for them in accordance with his means.[20]

2.12.10 In assessing the testator's capacity to make a valid will, the courts have also been concerned with the state of the testator's knowledge in relation to the property he means to dispose of. Such knowledge is an obvious yardstick of capacity, but is one which must be applied flexibly to the circumstances of the particular case. It might be unreasonable to expect a detailed and precise catalogue of his many and varied holdings in the will of an affluent testator, while lack of information in the will of a testator of humble means might raise questions about his capacity to make a valid will or, more particularly, throw doubt on his knowledge and approval of the contents of the will. The questions concerning capacity and knowledge and approval of contents are not the same, but they often run together with absence of knowledge and approval being argued as an alternative to lack

---

[18] Prior to the enactment of the Succession Act however the principle of freedom of testation allowed a testator to behave capriciously and mischievously towards his spouse and children. See *post* pp. 182 *et seq.*

[19] (1850) S. Hare 301, 306. See also *Re James's Will Trusts* [1962] Ch. 226, 234 (per Buckley J.)

[20] See *post* pp 184 *et seq.*

of testamentary capacity.[21] This has been particularly so in cases involving wills of testators who suffered from severe physical disabilities at the time of execution.

2.12.11 In *Ryan* v *Ryan*[22] the testator was at the time of execution paralysed in every part of his body save the throat and the features of his face. He was unable to render himself intelligible to any person save his wife who, having nursed him for fifteen years, was able to understand vocal sounds which to others were as unintelligible as a foreign language. The testator was otherwise of sound mind, memory and understanding, and his brothers and sisters who disputed the will did so on the ground that his bodily infirmities made it practically impossible for him to execute a will and to express knowledge and approval of its contents. His solicitor however had devised a plan, whereby the testator could express his wishes by answering questions in the affirmative by keeping his eyes closed for a certain time, and answering in the negative by keeping his eyes open. Barton J. was satisfied that the testator's solicitor had succeeded in ascertaining the testator's testamentary intentions and, despite what he described as the strange and unusual circumstances attending its execution, the learned judge could see no reason why he should not grant probate of it.[23]

2.12.12 A presumption was said to arise when a testator of sound mind, memory and understanding, had his will read over to him prior to execution, that he knew and approved of its contents.[24] Such presumption was considered by the Supreme Court in *In re Begley*[25] in which it had been proven in evidence that the disputed will had been read over to the testatrix before she signed it. The jury however had found that while the testatrix was of sound mind, memory and understanding at the time of execution, she did not know and approve the contents of the will. Hanna J. accordingly gave judgment condemning the will. The appellants sought to have the findings of the jury and the judgment of Hanna J. set aside on the grounds that they were contrary to the evidence, particularly in view of the presumption arising from the fact that the testatrix, who was of sound

---

[21] The two often run together where, as in *In the Goods of Corboy, supra*, the testator's medical condition, he was suffering from arteriosclerosis, made it virtually impossible for the legatee named in the codicil to show that the changes effected by the codicil had emanated from the testator. See *post* p. 68

[22] (1904) 4 N.I.J.R. 164

[23] The testator had made a number of wills each successive one being more favourable to his wife who conveyed his instruction for such wills to his solicitor, but Barton J. had no doubt that "the testator was fully able to estimate the respective claims on his bounty of his wife and family and had estimated them very justly." (*Ibid* at p.165)

[24] See *Fulton* v *Andrew* (1875) L.R. 7 H.L. 448, 463 (per Lord Cairns L.C.) and *Garnett-Botfield* v *Garnett-Botfield* [1901] P.335

[25] [1939] I.R. 479

mind, memory and understanding, had the will read over to her before she executed it.

2.12.13 Sullivan C.J. held that the jury's findings could not be disturbed since there were circumstances in connection with the preparation and execution of the will which might reasonably arouse the suspicion of the jury, and it was impossible therefore to say that the presumption of knowledge and approval applied, but he went on to consider the proposition that when a competent testator has had a will read over to him prior to execution, a presumption arises that he knew and approved of its contents. The Chief Justice agreed that there was clear authority for that proposition, but added, that

> "in order that the proposition should apply in any case it must be established to the satisfaction of the jury if the case be tried with a jury, that the will was read over and that it was read over in such a way as to make plain its contents to the testator."[26]

Whether a will was read over to the testator in such latter way will clearly depend on the circumstances of the particular case, and not least on the nature and extent of the testator's infirmity. The testator must be able not only to understand the nature of the testamentary act, but to signify approval of the contents of his will, and as we saw in *Ryan* v *Ryan* only considerable ingenuity on the part of his solicitor enabled the testator to do so.

2.12.14 While the reading over of the will to the testator prior to execution might not confirm unequivocally that he knew and approved of its contents, that fact taken in conjunction with other relevant factors might point to due execution. Such was held to be the case in *In the Goods of Glynn decd*[27] where the testator had suffered a massive stroke prior to the execution of his will. Medical evidence by the testator's doctor was to the effect that the testator was not fit to make a will at the date of execution, because he would not have been able to communicate his ideas or intentions with regard thereto, and it would have been extremely difficult to work out a code of communication. The doctor also pointed out that it is extremely difficult to assess the intellectual function of a person who is unable to speak. The disputed will had been drawn up by a Fr. Donohue, one of the witnesses, on the instructions of the testator prior to the date of the stroke but it had been executed by the testator after that date.

---

[26] *Ibid* at p.492

[27] Unreported judgment of Hamilton P. delivered 10 December 1986 1983 No. 671 See Also *In the Goods of O'Connor Decd.* [1978] I.L.R.M. 247. The finding of Hamilton J. was endorsed by the Supreme Court Walsh J. dissenting in a judgment delivered on 28 July 1989.

2.12.15 Hamilton P. who found in favour of the will was satisfied that when the will was produced and read to the testator prior to execution both Fr. Donohue and the other witness had an opportunity to, and did, satisfy themselves that the testator fully appreciated what was going on and that the terms of the document upon which he placed his mark fully represented what he wanted done with regard to his property.[28] An analogy can be drawn between the approach of Hamilton P. in *Glynn* and the rule in *Parker v Felgate*[29] under which the English courts have held, that if a testator is competent when giving instructions to another person to draw up his will, and the will is drawn up in accordance with those instructions, then the will is valid even though at the time of execution the testator is no longer competent to make a will.[30]

2.12.16 Old age, like infirmity is not, without more, proof of testamentary incapacity but, like infirmity, it may be invoked in support of a plea that the testator did not know and approve of the contents of his will, or that the will was procured as the result of undue influence. Palles C.B. issued this salutary warning in *Clery* v *Barry*:[31]

> "I am no admirer of instruments executed by gentlemen of ninety-two years of age, otherwise than in the presence of their professional advisers. I am no admirer of instructions for the will of any man being communicated to the person who prepares it, not by the testator himself, but by another in his absence. I am no admirer of the *dux facti* being a person (I care not how respectable) who takes a large interest under the will."[32]

The Court of Appeal held that in that case that it is a failure of duty on the part of a solicitor to prepare a will under any circumstances without seeing the testator, and it is utterly inexcusable to do so for an aged testator on the instructions of a person who is named an executor and is to receive a legacy.[33]

2.12.17 The court's suspicion of the circumstances attending the execution of a will has always been aroused when the will has been written, or otherwise prepared by a person who is to receive a benefit under it, and

---

[28] The fact that neither of the attesting witnesses had any interest in the will other than to give effect to the deceased's wishes weighed heavily with Hamilton P.

[29] (1883) 8 P.D. 171

[30] See *Battan Singh* v *Amirchand* [1948] A.C. 161 where the Privy Council advised great caution in the application of the principle where the testator's instructions are mediated through a lay person.

[31] (1889) 21 L.R. Ir. 152, 162

[32] *Ibid* at pp.175-6

[33] *Ibid* at p.167. See also *Re Hall* 50 D.L.R. (4th) 51

this suspicion attaches *a fortiori* to the will of an elderly or infirm testator. The principles of law applicable in such cases were reviewed by the Supreme Court in *In the Goods of Corboy decd.*[34] The issue in the latter case concerned the validity of a codicil to his will by the testator which was made when he was a very ill man, who had difficulty in speaking and expressing his wishes generally, and of whom it was difficult to say how much he understood of what was said to him. A Miss Healy who lived with the testator and looked after him prior to his death had drafted the disputed codicil, which had greatly increased the value of the legacies left to her in the will. The validity of the codicil was challenged, by the testator's nephew whose share in the deceased's estate was lessened by the codicil.

2.12.18 The circumstances surrounding the drafting of the codicil were calculated to arouse the court's suspicion, in that it gave effect to certain obliterations, interlineations and alterations in the will which the testator's solicitor only became aware of when the will was left with him by Miss Healy, apparently for safe keeping. The solicitor warned that these alterations would have no legal effect and allegedly suggested that they should be confirmed by a codicil, and that a solicitor would not be necessary for this purpose.[35] Despite the circumstances attending the execution of the codicil the President of the High Court found that it had been executed in accordance with the Wills Act 1837, and that at the time of its execution the deceased had been of sound mind, memory and understanding and that he had known and approved of the contents thereof.

2.12.19 The testator's nephew appealed to the Supreme Court on the grounds, *inter alia*, that as the said codicil was procured and prepared by Miss Healy, and as she was the sole beneficiary under the said codicil, the onus rested upon the person propounding the said codicil to prove affirmatively, unaided by presumption, that the testator knew and approved of the contents thereof, and that such onus had not been discharged. A further ground of appeal was that the learned President was wrong in law in failing to give due, or any, consideration to the nature of the onus required in the circumstances of the case to establish such knowledge and approval as aforesaid.

2.12.20 Budd J. in the Supreme Court took the view that Miss Healy was virtually in the position of propounding the codicil under which she was the beneficiary; it had been drawn up by her after consultation with the

---

[34] [1969] I.R. 148
[35] *Ibid* at p.153

testator's solicitor, and she had also procured its execution. Budd J. pointed out that there are certain well established principles concerning the onus of proof which is cast upon someone in Miss Healy's position, and he referred to *Fulton* v *Andrew*[36] in which Lord Cairns had applied the rules of law formulated by Parke B. in *Barry* v *Butlin*,[37] according to which, cases of this nature are to be decided. The first of these rules is that the *onus probandi* lies in every case upon the person propounding the will, who must satisfy the court that the instrument so propounded is the last will of a free and capable testator. The second, is that if a party writes or prepares a will under which he takes a benefit, that is a circumstance that ought generally to excite the suspicion of the court and calls upon it to be vigilant and jealous in examining the evidence in support of the instrument, in favour of which it should not pronounce unless the suspicion is removed. The principles of law stated in *Fulton* v *Andrew* were acted upon by the Supreme Court in *Re Begley*[38] and Budd J. was not aware that they had ever been departed from.[39]

2.12.21 The authorities reviewed by Budd J. clearly indicated that the circumstance that Miss Healy had prepared the codicil and procured its execution was one that ought to have excited the suspicion of the court and made it vigilant and jealous in examining the evidence in support of the codicil. The learned President, however, had not adverted anywhere in his judgment to the principles which should be applied in considering the evidence in the case, having regard to the surrounding circumstances; possible grounds for suspicion did not seem to have been weighed nor, it followed, were they dispelled. In perusing the judgment Budd J. found "little to indicate a suspicion or critical approach to the evidence adduced in support of the codicil but rather an indulgence in its acceptance".[40] In the absence of any apparent treatment of the evidence according to the rules laid down in *Fulton* v *Andrew* and the other cases reviewed, Budd J. concluded that the verdict in favour of the codicil could not stand.

2.13 Undue Influence

2.13.1 A distinction may be drawn between circumstances in which a beneficiary, who has written or otherwise been instrumental in the preparation of a will, incurs a heavy burden of proof that the will was that of a free and capable testator, and circumstances in which it is claimed that

[36] (1875) L.R. 7 H.L. 448
[37] (1838) 2 Moo. P.C. 480, 482
[38] [1939] I.R. 479
[39] [1969] I.R. 148, 157
[40] *Ibid* at pp.165, 166

a testator acted under the undue influence of another, in which case no presumption arises, and the person alleging undue influence must prove it.[41] The position relating to wills thus differs from that relating to *inter vivos* transactions, where equity will raise a presumption of undue influence when the parties stand in certain relationships with one another.[42] Although the existence of a particular relationship between a testator and beneficiary will not give rise to a presumption of undue influence, there may be other circumstances surrounding the making of a will which give rise to such presumption, and the courts have been more amenable to claims of undue influence when testators have been elderly or physically infirm when wills were made. An English author has suggested that because moral guilt is necessarily present in undue influence, the courts will require clear evidence of it, and where there is any doubt about the strengths of the evidence it is, where appropriate, better to issue process only requiring proof that the testator knew and approved the contents of the will.[43]

2.13.2 The principles of law applicable in cases of undue influence were considered by Costello J. in *Re Kavanagh: Healy* v *MacGillicuddy* and *Lyons*.[44] Costello J. referred to *Hall* v *Hall*[45] in which Sir J.P. Wilde pointed out that persuasion is not unlawful "but pressure of whatever character if so exerted as to overpower the volition without convincing the judgment of the testator, will constitute undue influence, though no force is either used or threatened".[46] Sir J.P. Wilde had gone on to say that

> "importunity or threats, such as the testator has not the courage to resist, moral command asserted and yielded to for the sake of peace and quiet, or for escaping from distress of mind or social discomfort, these if carried to a degree in which the free play of the testator's judgment, discretion or wishes is overcome, will constitute undue influence."[47]

2.13.3 Costello J. found the latter principles apposite to the facts of the instant case in which the plaintiff, Miss Healy, was claiming *inter alia*, that the defendant, Lyons, had exercised undue influence over the deceased, Patrick Kavanagh, in relation to a will under which the deceased had bequeathed to Lyons a twelve acre field subject to a life interest in the plaintiff, and had bequeathed legacies of £2000 to each of the two brothers

[41] See *Parfitt* v *Lawless* (1872) L.R. 2 P. & D. 462; *Craig* v *Lamoureux* [1920] A.C. 349; *Gregg* v *Kidd* [1956] I.R. 183

[42] See generally Keane "Equity and the Law of Trusts in the Republic of Ireland" at pp.338 *et seq.*

[43] Mellows "The Law of Succession" at p.68

[44] [1978] I.L.R.M. 175; See also *In the Estate of Johnston Decd* [1988] N.I.Y.B. 67

[45] (1868) L.R. 1 P. & D. 481

[46] *Ibid* at p.482

[47] *Ibid*

of Lyons. The plaintiff who was a cousin of the deceased had acted as his housekeeper for many years prior to his death, and had also helped in the running of his dairy business.

2.13.4 Costello J. concluded from the evidence, that the testator who had been in failing health, was physically feeble and his mental faculties had deteriorated when the will was made. He further concluded that the defendant, Lyons, had gradually over the years acquired domination over the deceased, partly by force of character, partly by his domineering manner towards the deceased and partly by ingratiating himself as a drinking companion and by making the deceased dependent on him for drink and entertainment. Costello J. was satisfied that the deceased who had genuine affection for Miss Healy, and was conscious of his moral duty to provide for her welfare after his death, had failed to express his affection and fulfill his duty in his will in which he had made the defendant the principal object of his bounty. Costello J. was also satisfied that the deceased had had no strong sentiments of friendship for the defendant and scarcely knew his two brothers and had no reason to make bequests in their favour. These findings of fact led Costello J. to the conclusion that the disputed will should be condemned on the grounds that it had been obtained by undue influence.

2.13.5 In the light of the conclusions of fact which he had reached, Costello J. was also satisfied that the defendant had failed to discharge the heavy burden of proof which rested on him to show that when the deceased executed his will he knew and approved of its contents.[48]

[48] [1978] I.L.R.M. 175, 190

Chapter 3

ALTERATIONS, OBLITERATIONS AND INTERLINEATIONS

3.1 Introduction

3.1.1 Section 86 of the Succession Act which substantially, but not altogether, reproduces section 21 of the Wills Act 1837 provides:

"An obliteration, interlineation or other alteration made in a will after execution shall not be valid or have any effect, unless such alteration is executed as is required for the execution of the will, but the will with such alteration as part thereof, shall be deemed to be duly executed if the signature of the testator and the signature of each witness is made in the margin or some other part of the will opposite or near to such alteration, or at the foot or end of or opposite to a memorandum referring to such alteration and written at the end of some other part of the will."

3.1.2 Alterations thus fall into two distinct categories, those made prior to the execution of the will and those made subsequent to execution. In the case of the former, if the testator intends that they should form part of his will when it is executed, they will be admitted to probate. This question of intention can be problematic when, for example, pencilled alterations are made in a will otherwise written in ink, a presumption arises that the pencilled alterations were deliberative only.[1] It is inadvisable therefore to pencil in alterations in a will written in ink. In any event, use of ink will not, without more, be conclusive proof that the alterations were made prior to execution.[2] Indeed it is often not apparent on the face of the will

---

[1] *Ante* p. 31 and see *In the Goods of Hall* (1871) L.R. 2 P. & D. 256

[2] *In the goods of Cadge* (1868) L.R. 1 P. & D. 543; *In the Goods of Benn* [1938] I.R. 313 and see *post* p. 74

that alterations were made prior to execution, and there is a presumption by law that unattested alterations were made subsequent to execution.[3] That being so it is clearly desirable that the testator and witnesses should sign, or initial, alterations whenever they are made. Section 86, like section 21 of the Wills Act, facilitates this prudent practice by permitting alterations to be duly executed by the placing of the signatures of the testator and the witnesses in the margin or near to the alterations, or at the foot or end of, or opposite to a memorandum referring to such alterations and written on some other part of the will.

3.2 Rebuttal of presumption as to time of alterations

3.2.1 The presumption that unattested alterations were made after the will was executed prevails only in the absence of evidence to the contrary, and in *In the Goods of Duffy*[4] Warren J. was of the opinion that "very slight affirmative evidence is sufficient to rebut that presumption, and sustain the alterations as made before execution, and therefore, valid".[5] Christian L.J. later agreed that very slight evidence would suffice to supply the want of any presumption that alterations were made before execution, but his Lordship was not happy with the use of a presumption that unattested alterations were made subsequent to execution. Christian L.J. pointed out that in the absence of evidence as to whether alterations were made before or after execution, they were to be rejected from probate, not because it was to be presumed that they were made after execution, but because the burden of proof which in this respect is cast upon the person claiming the benefit of such alterations, has not been discharged.[6] Christian L.J.'s criticism of the use of a presumption in such cases may be largely a matter of semantics, and judges and textwriters alike continue to speak of a presumption that unattested alterations were made after execution.[7]

3.3 Evidence in rebuttal of presumption

3.3.1 The courts have adopted a liberal approach to the kinds of evidence which may be admitted to prove that unattested alterations were made prior to execution and in *Moore* v *Moore*[8] Warren J. opined that "the court

---

[3] *Cooper* v *Bockett* (1846) 4 Moo. P.C. 419; *Doe d. Shallcross* v *Palmer* (1851) 16 Q.B. 747. Before the Wills Act 1837 the presumption was the other way.

[4] (1871) I.R. 5 Eq. 506

[5] *Ibid* at p.511

[6] *Duffy* v *Duffy* 1877 11 (ILTR) 126

[7] See e.g. Mellows, "The Law of Succession" (4th ed. 1983) at p.101 and Parry and Clark, "The Law of Succession" (8th ed. 1983) at p.71. See also *In the Goods of Benn* [1938] I.R.313, 319 (per Hanna J.)

is not confined to any species of evidence, but may act upon any evidence which, having regard to all the circumstances, reasonably leads the judgment to the conclusion that the alterations were made before execution".

3.3.2 External evidence that the alterations were made prior to execution may be provided (1) by attesting witnesses who may have seen the alterations on the will prior to execution;[9] (2) by the person who drafted the will and who can provide evidence to the effect that the alterations were made to the will before it was executed;[10] (3) by declarations made by the testator before or at the time of, but not after, execution.[11] Often however, attesting witnesses are dead, or forgetful, or simply did not see the alterations on the will prior to execution, and there may be no declarations by the testator which help to determine when the alterations were made.

3.3.3 In such cases the court can take cognisance of the internal evidence presented by the will itself. Thus in *In the Goods of Benn*[12] there was no direct evidence as to whether an interlineation in a holograph will was inserted before or after execution, but Hanna J. held, having regard to the internal evidence presented by the fabric of the will, that the interlined words were inserted before the will was executed. The interlined words were, in Hanna J.'s opinion, written with the same ink and pen as the rest of the will, while the signature of the testatrix and witnesses were written with other pens, and there was evidence that the will was executed at a different place and time. There was also evidence from a handwriting expert that the interlined words were written before the ink on the suceeding words was dry.[13]

3.3.4 The burden of proof which lies upon a person who alleges that alterations were made prior to execution is illustrated by the somewhat unusual circumstances in *In the Goods of Rudd*.[14] A testator had made a codicil to his will which contained, *inter alia* the words "My brother Wm. in

---

[8] (1872) I.R. 6 Eq. 166, 169

[9] Often an attesting witness will be the only person capable of providing the affidavit evidence required by Order 79 rule 11 of the Rules of the Superior Courts 1986.

[10] *Keigwin* v *Keigwin* (1843) 3 Curt. 607

[11] See *In the Goods of Duffy* (1871) I.R. 5 Eq. 506, 509. Cf. the position now in England under the Civil Evidence Act 1968.

[12] [1938] I.R. 313

[13] The opinion of the handwriting expert was based on the fact that if a fresh ink-link is made to intercept a bone-dry earlier line, no seepage occurs from the new line to the track of the old line. There was such seepage in the instant case.

[14] [1945] I.R. 180

South Africa is not to benefit by my decease" which words were claimed to be an alteration within section 21 of the Wills Act 1837. Maguire P. was satisfied that those words were in the handwriting of the testator, as was the rest of the codicil, but in a different ink and it appeared that before they were written the testator had gone over the last letter of the word immediately preceding them and added a full stop. It also appeared to Maguire P. that the writing of these words was more cramped than the rest of the document and that they were squeezed into a space less than they would require. There being nothing in the evidence to help the court to determine when the alteration was made Maguire P. fell back on the rule in *Granville* v *Tyler*[15] "that whoever alleges such alterations to have been done before the execution of the will is bound to take upon himself the *onus provandi*; *Cooper* v *Bockett*".[16] Since the onus had not been discharged Maguire P. granted liberty to apply for probate of the will and codicil excluding the words of the alleged alteration.[17]

3.3.5 There might be satisfactory evidence that some of a number of alterations in a will were made prior to execution and the question might then arise as to whether the court can ascertain which these were. Warren J. in *In the Goods of Duffy*[18] had acted upon the dictum of Wood V.C. in *Williams* v *Ashton*[19] to the effect, that evidence that some of several interlineations were made before execution did not prove that all were so made, but he was later overruled on that point by the Court of Appeal.[20] Accordingly, Warren J. held in *Doherty* v *Dwyer*[21] that where the attestation clause in a codicil contained a declaration that some alterations in the codicil had been made before execution, the court might infer from that circumstance, and from the appearance of the codicil, that all the alterations were made before execution.[22]

3.4 Circumstantial evidence as to time of alterations

3.4.1 The courts, in appropriate cases, have taken cognisance of circumstantial evidence that alterations were made prior to execution.

---

[15] (1851) 7 Moo. P.C.C. 320

[16] (1846) 4 Moo. P.C.C. 419. Maguire P. pointed out that the rule so stated was accepted and followed by Lord Cranworth in *Simons* v *Rudall* (18..) 1 Sim. N.S. 115 at p.137.

[17] See *post* p. 78

[18] (1871) I.R.5 Eq. 506

[19] (1860) 1 J. & H. 115

[20] *Duffy* v *Duffy* (1877) 11 I.L.T.R. 126

[21] (1890) 25 L.R. Ir. 297

[22] Warren J. used his own skill as an expert in the absence of professional evidence and having examined the document, and a photograph of it, he was satisfied that the alterations were written contemporaneously with the rest of the codicil.

Thus in *Moore* v *Moore*[23] the judgment of the court was influenced by the consideration that the testator, Mr Justice Moore, was an eminent property lawyer who knew that an unattested alteration made after execution would be void. Likewise, in *Doherty* v *Dwyer*[24] the court was clearly influenced by the fact that the testator was a solicitor acquainted with the law regulating the execution of testamentary instruments, who "knew the law on the subject, although he may not have always remembered it".[25] Warren J. said in *O'Meagher* v *O'Meagher*[26] of circumstances, one of which was that the testator was a solicitor of undisputed testamentary capacity, that "they constituted *prima facie* a strong case for presuming due execution – a presumption founded on probabilities, consonant with experience, commending itself to the judgment of intelligent men, learned or unlearned, and recognised by the law".

3.4.2 The language of section 21 of the Wills Act 1837 is substantially reproduced in section 86 of the Succession Act – with the omission of the provision that no obliteration, interlineation, or other alteration, made after execution, and not validly executed, shall have effect "except so far as the words or effect of the will before such alteration shall not be apparent".[27] The courts construed this to mean that words were not apparent unless they could be read by the naked eye, assisted, if necessary, by a magnifying glass but no physical interference with the will was permitted.[28]

3.4.3 The distinction between apparent and discoverable which ensued, can be seen in *Re Itter*[29] where a testatrix had pasted strips of paper containing unattested alterations over parts of her will. Although an infrared photograph revealed what had been written beneath the strips of paper it was held that the effect of the will before the alterations was not apparent.[30] The court did however admit the original words to probate under the doctrine of dependent relative revocation, since it was satisfied that the testatrix intended them not to have effect only if, the alterations on

---

[23] (1872) I.R. 6 Eq. 166

[24] (1890) 25 L.R. Ir. 297

[25] *Ibid* at p.305

[26] (1883) 11 L.R. Ir. 117, 118

[27] S.21 reads: "No obliteration, interlineation, or other alteration made in any will after the execution thereof shall be valid or have any effect, except so far as the words or effect of the will before such alteration shall not be apparent, unless such alteration shall be executed in like manner as hereinbefore is required for the execution of the will ..."

[28] See generally Mellows at (4th ed. 1983) pp.99 *et seq.* and Parry and Clark (8th ed. 1983) at pp.72 *et seq.*

[29] [1950] P.130

[30] *Ibid* at p. 132

the strips of paper did have effect.[31] Extrinsic evidence was likewise admitted in *In the Goods of Carmody*[32] where a testator had altered his will by wholly erasing certain words and drawing a pen line through other words which did not make them illegible. These alterations not having been properly executed, it was argued for the applicant, that the doctrine of dependent relative revocation applied to the words wholly erased, and that the words not rendered illegible formed an apparent part of the will. Both arguments suceeded and, as to the words wholly erased, the court ordered that they be admitted to probate, since evidence of the original terms of the will was available, from one Denis Curtin who had written out the will at the testator's request.

3.4.4 While the admission of such extrinsic evidence presents problems in cases not involving the doctrine of dependent relative revocation, there seems to be no reason in principle why scientific evidence of the will itself be confined to cases of dependent relative revocation.[33] Indeed, there is some evidence which suggests that the Irish Courts did not share their English counterparts' aversion to such evidence and, *In the Goods of Benn*[34] the motion before the court was adjourned so that obliterated words in a will might be deciphered, if possible, by infra-red photography. Also, in *Doherty* v *Dwyer*,[35] photographs of a will and codicil were taken by leave of the court in order to decipher, if possible, words that had been erased. There is arguably little difference in terms of physical interference with the will between infra-red photography and ordinary photography, since in each case a new document, the photograph, is brought into existence.[36]

3.4.5 Since the English courts' aversion to scientific evidence, such as infra-red photography, is based on a somewhat literal construction of the apparency requirement in section 21 of the Wills Act, its omission from section 86 of the Succession Act arguably removes any bar to the admission of such evidence by the Irish courts. The Explanatory Memorandum with the Succession Act is silent on the reasons for that omission, but, some guidance may be found in the following observations by Henchy J. on statutory interpretation in *Doyle* v *Hearn & others*:[37]

> "I consider it to be a general rule of statutory interpretation that when the legislature replaces a statutory provision by another, but differing,

---

[31] On the doctrine of dependent relative revocation see *post* pp. 96 *et seq.*

[32] (1944) 78 I.L.T.R. 112

[33] On the admission of extrinsic evidence generally see *post* pp. 113

[34] [1938] I.R. 313

[35] (1890) 25 L.R. Ir. 297

[36] See Mellows at (4th ed. 1983) p.100

[37] Unreported Supreme Court judgment delivered 31 July 1987.

statutory provision, the different wording of the latter provision must have been intended to produce a different effect. The legislature should not be considered to have enacted the new provision to no special or extra purpose."

3.4.6 Order 79 rule 12, of the Rules of the Superior Courts 1986 provides, that if no satisfactory evidence of the time when erasures and obliterations were made and the words erased or obliterated be not entirely effaced, but can upon inspection of the paper be ascertained, they must form part of the probate. Despite the echo of the apparency requirement in section 21 of the Wills Act contained in Order 70 rule 12 there is no reason in principle why inspection of the paper should not include processes like infra-red photography.

3.5 Effect of unattested alterations

3.5.1 If unattested alterations were made in a will after execution or, if made before execution, but there is no evidence to show that they were so made, the will can take effect as if there were blanks in the spaces which contain the alterations if the original words cannot be read.[38] Similarly, if words in a will are completely erased or obliterated, and extrinsic evidence is not admissible, or otherwise available, the will can take effect as if there were blanks in the spaces which contained those words.[39]

3.6 Unimportant alterations

3.6.1 Perhaps, not surprisingly, the clearest formulations of the principle that very slight affirmative evidence is required to prove that alterations were made prior to execution, are to be found in cases involving trivial and unimportant alterations. Thus in *In the Goods of Hindmarch*[40] the interlineations in a will were considered trifling. Sir J.P. Wilde went on to say that "the court may come to the conclusion that they were in the will at the time of execution upon any reasonable evidence, without insisting upon the oath of the attesting witness, or any other species of evidence".[41]

3.6.2 While section 86 makes no concessions to trivial or unimportant

---

[38] See *In the Goods of Benn* [1938] I.R. 313, 322; *In the Goods of Rudd* [1945] I.R. 180, 182

[39] *In the Goods of Morrell* (1935) 69 I.L.T.R. 79. See Mellows "The Law of Succession" (4th ed. 1983) at p. 103

[40] (1866) 1 P. & D. 307

[41] *Ibid* at p. 308 See also the judgement of Sir J.P. Wilde in *In the Goods of Cadge* (1868) 1 P. & D. 543 where the interlineations were necessary to complete the sentence in which they were.

alterations, the effect of the section is modified by Order 79 rule 11 of the Rules of the Superior Courts 1986, which provides:

"When interlineations or alterations appear in the will (unless duly executed, or recited in, or otherwise identified by the attestation clause), an affidavit or affidavits in proof of their having existed in the will before its execution shall be filed, *except when the alterations are of but small importance, and are evidenced by the initials of the attesting witnesses.*[42]

3.7 Validation of alterations by subsequent codicil

3.7.1 Alterations which have been made after the execution of the will, and which have not been properly executed, may be rendered valid by the re-execution of the will or, as is more commonly the case, by the execution of a codicil thereto. However, the execution of a codicil will not, without more, validate unattested alterations in the will, and such alterations will be presumed to have been made after the execution of both will and codicil unless there is evidence to rebut that presumption. Thus in *Doherty* v *Dwyer*,[43] Warren J., having found that all the alterations in a codicil were made prior to its execution, went on:

"The question remains, can I, by the aid of the codicil, give effect to the alterations and interlineations in the will? If these had been made between the dates of the execution of the will and the execution of the codicil, the codicil might have set up the will with the interlineations and alterations, but I have no evidence whatever to show that the alterations in the will were made before the execution of the codicil, or at any particular time."[44]

3.7.2 Since the testator must intend that the alterations be admitted to probate as part of his will, the codicil must be consistent with that intention. Thus, in *Re Hay*[45] where unattested alterations were made to a will by striking out three legacies, and a subsequent codicil revoked only one of them, it was held that the two other legacies were unrevoked. The requirement of intention applies *a fortiori* to the re-execution of a will, and it would be extremely unlikely that a will re-executed with proper formalities would not incorporate unattested alterations in the original will, if it was the testator's intention that they should be admitted to probate.

---

[42] See Order 79 rule 10 of the Rules of the Superior Courts 1986. In England the Non-Contentions Probate Rules 1954, Rule 129) allows the Registrar to grant probate of a will with alterations which are unattested, and where there is no evidence to show that they were made prior to execution, if the alterations appear to the Registrar "to be of no practical importance."

[43] (1890) 25 L.R. Ir. 297

[44] *Ibid* at p.306

[45] [1904] 1 Ch. 317. See also *In the Goods of Syres* (1873) 3 P. & D. 26

Chapter 4

REVOCATION, REPUBLICATION AND REVIVAL

4.1 Introduction

4.1.1 It is a fundamental principle of the law relating to wills that a will is revocable by the testator at any time before his death, and nothing which the testator says or does can alter that.[1] Thus mutual wills, which have been made in pursuance of an agreement not to revoke without the prior agreement of the other party, are revocable, although revocation without the necessary consent may give rise to an action for breach of contract against the estate of the person who has so revoked.[2]

4.1.2 The statutory provisions governing the revocation of wills are now contained in section 85 of the Succession Act which provides in subsection (1) that a will shall be revoked by the subsequent marriage of the testator, except a will made in contemplation of that marriage, whether so expressed in the will or not. Subsection (2) provides that, subject to subsection (1), no will or any part thereof, shall be revoked except by another will or codicil duly executed, or by some writing declaring an intention to revoke it and executed in the manner in which a will is required to be executed, or by the burning, tearing, or destruction of it by the testator, or by some person in his presence and by his direction, with the intention of revoking it. There are accordingly four ways in which a will may be revoked – (1) Marriage, (2) Another will or codicil, (3) Writing declaring an intention to revoke, and (4) Destruction.

---

[1] The only possible bar to revocation is a testator becoming mentally incompetent after the execution of his will.

[2] See *ante* p. 5

4.2 Marriage

4.2.1 The rule that a will is revoked by the subsequent marriage of the testator, which was contained in section 18 of the Wills Act 1837, is referable to the policy consideration that a person assumes obligations on marriage which should take precedence over any prior dispositions of his property.[3] Thus the object of the rule is "to prevent the 'accidental survival' of a forgotten will after the changed circumstances brought about by a subsequent marriage have occurred."[4] The revocation of a prior will by the subsequent marriage of the testator ensures that, in the absence of a will being made in favour of the new family, they will be taken care of by the intestacy rules.

4.2.2 The rule is considered by some commentators to be indefensible and anachronistic in the light of contemporary social conditions, not the least of which is the growing number of persons who eschew marriage to live in extra-marital or quasi-marital relationships.[5] It is conceded however by critics of the rule that if a pre-nuptial will is to be relevant, a statutory legacy should be given to the surviving spouse and some provision made for children of the deceased.[6] This is precisely the position in Irish Law since the Succession Act gives to the surviving spouse a legal right share in the estate of the deceased, and children may apply under section 117 to have proper provision made for them out of their deceased parent's estate.

4.2.3 Thus, while the rule has been restated in section 85(1) of the Succession Act, there are differences between that restatement and the rule contained in section 18 of the 1837 Act, and modifications made to the latter rule by subsequent English legislation. The most obvious difference is the omission from section 85(1) of the provision in section 18 of the 1837 Act that a will shall be revoked on marriage

"except a will made in exercise of a power of appointment, when the real or personal estate thereby appointed would not in default of such appointment pass to his or her heir, customary heir, executor, or

---

[3] Such policy reason is less cogent nowadays when surviving spouses are given legal right shares in the deceased's estate and children may make applications under s.117 of the Succession Act. See *post* pp. 183 *et seq.*

[4] Miller "The Machinery of Succession" at p.179. See Davey "The Making and Revocation of Wills" (1980) Conveyancer 64, at pp.101 *et seq.*

[5] The growing phenomenon of couples living together outside marriage was recognised by the Sub-Committee set up by the English Law Reform Commission to consider the law relating to the making and revocation of wills which pointed out however the difficulty in ascertaining the precise moment when co-habitation revokes a prior will by either party. See Davey at p.102

[6] *Ibid*

administrator, or the person entitled as his or her next-of-kin, under the Statute of Distributions, 1670."

Since it was the legislative intention in relation to powers of appointment to protect as much as possible, the interests of the testator's family there was no point in revoking a will exercising such a power unless on revocation the property appointed would pass to his next-of-kin on the testator's intestacy.[7]

4.2.4 The rights conferred on the surviving spouse and children of a deceased by Part IX of the Succession Act have superseded earlier legislative attempts to protect the interests of a testator's family, whether in relation to the exercise of powers of appointment or otherwise, and this no doubt accounts for the omission from section 85(1) of the exception provided in section 18 of the 1837 Act. That omission has the undeniable merit of sparing the Irish courts intractable problems such as that which arose in the English case *Re Gilligan*[8] where the court had to determine whether a widow was within the class of those entitled for the purpose of the exception in section 18. Pilcher J. held that the widow came within the next-on-kin under the Statute of Distribution and, as she would not benefit by the revocation of the will exercising the power, the appointment was not revoked.[9]

4.2.5 We are told in the Explanatory Memorandum with the Succession Act that section 85(1) introduces an important change in providing, that a will shall not be revoked by the subsequent marriage of the testator if the will was made in contemplation of that particular marriage, whether so expressed in the will or not.[10] The importance of this change can best be understood by reference to subsequent English legislative additions to section 18 of the 1837 Act which did not apply in Ireland. Thus section 177 of the Law of Property Act 1925[11] provided that "a will expressed to be made in contemplation of a marriage shall ... not be revoked by the solemnisation of the marriage contemplated."

4.2.6 This requirement was construed by Megarry J. in *Re Coleman*[12] to mean that the will as a whole, and not merely particular gifts in it, must be

---

[7] See Mellows "The Law of Succession" (3rd ed. 1977) at p.128

[8] [1950] p.32. See also *Re Master's Estate* (1968) 19 N.I.L.Q. 216

[9] See Mitchel (1951) 67 Law Quarterly Review, 351 and Russell (1952) 68 Law Quarterly Review, 455

[10] See the Explanatory Memorandum at para 54 p.8

[11] For the position in England with respect to wills made after 31 December 1982 see the Administration of Justice Act 1982, s.18

[12] [1976] Ch. 1. See also *Sallis v Jones* [1936] P.43 and *In the Estate of Langston* [1953] P.100

expressed to be made in contemplation of marriage. This construction was criticised as being "unduly narrow" by the English Law Reform Committee, whose recommendations for changes in the law relating to revocation by marriage were given effect to in the Administration of Justice Act 1982.[13] The latter Act amended section 18 of the 1837 Act to make it clear that revocation should not occur if it appeared from the will (1) that at the time it was made the testator was expecting to be married to a particular person, and (2) that he intended that the will, or a particular disposition in the will, should not be revoked by his marriage to that person.

4.2.7 There is a paucity of Irish case law on the problem which was the subject of the recommendations by the English Law Reform Committee, but it is arguable that the approach of the Irish courts would be on all fours with those recommendations, and, revocation by marriage of a will, or a particular disposition in a will, would depend on the construction of the particular will. This would also be a case where, in the absence of a clear and unambiguous intention on the face of the will, the courts would be able to take cognisance of extrinsic evidence under section 90 of the Succession Act.[14]

4.2.8 Allowing for the difference that in Irish law, the contemplation of marriage need not be expressed in the will, the English cases provide useful guidance on the use of language which may be construed as showing an intention that the will was made in contemplation of marriage. Thus expressions in a will such as "to my fiancee Mary" or "to my future wife Mary" have been construed as constituting evidence that the will was made in contemplation of marriage.[15] Of course if the testator marries someone other than Mary such marriage would cause revocation, since the will must be made in contemplation of a particular marriage and not marriage in general.[16]

4.2.9 Whether the will as a whole must be made in contemplation of the marriage of the testator if it is not to be revoked by that marriage has been a matter of some controversy in England.[17] Thus Megarry J. while holding

---

[13] See Law Reform Committee, 22nd Report at pp.14-16 and Edwards and Langstaff "The Will to Survive Marriage" (1975) 39 Conveyancer 121

[14] See *post* pp. 113 *et seq.*

[15] See e.g. *In the Estate of Langston* [1953] P.100. Compare the approach taken by the New Zealand Courts in *Burton* v *McGregor* [1953] N.Z.L.R. 487; *Public Trustee* v *Crawley* [1973] I N.Z.L.R. 695 and *Re Whale* [1977] 2 N.Z.L.R. 1 (all referred to in Parry and Clark "The Law of Succession" (8th ed. 1983) at p.58 n.8

[16] Section 85(1) of the Succession Act provides that a will shall not be revoked by the subsequent marriage of a testator if made in contemplation of *that* marriage.

[17] See Davey "The Making and Revocation of Wills" at p.102 and Edwards and Langstaff, *supra*.

in *Re Coleman*[18] that the use of the word "fiancee" would normally, by itself, express a sufficient contemplation of marriage to that person, went on to hold that while the gift to the testator's widow was made in contemplation of marriage, it could not be deduced that the will as a whole was made in contemplation of marriage and the will was accordingly revoked.[19] We have seen that the English Law Reform Committee was critical of Megarry J.'s construction of section 177 of the Law of Property Act but the Committee did recommend that the use of the word "fiancee" should not be conclusive of the question whether a will was made in contemplation of marriage, and particularly where the will contains only one trivial gift to the testator's "fiancee".[20] The foregoing could be said to represent the position in Irish law where the use of terms such as "my fiancee" or "my future wife" would normally lead the court to infer that the will was made in contemplation of marriage to that person. Whether a will was so made would depend however on a construction of the will, taking cognisance in appropriate circumstances of extrinsic evidence.[21] Thus it can be said with some confidence that the Irish courts are unlikely to find a single trivial gift to a beneficiary named as "my fiancee" conclusive of the question whether the will was made in contemplation of marriage.

4.2.10 In order for a will to be revoked by a subsequent marriage, it would seem axiomatic that the parties be free to marry, and that such marriage be valid in Irish law. There is a dearth of Irish authority on the matter, but the Irish courts are likely to follow English decisions such as that in *Mette* v *Mette*.[22] In that case the testator had purported to marry his deceased wife's half-sister which relationship made the marriage void. The court accordingly held that the void marriage did not revoke the testator's will.

4.3 Other Wills and Codicils

4.3.1 It is customary for a will to commence with a general revocation clause along the lines "I hereby revoke all former wills and testamentary instruments made by me and declare this to be my last will and testament". No particular form of words need be used in such a revocation clause, but, while the lay person might be forgiven for assuming that a clause in a will declaring it to be the "last will and testament" of the testator would be sufficient to revoke all previous testamentary dispositions, this is not

---

[18] [1976] Ch. 1

[19] It is of interest that because his will was revoked the testator died intestate and his widow took a greater benefit under the intestacy rules than she would have under the will.

[20] See Parry and Clark "The Law of Succession" (8th ed. 1983) at p.59

[21] See *post* pp. 113 *et seq.*

[22] (1859) 1 Sw. & Tr. 416. See Mellows "The Law of Succession" (4th ed. 1983) at p.96

necessarily the case. The case law reveals that such language, will not, without more, be construed as an express revocation of earlier wills and codicils.[23]

4.3.2 It is therefore desirable, if the testator wishes to revoke previous testamentary dispositions, to include an express revocation clause in the will, not least because it raises a presumption that the testator had the necessary *animus revocandi* in relation to earlier dispositions, and places a heavy burden of proof on the person who asserts that the testator did not have that intention.[24] MacDermott J. (as he then was) said of such a clause in *In b. Keenan:*[25]

> "For my own part, I incline to the view that where, as here, a will contains a clear revocatory clause couched in comprehensive terms and having the knowledge and approval of the testator, there is no room for such an inquiry and no ground for discriminating between different kinds of earlier testamentary dispositions which are fairly caught by the language of the clause."

4.3.3 The inquiry to which MacDermott J. referred had to do with, whether words in a revocation clause which revoked all previous wills should be construed as sparing the execution of a power of appointment contained in one or more of them. MacDermott J. pointed out that the authorities cited ranged from according testamentary appointments a special immunity from the operation of subsequent revocatory clauses, to suggesting that such appointments should be treated in this respect like any other testamentary dispositions.[26] MacDermott J. expressed a preference for the latter view, and went on to hold that, while an unambiguous general revocatory clause did not necessarily revoke a previous testamentary exercise of a power of appointment, the evidence in the instant case of the testatrix's intention to save the previous appointment from the operation of the revocatory clause was not sufficiently cogent.[27]

4.3.4 Since any act of revocation must be accompanied by an *animus*

---

[23] See *In b. Miller* [1940] I.R. 436; *Re Brennan* [1932] I.R. 633; *In b. Martin* [1968] I.R. 1; *Kitcat v King* [1930] P.266 and *Re Hawksley's Settlement* [1934] 1 Ch. 384

[24] See *Lowthorpe-Lutwidge v Lowthorpe-Lutwidge* [1935] P.151, (per Langton J.)

[25] (1946) 80 I.L.T.R. 1, 3

[26] Among the cases cited were *Sotheran v Denning* (1881) 20 Ch.D. 99; *Cadell v Wilcocks* (1898) p.21; *Lowthorpe-Lutwidge v Lowthorpe-Lutwidge* [1935] p.151 and *In the Estate of O'Connor* [1942] 1 All E.R. 546

[27] MacDermott J. further held that subsequent holograph confirmations of the exercise of the power of appointment could be admitted to probate since they were valid as testamentary dispositions according to Scots law and the provisions of s.2 of the Wills Act, 1861, (Lord Kingdown's Act) made them valid according to Northern Ireland law.

revocandi it follows that a revocation clause which is included in a will without the knowledge and approval of the testator will be ineffective.[28] The inclusion in a will of such clause will, as we have seen, raise a presumption that the testator intended the revocation of previous testamentary dispositions, but, while the onus of disproving such intention is not lightly discharged, the circumstances of the case may clearly show that the testator lacked the necessary *animus revocandi*. Thus in the English case *Re Phelan*[29] the testator, an expatriate Irishman, made a will leaving all his property to the people with whom he had lodged, but was then apparently advised that separate wills had to be made in respect of separate holdings of shares. Having acquired three standard will forms, he left each of three blocks of shares to his landlord and landlady, the wills all being executed on the same day. Each of the will forms contained a revocation clause which the testator had not deleted, but, Stirling J. held that since the surrounding facts disclosed that the testator did not know and approve of the revocatory nature of the clauses, the wills should be admitted to probate with the revocation clauses omitted.

4.3.5 If a revocation clause is included in a will without the knowledge and approval of the testator he can scarcely be said to have had an *animus revocandi*, but the position is less clearcut when such clause is included with the knowledge of the testator who is mistaken however as to its legal effect.

4.3.6 The general rule is, as we have seen, that a testator's mistake as to the legal effect of any of the terms of his will will not, without more, render those terms ineffective.[30] The occasionally harsh effect of this rule in relation to revocation clauses can be seen in *Collins* v *Elstone*[31] where, despite the fact that the testatrix was wrongly advised that a revocation clause in her new will would have only limited effect, it was held that since she intended its inclusion it must take effect as a revocation of her earlier will. This decision was subsequently criticised in *Lowthorpe-Lutwidge* v *Lowthorpe-Lutwidge*[32] and an English text-writer has argued that while it is in accord with the general principle that mistake of legal effect is not itself a reason for failing to give effect to the terms of a will, it is inconsistent with the other principle that a clause should operate only so far as is necessary to give effect to the testator's intention.[33] Since the

---

[28] See *In b. Oswald* (1874) L.R. 3 P. & D. 162 where the revocatory words were included *per incuriam* without instruction from the testator. See also *Re Swords* [1952] P.368

[29] [1972] Fam. 33

[30] See *In the Estate of Beech* [1923] P.46

[31] [1893] P.1

[32] [1935] P.151

[33] See Mellows "The Law of Succession" (4th ed. 1983) at p.85

intention of the testator is otherwise deemed to be of paramount importance in the construction of wills, there seems to be no reason in principle why a revocation clause should be given a wider effect than that ascribed to it by the testator. Indeed, there is authority to the effect that a revocation clause, in whole or in part, will be omitted from probate if there is no *animus revocandi*[34] and that a revocation clause couched in general terms may, on a proper construction, have a limited effect on previous dispositions.[35] The determination of the extent to which a testator intended a revocation clause to take effect would, arguably, involve the courts in no more difficult inquiries than those they are obliged to undertake when applying the doctrine of dependent relative revocation.[36]

4.4 Revocation by implication

4.4.1 There is a general rule of construction, that an earlier will or codicil is impliedly revoked by a later one which contains provisions inconsistent with, or merely repetitive of, those in the former will or codicil. The application of this rule is illustrated by the facts and decision in *In b. Martin*[37] where a second will of the testatrix, which contained no revocation clause but commenced with the words "This is my last will", purported to dispose of all her money. The deceased's estate consisted only of personalty, and a legatee under the second will applied to the High Court for liberty to apply for a grant of administration of the estate of the deceased with the second will annexed.

4.4.2 O'Keefe P., in granting the application, held, that the phrase "all my money" in the second will of the deceased, applied to her entire personal estate, other than her personal belongings, and constituted an implied revocation of her first will. O'Keefe P. referred to *In re Jennings*[38] and *Perrin v Morgan*[39] as demonstrating the modern position that while "money" means cash, the word in a will may cover much more, and may be the equivalent of "all my personal estate". While not inclined on a cursory reading of the second will to give so wide a meaning to the expression, O'Keefe P. considered that the consequences of a more restricted meaning would oblige him to fall back on the earlier will to find a valid residuary clause. If the deceased did not intend to revoke the earlier will by the later one the residuary clause in the earlier will stood, and, in that event, the deceased would be thought to have intended to allow to

---

[34] *Re Morris* [1971] P.62
[35] See *Re Wayland* [1951] W.N. 604
[36] See *post* pp.96 *et seq.*
[37] [1968] I.R. 1
[38] [1930] I.R. 196. See *post* p.108
[39] [1943] A.C. 399. See *post* p.109

stand, a gift to a person who had been dead for seven years at the date of the second will.[40]

4.4.3 Whether an earlier will is revoked entirely, or in part, by a later disposition is thus a matter of construction, and, in this respect, codicils are construed under the rule in *Hearle* v *Hicks*[41] on the basis that they interfere as little as possible with the clear provisions of the will. Judge McCarthy in the Circuit Court, in *Pakenham* v *Duggan and Ors,*[42] in holding that a residuary gift in a codicil operated as a revocation of a residuary gift in the will, followed *In re Stoodley.*[43] In the latter case a bequest of "the residue of my estate not bequeathed by the above will" was held to revoke a previous inconsistent testamentary bequest of the residue.

4.4.4 Since a will is not automatically or necessarily revoked by the execution of a later will, it follows that a will may consist of more than one testamentary document executed at different times. Thus in *In b. Wafer*[44] the testator had executed two wills, the first in 1945 and the second in 1958 shortly before his death. The second will contained no revocation clause and on its face was not executed in accordance with the Wills Act 1837 but evidence of its due execution was given on affidavit by the subscribing witnesses. Haugh J. accordingly made an order admitting both wills to probate as together constituting and forming the last will and testament of the deceased.

4.4.5 Although in ordinary circumstances only one testamentary instrument is taken as representing the testator's final intentions, it may not be possible in a particular case to say which one of several instruments this should be. Thus, in *In b. McCarthy*[45] the testator had made a will with a firm of solicitors in August 1957, and a further will, with a different firm of solicitors who were unaware of the first will, in September 1960. He then made a codicil to his first will in March 1963, with the firm of solicitors with whom he had made that will, but who were ignorant of his making of the second will in September 1960. It was argued for the applicant, who was one of the executors named in the first will and the sole executor named in the second will, that since there was a conflict in the terms of the instruments that could be decided only by a court of construction, both instruments stood to be construed and in designated sequence must be

---

[40] [1968] I.R. 1, 6
[41] (1832) 1 Cl. & Fin. 20
[42] (1951) 85 I.L.T.R. 21
[43] [1915] 2 Ch. 295
[44] [1960] Ir. Jur. Rep. 19
[45] [1965] Ir. Jur. Rep. 56

admitted to probate. Kenny J. in making the order sought followed the decision in *In b. Doyle*.[46]

4.4.6 Where there are two wills of the same date containing inconsistent provisions and it is not possible to determine which is the later will, then neither will will be admitted to probate.[47] However, that revocation clauses in such wills otherwise inadmissable to probate, may be effective in revoking an earlier will, is illustrated by the unusual facts in *Re Howard*.[48] There, a testator having first made a will leaving his estate to his son, later executed two wills on the same day, one in favour of his son and the other in favour of his wife, both containing general revocation clauses. It was held that neither will could be admitted to probate, since there was nothing to show the order in which they were executed and the revocation clauses in these wills were effective to revoke the earlier will.[49]

4.5 Writing declaring an intention to revoke

4.5.1 Section 85(2) of the Succession Act continues the provision in section 20 of the 1837 Act, that a will may be revoked in whole or in part by "some writing declaring an intention to revoke it and executed in the manner in which a will is required to be executed". The strictness with which the courts view the requirement that such writing be executed as a proper testamentary disposition, is illustrated by the decision in *In b. McCullagh*.[50] There, the testator's will dated 4 April 1945, was found after his death bearing a signed endorsement in his handwriting, stating that "This will made by me on April 4th is now cancelled as from 21-1-48." Enquiries were set on foot to discover if any other will could be found but these proved unsuccessful and the executors applied for a grant of probate of the will of 4 April 1945. Haugh J., in giving liberty to apply for a grant of probate, held that the endorsement on the will was not executed as a proper testamentary disposition and was therefore not sufficient to revoke the will, and, as no other will had been found it was impossible to say if such had ever in fact been executed and contained a revocation clause.

4.5.2 Haugh J.'s decision was absolutely correct in terms of the express language of section 20 of the 1837 Act, but can scarcely be said to have given effect to the testator's intention, which was to revoke his will. Be that

---

[46] (1881) 6 P.D. 207. See also *In b. Carleton* [1915] 2 I.R. 9; *In re Taylor Decd* [1938] 1 All E.R. 586 and *Re Pearson Decd* [1963] 3 All E.R. 763

[47] See *In b. Miller* [1931] I.R. 364

[48] [1944] P.39

[49] See Parry and Clark "The Law of Succession" (8th ed. 1983) at p.66

[50] [1949] Ir. Jur. Rep. 49 *Hellier v Hellier* (1884) 9 P.D. 237 was cited

as it may, the provision in section 20 has been substantially reproduced in section 85(2) of the Succession Act, and decisions like that in *In b. McCullagh* are likely to reoccur. If the principle that the testator's intention is paramount is to have more than token significance, then it is arguable that amending legislation should provide that a form of revocation in the testator's handwriting, and bearing his signature, should be treated as an effective revocation of his will. As we shall see such amending legislation might more appropriately provide for the addition of a category of symbolic destruction to the provisions on physical destruction contained in section 85(2).[51]

4.6 Revocation by destruction

4.6.1 Section 85(2) of the Succession Act, like section 20 of the 1837 Act, provides that a will is revoked by the burning, tearing, or destruction of it by the testator, or by someone in his presence and by his direction, with the intention of revoking it.[52]

4.6.2 The language of section 85(2) varies slightly from that of section 20, but it is clear that both contemplate acts of physical destruction. The courts construed the words "or otherwise destroying" in section 20 as being *eiusdem generis* with burning and tearing, and there is nothing to suggest that the slight variation in language in section 85(2) which refers simply to "destruction" was meant to embrace acts of symbolic destruction, such as that in the English case *Cheese* v *Lovejoy*.[53] There, a will was held not to have been revoked when the testator drew his pen through part of it, wrote "revoked" on the back, and threw it into a pile of waste paper. The testator did this in the presence of his housekeeper and maid, the latter of whom later retrieved the will from the pile of waste paper, kept it, and produced it on the death of the testator. The will was admitted to probate.

4.6.3 Decisions like that in *Cheese* v *Lovejoy*, have provoked much critical comment, and it has been argued, that the destruction required for revocation purposes should merely be a clear manifestation of the testator's wishes that he no longer considers his will to be effective, rather than the physical destruction of the will itself.[54] A suggested solution to the problem posed by cases such as *Cheese* v *Lovejoy* is the addition of the word "cancelling" to the language of section 20 which would, ironically, give effect to the recommendation of the Real Property Commissioners,

---

[51] See *post* p.91

[52] See Mellows "The Law of Succession" (4th ed. 1983) at pp.87 *et seq.*

[53] (1877) 2 P.D. 251

[54] See Davey "The Making and Revocation of Wills" at p.106

which preceded the enactment of the 1837 Act.[55] The addition of a word such as "cancelling" to the language of section 85(2) would also, arguably, allow the Irish courts to give effect to the clear intention of the testator in cases such as *In b. McCullagh*.[56] If such a statutory provision was inserted in section 85(2), there is no reason why the Irish courts should not follow the example of the American courts, and extend the meaning of such provision in cases where the intention of a testator to revoke his will is clear and manifest.[57]

4.6.4 The inclusion of precise words like "burning" and "tearing" in section 85(2) reflects the aversion which Irish legislators share with their English counterparts to more abstract concepts such as "cancelling", but, since much of the Succession Act is borrowed from civilian jurisdictions, the time may be ripe for a review of other of our legislative practices in respect of succession law.

4.7 Act of destruction and *animus revocandi*

4.7.1. An act of destruction must be done *animo revocandi,* and it follows that the destruction of a will through inadvertence, or by mistake, will not effect its revocation. Thus a will destroyed in the mistaken belief that it was invalid,[58] and a will destroyed in the mistaken belief that a later will had revoked it,[59] have been held not to have been revoked by their destruction. While a mistake by a testator as to the legal effect of language which he intends to include in his will will not normally result in the exclusion of such language from probate, the courts, as we shall see, are willing to employ the doctrine of dependent relative revocation in order to save wills where the testator mistakenly believed that on the revocation of his will some other disposition of his property would take effect.[60]

4.7.2 That the act of destruction be done *animo revocandi* would seem to require that the act and intention be concurrent phenomena, but there is some English authority to the effect that if an act of destruction by the testator himself is not done *animo revocandi* the testator may subsequently adopt his own act of destruction.[61] It is otherwise if the act of destruction is

[55] *Ibid*
[56] [1949] Ir. Jur. Rep. 49
[57] See Langbein "Substantial Compliance With The Wills Act" (1975) 88 Harvard Law Review 489. 522 n.117
[58] *Giles v Warren* (1872) 1 P. & D. 401. See also *In b. Taylor* (1890) 65 L.T. 230 and *Stamford v White* [1901] P.46
[59] *Scott v Scott* (1859) 1 Sw. & Tr. 258
[60] See *post* pp.96 *et seq.*
[61] *James v Shrimpton* (1876) 1 P.D. 431 Cf. *Mills v Millward* (1890) 15 P.D. 20

done by someone other than the testator, whose subsequent adoption of the act will be ineffective if the act was not done in his presence *and* by his direction.[62] The courts have interpreted these latter requirements strictly, and it has been held that a telephone call from a testator to his solicitor asking him to destroy the testator's will, is not an effective revocation if the act of destruction is carried out in the absence of the testator.[63] Likewise, a letter from a testator to his solicitor requesting the destruction of his will, will not be an effective revocation if the will is destroyed in the absence of the testator, but, if such letter is signed by the testator, and attested by at least two witnesses, it may constitute an effective written revocation within section 85(2).[64]

4.8 Extent of act of destruction

4.8.1 A will may be revoked in whole, or in part, by an act of destruction, and, in the absence of evidence of the testator's expressed intention in relation to the act, the testator's intention may be inferred from the state of the will after the act in question. If the destruction is of a vital part of the will, such as the testator's signature, or the signatures of the witnesses, it will be inferred that the testator intended to destroy his will *in toto*. Deasy L.J. pointed out in *In re White*[65] that the fact that the testator had torn off that portion of his will containing his signature and the attestation clause went a long way to showing that he intended to revoke the whole will.

4.8.2 The facts of *In re White* were somewhat unusual in that only that portion of the will which had been torn off by the testator was found after his death. That portion which contained the date of the will, the testator's signature and those of the attesting witnesses, and the appointment of an executor, had been torn off the dispositive part of the will which could not be found and was presumed to have been destroyed by the testator. Fitzgibbon L.J. who was also of the opinion that the testator must be taken to have intended the revocation of his will *in toto* pointed out, that the "*animus* must govern the extent and measure of operation to be attributed to the act in question, which act may be done with the intention of revoking the whole or part only of the will, or sometimes with no intention to revoke at all".[66]

4.8.3 An instance of partial revocation is to be found in *In b. Woodward*[67]

[62] See *Gill* v *Gill* [1909] P.157
[63] *In the Estate of de Kremer* (1965) 110 S.J. 18 See Parry and Clark at p.62
[64] See *ante* p.89
[65] (1897) 3 L.R. Ir. 413, 415
[66] *Ibid* at p.416
[67] (1871) 2 P. & D. 206. See also *In b. Nelson* (1872) 6 I.R. Eq. 569; *In the Estate of Nunn* (1936) 154 L.R. 498

which was referred to by Fitzgibbon L.J. in *In re White*.[68] There, a testator whose will was written on several sheets of paper, tore eight lines off one page and probate was granted of the rest. No part of the will which was essential to its valid execution was destroyed, and what remained of the original document was intelligible and workable as a will without the mutilated part. The court also took a benign view of the tearing off of a part of a will, in *In b. Leeson*.[69] There, the testator's will was found among his private papers after his death, written on a single sheet of paper, the entire of the left hand side of which was torn vertically, which suggested that it was originally the right hand portion of a double sheet of paper. There was no evidence as to when, or by whom, the paper had been torn, and the attesting witnesses were unable to recall the condition of the will at the time of execution.

4.8.4 While it appeared to Davitt P. that the will was written on a portion of what was originally a double sheet of paper, and, although no evidence had been produced to show how or when it had become torn, the learned President thought that in these circumstances it should be admitted to probate.

4.9 Mental capacity to revoke

4.9.1 The test of mental capacity, in relation to the revocation of a will by the testator, is the same as that required for the execution of a will, and, if the testator's mental faculties were impaired by, for example, drunkness at the time of the purported revocation, it will not be effective.[70] We have seen that the will of a testator, who being of sound mind at the time of the execution of the will, subsequently loses his mental capacity, may become irrevocable.[71] It may be otherwise of course if the testator's subsequent unsoundness of mind was not incurable, but a presumption will arise that a testator's mental incapacity persisted at the time of the purported revocation, and such presumption will only be rebutted by the clearest evidence.[72]

4.10 Lost wills

4.10.1 When a will, which was last known to be in the possession of the testator, cannot be found after his death, there is a presumption that he

---

[68] (1879) 3 L.R. Ir. 413, 416

[69] [1946] Ir. Jur. Rep. 33. Cf. *Leonard v Leonard* [1902] P.243 and *Treloar v Lean* (1889) 14 P.D. 49

[70] See *In the Goods of Brassington* [1902] P.1; *In the Goods of Hine* [1893] P.282

[71] See *ante* p.8

[72] See *Banks v Goodfellow* (1870) L.R. 5 Q.B. 549, 570

destroyed it *animo revocandi*. The rule was classically expounded by Parke B. in *Welch* v *Philips*:[73]

"Now the rule of the law of evidence on this subject, as established by a course of decisions in the Ecclesiastical Court is this: that if a will traced to the possession of the deceased and last seen there, is not forthcoming on his death, it is presumed to have been destroyed by himself; and that presumption must have effect unless there is sufficient evidence to repel it. The onus of proof of such circumstances is undoubtedly on the party propounding the will."

4.10.2 The presumption that a lost will which was in the testator's custody was destroyed by him *animo revocandi* will, as Cockburn C.J. pointed out in *Sugden* v *Lord St Leonards*,[74] be more or less strong, according to the character of the custody which the testator had over the will. The fact that Lord St Leonard's custody of his will had been "anything but a close custody" helped to rebut the presumption that he had destroyed the will *animo revocandi*.

4.10.3 Kenny J. referred in *In b Coster*[75] to Cockburn C.J.'s observations on the character of the testator's custody of his will, and also instanced the occurrence of a fire at the testator's home, and the possibility that a disappointed beneficiary had taken away the original will, as matters which may rebut the presumption that the will was destroyed *animo revocandi*.[76] In the *Coster* case, the will, which had been traced to the custody of the testatrix by coercive evidence, could not be found, despite exhaustive searches and inquiries, and Kenny J. could find nothing in the evidence to rebut the presumption that the testatrix had destroyed it *animo revocandi*.

4.10.4 If the presumption is rebutted by contrary evidence, the person seeking to prove a lost will must establish (1) that the will was duly executed, and, (2) the contents of the will.

4.10.5 Evidence of due execution may be given by one or more of the attesting witnesses, or by someone who was present at the execution of the will, and, if no such evidence is available, the maxim *omnia praesumuntur rite esse acta* may be invoked. Lindley L.J. said of the latter maxim, in *Harris* v *Knight*,[77] that

---

[73] (1836) 1 Moore's P.C. 299

[74] (1876) 1 P.D. 154, 217

[75] Unreported Supreme Court judgment delivered 19 January 1978. See Wylie "A Casebook on Irish Land Law" (2nd ed. 1986) at p.499

[76] *Ibid* at p.500. See also *Re Webb* [1964] 2 All E.R. 91 where evidence that the will was destroyed during an air raid rebutted the presumption

[77] (1890) 15 P.D. 170, 179

"it expresses an inference which may reasonably be drawn when an intention to do some formal act is established; when the evidence is consistent with that intention having been carried into effect in a proper way; but where the actual observance of all due formalities can only be inferred as a matter of probability."

Due execution was presumed in that case, on proof that the lost document was in the form of a will, and contained at the end three signatures, one of which was purported to be that of the testator.

4.10.6 There is no rule of law governing the sufficiency of evidence necessary to prove due execution, which question will depend on the circumstances of the particular case. Perhaps the best example of the courts' benignity in this respect is to be found in *Re Yelland*[78] where, both witnesses being dead, Oliver J. admitted evidence to the effect that one of the witnesses had told a neighbour that she had witnessed the disputed will.

4.10.7 The contents of a lost will, like those of any other document may be proved by secondary evidence, and, when such contents are not completely proved, probate will be granted to the extent to which they are proved. There has been some difference of judicial opinion as to whether declarations made by a testator after the execution of his will are admissible to prove the contents thereof. The majority in the English Court of Appeal in *Sugden* v *Lord St Leonards*[79] held that such declarations were admissible, but the House of Lords subsequently declined in *Woodward* v *Goulstone*[80] to express an opinion on whether post testamentary declarations were admissible to prove the contents of a lost will. Be that as it may, Warren J. in *In b. Ball*[81] could see no distinction between pre and post testamentary declarations, and Andrews L.J. in *In b. Gilliland*[82] approved *obiter* of the majority view in *Sugden* v *Lord St Leonards*. The preponderance of Irish and English case law supports the admissibility of post testamentary declarations, and an English textwriter has stated that, although the position cannot be regarded as settled, "it seems that *Sugden* v *Lord St Leonards* remains binding, though it will not be extended."[83]

4.10.8 If the missing will was drawn up professionally, the testator's solicitor might have retained a copy of it which could be admitted to

[78] (1975) 119 S.J. 562
[79] (1876) 1 P.D. 154. Mellish L.J. dissented on this point.
[80] (1886) 11 App. Cans. 469. See Mellows at (4th ed. 1983) p.266
[81] (1890) 25 L.R. Ir. 556
[82] [1940] N.I. 125
[83] Mellows *op. cit.* at (4th ed. 1983) p.266

probate, or he might have kept a note of the testator's instructions for his will from which the will could be reconstructed.[84] In the absence of such documentary evidence, a lost will may be reconstructed from the recollections of those who have read it. Thus in *In b. Regan*[85] where neither the original will, nor a contemporary copy, nor instructions therefor, were forthcoming, the court granted probate to a typed copy of the reconstructed will, made from statements of the next-of-kin of the testator.[86]

4.10.9 While the next-of-kin may be required to give oral evidence of the contents of the lost will and the circumstances of its execution, Davitt P. did not require the applicant, who was the son of the testator, or his sister, to give such evidence. As a general rule the court will not grant probate of a will on motion, but it may do so with the consent of all parties interested in the estate, and such consent may be dispensed with in the case of small estates.[87]

4.10.10 The contents of a lost will may be proved by the evidence of a single witness, though that witness be an interested party, if the evidence is otherwise unimpeachable. Thus in *Sugden* v *Lord St Leonards*[88] the contents of the lost will were proved by the evidence of the testator's daughter, who was a beneficiary under the will, her evidence being based on many conversations she had had with her father about the contents of his will. Perhaps the high point of the courts' liberality in this respect was reached in *Re Yelland*,[89] where a lost will was reconstructed from the recollections of the testatrix's daughter, also a beneficiary under the will, who had perused the will briefly for five minutes, some twenty years earlier.

4.11 Conditional Revocation

4.11.1 While an act of physical destruction will not revoke a will unless done *animo revocandi*, a further distinction has been made between an act of revocation which is intended to be absolute and effective forthwith, and one which is intended to take effect only on the fulfilment of some

---

[84] See Miller "Irish Probate Practice" (Dublin 1900) at pp.75-6

[85] [1964] Ir. Jur. Rep. 56

[86] It was held *semble* that the reconstructed terms of the will as contained in a typed copy thereof should be, as near as possible, in the same words as the lost original will and should be in *oratio recta*.

[87] See *In b. Merrigan Decd* (1899) 33 I.L.T.R. 131; *In b. Callan* (1874) I.R. 9 Eq. 484 and Miller "Irish Probate Practice" at p.73

[88] (1876) 1 P.D. 154

[89] (1975) 119 S.J. 562

condition. The condition may be a general one of the testator's choosing, or it may relate to the efficacy of some other disposition of the testator's property, when it is called "dependent relative revocation".[90]

4.11.2 The principle of "dependent relative revocation" has been applied where a testator purported to revoke a previous will on the assumption that a new will was valid,[91] and where a testator revoked his will on the mistaken assumption that the intestacy rules would effect the desired disposition of his property.[92] The principle may also apply where a testator has revoked his will with the intention of making a new will, but dies before doing so.

4.11.3 Thus in *In b. Coster*[93] a printed will form with nothing written on it was found among the personal papers of the deceased, giving rise to an inference that she had intended to make a new will. Gannon J., in the High Court, thought that the testatrix's missing will might have been mislaid, but, even if it had been destroyed, the revocation effected by this was conditional on the execution by the deceased of another valid will. Kenny J. in the Supreme Court disagreed:

"To make a destruction of a will by a testatrix a conditional revocation only, a mere general intention at the time of destruction to make another will is not, in most cases, effective to make the revocation by destruction conditional. The purchase of the printed form of will shows that the deceased had the making of another will in mind but this does not make the revocation conditional."[94]

4.11.4 The principle of "dependent relative revocation" will also apply where a testator revokes a later will, which has revoked an earlier will, on the mistaken assumption that the earlier will will thereby be revived. This was the precise circumstance which arose in *In the Goods of Hogan Decd.*[95] The deceased, Mrs Hogan, had made a will in August 1977, and a later one in July 1970, the effect of which was to revoke the earlier will. On the death of the testatrix only the will of August 1977 could be found among her personal papers, extensive searches failing to find the will of July 1979.

---

[90] See Newark (1955) 71 Law Quarterly Review 374
[91] See *Onions* v *Tyrer* (1716) 2 Vern. 741; *Re McMullan* [1964] Ir. Jur. Rep. 33
[92] See *In the Estate of Southerden* [1925] P. 177
[93] Unreported Supreme Court judgment delivered 19 January 1978. See Wylie "A Casebook on Irish Land Law" (2nd ed. 1986) at p.499
[94] Kenny J. referred to *Re Jones Decd* [1976] 1 All E.R. 593, 603 where Roskill L.J. had pointed out that the intention to make a new will, however clearly shown, is not enough of itself, as the authorities show, to make the revocation conditional. Kenny J. pointed out that Haugh J. had made the same point in *In the Goods of Walsh* [1947] Ir. Jur. Rep. 44
[95] Unreported judgment of Gannon J. delivered 18 February 1980. See "A Case of Dependent Relative Revocation" in (1981) 75 I.L.S.I. Gazette, 5

4.11.5 There was some evidence, from which the applicant, who was the daughter of the testatrix and the sole executrix of the 1979 will, drew the inference, which was deposed to in her affidavit, that the testatrix had destroyed the 1979 will by burning. Nevertheless, the applicant was seeking, with the consent of her brother and two sisters, who were beneficiaries under both the 1977 and 1979 wills, the admission to probate of a photocopy of the 1979 will, which had been kept by the testatrix's solicitor. It was contended for the applicant, that the testatrix had adopted the informal but effective method of revoking the 1979 will, viz. by burning it, only in the belief that by so doing the 1977 will would be revived. Since this belief was based on a mistaken assumption on her part of fact and of law, the condition upon which the 1979 will was revoked was not satisfied, and it followed that there was no true intention to revoke the 1979 will.[96] Gannon J. accordingly admitted the photocopy of the 1979 will to probate "in lieu of the original which was ineffectively revoked by destruction by the deceased by burning".

4.11.6 The decision in *In the Goods of Hogan Decd* raises some interesting questions, not the least of which is the extent to which the principle of "dependent relative revocation" can be said to depend on the intention of the testator. Decisions such as that in *In the Goods of Hogan* suggest that it has acquired an independent self-validating existence of its own, which has little to do with the intention of the testator. It is extremely unlikely that Mrs Hogan gave any thought to the possibility of the 1977 will being invalid and, that being so, the assumption that there was a conditional element in her revocation of the 1979 will was pure fiction. In so far as the intention of the testatrix could be ascertained, she did not wish the 1979 will to dispose of her property on death. The other certain intention that could be attributed to her was that she did not wish to die intestate, and the court clearly attached more weight to that consideration. Decisions like that in *In the Goods of Hogan* lend weight to the view of the English textwriter who said, of the application of the principle of "dependent relative revocation", that it "is, in most cases, in accordance with common sense, but it is only achieved by flagrant invention on the part of judges of an element of intention which in most cases was not present".[97]

---

[96] Counsel for the applicant cited *In the Goods of Irvine* [1919] 2 I.R. 485, 489 to the effect that if the act of revocation "whether by another will duly executed or by the destruction of the existing will, be without reference to any other act or event, the revocation may be an absolute one; but if the act be so connected with some other act or event that its efficacy is meant to be dependent on that other act or event, it will fail as a revocation. If that other act be efficacious, the revocation will operate; otherwise it will not. It is altogether a question of intention ..."

[97] Mellows "The Law of Succession" at p.94

4.12 Revival

4.12.1 The facts of *In the Goods of Hogan* suggest that it may well be a common misapprehension among lay persons that the revocation of a subsequent will, without more, revives an earlier will which has been revoked by the subsequent will. However, while revocation of a will by burning, tearing, or otherwise destroying it, can be simply effected, if done *animo revocandi*, the revival of a revoked will must be attended with rather more formality. Thus Gannon J. pointed out in *In the Goods of Hogan* that the statutory provisions governing the revival of a revoked will, which are contained in section 87 of the Succession Act are significantly more restrictive than those governing revocation which are contained in section 85.[98]

4.12.2 It is accordingly provided in section 87 of the Succession Act, which reproduces section 22 of the Act of 1837, that no will, or any part thereof, which is in any manner revoked, shall be revived otherwise than by the re-execution thereof, or by a codicil duly executed and showing an intention to revive it. It is furthermore provided in section 87 that when any will or codicil which is partly revoked, and afterwards wholly revoked, is revived, such revival shall not extend to so much thereof as was revoked before the revocation of the whole thereof, unless an intention to the contrary is shown.

4.12.3 In order for a will to be revived it must be in existence at the date of the instrument purporting to revive it, and it follows that a will which has been destroyed *animo revocandi* cannot be revived.[99] If a testator, having revoked his will by destroying it, changes his mind and wishes to dispose of his property in the manner of the revoked will, he can simply execute a new will containing similar dispositions to those in the revoked will. Whether the revoked will was destroyed or not, the testator who wishes to reinstate the provisions of the revoked will might well eschew the revival of such will in favour of the execution of a new will containing the desired provisions. The effect of revival in any event is the same as the making of a new will on the date of revival.[100]

---

[98] Gannon J. pointed out that the evidence of an intention to revive must be contained in the document effecting the revival which document must be executed in accordance with the formalities set out in s.78 of the Succession Act.

[99] See *In b. Reade* [1902] P. 75; *Re Hall* [1943] Ir. Jur. Rep. 25 and Miller "Irish Probate Practice" at p.170

[100]. Under s. 34 of the Wills Act 1837 a revived will was deemed, for the purposes of the Act, to have been made at the time of its revival. See generally *Goonewardene* v *Goonewardene* [1931] A.C. 647

4.12.4 While evidence of an intention to revive a will is required, it is not necessary that the reviving instrument should contain express words of revival. Nevertheless, prudence would dictate the use of such words, since the mere mention of a revoked will in a subsequent document will not necessarily revive the former.[101] The court must be able to ascertain from a subsequent testamentary document an intention to revive a revoked will.[102]

4.12.5 The revival of a will by a codicil may also confirm intervening codicils, but, where the reviving instrument refers to the will by its date and not to codicils to the will, the will only may be held to be revived.[103] Thus, in *French* v *Hoey*[104] the testator had made a will dated 21 October 1895, and a codicil thereto dated 31 October 1895. He made a new will on 18 November 1896, revoking all previous testamentary instruments, but he revoked this last-mentioned will by tearing it on 7 January 1897. He then made two codicils on 15 January 1897, one republishing the will of 21 October 1895 and written on the same sheet of paper as that will, referring to it as "my above-written will". The other was stated to be a codicil to that will, making a few different bequests but, in all other respects, confirming the same.

4.12.6 In an action to establish the will dated 21 October 1895 together with three codicils, one dated 31 October 1895 and the two others dated 15 January 1897, it was held that the codicil of 31 October 1895 was not revived, and probate should be granted only of the will of 21 October 1895 and the two codicils of 15 January 1897. In considering whether the codicil of 31 October 1895 had been revived within the terms of section 22 of the Wills Act 1837 Andrews J. said:

> "If the codicil of 31st October 1895, was revived its revival must have been effected by the instrument executed by the testator on the 15th January 1897, or one of them. It is no doubt true as a general rule that the word 'will', when used without limitation of its meaning, includes all the testamentary papers which, together, make up the whole of the testator's testamentary dispositions, and therefore includes codicils; but it may also be used in a restricted sense, so as to be applicable only to the instrument called the 'will', as distinguished from a codicil. I shall assume that the word 'will' may, under certain circumstances, have its

[101] See *Re Smith* (1890) 45 Ch. D. 632. Revocation of a revoking will does not, without more, revive an earlier will. See *In the Goods of Hodgkinson* [1893] P.339

[102]. See *In the Goods of Steele* (1868) L.R. 1 P. & D. 575 and *In the Estate of Davies* [1952] P.279 and generally the cases cited in Miller "Irish Probate Practice" at p.166

[103] See *In the Goods of Reynolds* (1873) 3 P. & D. 35 and Miller, *supra* at p.167

[104] [1899] 2 I.R. 472

largest signification, and include a codicil or codicils, even though it be referred to as a will of a specified date; but to effect by a subsequent codicil the revival of a codicil which stands revoked, the subsequent codicil must, by the express enactment of the 22nd section of the Wills Act, show an intention to revive it."[105]

4.12.7 If a codicil revives a revoked will it may have the effect of revoking an intermediate will which is inconsistent with the terms of the revived will.[106]

4.13 Republication

4.13.1 Republication differs from revival, in that it confirms an existing will or codicil, while the latter reinstates a will or codicil which has been revoked. The term republication has been something of an anachronism since section 5 of the Wills Act, 1837, which is reproduced in section 80 of the Succession Act, provided that every will executed in accordance with the Act should be valid without any other publication thereof.

4.13.2 Be that as it may, the term republication persists though there is much to be said for the use of the term "confirmation" as a more accurate description of the way in which republication has been used since 1837.[107] Indeed, that the courts often use the terms "republication" and "confirmation" synonymously can be seen in certain of the cases reviewed by Ronan L.J. in *Grealey* v *Sampson*.[108]

4.13.3 Republication must be attended with the same formalities necessary for the execution of a will, and it follows that the two ways in which republication can be effected are (1) by the re-execution of the original will, or (2) by a duly executed codicil which makes some reference to the will that is purported to be republished.

4.13.4 As with revival, no formal words of republication or confirmation are necessary, and the standard of proof required to establish republication is less stringent than that required to establish revival.[109] Thus, it has been said that a codicil described simply as a codicil to a particular will will republish that will.[110] The low level of proof required to establish

---

[105] *Ibid* at p.479
[106] See *In the Goods of Courtenay* (1891) 27 L.R. Ir. 507
[107] See Parry and Clark "The Law of Succession" (8th ed. 1983) at p.77
[108] [1917] 1 I.R. 280, 301
[109] See *ante* p.99
[110] *Re Taylor* (1880) 57 L.J. Ch. 430; *Re Champion* [1893] 1 Ch. 101 and *Re Harvey* [1947] Ch. 285

republication has been criticised by an English textwriter, who points out that in many situations a testator directs his attention to part only of his will which he wishes to alter, and yet a codicil giving effect to such alteration may be construed as republishing the entire will. He argues, that it would be more satisfactory to require positive proof of an intention to republish.[111]

4.13.5 The obvious advantage of republication, is that it allows the testator to provide specifically for persons who have come into existence, or property which has been acquired by the testator, between the date of the will and the republication thereof. Indeed, this latter aspect of republication provided its *raison d'etre* prior to 1837, when wills were not ambulatory in respect of realty which had been acquired between the date of the will and the death of the testator.

4.13.6 Republication, like revival, is said to bring the will down to the date of republication. Ronan L.J. put it thus in *Grealey* v *Sampson*:[112]

"With certain well defined exceptions, when a codicil republishes a will the effect is to bring the will down to the date of the codicil, and to make the devise in the will operate in the same way in which it would have operated if the words of the will had been contained in the codicil of later date, unless a contrary intention appears."

4.13.7 The rule that republication brings the will down to the date of the codicil in the absence of a contrary intention was accepted by the Court of Appeal in *Earl of Mountcashell* v *Smyth*,[113] but was qualified by the court in the light of the circumstances in that case. There, the testator by his will, dated 30 April 1836, had given to his daughter and six other named persons, a power to appoint in favour of any husband or wife the said daughter and other donees of the power might thereafter marry. The testator executed a codicil dated 18 June 1855, the effect of which was to republish his will, and the question arose as to whether the power in the will of 1836 was exercisable only in respect of persons the donees of the power might marry after the date of the codicil. If that were so, the power could only apply in the case of second marriages of the donees of the power if they were already married, as was the testator's daughter, at the date of the codicil.[114]

4.13.8 Perhaps not surprisingly, in the light of these circumstances, the Court of Appeal held, that although the codicil operated as a republication

---

[111] Mellows "The Law of Succession" (4th ed. 1983) at p.138
[112] [1917] 1 I.R. 286, 296
[113] [1895] 1 I.R. 346
[114] *Ibid* at p.357 (per Walker C.)

of the will, and for certain purposes brought it down to the date of the codicil, it did not alter the construction of the will, and the words "hereafter" and "may marry" were to be read as of the date of the will. Walker C. agreed that "the case must be considered as if the testator, in June 1855, made a will in the very words of the will of 1836, but how far the doctrine is to be pursued is the question".[115] Walter C. did not believe that the republication of the will did not interfere with its construction in regard to the objects of gifts but, if it was necessary for the construction of a will to refer to the date of its execution, that date remained a factor for determining its construction. Walker C. thought that authority and reason were in favour of that view.[116]

4.13.9 Ronan L.J. was later to point out in *Grealey* v *Sampson*[117] that the cases say that the will and codicil must be taken together as one document of the latter date, but nowhere, except in *Mountcashell* v *Smyth*[118] and *Long* v *Moore*,[119] had it ever been suggested, that the old date must be incorporated. Ronan L.J. confessed that he had some difficulty in understanding what a new will of a later date, but at the same time of the former date, meant, and he suggested the simple test of applying the statements in those two cases to section 24 of the Act of 1837 which would then read: "Every will shall be construed ... to speak and take effect as if it had been executed immediately before the death, but at the same time as if made at the time of its date."[120] It seemed obvious to Ronan L.J. that under section 24, and in cases of republication, the date of the will *may* be looked at for the purpose of ascertaining a "contrary intention", and he found it to be very remarkable that in *Mountcashell* v *Smyth* and *Long* v *Moore* this vital principle of contrary intention did not seem to have been considered.[121] Consideration of that principle would clearly have led to the same results in both cases by a less contentious route.

4.13.10 Barton J. underlined the court's willingness to effectuate the testator's intention in a celebrated passage in *Long* v *Moore*[122] where he said:

[115] *Ibid*

[116] *Ibid* at p.360. Walker C. thought that the absurdity which would follow from acceptance of the appellant's contention was like that in *Ogle* v *Sherborne* (1887) 34 Ch. D. 446. There the testator had bequeathed a silver cup to Lord Sherborne and his heirs as an heirloom. The person who was Lord Sherborne had died and left a successor to the title but the Court of Appeal held that the gift failed as it was to the Lord Sherborne who was alive at the date of the will despite the testator's intention that the gift should constitute an heirloom.

[117] [1917] 1 I.R. 286, 304

[118] [1895] 1 I.R. 346

[119] [1907] 1 I.R. 315

[120] [1917] 1 I.R. 286, 305

[121] *Ibid* at pp.299 *et seq*.

[122] [1907] 1 I.R. 315, 318

"The authorities ... lead me to the conclusion that the courts have always treated the principle that republication makes the will speak as if it had been re-executed at the date of the codicil not as a rigid formula or technical rule, but as a useful and flexible instrument for effectuating a testator's intentions by ascertaining them down to the latest date at which they have been expressed."

4.13.11 Barton J.'s observations were criticised by Ronan L.J. in *Grealey* v *Sampson*,[123] but have been judicially approved in England,[124] and have been cited by English textwriters in support of the principle that republication must not defeat intention.[125] They correctly focus attention on the primacy of the testator's intention, and can be said to be consistent with, and anticipatory of, the modern shift from principle to pragmatism in the administration of justice.[126]

4.13.12 The court's willingness to effectuate the intention of the testator also accounts for the general rule, that a duly executed codicil which republishes a will also republishes intervening codicils made between the date of the will and its republication.[127] Codicils which are not duly executed may also be held to be republished under the doctrine of incorporation.[128]

4.13.13 Unattested alterations made to a will or codicil after execution and before republication may also be held to have been republished by a subsequent codicil, if the testator intended them to form part of his republished will. Thus, where unattested alterations were made in a codicil to a will, it was held that another codicil which confirmed the will, republished the will and previous codicil in its altered state.[129]

4.13.14 The effect of republication on lapse[130] and ademption[131] is considered elsewhere.

---

[123] [1917] 1 I.R. 286, 304

[124] *Re Hardyman* [1925] Ch. 287, 291 (per Romer J.)

[125] See Parry and Clark "The Law of Succession" (8th ed. 1983) at p.78

[126] See Atiyah "From Principles to Pragmatism" (Oxford 1978)

[127] *Re Fraser* [1904] 1 Ch. 726 and see *Re Hay* [1904] 1 Ch. 317

[128] See *ante* p.56 *et seq.*

[129] *In the Goods of Wollaston* (1845) 3 N.C. 599; *In the Goods of Tegg* (1846) 4 N.C. 531; and see Miller "Irish Probate Practice" at pp.70-71

[130] See *post* p.154

[131] See *post* p.166

Chapter 5
THE CONSTRUCTION OF WILLS

5.1 Introduction

5.1.1 The function of the court in construing a will is to give effect to the testator's intention, as it is ascertained from the written terms of the will.[1] The statutory requirement of writing makes the will itself the primary evidence of the testator's intention and, unless extrinsic evidence is otherwise admissible,[2] the court may not attribute to the testator an intention which is not expressed in the will.[3] Nor may the court speculate upon what was in the testator's mind when he made his will.[4]

5.2 Reading the will as a whole

5.2.1 It is a fundamental rule of construction that a will is to be read as a whole, and thus a general intention will override a particular one.[5] Reading the will as a whole may show, as we shall see, that a testator used language in a particular way, and may help to resolve ambiguities in words and phrases used by a testator.[6] Such a reading of the will may also rebut presumptions in favour of the ordinary or technical meanings of words and

---

[1] See *Oliver* v *Menton* [1945] I.R. 6; *Re Moore* [1947] I.R. 205; *Re McCready* [1962] N.I. 43. See generally Hawkins and Ryder "Construction of Wills" (1965)

[2] See *post* pp.113 *et seq.*

[3] See *Fitzpatrick* v *Collins* [1978] I.L.R.M. 244

[4] See *In re Hogg* [1944] I.R. 244, 248 (per Murnaghan J.) and at p.258 (per Black J.)

[5] Ungood Thomas J. said in *Macandrew's Will Trusts* [1963] 3 W.L.R. 822, 834 that the "fundamental and over-riding duty binding the court is to ascertain the intention of the testator as expressed in his will read as a whole". Ungood Thomas J.'s words were cited by McWilliam J. in *Fitzpatrick* v *Collins* [1978] I.L.R.M. 244, 246. See also *Garnett* v *Garnett* (1854) 5 Ir. Jur. 89 and *Robinson* v *Moore* [1962-3] Ir. Jur. Rep. 29

[6] See *post* p.107

phrases,[7] supply, by implication, words omitted from a will,[8] and, allow the omission of words revealed as mere surplusage.[9]

5.3 The court will not rewrite a will.

5.3.1 The principle of freedom of testation, a commitment to which the Irish courts shared with their English counterparts prior to the enactment of the Succession Act 1965, meant that a testator could dispose of his property more or less as he pleased.[10] The courts could not, consistent with that principle, purport to remake wills for capricious testators, and the law reports are replete with cases in which wills have been admitted to probate despite the often cruel indifference of testators towards those most deserving of their bounty. Black J. had put it bluntly in *In re Hogg*[11] when he said, of certain residuary provisions in a will, that although they seemed peculiar, that was no reason for inferring that they were not so intended. He went on:

> "After all, testators do sometimes deliberately make peculiar dispositions. Moreover, these provisions might not really be peculiar but may merely seem to be so to those who are necessarily unable to put themselves in the position of the testator and understand his ideas on matters affecting his relations."[12]

5.3.2 Certain provisions in the Succession Act 1965 have eliminated the malign effects of the principle of freedom of testation in relation to a testator's surviving spouse and children, but, those provisions apart, testators remain relatively free to make eccentric or capricious dispositions of their properties.

5.3.3 A distinction can be drawn between rewriting a will, which the court may not do, and making alterations in a will which, as we have seen, the court may do to ensure that the written document is consistent with the testator's intention.[13] If the words used by the testator are clear and

[7] See *Perrin* v *Morgan* [1943] A.C. 399, 406 (per Viscount Simon L.C.)

[8] *In the Goods of Duffy* (1871) I.R. 5 Eq. 506, 509; *Re Redfern* (1877) 6 Ch. D. 133. The substance of the omitted words must be clear on the face of the will. See *Re Follett* [1955] 1 W.L.R. 429

[9] The court may omit one of the two provisions in a will which are not consistent with each other if it is clear from the will which of the two represents the testator's wishes. See e.g. *Re Isaac* [1905] 1 Ch. 427

[10] See *post* pp.182 *et seq.*

[11] [1944] I.R. 244, 258

[12] *Ibid*

[13] McWilliams J. pointed out in *Fitzpatrick* v *Collins* [1978] I.L.R.M. 244, 247 that had the testator adverted to the possibility of his wife predeceasing him he would have made dispositions similar to those he made if she died within two months of his death "but I am not entitled to make a will for a testator to cover circumstances which he has overlooked and such speculation is irrelevant".

unambiguous that is generally an end of the matter, and effect must be given to the words used.[14] If, however, reading the will as a whole reveals that particular words do not accurately reflect the testator's intention, the court may change the words used, or, in appropriate cases omit them altogether.[15]

5.3.4 Reading the will as a whole might also reveal that words have been unintentionally omitted. The courts are loath to add words to a will, but, if it is clear from the will that words have been omitted, and the substance of the omitted words is also clear, the court will add words to the will in order to give effect to the testator's intention.[16]

5.4 Meaning of words and phrases

5.4.1 The general rule of construction is, that a testator is presumed to have intended that a word or phrase is to be given its ordinary grammatical meaning unless there is something in the context, or other admissible circumstances, which proves otherwise.[17] Of course the same collocation of ordinary words may mean different things to different people, a point illustrated by the Northern Ireland case *Heron* v *Ulster Bank Ltd*[18] in which the Court of Appeal, reversing the decision of Lord MacDermott, held, that if a testator mentions one of his children, and then refers to "my other children", the ordinary meaning of the latter phrase is "all my children except the one already mentioned".[19]

5.4.2 A particular difficulty arises when a testator uses a word or phrase which has more than one ordinary meaning, an example of which is the word "money", which in its widest popular sense embraces all one's property, but, in its strict legal sense, came to mean cash in hand or choses in action, such as money in a drawing account in a bank.[20] In applying what became a strict rule of construction, judges often admitted to defeating the testator's intention.[21] In view of this, it was not surprising that the attitude of the courts began to soften and in *In re Jennings*[21] in a judgment later

---

[14] See *Rowe* v *Law* [1978] I.R. 55 and *post* p.116

[15] Murnaghan J. pointed out in *In re Hogg* [1944] I.R. 244, 251 that "there is no magic in words".

[16] See *In the Goods of Duffy* (1871) I.R. 5 Eq. 506,509

[17] *Perrin* v *Morgan* [1943] A.C. 399, 406 (per Viscount Simon L.C.)

[18] [1974] N.I. 44

[19] *Ibid* at p.53 (per Lowry L.C.J.)

[20] See the comments of Lord Atkin in *Perrin* v *Morgan* [1943] A.C. 399, 415 and those of Meredith J. in *In re Jennings* [1930] I.R. 196, 201. See also *Lowe* v *Thomas* (1854) 5 De G.M. & G. 315 and *In re Hodgson* [1936] Ch. 203

[21] [1930] I.R. 196

described by Viscount Simon L.C. as "pungent and entertaining"[22] Meredith J. construed a provision in a will, that the testator's granddaughter was "to have the use of all my money for her lifetime" as including, *inter alia,* an undivided share in leasehold property.[23] Meredith J. did not accept that the authorities obliged the court to hold that there was no derivative or secondary meaning of the word money and, as he put it colloquially, it was time for the courts to hoist the white flag since testators "evidently prefer to say 'cash' when they mean 'cash'".[24]

5.4.3 The House of Lords later took much the same view in *Perrin* v *Morgan*[25] when it held, that in interpreting a will the court is not bound, in the absence of special circumstances, to adopt a fixed meaning of the word "money" as being its legal as opposed to its popular meaning, but must ascertain as between various usual meanings which is the correct interpretation of the particular document, in the light of the context and other relevant circumstances.[26] Previous decisions of courts of coordinate jurisdiction had obliged the Court of Appeal to apply the strict rule of construction of the word "money" but Lord Greene M.R. had expressed the court's disapproval of the rule when he referred to it as "a blot upon our jurisprudence".[27] Gavan Duffy J. expressed similar sentiments in a typically discursive judgment in *In re Moore,*[28] in which he held that National Savings Certificates passed, under a bequest in a will of "my moneys on deposit in England".[29]

5.4.4 As we have seen, a testator is not obliged to use any particular form of words or mode of language when making his will, the only requirement being that his language is intelligible.[30] Lord Cranworth L.C. pointed out in *Windus* v *Windus,*[31] that there is no magic in words, and "any man may use his own nomenclature, if he only expresses what he means". A testator may explicitly create his own dictionary for the purposes of his will, by

[22] [1943] A.C. 399, 414

[23] [1930] I.R. 196, 208. Meredith J. respectfully adopted the entire reasoning of the judgments in *In re Taylor* [1923] 1 Ch. 99

[24] *Ibid* at p.200

[25] [1943] A.C. 399

[26] *Ibid* at p.408 (per Viscount Simon L.C.)

[27] [1942] Ch. 345, 346

[28] [1947] I.R. 205

[29] *Ibid* Having referred to *Perrin* v *Morgan* Gavan Duffy J. went on to say (at p.212) that he saw no reason why he should not welcome a breath of fresh air from across the channel and "*stare decisis* cannot mean persisting in error after the most authoritative judges of a particular precedent have demonstrated it to be both mischievous and misconceived".

[30] *Ante* p.32

[31] (1856) 6 D.M. & G. 549

[32] *Ibid* at p.187. See also *Singleton* v *Tomlinson* (1878) 3 App. Cas. 304

including in it a definition clause or explanatory note setting out the meaning which he wishes to be attributed to the language used. On the other hand, the will read as a whole might implicitly reveal that the testator has used language in a particular way and, as Murnaghan J. pointed out in *In re Hogg*,[33] the court is not confined to the interpretation of distinct clauses in a will but may be guided by the whole tenor of the will.

5.5 Technical words

5.5.1 When a testator uses technical terms in his will he is presumed to have intended them to be given their usual technical meaning, which is a question of fact to be determined from expert evidence.[34] Thus, when a testator uses technical legal terms in his will he is presumed to use them in their legal signification, unless the context clearly indicates the contrary.[35] Such a contrary intention was found in the rather unusual circumstances of *Oliver* v *Menton*[36] where a testatrix had left a leasehold dwellinghouse and a freehold garage to two named daughters and three named granddaughters, all spinsters, as joint tenants "as long as they remain unmarried". Gavan Duffy J. held that the words used indicated an intention that the property in question should be used as a house for the five named donees so long as, remaining spinsters, they would probably need it. Since a literal construction would defeat the testator's intention, the learned judge construed the gift as conferring, not a joint tenancy, but a tenancy in common, with the benefit of survivorship on death and the like benefit of accruer on marriage.

5.5.2 The decision in *Oliver* v *Menton* comes perilously close to rewriting the will for the testatrix, but has the undeniable merit of giving effect to the clear intention of the testatrix. The language used by the testatrix's draftsman was ill-adapted to its purpose, but not so ill-adapted as to leave her clear purpose in doubt and, Gavan Duffy J. observed the Fates had been kind to the draftsman "in giving him a will, and not a deed, for his experiment".[37]

---

[33] [1944] I.R. 244, 248

[34] See generally *Re Harcourt* [1922] A.C. 473; *Re Cook* [1948] Ch. 212 and *Falkiner* v *Commissioner of Stamp Duties* [1973] A.C. 565

[35] Meredith J., however, pointed out in *In re Jennings* [1930] I.R. 196, 204, that the authorities which suggest "that the lawyer's dictionary is to be rigidly adhered to unless the context happens to provide an excuse for looking to a wider interpretation of the word may be explained as cases in which the Court, for some reason or another, held that the will was to be regarded as one adopting the strict language of lawyers".

[36] [1945] I.R. 6

[37] *Ibid* at p.10

5.5.3 An interesting contrast in judicial interpretations of technical legal language in a will is to be found in *In re Hogg*,[38] where a testator had appointed his sister residuary legatee and, in the event of her predeceasing him, he appointed her children residuary legatees and devisees. His sister having survived the testator, the question arose as to whether the residuary gift to her carried the real estate. Gavan Duffy J. could find no rational basis for the distinction in the language of the residuary gifts to the sister and her children, but he felt constrained by the authorities to hold that the residuary gift to the sister did not carry the real estate.[39]

5.5.4 On appeal the Supreme Court being evenly divided Gavan Duffy J.'s judgment was affirmed. O'Byrne J. and Black J. agreed with Gavan Duffy J. that the testator had made a distinction between his sister as residuary legatee and her children as residuary legatees and devisees, and the court could not hold that no distinction had been made.[40] Murnaghan J. however, with whom Geoghegan J. concurred, held that the precise technical meaning of the words used could not be attributed to the testator, and the will, taken as a whole, showed that the testator's sister was intended to take the undisposed of real estate.[41]

5.5.5 If there is evidence before the court, and such was not the case in *In re Hogg*, that the will was the work of a skilled draftsman, or was made with professional assistance or advice, the court would be justified in interpreting strictly technical legal terms used but, in the absence of such evidence, the approach of Murnaghan J. is much to be preferred.[42]

5.5.6 A testator who does not have the benefit of professional legal advice when drawing up his will may use words which have a popular connotation which does not coincide with their technical legal connotation and, if his intention is not apparent on the face of the will, or ascertainable from admissible extrinsic evidence,[43] the technical meaning will prevail. Certain commonplace words were calculated to raise problems of interpretation and construction. One such word was "land" and, prior to the Wills Act 1837, a disposition of a testator's "land" was construed as referring to the

[38] [1944] I.R. 244

[39] *Ibid* at p.247

[40] O'Byrne J. referred (at p.252) to the well established canon of construction that where a testator uses technical words he is presumed to employ them in their legal significance, unless the context clearly indicates the contrary. Black J. pointed out (at p.258) that because the residuary provisions as construed by Gavan Duffy J. may seem peculiar was no reason for inferring that they were not so intended.

[41] *Ibid* at p.252

[42] See *Read* v *Backhouse* (1831) 2 Russ. & M. 546; *Hall* v *Warren* (1861) 9 H.L. Cas. 420 and Mellows "The Law of Succession" (4th ed. 1983) at p.158

[43] On extrinsic evidence generally see *post* pp.113 *et seq.*

testator's freehold interest, if he had such. The intention of the testator was not altogether irrelevant and, if he had no freehold interest in the land, his disposition was construed as referring to any leasehold interest he might have in the land.[44] Things were made easier for testators by section 26 of the Wills Act 1837 which provided that a general devise of land would include the customary, copyhold and leasehold estates of a testator, unless a contrary intention appeared in the will. This provision is restated for leasehold interests by section 92 of the Succession Act which provides: "A general devise of land shall be construed to include leasehold interests as well as freehold estates, unless a contrary intention appears from the will."

5.5.7 Of course a testator is free to dispose of his realty and personalty separately, and he may use technical terms in his will in such a way as to make clear his intention to do so. The fact that a will has been drawn up professionally will invariably lead the court to put a technical construction on the words used, and if, for example, such a will disposed of the testator's "real estate" such term will be construed by reference to section 4(a) of the Succession Act, which defines it as, including

"chattels real, and land in possession, remainder, or reversion, and every estate or interest in or over land (including real estate held by way of mortgage or security) but not including money to arise under a trust for sale of land, or money secured or charged on land."

5.5.8 The attitude of the courts to the construction of wills which have been drawn up by skilled practitions can be shown by reference to *Re Fetherstonhaugh — Whitney's Estate*.[45] There the Court of Appeal held, reversing Wylie J., that the residuary clause in a will which had been drawn up by an experienced practitioner, did not carry the real estate, inasmuch as (1) the will showed a clear division between real and personal property, and made a complete disposition of each, and used appropriate words exclusively for the gifts of each; (2) the testatrix had no real estate other than that of which the will contained complete dispositions; (3) that the will showed that the use of the word "property" in the residuary clause was limited by its context to personal estate.[46]

5.5.9 The majority in the Court of Appeal was clearly satisfied that effect was being given to the testator's intention by excluding the real estate from the residuary gift, but it is clear that if a contrary intention had been deduced from the evidence, it would have been included in the residuary gift. The courts do not routinely invoke technical distinctions to frustrate

---

[44] See Wylie "Irish Land Law" (2nd ed. 1986) at p.739
[45] [1924] 1 I.R. 153
[46] *Ibid* at p.162

the intentions of testators if those intentions are otherwise apparent, or ascertained from admissible extrinsic evidence.

5.5.10 Despite the relative benignity of courts and legislature testators are well advised, when disposing of interests in land, to eschew words which do not clearly delineate those interests. The problems which might otherwise arise can be seen in *Re Curneen*[47] where the court had to determine, whether the words "all the remainder of my belongings" in a residuary clause, included the testator's interest in registered freehold land. It was contended for the next-of-kin that the relevant authority was *Re Price*,[48] where it had been held that a gift of "all my belongings" did not include the testator's freehold house, which accordingly passed as on an intestacy. It was countered for the plaintiffs, that freehold land registered under Part IV of the Local Registration of Title (Ir.) Act, 1891, had assimilated some of the characteristics of personalty for the purpose of devolution, and counsel for the plaintiffs cited *McInerney* v *Liddy*,[49] where the designation of two persons as "residuary legatees" was held to be sufficient to pass to them the testator's interests in freehold registered land not specifically disposed of in the will.

5.5.11 Murnaghan J. was of the opinion that the words "my belongings" were, of themselves, inappropriate to pass the freehold registered land comprising, as a general rule, chattels and personal property.[50] Nor was there anything in the will taken as a whole to indicate a contrary intention. Rather, as Murnaghan J. pointed out, the same expression "my belongings" was used by the testator in an earlier context when confined to pure personalty, and this suggested that the expression was not intended to include land when used in the second instance.[51]

5.5.12 In holding that the testator had died intestate, in so far as the freehold registered land was concerned, Murnaghan J. also took cognisance of the fact that the purpose of the residuary bequest was the provision of money for the saying of Masses for the testator's soul, for which purpose a large sum was already available from the pure personalty. Whether or not some such phrase as "my belongings" will include any freehold interest which the testator may have had, thus can be said to depend on the circumstances of the particular case and *Re Curneen* is authority for nothing more than that the courts should adopt a pragmatic approach to the resolution of these problems of construction.

[47] (1957) 91 I.L.T.R. 55
[48] [1950] 1 Ch. 242
[49] [1945] I.R. 100
[50] (1957) 91 I.L.T.R. 55, 56
[51] *Ibid*

5.6 Extrinsic Evidence

5.6.1 The statutory requirement of writing, as we have seen, made the will itself the primary evidence of the testator's intention, and precluded the court from attributing to the testator an intention not expressed in the will.[52] When construing the terms of a will the court was not precluded, however, from admitting extrinsic evidence which explained or clarified what the testator had written. A careful distinction was made between extrinsic evidence which was merely explanatory of the language used by the testator, which was admissible, and such evidence which sought to establish the testator's intention as an independent fact, which was inadmissible.[53]

5.6.2 The language used by a testator in relation to persons and property mentioned in his will reflected facts and circumstances within his peculiar knowledge, and the so-called "armchair principle" allowed the court to take cognisance of the facts and circumstances by which the testator "was surrounded when he made his will to assist in arriving at his intention".[54] Reference to the surrounding circumstances, which followed and could not precede a literal construction of the will, might show that the testator had used language in a particular way, and evidence could be adduced to show the usage of the class of persons to which the testator belonged.[55] Thus in determining whether National Savings Certificates passed under a bequest in the testatrix's will of "any moneys on deposit in England" Gavan Duffy J. said in *In re Moore*:[56]

> "Not only does the nature of the transaction make the use of the word 'deposit' reasonable, but we have the authority of Lord Greene M.R. and Lord Thankerton for believing that the modest class for whom the savings certificates were invented would be expected in England to speak of those investments as their 'money'; see *In re Morgan; Morgan v Morgan*[57] and *Perrin v Morgan*;[58] and I may reasonably suppose that a lady who spent a lifetime in England as a hospital nurse would use the same language."

Gavan Duffy J. also employed the most probable meaning test which Lord Atkin had formulated in *Perrin v Morgan*.[59] Lord Atkin had pointed out

---

[52] See the passage in Wigram on *Extrinsic Evidence in Aid of the Interpretation of Wills* (5th ed.) quoted by Henchy J. in *Rowe v Law* [1978] I.R. 55, 70-1

[53] See *In re Grainger* [1900] 2 Ch. 756; *In re Hall* [1944] I.R. 54; *In re Carlisle* [1950] N.I. 105

[54] *Boyes v Cook* (1880) 14 Ch. D. 53, 56; See also *Fitzgerald v Ryan* [1899] 2 I.R. 637

[55] See generally Mellows "The Law of Succession" (4th ed. 1983) at pp.126 *et seq.*

[56] [1947] I.R. 205, 209

[57] [1942] Ch. 345

[58] [1943] A.C. 399

[59] *Ibid* at p.414

that no will can be analysed *in vacuo* and the construing court, having regard to the admissible circumstances, "must adopt the most probable meaning".

5.6.3 While the "armchair principle" could thus be used in clarifying any imprecision in the language used in the description of persons or property in a will, the narrowness of the rule of construction that extrinsic evidence was admissible to explain what the testator had written, but not what he had intended to write, was starkly underlined by the decision in *In re Julian*.[60] The latter case involved a bequest of a sum of money in the will of a Protestant lady to "The Seamen's Institute, Sir John Rogerson's Quay, Dublin" which bequest was claimed by two bodies, the Catholic Seaman's Institute, Sir John Rogerson's Quay, and the Dublin Seaman's Institute, a Protestant body whose address was Eden Quay, Dublin.

5.6.4 At the hearing of a construction summons it was sought to prove the intention of the testatrix by introducing parol evidence of her religion and her long association with the Protestant Institute on Eden Quay. It was also sought to introduce evidence to show that the solicitor who drafted the will had made a mistake with regard to the address of the institute to be benefitted.[61]

5.6.5 Kingsmill Moore J. held, reluctantly, that parol evidence was inadmissible to show the intention of the testatrix, since such evidence was admissible only to determine which of several persons or objects was designated in a truly equivocal description in a will, and no such doubt was disclosed by the language in the instant will. Kingsmill Moore J. added:

"This is by no means the first – and equally certainly will not be the last – case in which a judge has been forced by the rules of law to give a decision on the construction of a will which he believed to be contrary to the intentions of the testator. The law reports are loud with the comments of judges who found themselves in a similar plight ..."[62]

5.6.6 In the light of cases like *In re Julian* it is not surprising that some modification of the existing law was attempted in the Succession Act 1965, section 90 of which provides: "Extrinsic evidence shall be admissible to show the intention of the testator, and to assist in the construction of, or to explain any contradiction in, a will."

[60] [1950] I.R. 57

[61] The testatrix in giving her instruction for her will to her solicitor had expressed some doubt as to the correct address of the Seamen's Institute she wished to benefit, whereupon the solicitor had consulted a reference book in which the only Institute listed was the Catholic one on Sir John Rogerson's Quay.

[62] [1950] I.R. 57, 66

5.6.7 Parke J. had to consider the effect of section 90 in *Bennett* v *Bennett*[63] where the deceased had devised his lands to his wife for life and, on her death, to his nephew, Dennis Bennett absolutely. The testator had also appointed his wife and said nephew Dennis Bennett executrix and executor of his will. It transpired that the deceased had no nephew called Dennis Bennett, his only relative of that name being his brother, but the testator's nephew William Bennett, one of the defendants, contended that he should be allowed to adduce evidence to show that the testator had intended him to be the beneficiary and executor named in the will.

5.6.8 It seemed clear to Parke J., having regard to the terms of section 90, that such evidence was admissible "bearing in mind that the onus of proof rests upon he who asserts such a proposition". The defendants' evidence, and the circumstances existing at the date of execution of the will, led Parke J. to the conclusion that the testator intended to benefit his nephew, William Bennett, whose name should be substituted for that of Dennis Bennett wherever the latter appeared in the will. The learned judge rejected the submission of counsel for the plaintiff, that section 90 was merely declaratory of the position obtaining prior to the Succession Act that extrinsic evidence was admissible only to ascertain the testator's intention as expressed in the will:

> "It seems to me that section 90 is fundamentally novel in that it places no such limitation on the purpose for which extrinsic evidence may be admitted. I believe that it does amend the common law and directs the courts in a proper instance to look outside the will altogether in order to ascertain the testator's intention *if (but only if) the will can not be construed literally having regard to the facts existing at the testator's death*".[64]

5.6.9 Parke J.'s concluding italicised sentence is scarcely compatible with his description of section 90 as being fundamentally novel, and, it is certainly the case that prior to the Succession Act, extrinsic evidence would have been admissible in circumstances like those in the *Bennett* case.[65] The somewhat less than fundamentally novel character of section 90 was underlined in *Rowe* v *Law*[66] in which Parke J.'s view of the scope of section 90 found favour with Kenny J. in the High Court and the majority in the Supreme Court. The question at issue in *Rowe* v *Law* was, whether, when a phrase in the testatrix's will made a clear and unambiguous disposition of

---

[63] Unreported High Court judgment of Parke J. delivered on 24 January 1977. See note in [1978] I.R. 56-7

[64] *Ibid* at pp.6,7

[65] See generally Jarman on *Wills* (8th ed) Chapter 37 on the admissibility of parol evidence in cases where the subject or object of a devise or bequest is erroneously described in a will.

[66] [1978] I.R. 55

a portion only of a trust fund, evidence was admissible under section 90 to show that the testatrix intended to dispose of the entire trust fund.

5.6.10 Kenny J. found that the disputed phrase in the testatrix's will referred clearly and unambiguously to a portion only of the trust fund and, that being so, section 90 did not make extrinsic evidence available to show the intention of the testatrix. Kenny J. went on:

> "It is only when the court requires assistance because the will is ambiguous or because there is a contradiction in it that the intention is in doubt. The intention cannot be in doubt if the will itself is unambiguous. The alternative construction of section 90, that extrinsic evidence is always admissible to show the intention of the testator, has the remarkable result that everything the testator said before and after he made the will would be admissible in evidence. The result of this would be that a construction summons would in many cases become almost a probate suit."[67]

5.6.11 Henchy J., who reached the same conclusion as Kenny J., read section 90 as allowing extrinsic evidence only if it met the double requirement of (a) showing the intention of the testator, *and* (b) assisting in the construction of, or explaining by contradiction in, a will. It would be unreasonable and contradictory, Henchy J. felt, for the legislature on the one hand to lay down formal requirements for the execution of wills in section 78 and, on the other hand, to allow by section 90 the admission of extrinsic evidence of the testator's intention without qualification or limitation as to purpose or circumstance. Such a sweeping and disruptive change "fraught with possibilities for fraud, mistake, unfairness and uncertainty should not be read into the section if another and reasonable interpretation is open".[68] Henchy J. went on:

> "The alternative reading would treat the section as making extrinsic evidence admissible if it meets the requirement of either (a) or (b). That, however, would produce unreasonable and illogical consequences which the legislature could not have intended. If the section makes extrinsic evidence admissible merely because it satisfied requirement (a), then in any case the court could go outside the will and receive and act on extrinsic evidence as to the intention of the testator. The grant of probate would no longer provide an exclusive and conclusive version of the testamentary intention as embodied in a will."[69]

5.6.12 Griffin J. was likewise of the opinion that the effect of admitting extrinsic evidence of the dispositive intention of a testator, without

---

[67] *Ibid* at p.60
[68] *Ibid*
[69] *Ibid* at p.72

116

qualification, would be to nullify the provisions of section 78 "and to render ineffective the safeguards provided therein".[70]

5.6.13 While O'Higgins C.J. agreed with both his learned brethren, and with Kenny J. in the High Court, that the language used in the testatrix's will referred unambiguously to a portion only of the trust fund, he disagreed with their interpretation of section 90 which, in his opinion, was intended to modify the state of law which had led to decisions such as those in *Higgins* v *Dawson*[71] and *In re Julian*.[72] Thus O'Higgins C.J. could not agree with the view that it was only when the language of a will was ambiguous or contradictory that extrinsic evidence was admissible under section 90, since that construction regarded the section as doing little more than giving effect to the existing law, whereas the description of section 90 in its marginal note shows that it ws intended to effect a change in the existing law.[73] That change O'Higgins C.J. believed, was intended to ensure that the intention expressed in the written will could be tested against the available extrinsic evidence.[74]

5.6.14 While O'Higgins C.J.'s interpretation of section 90 derives considerable support from the legislative history of the section, the legislators clearly failed to address the problem which would inevitably ensue from the tension between the formal requirements in section 78 and an open-ended admission of extrinsic evidence under section 90. The Minister for Justice had said during the Committee Stage of the Succession Bill, that he thought it desirable that documentary or oral evidence of what the testator had said, or not said, at the time of making the will, should be admissible to show intention, but, section 90 contains no such limitation as to time or circumstance.[75] That being so, it is arguable that the court has no alternative but to construe the section in the manner of Kenny J. and the majority of the Supreme Court in *Rowe* v *Law*.

5.6.14 It is an interesting fact that all three judges in the Supreme Court, in *Rowe* v *Law*, expressed the opinion that had section 90 been in force when

---

[70] *Ibid* at p.77

[71] [1902] A.C.1

[72] [1950] I.R. 57

[73] Section 90 is described in its marginal note as "new".

[74] Indeed the Chief Justice believed that s.90 made it mandatory to admit evidence to show the intention of the testator when it comes to construing a will. If the section had been intended to do little more than put in statutory form the position at common law, it would, in the Chief Justice's opinion, have been worded very differently. See [1978] I.R. 55, 66-7.

[75] See Dail Debates Vol. 215 para. 2015. The Minister reminded Deputies of the ambiguity in the will that led to tragedy in Sean O'Casey's play *Juno and the Paycock*.

In re Julian was decided that decision would have gone the other way.[76] O'Higgins C.J. had no doubt however that if section 90 was to be interpreted as Kenny J. had interpreted it "no change would be possible in cases such as *In re Julian* because, as in this case, the words used in the will are unambiguous and clear and no contradiction appears".[77] It is at least arguable, however, that the language of the will in *In re Julian* was not clear or unambiguous since the Catholic Seaman's Institute on Sir John Rogerson's Quay was not referred to by its full title, the use of which would surely have alterted the testatrix to the solicitor's mistake. It is difficult to resist the conclusion that Kingsmill Moore J. was wrong in not finding an equivocation in the language of the will, and that the effect of section 90 on the outcome of a similar case would not depend on that section having made a radical alteration in the law governing the admissibility of extrinsic evidence. In any event, if the view of Kingsmill Moore J., with which O'Higgins C.J. later agreed, on the clarity and unambiguity of the language in the will in *In re Julian* is correct, then section 90 would not have altered the result in that case, given the construction of section 90 adopted by the majority in *Rowe* v *Law*.

5.7 Inconsistent and contradictory clauses

5.7.1 Section 99 of the Succession Act, which like section 90, imports a new rule of interpretation for the construction of wills, provides: "If the purport of a devise or bequest admits of more than one interpretation, then in case of doubt, the interpretation according to which the devise or bequest will be operative shall be preferred." Statutory effect is thus given to the long established principle that the court leans against intestacy, which found expression in the so-called Golden Rule that the court should endeavour to adopt a construction which would not lead to intestacy.[78] Whatever about the similarity between section 99 and the aforementioned Golden Rule, the Explanatory Memorandum with the Succession Act makes it clear that the new rule of construction is borrowed from the German Civil Code and section 99 corresponds precisely with para. 2084 of that code.[79]

5.7.2 The courts had adopted a general rule of construction that the later of two contradictory or inconsistent clauses was to prevail on the ground that it was the last expression of the testator's wishes.[80] The somewhat arbitrary

---

[76] See Griffin J. at p.78; Henchy J. at p.73; O'Higgins C.J. at p.66

[77] *Ibid* at p.67 See also *In re Clinton* [1988] I.L.R.M. 80 and *In re Egan Decd.* Unreported judgement of Egan J. delivered 16th June 1989; 1988/399 Sp.ct 5

[78] See Mellows "The Law of Succession" (4th ed. 1983) at pp.162 *et seq*.

[79] See the Explanatory Memorandum at para. 59, p. 8.

nature of what Lord Greene M.R. called this "rule of despair"[81] led to a judicial reluctance to follow it, more particularly if its adoption would lead to an intestacy. In such cases the court would often seek to avoid an application of the rule by deducing from the will, read as a whole, that the testator intended the earlier of inconsistent clauses to prevail. The intellectual gymnastics involved in the search for such intention led to a certain inconsistency in decision making which the Irish courts are now arguably spared, given the express language of section 99.

5.7.3 If there is no question of intestacy in a particular case from the application of the rule that the last of inconsistent clauses prevails, there seems to be no reason in principle why the courts should not employ the rule. Of course an inconsistency or contradiction in the language of the will would come within the allowable grounds for the admission of extrinsic evidence as set out by the majority in *Rowe* v *Law*,[82] but, if no such evidence is available, the court could fall back on the rule that the last of inconsistent clauses should prevail.

5.8 *Favor testamenti*

5.8.1 Section 99, together with section 90, was intended to incorporate into Irish Law the principle of *favor testamenti* which is to be found in Civil Law jurisdictions and which, particularly in Germany, allows the court to adopt supplementary interpretations to resolve the difficult problems which may arise in the construction of wills.[83] In adopting the principle of *favor testamenti* the Irish legislature clearly wanted to make it easier for the court to "get at" the intention of the testator, but, as we have seen, the courts have held, that an unbridled power to look outside the will would subvert the formal requirements for the execution of wills set out in section 78 of the Succession Act.[84] Be that as it may, the principle of *favor testamenti* is now, arguably, part of Irish law and, applied within acceptable parameters, subsumes more traditional rules of construction.

5.9 *Falsa demonstratio*

5.9.1 One such rule of construction is the maxim *falsa demonstratio non nocet cum de corpore constat* which provides, that where there is more than one part in the description of a person or property in a will, and one part is true and identifies the person or property with sufficient clarity, the other

---

[81] *Re Potter's Will Trusts* [1944] Ch. 70, 77
[82] See *ante* p.116
[83] See Brady "The *Favor Testamenti* in Irish Law" in (1980) Irish Jurist (N.S.) 1
[84] See *ante* p.116

or false parts can be ignored.[85] The maxim *falsa demonstratio* was also applied in cases where the description of persons or property in a will was wholly false, but the context or the surrounding circumstances showed clearly and unambiguously what the testator had intended.[86] Since the description of persons or property in a will is always subject to verification by reference to the context, and the surrounding circumstances, it can be seen that the use of the *falsa demonstratio* maxim, had it been argued, would have brought about the same result in *Bennett* v *Bennett* as reliance on section 90.

5.10 Particular rules of construction

5.10.1 A will speaks from death. The rule that a will speaks from death which was contained in section 24 of the 1837 Act, is re-enacted in section 89 of the Succession Act, which provides, that every will

> "shall, with respect to all estate comprised in the will, and every devise or bequest contained in it, be construed to speak and take effect as if it had been executed immediately before the death of the testator, unless a contrary intention appears from the will."

Thus a testator may dispose of property in his will which he acquires after its execution but before his death.

5.10.2 The inclusion of the rule in the 1837 Act has been attributed to the fact that prior to 1837 the gift of a leasehold interest would pass only that interest in existence at the date of the will, which meant that if the lease had expired and been renewed by the testator before his death the renewed lease would not pass under the will.[1] Although section 24 of the 1837 Act made the date of the testator's death the significant time the intention of the testator remained the paramount consideration, and, the language used in the will must be consistent with, and capable of encompassing, the renewed lease, if the latter is to pass under the will. If the testator's language refers specifically and unequivocally to the interest in existence at the date of the will, the court might construe such reference as amounting to a contrary intention which will exclude the rule introduced by section 24.[2]

---

[85] See *Re Brockett* [1908] 1 Ch. 185 and generally Mellows "The Law of Succession" (4th ed. 1983) at pp.124 *et seq.*

[86] *Ibid*

[1] *Ibid* at p.142

[2] See *Lady Langdale* v *Briggs* (1856) 8 De G. M. & G. 391; *Re Gibson* (1866) L.R. 2 Eq. 669; *Saxton* v *Saxton* (1879) 13 Ch. D. 359. See Parry and Clark "The Law of Succession" (8th ed. 1983) at pp.410 *et seq.*

5.10.3 That the courts have adopted a flexible and discretionary approach to this question is illustrated by Gavan Duffy J.'s characteristically discursive judgement in *In re Farrelly*.[3] There, the testator had bequeathed, *inter alia,* certain Irish Free State 5 per cent National Loan Stock which he held at the date of the will, on trust for his sister for life, and, upon her death, for his two nephews upon their attaining 21 years of age. The testator had further provided, that if the said Irish Free State National Loan should mature and be redeemed while subject to the above trusts, the proceeds of redemption were to be invested in trustee securities. The testator also referred to the "said investments or the securities representing the same" on his sister's death but the will was silent as to the "securities representing the same" on his own death. At his death the testator held certain Irish Free State 3½ per cent National Loan Stock, bought after the date of the will and certain Irish Free State 4 per cent Conversion Loan, which represented the statutory conversion of the 5 per cent National Loan Stock which he held at the date of the will.

5.10.4 In these circumstances, Gavan Duffy J. held, that the words in the will referring to the maturity and redemption of the Irish Free State National Loan Stock disclosed a contrary intention within the meaning of section 24 of the 1837 Act, by indicating *quoad* that bequest, that the testator meant the will to speak as at its own date. It followed that since the testator's only holding at the date of the will was in the 5 per cent National Loan Stock his holding in the 4 per cent National Loan Stock would be excluded, unless the latter, which replaced the former on conversion was substantially the same. Gavan Duffy J. had no difficulty in holding that the difference between 5 per cent and 4 per cent did not make a substantially different security, nor did the alteration in redemption rights. Gavan Duffy J. believed that his conclusion had the double merit of giving the legatees the stock that any layman would say that the testator really meant them to have, while depriving them of stock which, in the common sense view of the man in the street, was not intended for them.[4] This latter reference was to the 3½ per cent National Loan Stock which the learned judge held to be adeemed.[5]

5.10.5 A similar result was achieved in *In re Faris decd*[6] where the testatrix had bequeathed to A, B, and C "my one hundred and seventy pounds Guinness & Co. Ordinary Shares". Between the date of the will and the death of the testatrix, a bonus of one new share for each original share was

[3] [1941] I.R. 261
[4] *Ibid* at p.276
[5] See *post* p.166
[6] [1911] 1 I.R. 165

distributed to the shareholders of Guinness & Co. and converted into stock. The result of this distribution was to reduce the stock in Guinness & Co. to half its original value, so that the holding of £340 stock, consisting of the original shares and the bonus, was worth no more than the original holding of £170 stock.

5.10.6 It seemed to O'Connor M.R. to be manifest on these facts that he would be depriving the legatees of the benefit the testatrix intended to confer on them if he did not hold that the £340 Stock which the testatrix held at her death passed under the bequest of £170 stock in her will.[7] In so holding, the Master of the Rolls asked could anyone doubt, on the evidence, that the £170 Guinness & Co. stock had been changed in name and form only, and was still substantially the same.[8] O'Connor M.R. referred to a number of authorities in support of the proposition that when a testatrix gives shares she gives all the "accidents" and "incidents" and rights arising out of possession and ownership of the shares.[9]

5.10.7 The Master of the Rolls concluded his judgment on that point by citing the passage from the judgment of the Vice-Chancellor in *Longfield* v *Bantry*[10] which reads:

> "The principle of law to be deduced from the many authorities on this subject may be shortly stated to be that a specific legacy will be adeemed if the subject of the bequest be not in existence as the same specific thing at the testator's death. The intention of the testator in his dealing with the subject of the gift, after the making of the bequest, cannot be taken into consideration. A change in the accidents, however, will not operate as an ademption if the substance and essence of the subject remains the same."

5.10.8 It is tempting for the textwriter to draw a clear distinction between specific gifts and general gifts, but while the case law shows that a specific gift is more likely to be construed as manifesting a contrary intention to the rule that a will speaks from death, much depends on the context. That pitfalls remain for testators is underlined by decisions in cases where the use of commonplace and apparently unambiguous words is not calculated to have a predictable effect. Such a word is "now" as used in the gift of "the house which I now own". Different interpretations have been put on that word, it being interpreted in some cases to mean the date of the will and in

---

[7] *Ibid* at p.174
[8] *Ibid*
[9] See e.g. *Slater* v *Slater* [1907] 1 Ch. 665, 672
[10] (1885) 15 L.R. Ir. 101, 128

others the death of the testator.[11] This variance has led an English textwriter to the conclusion that the courts exercise a wide freedom of action in this area, and that judges often take cognisance of facts which are technically irrelevant in their desire to achieve just solutions.[12] In defence of such judges, it could be argued that since the testator's intention is the paramount consideration the courts ability to ascertain that intention should not be unduly hampered by technical considerations, a fact which the Succession Act recognised by facilitating the admission of extrinsic evidence.[13]

5.10.9 The effect of a contrary intention in a will on the rule that the will speaks from death arose in a different context in *In re Goodbody decd.*[14] There, a testator had left the residue of the proceeds of sale of his real and personal estate, after the death of his wife, to whom he gave a life estate therein, "in trust for my next-of-kin living at her death according to the Statute of Distributions". At his death the testator was survived by his widow, his mother and twelve brothers and sisters. The testator's mother, and brothers and sisters, predeceased his widow, at the time of whose death there were twenty seven nieces and nephews of the testator alive. The question before the court was, whether the testator's next-of-kin were to be ascertained at his death or at the death of his widow.

5.10.10 Dixon J. pointed out that the authorities opened established the principle that next-of-kin are to be ascertained as at the death of a testator, but this principle does not apply where there is a contrary intention on the part of the testator. However, a clear indication of such contrary intention is necessary, and Dixon J. could find no evidence of that intention in the will before him. Dixon J. also pointed out that where a testator fixes a time for distribution, enjoyment of the benefits so conferred is limited to those living at the time so fixed. Since all the testator's next-of-kin, as ascertained at his death, had predeceased his widow, whose death was the time fixed for distribution, the residuary bequest lapsed and should be distributed as an intestacy.[15]

5.11 The rule in *Wild's Case*[16]

5.11.1 This somewhat anomalous rule determined the effect of a devise of

---

[11] See *Wagstaff* v *Wagstaff* (1869) L.R. 8 Eq. 229; *Re Fowler* (1915) 139 L.T.Jo. 183 and Mellows "The Law of Succession" (4th ed. 1983) at pp.142–3
[12] *Ibid* at p.143
[13] See *ante* p.114
[14] [1955-56] Ir. Jur. Rep. 73
[15] *Ibid* at p.75

land to "A and his children". If A had no children when the will was executed he took an estate tail. This was so even if children of A were born before the death of the testator, the word "children" being construed as a word of limitation. However, if A had children living when the will was executed the word "children" was treated as a word of purchase, and A took jointly with all his children living at the testator's death.[17] The rule in *Wild's Case* thus continued to obey the old principle, that the time of execution of the will was the significant time, despite the adoption of the modern rule that a will speaks from death, in 1837.

5.11.2 The re-enactment of that rule in section 89 must be read in conjunction with section 95(1) of the Succession Act, which provides that an estate tail (whether general, in tail male, in tail female or in tail special) in real estate may be created by will only by the use of the same words as those by which a similar estate tail may be created by deed.[18] The combined effect of sections 89 and 95(1) is that, if A has children living at the testator's death then, in the absence of precise words of limitation setting up an estate tail, he will take the devise jointly with them. If there are no children living at that time A will take an estate in fee simple, or whatever estate the testator had power to transmit.[19]

5.12 Meaning of "die without issue"

5.12.1 In the case of a gift by will "to A, but if he dies without issue to B" it was assumed, in the absence of a contrary intention in the will, that the testator intended that B should not take unless A and his issue had died out.[20] This presumed intention of the testator was given effect to, if the gift concerned realty, by giving A a fee tail estate, but, since personalty could not be entailed, A took an absolute interest if the gift concerned personalty.

5.12.2 The way in which the words "die without issue" were construed was altered by section 29 of the Wills Act 1837, which provided, that those words, or any other words which may import either a want or failure of issue of any person in his lifetime, at the time of his death, or an indefinite failure of his issue, should be construed to mean a want or failure of issue in the lifetime, or the time of death of such person, unless a contrary

---

[16] (1599) 6 Co. Rep. 16a
[17] See Wylie "Irish Land Law" (2nd ed. 1986) at p.226
[18] On the relevant words of limitation see Wylie at pp.224 *et seq.*
[19] See the Explanatory Memorandum with the Succession Bill at para. 55 p.8
[20] See generally Wylie "Irish Land Law" (2nd ed. 1986) at p.737

intention appeared in the will.[21] The effect of section 29, which is substantially reproduced in section 96 of the Succession Act, was to give the words used by a testator their more natural meaning, and so in the case of a gift of realty, A took a fee simple, and in the case of a gift of personalty A took an absolute interest.[22]

5.12.3 The uncertainty as to whether A would have issue living at his death would clearly affect the value of his interest, and section 10 of the Conveyancing Act 1882 sought to ameliorate A's position by providing that, in relation to *land*, the executory gift over to B became void as soon as any of A's issue reached the age of twenty one years. The restriction on executory limitations in section 10 of the 1882 Act has been reproduced and extended in two important respects by section 100 of the Succession Act. Firstly, it is no longer confined to interests in land but applies to "any interest in other property".[23] Secondly, where a person is entitled under a will to any such interest

> "with an executory limitation over in default or failure of any of his issue, whether within a specified period of time or not, that executory limitation shall be or become void and incapable of taking effect, if and as soon as there is living any issue of the class in default or failure of which the limitation over was to take effect".[23a]

5.13 Gifts to Individuals

5.13.1 While references to property in a will are generally construed in the light of the rule that a will speaks from death, this is not the case with persons named in the will as donees of the testator's bounty, whether as legatees or devisees. In the latter case there is a not unreasonable assumption that it is the person who conforms to the description in the will at the date of its execution who is the intended donee.[24] This presumption will give way to a contrary intention in the will, and it has been suggested that the court will be less likely to find such contrary intention in a will where the relationship between a beneficiary and the testator is a close one.[25] Thus in the case of a gift to "my wife" there is a strong presumption

---

[21] A contrary intention appeared in the will by reason of such person having a prior estate tail or of a preceding gift, being without any implication arising from such words, a limitation of an estate tail to such person or issue, or otherwise.

[22] *Re Mooney* (1925) 59 I.L.T.R. 57; *Weldon* v *Weldon* [1911] 1 I.R. 177; *Re Conboy* [1916] 1 I.R. 51 and see Wylie "Irish Land Law" (2nd ed. 1986) at p.737

[23] Section 100 (b)

[23a] Section 100

[24] See *Re Coley* [1903] 2 Ch. 102; *Amyt* v *Dwarris* [1904] A.C. 268

[25] See Mellows "The Law of Succession" (4th ed. 1983) at p.130

that the intended donee is the person who is married to the testator at the date of the will. In these modern times when marital vows, even in divorce free Ireland, are no longer as universally sacrosanct as they once were, testators are well advised to eschew terminology which has the effect of limiting their bounty to those persons with whom they are cohabiting when wills are made, unless of course that is their intention. If a testator intends otherwise he must use language which clearly shows that the intended donee is the person with whom he is living at the time of his death. The use of a term such as "my present wife", much favoured in his comic writings by a distinguished Irish author, is not calculated to make the intention of the testator any clearer since "present" may refer either to the date of the will or the death of the testator. Testators should, in any event be aware of the possibility that, in the absence of a contrary intention, the gift might lapse if the person who satisfies the description in the will at the date of its execution, predeceases the testator.[26]

5.14 Class gifts

5.14.1 While the identify of an individual legatee or devisee is determined, in the absence of a contrary intention in the will, by reference to the date of the will and not the death of the testator, the converse is true in the case of a class gift.[27] We have seen how such a gift was construed in *In re Goodbody Decd,*[28] where the testator left the residue of the proceeds of sale of his real and personal estate in trust for his next-of-kin who were alive at the death of his wife, to whom he had given a life interest therein. Dixon J. applied the general principle that next-of-kin are to be ascertained at the testator's death, and held that only those so ascertained who were alive at the wife's death could take.[29]

5.14.2 It could be argued of course that the determination of a man's next-of-kin can only sensibly be made at the time of his death, but there are other good reasons why the death of the testator should be the crucial time in the construction of class gifts. One such reason can be found in the long established principle of English property law, which we in Ireland inherited, that a man's property and assets should be freely alienable and

---

[26] In *Re Whorwood* (1837) 34 Ch.D. 486 a bequest to "Lord Sherborne" was held to lapse because the person who held the title at the date of execution of the will predeceased the testator.

[27] See generally Wylie "Irish Land Law" (2nd ed. 1986) at pp. 291 *et seq.*; Mellows "The Law of Succession" (4th ed. 1983) at pp. 139 *et seq.* and Parry and Clark "The Law of Succession" (8th ed. 1983) at pp. 421 *et seq.*

[28] [1955–56] Ir. Jur. Rep. 73

[29] Dixon J. pointed out, however, (at p.75) that where a testator fixes a time for distribution, enjoyment of the benefits conferred is limited to those living at the time so fixed. This principle will give way if there is clear evidence of a contrary intention on the part of the testator. See *Valentine v Fitzgibbon* [1894] I.R. 93

not unduly tied up. Class gifts presented particular problems in this respect, since membership of a class might not be finally determined until long after the death of the testator and distribution of his estate would be thereby delayed. The courts accordingly developed certain class closing rules to facilitate the early distribution of a deceased's estate.[30]

5.14.3 The clearest example of such class closing rules applies where there is an immediate disposition in favour of children as a class, and there are such children living at the testator's death. The children then so living, and no others, will comprise the class and be the objects of the disposition, unless a contrary intention appears in the will.[31] Apart from this possibility of the rule being excluded by a contrary intention in the will, it has nothing to do with the intention of the testator, and such rules have been described by an English textwriter as "frankly and blatantly rules of convenience".[32]

5.14.4 Another such rule, otherwise known as the rule in *Andrews* v *Partington*,[33] provides, that where a disposition in favour of children as a class is accompanied by a provision postponing payment or distribution of the share of each child until the attainment of a certain age, the class is automatically closed when the first child reaches that age and children from thereafter are excluded. This is again a rule of conveience but, as Chitty J. said in *In re Wenmoth*,[34] it must be very inconvenient for those children born after the date of distribution. Its convenience, as Black J. pointed out in *Re Poe*,[35] lies in obviating the inconvenience of making the child who has attained the age of distribution wait an indefinite period for his or her share.

5.14.5 Although the class closing rules were not developed specifically to save dispositions from the vice of remoteness, they could operate in that way since they could be used to obviate the requirement of the rule against perpetuities that each member of a class should take a vested interest within the perpetuity period of the whole gift would fail.[36] This operation of the class closing rules is illustrated by the decision in *Picken* v

---

[30] See Wylie "Irish Land Law" (2nd ed. 1986) at pp.292 *et seq.*

[31] See Mellows "The Law of Succession" (4th ed. 1983) at p. 141

[32] *Ibid* at p.139

[33] (1791) 3 Bro. C.C. 401; See also *Re Burke* [1945] Ir. Jur. Rep. 12 and *Williamson* v *Williamson* [1974] N.I. 92

[34] (1887) 37 Ch. D. 266, 270

[35] [1942] I.R. 535, 538; See Wylie *A Casebook on Irish Land Law* (2nd ed. 1986) at p.268

[36] Black J. pointed out in Re Poe [1942] I.R. 535, 536, that the terms of the will before him raised in an acute form what is very often one of the most difficult of all technical legal problems viz. the effect of the rule against perpetuities upon the validity of a particular testamentary disposition. See generally Maudsley "The Modern Law of Perpetuities" (1970) at pp.15 *et seq.*

Matthews,[37] where property was left on trust for such children of the testator's daughters as should attain twenty five years. One daughter had a child who had attained twenty five years at the testator's death, and as this closed the class and confined it to children living and ascertained at the testator's death, subject to their attaining twenty five years, the gift was valid.

5.14.6 The class closing rules, being rules of convenience, must, as we have seen, give way to a contrary intention in the will, and Black J. had to determine in *Re Poe*[38] whether the will before him contained such a contrary intention. The testator had devised and bequeathed certain property to be divided in equal shares between the children of his brother, and ordered that his trustees should have the power to use the money and other property to the best advantage of the children of his said brother until each of them attains the age of twenty five years, when each was to receive his or her share. The testator had also provided however that the children of his said brother were "to include any children he may have at a future date". One of the questions before Black J. was whether these latter words constituted a contrary intention.

5.14.7 It had been impressed upon Black J. that the words used by Lord Selborne L.C. in *Pearks* v *Moseley*[39] precluded the court from taking account of the rules on remoteness when construing a will. Lord Selborne had said:

> "you do not import the law of remoteness into the construction of the instrument, by which you investigate the expressed intention of the testator. You take his words and endeavour to arrive at their meaning exactly as if there had been no such law, and as if the whole intention expressed by the words could lawfully take effect."[40]

Black, J., however, thought that Lord Selborne's language could not be taken to mean that he must leave the law on remoteness entirely out of account in all circumstances since Lord Selborne himself had conceded that "in dealing with words that are obscure or ambiguous, weight, even in a question of remoteness, may sometimes be given to the consideration that it is better to effectuate than to destroy the intention".[41]

---

[37] (1878) 10 Ch.D. 264
[38] [1942] I.R. 525
[39] (1880) 5 App. Cas. 714
[40] *Ibid* at p.719
[41] *Ibid*

5.14.8 Black J. considered the words of the will before him to be ambiguous and indeterminate such that in construing them he should be justified in giving some weight, if neessary, to the consequence that would ensue from adopting a construction which would not give effect to the testator's intention. But even without such consideration of consequences Black J. was prepared to take the same view albeit with the doubt which so many conflicting authorities rendered inevitable.[42]

5.14.9 There is ample authority for the proposition that where a gift is void for remoteness all limitations ulterior to and dependant on such remote gift are also void.[43] There is also authority for the further proposition however that a limitation following one which is void as being too remote may be good if it can take effect independently of the void limitation and Andrews L.J. was of the opinion in *Re Hay*[44] that the gift over in default of appointment took effect independently of the preceding power and was good though the power was void for remoteness.

5.15 Exercise of powers of appointment

5.15.1 Section 93 of the Succession Act, which substantially reproduces section 27 of the Wills Act 1837, provides

"that a general devise of land shall be construed to include any land which the testator may have power to appoint in any manner he may think proper, and shall operate as an execution of such power, unless a contrary intention appears from the will; and in like manner a general bequest of the personal estate (other than land) of the testator shall be construed to include any such estate which he may have power to appoint in any manner he may think proper, and shall operate as an execution of such power, unless a contrary intention appears from the will."

5.15.2 There is, accordingly, a statutory presumption that a general devise or general bequest of property which is the subject of a general power of appointment is intended as an exercise of the power. It is not proposed to consider here the distinction between general and special powers, other than to say that the acquisition of a general power approximates to full ownership of the subject matter of the power since the donee may appoint to whomever he pleases, while the donee of a special power may only appoint to particular persons or a particular class of persons.[45] A special

---

[42] [1942] I.R. 525, 545
[43] See e.g. In re Abbott [1893] 1 Ch. 54
[44] [1932] N.I. 215 (See Wylie "A Casebook on Irish Land Law" at p.275)
[45] See generally Wylie "Irish Land Law" (2nd ed. 1986) at pp.593 *et seq.*

power is thereby excluded from section 90 since the donee may not "appoint in any manner he may think proper". Also excluded from section 90 is the so-called hybrid power which permits the donee to appoint to anyone with the exception of a certain person or certain persons. It is argued, by an English textwriter, that a power which is a hybrid power when the will is executed may become a general power amenable to section 27 of the 1837 Act, if the person in whose favour the power may not be exercised dies before the will takes effect on the death of the testator.[46]

5.15.3 While a general power leaves the donee free to appoint to whomever he pleases, certain conditions may be attached to the exercise of the power and non-compliaance with those conditions may invalidate its exercise. Thus, a power may be exercisable only be deed and not by will, and, if the power is exercisable by will, it may be required by the instrument creating the power that the will refers specifically to the exercise of the power.[47]

5.15.4 While the operation of section 93 will be precluded if a contrary intention appears in the will, the onus of proving such contrary intention lies on he who asserts it, and, in practice, the courts have rarely found that such onus has been discharged. If a testator wishes to exclude the operation of section 93 then he should make it absolutely clear in his will that any general disposition therein is not intended as an exercise of his power of appointment.

5.15.5 With regard to special or hybrid powers, the person asserting that a disposition in a will represents an exercise of the power must prove that the testator intended it to be so. The testator may of course have made an express reference to the exercise of the power in his will, but it is not necessary that he should have done so. Thus an intention to exercise the power may be inferred from a mention of the power which doesn't constitute an express exercise of it or, from a reference in the will to the property which is the subject matter of the power. Budd J. pointed out in *Hennessey* v *Murphy & Others*[48] that in cases of construction of wills one is "ultimately driven back to the actual wording used by the testator having regard to the facts as known to the testator with regard to his estate".

5.15.6 Budd J.'s decision in *Hennessey* v *Murphy & Others* is a fine example of the flexible approach of the courts to the question of whether a special power has been exercised. There, a testatrix who had a testamentary

---

[46] Mellows "The Law of Succession" (4th ed. 1983) at p.145
[47] *Ibid*
[48] (1953) 87 I.L.T.R. 29

power of appointment over certain property, appointed by her will to persons who were not objects of the power, and added a residuary gift of her property "of every nature, kind and description of which I die seized" to her son who was an object of the power. The question before Budd J. was whether the property invalidly appointed was caught by the residuary clause which constituted an exercise of the power.

5.15.7 Budd J. held, that since the will showed an express intention by the testatrix to exercise the power, and, since the residuary clause referred to the property which was the subject of the power, the residuary gift operated as an appointment to the testator's son of the property which had been invalidly apointed. Budd J. said, of the use of a residuary clause, that he thought that it

> "is looked on by most lawyers and laymen as a means whereby not only is property gathered in which is not otherwise dealt with specifically, but whereby a testator also makes sure that if there is any mistake in the will, and any property is not covered, such property will be captured by such residuary clause and there will not be an intestacy".[49]

The particular residuary clause could thus be regarded in the light that the testatrix was making sure that if the appointment was invalidly executed the property would pass to her son.[50]

5.15.8 Kenny J. took a less benign approach to the purported exercise of a general power in *In re Boland*.[51] There the testatrix referred in her will to all the real and personal estate "which I can dispose of in any manner either as beneficially entitled thereto or under any general power". The question before Kenny J. was, whether a special power was exercised by these general words in the appointor's will. The problem was exacerbated by the fact that the testatrix was the donee of two powers of appointment, one under her father's will and the other under her marriage settlement.

5.15.9 Kenny J. pointed out that the later authorities establish that a document which does not contain a reference to the special power or to the property which may be appointed under the power, may be an exercise of the power if such intention is shown by the document. The learned judge could find no such intention in the will before him, the elaborate nature of which showed that the testatrix had professional advice which made it unlikely that the words used were selected with the intention of exercising the special powers of appointment.[52] Even if the words used in the will

---

[49] *Ibid* at p.34
[50] *Ibid*
[51] [1961] I.R. 426
[52] *Ibid* at p.436

showed an intention to exercise a power of appointment, and Kenny J. did not think that they did, he did not know which of the powers the testatrix intended to exercise.

5.15.10 Kenny J. declined counsel's invitation not to follow the decision in *In re Robertson's and Cardew's Trusts*[53] where Dixon J. held that a testatrix's disposition of "any property over which I may have any power of disposition or appointment" did not constitute an effective exercise of the power of appointment which the testatrix had. The authorities clearly did not support the proposition that when a will contains a reference to a power of disposition, or a general power, that can be taken as a reference to any special power which the person making the will had.[54]

5.16 Conditions attached to gifts

5.16.1 It is not uncommon for a testator to impose a condition on a gift in his will, non-compliance with which by the donee will bring about a forfeiture of the gift. Such condition may be a condition precedent, in that compliance with it may be a precondition to the vesting of the gift in the donee, or it may be a condition subsequent which governs the retention of the gift by the donee.[1]

5.16.2 If a condition precedent is void as being for example offensive to public policy, or on grounds of uncertainty, a gift of realty fails altogether, but there is authority to the effect that if a condition is void as involving *malum prohibition*, and not *malum in se*, the beneficiary will take a gift of personalty free of the condition.[2] The different effects of a condition which is said to be *malum in se* and one which involves a mere *malum prohibition* have been attributed to the presumed intention of the testator, but this attribution was criticised by Dixon J. in *Re Blake*[3] on the ground that it is unreal to presume that a testator knew of such an esoteric distinction. Dixon J.'s criticism is a cogent one, and has led an eminent Irish textwriter to the conclusion that whether a condition is *malum prohibition* or *malum in se* the gift should be void.[4]

5.16.3 The distinction between a condition precedent and a condition subsequent can be stated clearly, but it is often difficult in practice to

---

[53] [1960] I.R. 7

[54] [1961] I.R. 426, 439

[1] Jarman on Wills (8th ed. 1951) Vol. 2 at p.1458

[2] See *In re Elliott* [1952] Ch. 217; *Re Piper*[1946] 2 All E.R. 503

[3] [1955] I.R. 89, 100

[4] Keane "Equity and Trusts in the Republic of Ireland" at p.193

determine from the language of the will which one the testator intended.[5] As with other problems of construction, the intention of the testator must be gathered from the will read as a whole together with any admissible extrinsic evidence. Lowry L.C.J put it thus in *In re Porter*:[6]

> "Whether the condition is precedent or subsequent to the vesting of the interest given depends on the intention of the testator as gathered from the words used. It has been stated that there are no technical words to distinguish a condition precedent from a condition subsequent and that, where it is doubtful whether a condition is precedent or subsequent, the court leans towards a construction which will hold it to be a condition subsequent, for that construction will lead to the early vesting of the gift, and there is a presumption in favour of early vesting."

Lowry L.C.J went on to say, that if the nature of the interest is such as to allow time for the performance of the act before the interest can be enjoyed, it is generally precedent, whereas, if it is reasonable to suppose that the interest must vest in possession before the donee can be expected to comply with the condition, it will be subsequent.[7]

5.16.4 In line with their preference for early vesting, the courts have adopted a lenient approach to the question whether a condition precedent is sufficiently certain and the question whether the condition has been performed. The donee need only satisfy a reasonable test of compliance and the courts are "willing to facilitate the taking of a gift by a person who comes within any reasonable meaning of the condition but unwilling to divest a vested interest unless the circumstances which could lead to divesting are clear".[8]

5.16.5 An interesting example of a condition precedent, and the approach of the courts thereto, is to be found in *In re Farrelly*[9] where the testator, who was an agent of an Insurance Society, bequeathed his collecting book to his two nephews to be divided between them on their attaining the age at which the Society usually sanctioned the appointment of their agents. An agent was entitled to appoint his successor subject to the Society's Approval, but the Society refused to appoint the testator's nephews as agents of the Society.[10] The question accordingly arose as to whether the

---

[5] Jarman at p.1458

[6] [1975] N.I. 157, 160

[7] *Ibid* Lowry L.C.J. referred to *Williams on Wills* (3rd ed) at pp.266-7 and Theobald on *Wills* (13th ed.) para. 1564 and Jarman (8th ed.) pp.1458-1465

[8] [1975] N.I. 157, 161

[9] [1941] I.R. 261

[10] The nephews were minors at the time of the testator's death.

condition attached to the bequest was a condition precedent or a condition subsequent, and whether there had been non-performance of a condition precedent.

5.16.6 Gavan Duffy J. held that the testator's intention was to transmit the agency in moities to his two nephews upon an uncertain contingency and, therefore, neither nephew took a vested interest at the testator's death. The bequest to each nephew was thus subjet to a condition precedent and, Gavan Duffy J. further held, that the condition was a mixed one, the performance of which was partly within the legatee's power and partly within the power of another party. Gavan duffy J. concluded that since the condition was impossible to perform because of the Society's refusal to appoint the nephews as agents, the condition must be taken to have been fulfilled, and the interest of the nephews in the legacy absolute.[11]

5.16.7 Since failure to comply with a condition subsequent results in divestiture the courts have required that such conditions satisfy a higher test of certainty. This more stringent approach to conditions subsequent was classically expounded by Lord Cranworth L.C., who said in *Clavering* v *Ellison*,[12] that where a vested interest is to be defeated by a condition involving a contingency that is to happen afterwards "the condition must be such that the court can see from the beginning, precisely and distinctly, upon the happening of what event it was that the preceding vested estate was to determine".

5.16.8 The approach of the courts to conditions subsequent is graphically illustrated by the decision in the Northern Ireland case *In re Johnston Decd.*[13] There, the testator had bequeathed his residence to his sister for life with remainder to his grand-nephew on condition that he resided in the premises with the testator's sister until her death. There was a gift over to certain charitable institutions of the proceeds of sale of the premises on his sister's death, if the grand-nephew failed to satisfy the terms and conditions attached to the gift.

5.16.9 The nephew's performance of the condition was rendered impossible by the life tenant's refusal of his offer to reside with her after the testator's death, and the court had to determine the nephew's entitlement to the gift in the light of that. Carswell J., who considered the obligation on the

---

[11] To determine the effect of the proved impracticability of the legatees satisfying the condition Gavan Duffy J. eschewed the more familiar names of Jarman, Theobald, Hawkin *et al.* and plunged, characteristically into Swinburne on *Wills* the 7th edition of which was published in Dublin in 1793. See [1941] I.R. 261, 269

[12] (1859) 7 H.L.C. 707, 725

[13] Unreported judgment of Carswell J. delivered 8 September 1986, (1986) N.I.Y.B. 16

nephew to reside with the testator's sister to be in the nature of a condition subsequent, did believe that her refusal to allow the nephew to reside with her made the performance of the condition impossible in law. It followed, that however hard it might be on the beneficiary that his honest efforts to comply with the condition could be frustrated at the will, or even by the whim, of the life tenant, that did not make the condition invalid for impossibility.[14]

5.16.10 Nor was Carswell J. able to exercise the jurisdiction to grant relief against the breach of a condition where it is equitable to do so, since such jurisdiction is not available when there is a gift over on failure to perform the condition.[15] Carswell J. however was able to avoid the patently inequitable result that the nephew's interest was forfeit, despite his best efforts to fulfill the condition, by finding that the condition was invalid as (1) offending public policy and (2) lacking the degree of certainty required of such condition.

5.16.11 Carswell J. pointed out that conditions are against public policy when the state has, or may have, an interest that they should remain unperformed or unfulfilled, and it is well settled that a condition tending to bring about the separation of parent and child falls into this category, whether or not it was designed by the testator to have this effect.[16] The grand-nephew was only fifteen years of age at the testator's death and the condition clearly envisaged that he would cease to reside with his own parents and would reside with the testator's sister. Carswell J. rejected the argument that if the condition was void as against public policy its operation was not completely avoided but only suspended during the beneficiary's minority, during which time he was excused from performance of it. The learned judge considered, both on the authorities and on general principle, that a condition which is void as being against public policy is altogether void and inoperative, and is not merely suspended during the minority of the beneficiary or operative after that time. It followed that the beneficiary took the premises free of condition.[17]

---

[14] *Ibid* at pp.23, 24. On the exacting standards sufficient to make performance impossible in law Carswell J. referred to Williams on *Wills* (5th ed.) at p.311; Jarman (8th ed.) at pp.1454, 1472 ff; Halsbury's Laws of England (4th ed.) Vol. 50 para. 331

[15] Carswell J. referred to *Lloyd* v *Branston* (1817) 3 Mer. 108 in support of the proposition that a direction that a gift should fall into residue is treated as a gift over for this purpose.

[16] Carswell J. referred to *In re Boulter* [1922] 1 Ch. 75 where the condition was that infants, whose mother was of German origin, should not reside abroad except for limited periods. See also Halsbury's Laws of England (4th ed.) Vol. 50 para. 319

[17] The learned judge referred to *In re Sandbrook* [1912] 2 Ch. 471 and *Re Piper* [1946] 2 All E.R. 503 in support of his conclusion

5.16.12 While decisions abound in which the word "reside" has been discussed at length, Carswell J. was mindful of the warning given by Andrews L.C.J. in *In re Doherty*[18] against over-reliance on decided authorities in cases concerning the construction of wills. Considering the motive behind the devise of the testator's residence to his grand-nephew, Carswell J. did not think it insuperably difficult to attach sufficient certainty to the phrase "come to live in the said property after my death".[19] The learned judge had more difficulty with the phrase "continues to reside therein with my said sister Minnie Johnston". That phrase, in Carswell J.'s opinion, was flawed with "conceptual uncertainty" since it didn't indicate whether for example the grand-nephew could go off for periods to residential educational establishments or whether he could marry and bring a wife to live on the premises.[20] In these circumstances Carswell J. considered that the degree of uncertainty was too great for the beneficiary to be able to tell properly in advance the content of the obligations placed upon him if he was to comply with the condition.

5.16.12 Carswell J. also rejected the argument, which was based on Lord Denning's judgment in *In re Tuck*,[21] that the defect in the condition was cured by making the decision of the executors and trustees final of the question whether the grand-nephew complied with the condition. While the decision of the executors and trustees can cure a defect in relation to "evidential uncertainty" this was not so when it came to "conceptual uncertainty". Carswell J. respectfully adopting what Jenkins J. said in *In re Coxen*,[22] of a condition which read, 'if in the opinion of my trustees she shall have ceased permanently to reside':

> "If the testator had insufficiently defined the state of affairs on which the trustees were to form their opinion, he would not, I think, have saved the condition from invalidity on the ground of uncertainty merely by making their opinion the criterion, although the declaration by the trustees of this or that opinion would be an event about which in itself there could be no uncertainty."

[18] [1950] N.I. 83, 85

[19] Carswell J..pointed out that it is well constantly to remind oneself when construing a will that the context of the wording is likely to have a profound, if not a controlling, effect on the meaning to be given to individual words. It was readily apparent in the instant case that the testator's motive in making a devise to his grandnephew was his desire to have someone live with his sister and its construction was governed by this context.

[20] Lord Denning's criticism of the distinction between "conceptual uncertainty" and "evidential uncertainty" in *In re Tuck* [1978] Ch. 49, 59 was considered by Carswell J. who felt however that the distinction was too well established to be disregarded. The uncertainty in the instant case, Carswell J. believed, was one of "conceptual uncertainty".

[21] [1978] Ch. 49

[22] [1948] Ch. 747, 761-2

5.16.13 The meaning of the phrases "come to reside" and "continue to reside" are surely not as distinct, and the difference between them as problematic, as Carswell J. purported to find. The learned judge was right in not allowing the non-performance of the condition, which the beneficiary had honestly tried to perform, to cause forfeiture of the gift, but the condition was clearly void on grounds of public policy and the finding of uncertainty was not essential to prevent forfeiture.

5.16.14 Another example of a condition subsequent which was held to be both uncertain and against public policy is to be found in *In re Dunne Decd.*[23] There, the testator had devised and bequeathed all his property to one Samuel Le Blanc and his wife, subject only to the condition "that my dwelling house and lands or any part thereof shall not be sold or otherwise conveyed or transferred by them or either of them, their successors or assigns, to any member of the Meredith families of O'Moore's Forest, Mountmellick".

5.16.15 In determining the validity of this condition O'Hanlon J. referred to Wylie's "Irish Land Law", where it is said, that where the condition is not a total restriction, it is a question for the court as a matter of public policy to decide whether it is so restrictive as to be void and in so deciding the court has to balance the competing interests of free disposition of property by grantors and the general policy of ensuring marketability of freehold land.[24] For his part O'Hanlon J. had reservations about the consistency with public policy

"of incorporating conditions in the grant or devise of freehold property, the obvious purpose of which is to perpetuate old resentments and antagonisms and bind the grantee or devisee to bear them in mind and give effect to them when contemplating any further disposition of the property."

5.16.16 O'Hanlon J. also found the condition void on grounds of uncertainty, since he found it impossible to say with any degree of certainty at what time in the future, and by what combination of circumstances a descendant of the present Meredith families of O'Moore's Forest, Mountmellick, could be regarded as no longer belonging to the category described by the testator.

5.16.17 The vices of uncertainty and contrary to public policy have often

---

[23] Unreported High Court judgment of O'Hanlon J. delivered 1 July 1988. 1988 No. 336 Sp. Ct. 6

[24] Wylie "Irish Land Law" (2nd ed. 1986) at p. 186. A total restriction on alienation is clearly void but O'Hanlon J. found support for the validity of a partial restriction in the judgment of O'Brien J. in *Billings* v *Welch* (1871) I.R. 6 C.L. 88,101

been relied upon to impugn conditions which are all too common in Irish wills, viz. conditions obliging the donee to eschew conversion to another religion or not to marry a person of another religion. Thus in *In re McKenna Decd*[25] the testator left a fund to trustees to pay the income to his daughter, provided that she did not marry a Roman Catholic, in which event she would forfeit all benefit under the will. The daughter, who was twenty years of age at the testator's death, married a Roman Catholic three years later and the trustees ceased to pay her any income from the trust fund.

5.16.18 On the daughter's application to have the will construed, Gavan Duffy P. dealt shortly with the argument that the condition was void for uncertainty. He said:

"I am confronted by a familiar expression used by a Protestant farmer in his will: I know what he meant and practically every citizen in every walk of life, be he Catholic or Protestant, knows the meaning conveyed by the words 'marry a Roman Catholic'. I wish to state emphatically that I do not concern myself with any theological definition of membership of the Church; I have only to construe the plain words used by a plain man in a sense plain to all of us; and I shall not make the law justly ridiculous in the eyes of persons of common sense by declaring a common expression, which the People know and understand, to be unintelligible in the High Court of Justice in Ireland."[26]

5.16.19 The Northern Ireland Court of Appeal adopted the same approach in *McCausland* v *Young*,[27] holding in relation to the construction of a similar condition in a will, that the term "Roman Catholic" was to be interpreted as reasonably understood by ordinary persons. Andrews L.C.J. found the evidence of two eminent Catholic Canonists to be of no real assistance in construing the will, preferring what he called the common sense approach of Gavan Duffy P. in *In re McKenna*.

5.16.20 Conditions in general restraint of marriage which require the donee to remain unmarried for the rest of his or her life are clearly contrary to public policy, and void for that reason, but whether contracts in partial restraint of marriage are valid depends on the circumstances of the particular case.[29] We have already noted the unwillingness of the courts to

---

[25] [1947] I.R. 277

[26] *Ibid* at p.285. In holding the condition not void for uncertainty Gavan Duffy P. distinguished *Clayton* v *Ramsden* [1943] A.C. 320 and approved the principles stated by Lord Green M.R. in *In re Samuel* [1942] Ch. 1, 13

[27] [1947] N.I. 49

[28] *Ibid* at p.57

[29] An example of a condition in partial restraint would be one not to marry below a certain age. See *Kiersly* v *Flahavan* [1905] 1 I.R. 45

give effect to the divestitive nature of conditions subsequent and a clear example of this in relation to such a condition in partial restraint of marriage is to be found in *In re McKenna*. There Gavan Duffy J. held, that where a legacy is to vest or become payable at a certain age, a restrictive condition as to marriage will be read as relating to marriage under that age, and the learned judge read the restrictive conditions in that case as relating only to the daughter's marriage with a Roman Catholic before she attained the age of twenty-one years.[30]

5.16.21 Conditions in partial restraint of marriage have come under close scrutiny in the light of the development by the Irish courts of a doctrine of unspecified rights derived from Article 41 of the Constitution, one of which is the right to marry.[31] This development has led an eminent Irish textwriter to argue, that such conditions should now be treated as being in restraint of the constitutional right to marry and thus void.[32] There is however a counter argument that there is no public policy reason why a testator should not be free to attach a condition to a gift requiring the beneficiary to eschew membership of a particular religion, or requiring the beneficiary not to marry a member of a specified religion. The donee is after all free to choose whether or not to comply with the condition.

5.16.22 Support for the latter argument is to be found in the decision of the House of Lords in *Blathwayt* v *Baron Cawley*,[33] where the settlement creating a trust provided that if a beneficiary should become a Roman Catholic his interest would be forfeited. Their Lordships had no difficulty in finding this restrictive condition valid, since they took the view that it involved no trace of religious discrimination, but was rather a matter of personal choice and testamentary freedom. It is arguable that what remains of the concept of testamentary freedom after the enactment of the Succession Act should dictate a similar approach by the Irish courts.[34] It is also unlikely that the Irish courts would dissent from the view of the Law Lords that the restrictive condition in that case did not offend public policy, since it would not be binding on the infant beneficiary until he had attained his majority, after which he would have a reasonable time within to decide whether or not he should comply with the condition.

5.16.23 In so far however as the Law Lords were saying that such a restrictive condition does not offend public policy, whether it applies to an

---

[30] Gavan Duffy J. followed the decision and reasoning in *Duggan* v *Kelly* (1847) 10 Ir. Eq. R. 295

[31] See *Ryan* v *Att.-Gen.* [1965] I.R. 294 and *McGee* v *Att.-Gen.* [1974] I.R. 284

[32] See Keane *op. cit* at p.194

[33] [1976] A.C. 397

[34] See *post* pp.182 *et seq.*

adult or infant beneficiary, the Irish courts would be bound by authority to make a distinction between the two kinds of gift. Gavan Duffy J.said in *In re McKenna*:[35]

"A girl's father, who strives by his will and by other means to protect her during her minority against contracting a marriage with any man of a religion which he abhors, is doing his duty by the child and is acting within his rights; that is his legitimate exercise of *patria potestas* over a young girl whose moral welfare is committed to his care; but, so much being conceded, he ought to recognise that new status acquired upon her majority."

5.16.24 While a conditional gift by a parent to his or her child is thus defensible as a legitimate exercise of *patria potestas* a similar gift by a stranger to a child may be invalid on the grounds that it is inconsistent with that same *patria potestas* which is now solemnly guaranteed by the constitution. Thus in *Re Blake*[36] Dixon J. held, that a condition which required that the grandchildren of the testator be brought up as Roman Catholics was void since it interfered with the parents' rights and duties under Article 42.1 of the constitution. This finding of Dixon J. could be said to be unexceptional in that it's inconceivable that an Irish Court would enforce a condition which is subversive of those parental rights and duties.

5.16.25 There is another aspect of Dixon J.'s judgment in *Re Blake* however which merits close attention. Dixon J. held, that since the condition in that case was a condition precedent and was void on grounds of public policy, it followed that both the condition and the gift failed. Some doubt has been thrown on this latter conclusion by the decision in *Re Doyle*,[37] where Kenny J. held that a condition which required that the donee be a Roman Catholic at the testator's death, and have given an undertaking to her parish that she would remain so, was void as being impossible to perform. Kenny J. added that the condition was void as being contrary to the guarantee of freedom of conscience and the free profession and practice of religion contained in Article 44.2.1 of the constitution. Kenny J. went on to hold that the donee took the gift free from the condition.

5.16.26 In so far as Kenny J. held that the donee would take the gift free from a condition which was impossible to perform his judgment is consistent with authority[38] but there is no authority to support the wide

[35] [1947] I.R. 277, 287
[36] [1955] I.R. 89
[37] Unreported High Court judgment 1972 (No. 143 Sp.)
[38] See *ante* p.134

view that a gift will take effect free from the condition where the condition is void on the grounds of public policy. Be that as it may, it is arguable that a testator who imposes a condition which is void on grounds of public policy should be in the same position, as it were, as one who imposes a condition which is impossible to perform, and in either case the donee should take the gift free from the condition.

5.16.27 What is left of the concept of testamentary freedom after the enactment of the Succession Act should dictate that a testator be reasonably free to attach conditions to his bounty and, if such conditions do not impair the constitutional rights of others, and are otherwise consistent with general legal and equitable principles, they should be enforced.

5.17 Meaning of "children" and "issue"

5.17.1 While the Succession Act made radical changes in our law of inheritance by giving statutory effect to the moral claims of the surviving spouse and children of a deceased testator, it stopped short of conferring succession rights on illegitimate children of the deceased. The social and moral climate of the early nineteen sixties did not permit the conferring of such rights, and ensured the survival of the rule of construction that words such as "children" or "issue", when used in wills or other instruments, were to be intterpreted as referring only to legitimate or legitimated children, and those claiming a relationship to the deceased through such children.[39] Of course the intention of the testator remained paramount, and if it was clear on the face of the will, or could reasonably be inferred therefrom, that the testator intended an illegitimate child to take, effect would be given to that intention.[40]

5.17.2 The public perception of illegitimacy and the legal disabilities that should attach to it has changed since the mid nineteen sixties, and the quickening pace of social change has seen the enactment of the Status of Children Act, 1987, the main purpose of which is the equalisation of the rights under the law of all children, whether born within or outside marriage.[41] Thus, the general principle is stated in section 3 of the Act, that relationships between persons are to be determined without regard to whether any person's parents are, or have been, married to each other. The Act seeks to give effect to this general principle in relation to

[39] See *In re Walker Decd* [1985] I.L.R.M. 86 and generally *The State Nicholaou* v *An Bord Uchtala* [1966] I.R. 567
[40] See *O* v *D* [1916] 1 I.R. 364
[41] See the Law Reform Commission's Report on Illegitimacy (L.R.C. 4 – 1982)

guardianship, maintenance and property rights, by putting children whose parents have not been married in the same position, as nearly as possible, as children whose parents have been married.

5.17.3 The application of the general principle stated in section 3 to the Succession Act, and to wills and other dispositions, is dealt with in Part V of the Act under the rubric "Property Rights". Section 27(1) provides, that in relation to the construction of dispositions made after the commencement of Part V words denoting a family relationship are to be interpreted, in the absence of a contrary intention, in accordance with section 3 of the act, that is without regard to whether the parents of any person involved are, or were married, to each other.

5.17.4 The consequences of section 27(1) for legitimated children are dealt with in section 27(2) which provides, that certain provisions of section 3 of the Legitimacy Act, 1931, under which legitimated persons, and persons related through legitimated persons, are entitled to take interests in property as though born legitimate, will not apply in relation to dispositions made after the commencement of Part V of the Act "except as respects any interest in relation to which the dispostion refers only to persons who are, or whose relationship is deduced through, legitimate persons". The purpose of section 27(2) is explained in the Explanatory Memorandum with the Status of Children Bill, 1986, by reference to the following examples. If a disposition is expressed to be "to the children of X", then, under section 27(1), X's legitimate, legitimated and illegitimate children are entitled to benefit and subsection (2) will ensure equality of treatment as between legitimated persons and others. If however the disposition is expressed to be "to the legitimate children of X" subsection (1) is not applicable but the exception provision in subsection (2) will ensure that, as under existing law, legitimated children of X wil be entitled, as if born legitimate to benefit under the disposition.[42]

5.17.5 Additions to the law governing the property rights of adopted children are contained in two other subsections of section 27. Subsection (3) extends the provisions of section 26 of the Adoption Act, 1952, which relates to the property rights of persons adopted under the Adoption Acts, to persons adopted abroad whose adoptions are recognised under Irish law. Subsection 4(a) provides that the section is without prejudice to section 26 of the Adoption Act, 1952, but, paragraph (b) of subsection (4) ensures that a reference to a child in a will or other disposition is to be interpreted as including a child adopted subsequent to the will or other disposition. Under existing law a disposition by will "to the children of X"

---

[42] See the Explanatory Memorandum with the Status of Children Bill 1986 at p.6

included X's children adopted at the time the will was made, but excluded those subsequently adopted.[43]

5.17.6 Any rule of law which renders void as contrary to public policy, a disposition in favour of an illegitimate child not in being when the disposition takes effect, is abrogated by section 27(5) as respects such disposition made after the commencement of Part V. Subsection (6) provides, that the section will not operate retrospectively to affect dispositions made before the commencement of Part V or, to widen the class of persons in whose favour an appointment may be made under a special power of appointment.

5.17.7 "Disposition" is defined in subsection (7)(a), for the purposes of the section, as including an oral disposition of real or personal property whether *inter vivos* or by will or codicil. Subsection (7)(b) provides, that notwithstanding any rule of law, a disposition made by will or codicil executed before the commencement of Part V, shall not be treated as having been made later by reason only of the fact that such will or codicil is confirmed by a later codicil.

5.17.8 The definition section (section 3) of the Succession Act, 1965, is amended by section 28 of the Status of Children Act, 1987, by changing the meaning of the term "issue", to accord with the new section 4A being inserted into the Succession Sct by section 29 of the 1987 Act, and by importing into the Succession Act the construction of expressions such as "a person whose parents have not married each other" provided for in section 4 of the 1987 Act.

5.17.9 The new section 4A being inserted into the Succession Act by section 29 of the 1987 Act provides in 4A(1) that, in deducing any relationship for the purposes of the Succession Act, the relationship between every person and his father and mother shall, subject to section 27A (inserted in the Succession Act by section 30 of the 1987 Act) be determined in accordance with section 3 of the 1987 Act, that is without regard to marital status.

5.17.10 Section 75(1) of the Succession Act provided that references to any Statutes of Distribution in an instrument made *inter vivos*, or in a will coming into operation, after the commencement of the Act, should be construed, unless a contrary intention appeared, as references to Part VI of the Succession Act. Section 4A(3) now provides that the references in section 75 (1) to Part VI of the Succession Act shall, in relation to an

---

[43] See s.26(2) of the Adoption Act, 1952

143

instrument made *inter vivos*, or a will coming into operation, after the commencement of Part V of the 1987 Act, be construed as including references to section 4A.

5.18 Conflicts of Law

5.18.1 Problems of construction may arise in relation to wills which dispose of property located in a foreign jurisdiction, and foreign wills which dispose of property located in the domestic jurisdiction. The approach of the courts and textwriters alike, to the construction of such wills has varied in accordance with the nature of the property disposed of.[44]

5.18.2 The construction of a will dealing with immovables has generally been governed, in the absence of a contrary intention on the part of the testator, by the *lex loci rei sitae*, and that of a will dealing with movables by the *lex domicilii*, the law of the place which was the testator's domicile at the relevant time.[45] There is some dispute among textwriters as to whether the relevant time is the death of the testator or the time the will is made, but, that the latter is to be preferred, derives support from the provision in section 107(1) of the Succession Act that the construction of a testamentary disposition "shall not be altered by reason of any change in the testator's domicile after the making of the disposition".[46]

5.18.3 Section 107, in neither subsection (1) nor (2), makes any distinction between movables and immovables, and this omission lends support to the view of certain textwriters that there is much to be said for applying the *lex domicilii* to the construction of a will of immovables unless the testator has manifested a contrary intention.[47] There are certain difficulties in the way however of applying the *lex domicilii* to wills of immovables not the least of which is the provision in section 102 (1) (e) of the Succession Act, that the validity of such wills is to be determined in accordance with the internal law of the place where they are situated. Such internal law will also determine "what is included in a general devise of an estate, for instance, whether it means the lands and buildings thereon only, or includes livestock or other movables necessary for the work of the estate".[48]

[44] See Halsbury's Laws of England (3rd ed.) Vol. 7 at p.63

[45] See O'Hanlon J.'s comments in *In re Bonnet* (1983) I.L.R.M. 359

[46] Section 107(2) provides that in determining whether or not a testamentary disposition complies with a particular law, regard shall be had to the requirements of that law at the time of making the disposition, but this shall not prevent account being taken of an alteration of law affecting testamentary dispositions made at that time if the alteration enables the disposition to be treated as valid.

[47] See Binchy "Irish Conflicts of Law" at p.545

[48] See Dicey and Morris "Conflicts of Law" (10th ed. 1980) Vol. 2 at p.629

5.18.4 Whichever legal system governs the construction of a will, the intention of the testator remains paramount, and, in the absence of some illegality or impossibility attaching to a disposition of immovables in the light of the *lex situs*, the task of construction will invaraiably present the same problems whether the *lex situs* or the *lex domicilii* is employed. Such was the case in *In re Bonnet Decd*[49] which involved the construction of a will made in Germany by a Ms. Bonnet, a German national who was at the time of her death, and at all other times, domiciled in Germany. The text of the original will and the codicil thereto was in German. The particular clause which required to be construed by the court referred to the disposition of a "farm" in Ireland in favour of the "Protestant Church in Ireland".

5.18.5 O'Hanlon J. did not feel obliged to choose between German law and Irish law in the construction of the will since he was satisfied, from the evidence given by experts in German law, that the German legal code incorporates the primary principle of construction which is applicable in Irish law, "namely, that whether or not the case contains a foreign element, a will is to be construed in accordance with the intention of the testator to be gathered from the will".[50] The application of that primary principle to the circumstances of the instant case enabled O'Hanlon J. to answer the question of construction raised.

5.18.6 One such question concerned the identity of the beneficiary, who was referred to in the English translation of the will as "the Protestant Church in Ireland". The original German text referred to the beneficiary in the words "der Evangelischen Kirche in Ireland" which all parties were agreed was a reference to the Lutheran Church, of which the textatrix ws a member. O'Hanlon J. accordingly gave effect to this agreed construction, holding that the bequest was one "to the Ministers and members of the Church known as the Lutheran Church in Ireland for the use of the said Church in Ireland".

5.18.7 A second problem of construction arose from the fact that the testatrix was not, in her personal capacity, the owner of a "farm" in Ireland, but she or her nominees held the entire shareholding in a private company which owned three parcels of land in Co. Laois, comprising 175 acres, together with buildings, livestock and farm machinery on the said lands. The company also had a small holding of bank stock and a small amount of cash in the bank. O'Hanlon J. concluded that there was clearly an intention on the part of the testatrix to give her lands in Ireland to the

[49] [1983] I.L.R.M. 359
[50] *Ibid* at p.361

beneficiary named in the will, but, the will had all the appearance of having been prepared in haste, and it appeared that the notary who drafted it must not have discussed with the testatrix the manner in which she had acquired the beneficial interest in the lands in Ireland. Nor did he appear to have been conscious of the fact that the legal owner of the lands was a limited company and not the testatrix herself. In all these circumstances, and having regard to the fact that the expression "farm" was used in the German text of the will, which the experts in German law who gave evidence agreed, was one generally used in German only when referring to lands held abroad, O'Hanlon J. considered that the text of the will was loosely drawn and should be construed as referring to her property in Ireland.

5.18.8 The testatrix and her husband had formed a small private company whose whole *raison d'etre* appeared to be the acquisition and running of the farm in question, and O'Hanlon J.'s impression was that the testatrix "intended to hand over the entire enterprise, lock, stock and barrel, with its assets and liabilities as they then stood, to the beneficiary named in the will".[51]

5.18.9 It could be said of course that O'Hanlon J. was able to decline to choose between the *lex domicilii* and the *lex situs* because the principles of construction in German and irish law happily coincided in the ascertainment of the testatrix's intention. It might have been otherwise if such principles had been widely diverse, but since the intention of the testator is crucial in the first instance in determining which legal system wil apply, it should be possible for an adroit judge to find the initial intention which facilitates his giving effect to what he perceives to be the testator's intention.

5.19 Meaning of domicile

5.19.1 The application of the *lex domicilii* to the construction of wills of immovables has the apparent advantages of simplicity and consistency with its application to wills of movables, but, case law in the latter area reveals that the courts are often faced with difficult problems in determining domicile, despite the apparent ease with which the law on such can be stated.

5.19.2 Each person acquires a domicile of origin at birth but can subsquently acquire a domicile of choice, which requires an intention of permanent or indefinite residence in the particular place. Residence,

[51] *Ibid* at p.362

without more, is not enough, since there must be evidence of an intention to change domicile. Thus, even prolonged residence must be accompanied by facts and circumstances supportive of the necessary intention to change domicile. Budd J. put it thus in *In re Sillar*:[52]

"From a consideration of the case law it is clear that it is a question of fact to determine from a consideration of all the known circumstances in each case whether the proper inference is that the person in question has shown unmistakably by his conduct, viewed against the background of the surrounding circumstances, that he had formed at some time the settled purpose of residing indefinitely in the alleged domicile of choice. Put in more homely language, that he had determined to make his permanent home in such place."

5.19.3 The question before the court in *In re Sillar* was whether the will of an English national, who had resided in Ireland for well over forty years, was to be construed in accordance with Irish or English law. In his will the testator described himself as a British subject, domiciled in England and resident in Ireland. He had also asserted in an earlier statement to the Revenue Commissioners that he had not abandoned his English domicile and that it was his intention to return to England when circumstances would permit. Nevertheless, Budd J. held that the testator was domiciled in Ireland at the date of his will and that of his death, and, he not having indicated an intention that his will should be construed according to English law, it should be construed in accordance with Irish law.

5.19. 4 Budd J. pointed out that a will is *prima facie* to be construed in accordance with the law of the testator's domicile, but this was a rule of construction "which may be departed from where it can be shown that the testator wrote with reference to the laws of some other country".[53] Budd J. failed to find such contrary intention in the instant case despite the fact that a large part of the testator's estate consisted of English assets, he was by nationality an Englishman and there were many English legatees. Of particular interest is Budd J.'s treatment of the fact that the testator habitually referred to himself as a British subject domiciled in England, and had held a British passport. Budd J. believed that such evidence was important and of great weight, but, if a person was physically resident in a place and the proper inference from all the known circumstances was that he had formed the intention of remaining indefinitely in that place "he cannot alter the fact that he has acquired a domicile of choice by stating something to the contrary".[54] Likewise a passport, to Budd J.'s mind, was more connected with nationality and allegiance than domicile, and there

[52] (1956) I.R. 344, 350
[53] *Ibid* at p.361. Budd J. referred to *In re Price* [1900] 1 Ch. 442
[54] *Ibid* at p.355

was no reason in law why the testator, or any of his fellow countrymen who became domiciled in Ireland, should not retain their British nationality.[54a]

5.19.5 The statement by a testator that he was domiciled in Ireland was likewise not conclusive in *In re Rowan Decd*[55] where Costello J. held that such statement was a conclusion of law rather than a statement of what his past intentions had been, and as such did not disprove the evidence which tended to show that he had previously decided that he would reside permanently in France, where he had acquired a domicile by choice. At most, such evidence supported the view that the deceased had formed the intention to return to live in Ireland but, it was ineffective in law, as the deceased had not in fact changed his residence before his death.

5.19.6 Budd J. held in *In re Adams Decd*[56] that the national validity of a will or codicil depended upon a testator's domicile at the time of his death, but that the ascertainment of such domicile was governed by the *lex fori* which in that case was Irish law.[57] The testator had acquired a domicile of choice in France, which he had not abandoned prior to his death and French law wuld determine the construction of the codicil in question, unless the testator had manifested a contrary intention. Budd J. found such contrary intention and gave his reasons thus:

> "Turning then to the question of interpreting the codicil according to the law intended by the testator, the nature of the indications given on this matter have to be considered. Here the codicil is in the English language and in the form appropriate to an Irish will or codicil, in that executors are appointed and it is attested in the Irish form. The executors are Irish companies. It is not in the holograph form as required by French law. Apart from the testator's anxiety to have his estate administered in Ireland it would apear to me that there are sufficient indications contained in the will itself for me to come to the conclusion that it was the testator's intention that his will should be interpreted as regards matters of construction in accordance with Irish law."[58]

---

[54] *Ibid* at p.353

[55] Unreported judgment of Costello J. delivered 17 December 1986 (1985 No. 344)

[56] [1967] I.R. 424

[57] Budd J. accepted the law on the question of domicile as that stated by Russell J. in *In re Annesley* [1926] Ch. 692

[58] [1967] I.R. 424, 459

Chapter 6
FAILURE OF BENEFIT

6.1 Introduction

6.1.1 A gift by will, whether by legacy or devise, may fail to take effect for one of more of several reasons, the more prominent and usual of which are considered in detail in this chapter. The list of reasons so considered does not purport to be exhaustive and, where appropriate, readers are referred to standard works on Land Law, Equity and Trusts, for further reading.

6.2 Disclaimer

6.2.1 The beneficiary of a gift made by will cannot be forced to accept it, and he may accordingly disclaim such gift by refusing or renouncing it.[1] The reasons for a beneficiary's disclaimer may be that a gift of leasehold property imposes liabilities on him which exceed the value of the property to him, or, a gift is subject to a condition which the beneficiary finds unacceptable. In the latter case, depending on the closeness of the beneficiary's relationship with the testator, the beneficiary might still be entitled to the property under the intestacy rules, free from any unacceptable condition.

6.2.2 Disclaimer may be made formally by deed, by writing only, or may be implied from conduct.[2] A beneficiary may disclaim a gift at any time before he has derived any benefit from it, but, by accepting such benefit, he will be taken to have affirmed the gift. A beneficiary who is given two separate gifts in the same will may, as a general rule, disclaim one and take the other

---

[1] Abbott C.J. put it bluntly in *Townson* v *Tickell* (1819) 3 B. & Ald. 31 when he said that the law "is not so absurd as to force a man to take an estate against his will".

[2] See *Re Birchall* (1889) 40 Q.D. 436; *Re Clout and Frewer's Contract* [1924] 2 Ch. 230.

but, it will be a matter of construction in each case whether the will requires the beneficiary to take both of the gifts or neither of them.[3] If a single gift consists of more than one asset a beneficiary is not able to disclaim certain of the assets and take others. Such a gift must be disclaimed as a whole.[4]

6.2.3 Disclaimer of a prior interest will normally accelerate subsequent interests, unless there is a contrary intention in the will. The doctrine of acceleration may apply where for example, a testator leaves property to X for life with remainder to Y absolutely. If X should disclaim his interest, or his interest should otherwise fail because for example, he had witnessed the will, Y's remainder interest is accelerated and takes effect in possession immediately.[5]

6.3 Lapse

6.3.1 It follows from the ambulatory nature of wills that a gift by will fails if the beneficiary predeceases the testator. Likewise if a gift is made to a corporate body which is dissolved before the death of the testator, but gifts to charitable bodies may be applied *cy-pres*, if the testator has manifested a general charitable intention.[6] The nature of the interest given by the will may also preclude the operation of the doctrine of lapse, in that if the testator leaves property on a joint tenancy the deaths of one or more joint tenants before that of the testator will not cause the gift to lapse. It will be otherwise of course if all the joint tenants predecease the testator.[7] If the testator has used words of severance in his will the death of a tenant in common before that of the testator will bring about the lapse of that tenant's share.

6.3.2 It is not enough to preclude the doctrine of lapse for a testator simply to state in his will that it is not to apply.[8] A testator may of course provide

---

[3] See *Talbot* v *Earl of Radnor* (1834) 3 M. & K. 252; *Fairclough* v *Johnstone* (1863) 16. Ir. Ch. r442.

[4] See *Guthrie* v *Walrond* (1862) 22 Ch. D. 573, 577 where Fry L.J. said that it appeared plain to him "that when two distinct legacies or gifts are made by will to one person, he is as a general rule, entitled to take one and disclaim the other, but that his right to do so may be rebutted if there is anything in the will to show that it was the testator's intention that that option should not exist". Cf. *Re Joel* [1943] Ch. 311.

[5] See *Re Hodge* [1943] Ch. 300 and, generally, Parry and Clark "The Law of Succession" (8th ed. 1983) at pp.344 *et seq.*

[6] See Keane "Equity and the Law of Trusts in the Republic of Ireland" at pp.150 *et seq.* and Wylie "Irish Land Law" at pp.519 *et seq.*

[7] See *Morley* v *Bird* (1798) 3 Ves. 629 and Parry and Clark "The Law of Succession" (8th ed. 1983) at pp.326-7.

[8] *Re Ladd* [1932] 2 Ch. 219

for the eventuality of a beneficiary or beneficiaries predeceasing him and make alternative or substitutory arrangements.[9]

6.3.3 If a gift in a will lapses section 91 of the Succession Act, which reproduces section 25 of the Act of 1837, provides that, unless a contrary intention appears from the will,

> "any estate comprised or intended to be comprised in any devise or bequest contained in the will which fails or is void by reason of the fact that the devisee or legatee did not survive the testator, or by reason of the devise or bequest being contrary to law or otherwise incapable of taking effect, shall be included in any residuary devise or bequest, as the case may be, contained in the will."

If the will contains no residuary clause the property in question will devolve as on intestacy.

6.3.4 We have seen that the doctrine of lapse does not apply in the case of certain charitable gifts, nor where the testator has made provision for alternative or substitutory gifts.[10] There are other exceptions to the doctrine of lapse in relation to gifts by will.

6.3.5. (a) Gifts of entails

Section 97 of the Succession Act, which re-enacts section 2 of the Act of 1837, provides, that where

> "a person to whom real estate is devised for an estate entail or an estate in quasi entail dies in the lifetime of the testator leaving issue who could inherit under the entail, and any such issue is living at the time of the death of the testator, the devise shall not lapse, but shall take effect as if the death of that person had happened immediately after the death of the testator, unless a contrary intention appears from the will."

6.3.6 The language of section 97 is so clearly calculated to give effect to the intention of the testator who, by giving an entailed interest, clearly intends to benefit not only the immediate beneficiary but also his heirs, that reference to the exclusion of a contrary intention in the will seems unnecessary. Be that as it may, the reference in section 97 to the absence of a contrary intention in the will underlines the primacy of the testator's intention in all matters concerning the construction of wills.

6.3.7 It has been argued that the provision in section 97 does not

---

[9] See e.g. *Re Greenwood* [1912] 1 Ch. 393
[10] See *ante* p.150

necessarily mean that the issue will take on the death of the primary devisee, but merely provides that the gift is to take effect as if the primary devisee died immediately after the testator, and, if the primary devisee dies bankrupt his trustee in bankruptcy or the Official Assignee can claim the entail.[11] The authority cited for this proposition is *Re Pearson*[12] where a testator had made a gift to his son, who predeceased him but left issue living at the testator's death, who thus saved the gift from lapse under section 33(1) of the Act of 1837. The testator's son having died an undischarged bankrupt, it was held that the gift passed to his trustee in bankruptcy.

6.3.8 It is eminently fair that the son's trustee in bankruptcy should have access to the assets donated to him under his father's will, and the exclusion from benefit of the son's issue is referrable to the fact that they would only be beneficially entitled to the subject matter of the gift under the son's will or on his intestacy. They did not stand in the son's shoes in relation to the gift but by being alive at the date of the testator's death, allowed it to happen.[13] Where an entailed interest is concerned however, the primary devisee's issue are not reliant on being beneficially entitled under his will or on his intestacy, and with respect to their entitlement to the subject matter of the gift a distinction can be made between an entailed interest and an interest simpliciter.[14] In the case of an entailed interest it is arguable that the primary donee's trustee in bankruptcy can dispose of no more than a commercially unattractive base fee.

6.3.9 (b) Gifts to children and issue

It was provided in section 33 of the Act of 1837, that where a testator made a gift in favour of his child or more remote issue, and the child or issue predeceased him, the gift would be saved from lapse if the primary beneficiary himself left issue living at the death of the testator, unless a contrary intention appeared from the will. This provision is re-enacted in section 98 of the Succession Act but is extended to cases where (i) the gift to the child or issue is made by the exercise of a special power of appointment, and, (ii) where the gift is made to the person concerned as a member of a class.

6.3.10 The language of section 33 made specific reference to a devise or bequest to a testator's child or more remote descendant, and the section was held not to preserve from the doctrine of lapse gifts made under a

---

[11] See Wylie "Irish Land Law" (2nd ed. 1986) at p.729

[12] [1920] 1 Ch. 247

[13] See Parry and Clark "The Law of Succession" (8th ed. 1983) at p.332

[14] On entailed interests generally see Wylie "Irish Land Law" (2nd ed. 1986) at pp.217 *et seq.*

special power of appointment.[15] The saving provision in section 33 did apply however to gifts made under a general power of appointment, and section 98 now equates the two kinds of power in this respect.[16]

6.3.11 The rule, with respect to class gifts, that membership of a class is ascertainable at the testator's death meant the exclusion from a class of a potential member who predeceased the testator. It followed that if a testator left a gift "to all my children" a child who predeceased the testator failed to become a member of the class and, the doctrine of lapse having no application to a class gift, the saving provision of section 33 did not apply. The inclusion of class gifts in section 98 now ensures that the issue of such child will take his share and brings about the same result as if the testator's children in the above example had all been identified as individuals, in which case section 33 of the Act of 1837 was held to save the gift from the doctrine of lapse.[17]

6.3.12 The provision in section 98 will not apply to gifts, such as a life interest, which terminate naturally on the donee's death,[18] nor, apparently, will it apply to gifts which are contingent on the donee reaching a certain age. Thus, in *Re Wolson*[19] a testator made a gift to his daughter which was contingent on her reaching the age of 25 years. The daughter predeceased the testator, dying at the age of 24 years, and leaving issue, but it was held that section 33 did not preserve the gift from lapse.[20]

6.3.13 The requirement in section 33, that the donee child, who predeceased the testator, leave issue living at the testator's death, was construed in *Elliott* v *Joicey*[21] to exclude a child *en ventre sa mere*. That requirement, which is repeated in section 98 must be read however in the light of the interpretation section of the Succession Act which provides, in section 3(2), that descendants and relatives of a deceased person "begotten before his death but born alive thereafter shall, for the purposes of this Act, be regarded as having been born in the lifetime of the deceased and as having survived him"[22] An illegitimate child or issue will now be treated for the purposes of section 8 as a legitimate child or issue.[23]

---

[15] See *Holyland* v *Lewin* (1883) 26 Ch. D. 266

[16] On the exercise of powers generally see *ante* pp.129 *et seq.*

[17] See e.g. *Re Stansfield* (1880) 15 Ch. D. 84

[18] See *Re Butler* [1918] 1 I.R. 894

[19] [1939] Ch. 80

[20] Cf. *Re Wilson* (1920) 89 L.J. Ch. 216

[21] [1935] A.C. 209 disapproving *Re Griffiths Settlement* [1911] 1 Ch. 246

[22] The Explanatory Memorandum with the Succession Act makes it clear (at p.1) that s.3(2) is intended to exclude the effect of *Elliott* v *Joicey*.

[23] See Status of Children Act 1987.

6.3.14 (c) Gift in discharge of a moral obligation

Another exception to the doctrine of lapse is provided by the principle that a gift which is made in satisfaction of some moral obligation owed by the testator, will not lapse.[24] This exception has been held to apply when the moral obligation existed at the testator's death even though he was not legally bound to discharge the obligation.[25] The discharge of the obligation may be in respect of a debt owed, not by the testator himself, but, as in *Re Leach's W.T.*,[26] by the testator's deceased son.

6.3.15 The ambit of the exception is uncertain however, and it has been suggested that it may be confined to the recognition by a testator in his will of a moral obligation to pay one or more debts, but does not extend to other forms of moral obligation.[27]

6.4 Lapse and republication

6.4.1 Although a will is read as though it had been executed at the date of a codicil which republishes it, this will not save from the doctrine of lapse a gift to a beneficiary who dies after the execution of the will and before its republication by codicil.[28] However, republication may alter the construction of the will in relation to the identity of a beneficiary so as to save the gift from lapse. Thus in *Re Hardyman*[29] the testatrix had left a legacy in trust for her cousin, his wife and their children which clearly referred to the cousin's wife living at the date of the will. The cousin's wife died after the will was made, and the testatrix later republished the will in general by a codicil which did not refer to the gift to the cousin and his wife in particular. The cousin having remarried Romer J. held, that as a result of its republication, the will referred to any woman the cousin might marry and not exclusively to his deceased first wife. Of course if the will had not been republished the gift to the cousin's wife would have lapsed, as it would if she had been identified by name or in such a way that its republication would not have altered the construction of the will.

6.5 Commorientes

6.5.1 As we have seen, a beneficiary's entitlement to a gift under a will depends as a general rule, on him surviving the testator, and, if he

---

[24] See Farwell J.'s judgment in *Stevens* v *King* [1904] 2 Ch. 30,33.

[25] *Williamson* v *Naylor* (1838) 3 Y. & C. 208 (the discharge of a statute barred debt).

[26] [1948] Ch. 232

[27] See Parry and Clark "The Law of Succession" (8th ed. 1983) at p.334

[28] *Re Woods Will* (1861) 29 Beav. 286

[29] [1925] Ch. 287

predeceases the testator, the gift will lapse. A particular difficulty arises when a testator and beneficiary, or an intestate deceased and intestate successor, die in circumstances, such as an airline or shipping disaster, in which it is not clear who died first.

6.5.2 There was no presumption at common law as to the order of deaths in such circumstances, and the onus of proof lay on the person asserting the order of deaths.[30] In the absence of affirmative evidence of survivorship the courts deemed it more reasonable to consider that the parties had died at the same time, in which case no party would have a claim to the estate of another party who perished in the same accident.[31] The position was altered in England by section 184 of the Law of Property Act, 1925, which provides, that where two or more persons die in circumstances rendering it uncertain which of them survived the other, there is a statutory presumption that the parties died in order of seniority, the eldest first and the youngest last.[32]

6.5.3 The Succession Act eschews the English model and section 5 provides that where, after the commencement of the Act, two or more persons have died in circumstances rendering it uncertain which of them survived the other or others, then, for the purposes of the distribution of the estate of any of them, they shall be deemed to have died simultaneously.[33] The Explanatory Memorandum with the Succession Act tells us that the new rule is borrowed from Article 20 of the German Civil Code, as amended in 1951.[34] A similar rule is to be found in Article 32 of the Swiss Civil Code.

6.6 Gifts to witnesses

6.6.1 Section 82 of the Succession Act, which substantially reproduces section 15 of the Act of 1837, provides in subsection (1) that, if a person

"attests the execution of a will, and any devise, bequest, estate, interest, gift or appointment, of or affecting any property (other than charges and directions for the payment of any debt or debts) is given or made by the will to that person or his spouse, that devise, bequest, estate, interest,

---

[30] See *Underwood* v *Wing* (1855) 4 De G.M. & G. 633; *Wing* v *Angrave* (1860) 8 H.L. Cas. 183; *Re Nightingale* (1927), 71 Sol. J. 542 and *Re Rowland* (1963) Ch. 1

[31] See *Wright* v *Netherwood* (1793), 2 Salk. 593; *Re Phene's Trusts* (1870) 5 Ch. App. 139

[32] Section 184 was amended by the Intestates Estates Act 1952, in so far as it applied to the deaths of spouses where the elder of the two was intestate in which case s.1(4) of the 1952 Act provides that the younger spouse is deemed not to have survived the elder.

[33] If joint tenants die in circumstances which make it unclear which died first the apparent effect of s.5 of the Succession Act is that the estate will pass to their heirs on a joint tenancy. See Wylie "Irish Land Law" (2nd ed. 1986) at p.388 citing *Bradshaw* v *Toulmin* (1784) Dick 633.

[34] Explanatory Memorandum with the Succession Act at p.2

gift or appointment shall, so far only as concerns the person attesting the execution of the will, or the spouse of that person, or any person claiming under that person or spouse, be utterly null and void."

Subsection (2) provides, that

"the person so attesting shall be admitted as a witness to prove the execution of the will, or to prove the validity or invalidity thereof, notwithstanding such devise, bequest, estate, interest, gift, or appointment

6.6.2 There are limits however to the general rule that a beneficiary who signs a will is precluded from taking a benefit under the will, and the rule will not apply in the following circumstances.

6.6.3 (a) If the beneficiary signs the will not *qua* witness, but in some other capacity, he will not be precluded from benefit. Thus in *Re Parker*[35] an executor who was also a legatee signed the will after the testator, but above the attestation clause and the signatures of the two witnesses, in the belief that it was necessary for an executor so to sign a will. Barton J. pointed out, that while every such signature to a will must be presumed to be made as a witness such presumption may be disproved. Since it appeared from the affidavit evidence of the executor that he had not intended to sign the will *qua* witness, Barton J. held that the legacy to the executor was not void under section 15 of the Wills Act, 1837.

6.6.4 (b) A gift will not be avoided by the fact that the beneficiary has attested the will if the beneficiary is not to take the gift beneficially but as trustee. The point is illustrated by the decision in *Kelly* v *Walsh*[37] where the testator had bequeathed a sum of £40, and also his residuary estate to a Father Walsh, for the purpose of having Masses celebrated for the repose of the donor's soul. The executors having brought proceedings to have the validity of the gifts determined, Dixon J. held, that as the bequests were charitable bequests the donee did not take a beneficial interest or devise within the meaning of section 15 of the Wills Act, 1837, although he might himself benefit incidentally in a material sense thereby.[38]

6.6.5 Where a witness to a will is also a beneficiary under a secret trust which has been accepted by a legatee or devisee under a will, there seems to be no reason in principle why such beneficiary should be deprived of his

[35] (1905) 39 I.L.T.R. 6

[36] *Ibid* at p.7

[37] [1946] I.R. 388. See also *Re Ray's Will Trusts* [1936] Ch. 520

[38] *Ibid* at p.389. The benefit to the donee would come from the honoraria he could claim for the saying of Masses but, as Dixon J. pointed out, the Masses need not be said by the donee who could arrange for them to be said by other priests.

beneficial interest by his attestation of the will.[39] Indeed the retention of his interest by such beneficiary would be consistent with the principle that a secret trust operates debors the will.[40]

6.6.6 (c) The courts have construed narrowly the provision that the spouse of an attesting witness may not benefit under the will, and it has been held not to invalidate a gift to a beneficiary who marries an attesting witness after the execution of the will and before the death of the testator.[41]

6.6.7 (d) A gift to an attesting witness takes effect if it is confirmed by a testamentary instrument which the witness beneficiary does not attest.[42] The point is neatly illustrated by the decision in *Re Marcus*.[43] There, a testator left gifts in his will to two persons, one of whom attested both the will and subsequent codicils and was held not to take the gift under the will. The other party who attested the codicils but not the will was held entitled to take under the will. The latter party's interest derived from a testamentary instrument which he had not attested.

6.6.8 The benign effect of the above rule can be seen in *Gurney* v *Gurney*[44] where, a testator had revoked certain legacies in his will by a codicil thereby increasing the value of his residuary estate. Those entitled to the testator's residuary estate under the will had not attested the will, but had attested the codicil, the effect of which was to increase the value of their residuary interest. Even so they were held entitled to the whole of the residuary estate under the will as increased by the codicil.[45]

6.6.9 The fact that the attestation of a person who receives a gift under a will is superfluous to the due execution of the will does not, without more, save the gifts from lapse. If the will was signed by such person *qua* witness the gift will not take effect, but the Irish courts, as we have seen, have shown a willingness to construe the signature of a beneficiary as having been made by him other than as a witness.[46] Thus, in *In the Goods of Shaw Decd.*[47] a legatee, one Hugh Wilson, had signed the will below the signatures of the testator and two attesting witnesses with the words

[39] *O'Brien* v *Condon* [1905] 1 I.R. 51; *Re Young* [1951] Ch. 344. Cf. *Re Fleetwood* (1880), 15 Ch.D. 594

[40] See *ante* p.19

[41] *Tee* v *Bestwick* (1881), 6 Q.B.D.311

[42] See *Re Trotter* (1899) 1 Ch. 764; *Gaskin* v *Rogers* (1866), L.R. 2 Eq. 284

[43] (1887) 57 L.T. 399

[44] (1855) 3 Drew 208

[45] Cf. *Gaskin* v *Rogers* (1866), L.R. 2 Eq. 284; See Mellows "The Law of Succession" (4th ed. 1983) at p.61

[46] See *ante* p.156

[47] [1944] Ir. Jur. Rep. 77

"Above signatures also witnessed by Hugh Wilson". Maguire P. pointed out that the evidence of a beneficiary must be carefully considered, but he accepted the evidence of Hugh Wilson that he did not sign as a witness, or at the request of the testator, and was accordingly entitled to the legacy.

6.6.10 A similar benign result was achieved in *In the Goods of Willis*[48] where the testator had expressed the desire that his sister, to whom he bequeathed all his property should also sign his will after the attesting witnesses. The evidence before the court disclosed that she had done so to placate the whim of her extremely ill brother, believing that it would have no effect, one way or the other, on the validity of the will. Sullivan P. made an order for probate directing that the sister's signature be omitted from the grant.

6.6.11 The foregoing cases may be compared with the English case *In the Estate of Bravda*[49] where gifts in his will to the testator's two daughters were held to be ineffective by the Court of Appeal because the daughters had signed the will at the testator's request "to make it stronger." The gifts to the two daughters were held to be ineffective, despite the fact that there were two other attesting witnesses and the signatures by the daughters were superfluous to the due execution of the will.

6.6.12 The manifestly harsh and unsatisfactory outcome of cases such as *In the Estate of Bravda* has been precluded in England with the enactment of the Wills Act, 1968,[50] section 1 of which provides, that the attestation of a will by a beneficiary, or his spouse, can be disregarded if the will is otherwise duly executed without them. Although the Irish courts have, arguably, adopted a more liberal approach to the question of superfluous witnesses than that shown by the English Court of Appeal in *In the Estate of Bravda*, prudence would dictate the enactment in Ireland of legislation similar to section 1 of the English Wills Act, 1968.

6.7 Illegality and rules of public policy

6.7.1 It is a long established rule of public policy that a person may not profit from his or her own crime, and it follows that a person guilty of murder, or manslaughter, can take no benefit under the will, or on the intestacy of his victim.[51] The exclusion from succession of such persons is

---

[48] (1927) 61 I.L.T.R. 48
[49] [1968] I.W.L.R. 492
[50] C. 28
[51] *In the Estate of Hall* [1914] P.1; *In the Estate of Crippen* [1911] P.108; *Re Sigsworth* [1935] Ch. 89 and *Re Giles* [1972] Ch. 544.

now contained section 120 (1) of the Succession Act, which provides, that a sane person who has been guilty of the murder or manslaughter of another shall be precluded from taking any share in the estate of that other, except a share arising under a will made after the act constituting the offence.[52] Subsection (5) of section 120 provides, that any share which a person is precluded from taking under the section shall be distributed as if that person had died before the deceased.

6.7.2 The express language of section 120 (1) would seem to allow the perpetrator of a lesser offence than murder or manslaughter to benefit under the will, or on the intestacy, of his victim.[53] Certainly the case law on this rule of public policy prior to the enactment of the Succession Act deals with murder and if manslaughter, and there is no authority to suggest that the rule should extend beyond those particular offences. Indeed, the limitation of the rule to murder and manslaughter also derives implicit support from the provision in section 120 (4) which, precludes from taking a share as a legal right, or making the application under section 117, a person found guilty of an offence against the deceased, or the spouse or any child of the deceased, punishable by imprisonment for a maximum period of at least two years.[54]

6.7.3 The lay person may well be surprised to learn that a beneficiary who was guilty of an act, such as dangerous driving, which caused the death of a testator, is not precluded from taking a benefit under the will of his victim if the act falls short of the offence of manslaughter, but the exclusionary rule is well settled, and it is extremely unlikely that the courts will feel free to extend the ambit of the rule beyond the designated offences of murder and manslaughter.[55]

6.7.4 The other side of that coin is the argument that the rule which excludes from benefit a person guilty of manslaughter should not be treated as an absolute rule of law, but should be applied with due regard to the particular circumstances of the individual case. An example of the strict rule of law approach is to be found in the English case *Re Giles*[56] where a wife who would have succeeded to her husband's entire estate under the terms of his will, had killed him by striking him with what was coyly

---

[52] Section 120(1) also provides that such person shall not be entitled to make an application under s.117. See *post* pp.197 *et. seq.*

[53] Cf Mellows "The Law of Succession" (4th ed. 1983) at p.393 and see *McKinnon* v *Lundy* (1894) 210 AR 560 where the degree of moral guilt was held to be irrelevant to the application of the rule.

[54] See the Exploratory Memorandum with the Succession Act at para.74 p.10

[55] See *Gray* v *Barr* [1971] 2 Q.B. 554; *R* v *Chief National Insurance Commissioner* [1981] Q.B.758 and generally Youdan *Acquisition of Property by Killing* (1973) 89 Law Quarterly Review 235

[56] [1972] Ch 544

described as a bedroom utensil, otherwise a domestic chamber-pot. The wife was charged with the murder of her husband but was found guilty of his manslaughter by reason of diminished responsibility, the court accepting certain medical evidence as to her mental condition at the time of the offence. She was accordingly ordered to be detained in Broadmoor Hospital without limit of time. Despite this, Pennycuick V.C. subsequently held that the wife was precluded from taking any benefit under the will or the intestacy rules, and the Vice-Chancellor rejected the argument of counsel for the widow that the exclusion from benefit rule should apply only to offences deserving of punishment or carrying a degree of moral culpability. Pennycuick V.-C.'s decision in *Re Giles* prompted an English textwriter to observe: "The cold, unfeeling hand of the law is laid upon us"[57]

6.7.5 That the position is now much improved in England following the enactment of a Forfeiture Act, 1982,[58] can be seen in *Re K. (Decd.).*[59] There the testator had, for a number of years, committed frequent violent and unprovoked assaults on his wife, who remained loyal to him, however, apparently on the ground that his behaviour was attributable to mental illness. The deceased had attacked his wife on the day he died and she sought to escape to her bedroom taking with her a shotgun, the sight of which she hoped would deter her husband from further assaults on her. She had however released the safety catch on the gun, and as her husband moved towards her the gun went off killing him. At her subsequent trial, during which she pleaded guilty of manslaughter, the trial judge did not impose a custodial sentence but put her on probation for two years.

6.7.6 It fell to Vinelott J. to determine whether the widow was precluded from benefit under her deceased husband's will. Despite his expression of great sympathy for the widow, Vinelott J. held, that the death of the testator was the unintended but unfortunate consequence of her conduct, and she was therefore not entitled to benefit under her deceased husband's will. Vinelott J. went on to hold however that the court had power under the Forfeiture Act, 1982, to modify the effect of the exclusion from benefit rule, and he allowed the widow to take the benefit under her husband's will. The relevant part of the Forfeiture Act is section 2 which in subsection (1) permits a court to make an order modifying the effect of the rule which excludes from benefit a person who had unlawfully killed another, where, as provided in subsection (2), the court is satisfied that, having regard to the conduct of the offender and of the deceased, and to such other

---

[57] Mellows "The Law of Succession" (3rd ed. 1977) at p.531
[58] c. 34
[59] [1985] Ch. 85; affirmed [1986] Ch. 180

circumstances as appear to the court to be material, the justice of the case requires the effect of the rule to be so modified in that case.

6.7.7 While a strong case can be made for the introduction of similar legislation in Ireland there is much to be said, pending its introduction, for the Irish courts following the approach taken by the New South Wales Supreme Court 1 in *Public Trustee* v *Evans*.[60] There, in the absence of legislation similar to the English Forfeiture Act 1982, the court had to determine whether the killing of her husband by a wife in circumstances not dissimilar to those in *Re K. (Decd.)* precluded the wife from benefitting under the intestacy rules. The wife was charged with manslaughter but the trial judge held, having regard to all the circumstances of the case, that the jury should be discharged from giving a verdict, such discharge operating as an acquittal.[61] A killer's acquittal in criminal proceedings however does not automatically bar the operation of the exclusion from benefit rule,[62] and, the Public Trustee, as administrator of the deceased's estate, made an application to the court to determine whether the widow was entitled to any benefit on the administration on intestacy of the deceased's estate.

6.7.8 Young J. in the New South Wales Supreme Court observed that the ambit of the exclusion from benefit rule was still in doubt and ill-defined and he had to decide

"whether in 1985 in New South Wales there is a rule of public policy which makes it anti-social to permit a wife who has been threatened by her husband that he will kill her and her children, and who has shot him to prevent mayhem, to be debarred from recovery."[63]

Young J. went on to point out that the exclusion from benefit rule was essentially a judge-made rule, and he believed that it would be socially unreal for a court of equity and good conscience not to take cognisance of the prevailing ethos which commonly recognises that unfortunate situations may occur in family groups whereby a death regrettably occurs because of a situation of domestic violence.[64]

6.7.9 Young J.'s approach to the application of the exclusion from benefit rule is commendable, and it is earnestly to be hoped that the Irish courts will likewise follow the path of judicial pragmatism and eschew the

---

[60] (1985) 2 N.S.W.L.R. 188
[61] Under S.24 of the Crimes Act, 1900 (New South Wales) and see Mackie "Manslaughter and Succession" (1988) 62 A.L.J. 616, 620.
[62] See *Gray* v *Barr* [1971] 2 Q.B. 554
[63] (1985) 2 N.S.W. L.R. 188, 192
[64] *Ibid*

absolutist rule of law approach favoured by the English courts and modified in England only with the enactment of the Forfeiture Act 1982.[65]

6.8 Rules against perpetuities and accumulations

6.8.1 A disposition of real or personal property in a will, or *inter vivos* settlement, fails to take effect if it offends the rule against perpetuities, which places limits on a person's ability to control the vesting of his property in the future. The so-called perpetuity period within which property must vest in the donee has been settled by the courts as a life or lives in being, plus twenty one years and any period of gestation.[66] It is not proposed to deal further in this book with the rule against perpetuities and readers are referred to specialised works on the topic and to standard works on property law.[67] Readers are likewise referred to standard works on property law in relation to the analogous rule against accumulations, which prevents settlors from directing that the income from property be tied up or accumulated for unreasonable periods of time.[62] The rule against accumulations has a limited application in Ireland.[69]

6.9 Uncertainty

6.9.1 A gift in a will may fail for uncertainty if, either the subject matter of the gift, or the object or objects, are not stated with sufficient clarity to enable the court, having regard to admissible extrinsic evidence,[70] to enforce its terms. The courts however have gone to great lengths in order to save gifts which appear to be too vague to take effect, and, as Lord Hardwicke L.C. put it in *Minshull* v *Minshull*.[71] "a court never construes a devise void, unless it is so absolutely dark, that they cannot find out the testator's meaning." The policy reasons underlying the courts' benignity in this respect were expressed in an oft-quoted dictum of Lord Esher M.R. in In *re Harrison*[72]:

---

[65] See the judgment of Geoffrey Lane J. in *Gray* v *Barr* (1970)2 Q.B. 626, 640

[66] Legislative changes have been made to the rule against perpetuities in England (see sections 162–3 of the Law of Property Act, 1925, and the Perpetuities and Accumulations Act (1964) and in Northern Ireland (see the Perpetuities Act (N.I.) 1966. There is as yet no comparable legislation in the Republic of Ireland.

[67] See Morris and Leach "The Rule Against Perpetuities" (2nd ed. 1962); Maudsley "The Modern Law of Perpetuities" (1979); Wylie "Irish Land Law" (2nd ed. 1986) at pp. 278 *et seq.* and Megarry and Wade "The Law of Real Property" (4th ed. 1975) at pp. 207 *et seq.*

[68] Wylie "Irish Land Law" (2nd ed. 1986) at p.319

[69] *Ibid*

[70] See *ante* p.113

[71] (1737) 1 Atk. 411, 412.

[72] (1885) 30 Ch.D. 390, 393

"There is one rule of construction which to my mind is a golden rule, viz., that when a testator has executed a will in solemn form you must assume that he did not intend to make it a solemn farce – that he did not intend to die intestate when he has gone through the form of making a will. You ought, if possible, to read the will so as to lead to a testacy, not an intestacy. This is a golden rule."

6.9.2 That the Irish courts have been no less inclined to give effect to what might fairly be described as uncertain wills is illustrated by the decision in *Makeown* v *Ardagh*.[73] There a testatrix had made a number of bequests including one to her nephew J.A. of "the sum of – hundred pounds." Chatterton V.C. took the view that it was manifest that the testatrix intended to leave to her nephew a legacy, and that it was to be of a sum not less than one hundred pounds. The testatrix had probably intended, when writing that portion of her will, to leave it open to her to fill the space with either one or some higher number, but, the Vice-Chancellor pointed out he must, in order to give effect to the words she had used, read them as he found them, and see if they were capable of a sensible interpretation. The words used by the testatrix, though not forming a grammatical sentence had, the Vice-Chancellor thought, an intelligible meaning and he decreed a payment of one hundred pounds to the legatee.[74]

6.9.3 A similarly benign outcome occurred in the English case *Re Stevens*[75] where a testatrix, by her will made on a printed form, after leaving blanks in the spaces for the names of the executors continued "I give, devise and bequeath unto my brother H, also sister J, also sister E." After a further blank space, the will was signed and attested in proper form. On the hearing of a summons taken out to ascertain the effect of the provisions of the will Wynn-Parry J. held that the testatrix intended to deal with the whole of her property by leaving it to the named beneficiaries and, J. having predeceased the testatrix, the surviving brother and sister took the estate in equal shares as joint tenants.[76] Wynn-Parry J. did not believe that the omission of any appointment of executors precluded him from giving effect to the intention of the testatrix to deal with the whole of her property which intention sufficiently appeared from the form in which the will was admitted to probate.[77]

---

[73] (1876) I.R. 10 Eq. 445

[74] *Ibid.* at p. 453

[75] (1952) Ch. 323

[76] Wynn-Parry J. applied the so-called golden rule formulated by Lord Esher M.R. in In re Harrison (1885) Ch. D. 390, 393.

[77] In this respect Wynn-Parry J. followed *In re Bassett's Estate* (1872) L.R. 14 Eq. 54; In *re Messenger's Estate* [1937] 1 All E.R. 355 and *In re Turner* [1949] 2 All E.R. 935.

6.9.4 The distinguished English judge and jurist R.E. Megarry has written that some testators invite litigation, and, high in the list of precedents destined never to achieve immortality in the pages of *Key* and *Elphinstone* must come the clause construed in *Re Golay*[78] which ran

> "I direct my executors to let Tossy – Mrs. F. Bridgewater – to enjoy one of my flats during her lifetime and to receive a reasonable income from my other properties; she is, if she so wish, to wear any of my jewellery, car etc. until her death."[79]

On a summons by the executor of the will to determine, *inter alia,* whether that direction was void for uncertainty Ungood-Thomas J. held, that by the words "reasonable income" the testator had provided an effective determinant, by which, effect could be given to his intention. Ungood-Thomas J. was of the opinion that by the use of those words the testator intended that the yardstick was not what he or some other specified person subjectively considered reasonable, but that objective yardstick which the court, which was constantly involved in making such objective assessments, could and would apply in quantifying the amount.[80] The gift of a "reasonable income" accordingly did not fail for uncertainty because it had not specified any person to quantify it.

6.9.5 What is of particular interest to the Irish lawyer is that the principal case relied upon by Ungood-Thomas J. to support the gift was the Irish case *Jackson* v *Hamilton*.[81] There a testator had directed in his will that the trustees should from time to time retain in their hands any reasonable sum or sums of money which would be sufficient to remunerate them for the trouble they would have in carrying the trusts of the will into execution. The master, when the matter came before him, had no difficulty in quantifying a "reasonable" remuneration at £250 for each trustee, and Sir Edward Sugden confirmed the course which the master had taken. Ungood-Thomas J. rejected the argument that since in that case a discretion was in the first place given to the trustees, the court had merely been exercising the discretion given to the trustees.[82]

6.9.6 R.E. Megarry is critical of the lack of discussion in *Re Golay* of the principle which emerged from *Re Gape*[83] which is, that what makes a gift void for uncertainty is not difficulty of ascertainment but uncertainty of

---

[78] [1965] I W L.R. 969
[79] See R.E.M. (1965) 81 Law Quarterly Review 481
[80] [1965] I W L.R. 969, 971
[81] (1846) 3 Jo. & Lat. 702
[82] See the judgment of Ungood-Thomas 3. at [1965] I W.L.R. 969, 971
[83] [1952] Ch. 418, 743

concept.[84] The learned author concedes however, that some degree of imprecision in the concept must be permissible before the court can "repose on the easy pillow of saying that the whole is void for uncertainty."[85] Whether that degree of imprecision was exceeded in *Re Golay* may have to be explored in future cases, and that exploration "cannot fail to be of the greatest interest."[86]

6.9.7 A gift by will fails if the object or objects are uncertain, or cannot be rendered certain by the court, but, as we have seen, the misdescription of an object will not cause the gift to fail for uncertainty if extrinsic evidence is admissible under section 90 of the Succession Act to cure the misdescription.[87] If the description of an object in a will can be applied to a person living at the testator's death, then it would appear that extrinsic evidence is not admissible under section 90 to show that the testator intended to benefit someone else.[88] If it is not possible for the court to ascertain, extrinsic evidence notwithstanding, which of several possible beneficiaries were intended to benefit, the gift will fail for uncertainty.[89]

6.9.8 It is sometimes said that "a charitable bequest never fails for uncertainty"[90], but this must be qualified by adding the rider that the testator must have manifested a general charitable intention.[91] If the testator has manifested such an intention and the particular object of his bounty has ceased to exist, or never did exist, then the gift will be applied *cy-pres*.

6.9.9 These points are neatly illustrated by certain of the facts in *Makeown v Ardagh*.[92] There the testatrix had bequeathed £200 to the institution "C", which had ceased to exist before the date of the will, its funds and liabilities having been taken over by a similar institution. It was held however, that the intention being to benefit the particular institution named, the bequest could not be carried out *cy-press* and therefore failed altogether. The testatrix had also bequeathed £500 to the "P.C. and P. Missionary Society" which did not exist but there was in existence the "S.A. Missionary Society"

---

[84] (1965) 81 L.Q.R. 481, 482

[85] *Re Roberts* (1881) 19 Ch. D. 520, 529 (per Jessel M.R.)

[86] (1965) 81 L.Q.R. 481, 483

[87] See *Bennett* v *Bennett* Unreported High Court judgment by Parke 3. delivered 24th Jan. 1977 and see ante p.115

[88] See *ante* p.116

[89] See e.g. *Re Stephenson* [1897] 1 Ch. 75

[90] *Re White* [1893] 2 Ch. 41, 53.

[91] See *Re Royal Hospital Kilmainham* [1966] I.R. 451 and generally Keane "Equity and the Law of Trusts in the Republic of Ireland" at pp. 150 *et seq.*

[92] (1876) I.R. 10 Eq. 445

which carried on missions in P.C. and P., of which the testatrix knew, and to which she subscribed funds. It was accordingly held that the reference to the "P.C. and P. Missionary Society" was a mere misdescription of the "S.A. Missionary Society" and that the latter was entitled to the bequest.

6.10 Ademption

6.10.1 The term ademption is used to cover several different situations but, in the context of failure of benefit, it is most commonly used where the subject matter of a gift by will had ceased to exist, or conform to the description of it in the will, or has ceased to be subject to the testator's power of disposition, at the time of his death. In such a case the gift is said to be adeemed.[93]

6.10.2 Ademption applies only to specific legacies and not to general or so-called demonstrative legacies.[94] The distinction between specific legacies and others was formulated by Romilly M.R. in *Duncan* v *Duncan*[95] thus:

"If a person bequeathed a debt which is due to him, that is a specific legacy. It is equally so if he bequeath it to several persons in certain shares and proportions, as in equal moities or in equal fourths; or if he say 'I give £1000 out of it to A.B. and the residue to C.D.' In all these cases the legacies are specific. But if he says, 'I give a legacy of £40 to A., and I desire it to be paid out of the debt due to me from B.,' this is not a specific legacy. Testator gives a legacy, and merely points to a fund out of which it is to be found. The question is, whether the testator has given the thing itself, and if that be so, it cannot be treated otherwise than as a specific bequest."

6.10.3 The effect of the principle of ademption on specific legacies has led the courts, whenever possible, to find that a legacy is general or demonstrative rather than specific.[96] That the facts of the particular case may preclude such a finding however is illustrated by the decision in *Kelly* v *Frawley*.[97] There a testator, having made certain specific bequests, bequeathed all his remaining property to his executor

---

[93] See generally Keane "Equity and the Law of Trusts in the Republic of Ireland" at pp. 309 *et seq*.

[94] A demonstrative legacy is general in nature but is directed to be paid out of a specific fund or satisfied out of the testator's property and is not liable to ademption by an act of the testator during his lifetime. See Wylie "Irish Land Law" (2nd ed. 1986) at p.728

[95] (1859) 27 B. 386, 389 cited by Powell J. in *McCoy* v *Jacob* [1919] 1 I.R.134, 138

[96] E.g. *Re Gage* [1934] Ch. 536

[97] (1944) 78 I.L.T.R. 46

"upon trust as to the sum of £121 or thereabouts due to me by the representatives of the late P.McI. (secured by the lands of the said P.McI.) for P.K. absolutely."

After the execution of the will, and before the death of the testator, a cheque for £100 drawn by solicitors acting for the representatives of P. McI. was forwarded to the testator's solicitors in full satisfaction of the debt due, and a release of the charge on P.McI.'s lands was then executed by the testator. The testator's solicitors indorsed the cheque, and forwarded it to the testator who did not present the cheque for payment but retained it in his possession until he died.

6.10.4 In these circumstances Judge O'Briain in the Circuit Court held, that the legacy to P.K. was a specific legacy and had been adeemed. Judge O'Briain referred to *Humphreys* v *Humphreys*[98] in which the Lord Chancellor said, that the only rule to be adhered to was to see whether the subject of the specific bequest remained *in specie* at the time of the testator's death, for if it did not, then there must be an end of the bequest. Judge O'Briain thought that in the instant case there had been a specific legacy of a particular debt, which debt was so altered in form by the subsequent transactions that the subject matter of the legacy was extinguished, and a new debt, the liability on the cheque, created.[99]

6.10.5 A change in the name or form of a specific gift will not cause the gift to be adeemed if its substance remains unaltered.[100] The Vice-Chancellor put it thus in *Longfield* v *Bantry*[101]:

"The principle of law to be deduced from the many authorities on this subject may be shortly stated to be that a specific legacy will be adeemed if the subject of the bequest be not in existence as the same specific thing at the testator's death. The intention of the testator in his dealing with the subject of the gift, after the making of the bequest, cannot be taken into consideration. A change in the accidents, however, will not operate as an ademption if the substance and essence of the subject remain the same."

---

[98] (1789) 2 Cox. 184
[99] Judge O'Briain thought the instant case indistinguishable from *Sidney* v *Sidney* (1873) L.R. 17 Eq. 65
[100] See *Re Slater* [1907] Ch. 665
[101] (1885) 15 L.R. Ir. 191, 128. See also *Re Faris* [1911] 1 I.R. 165; *Re Farrelly* [1941] I.R. 261 and *ante* p.122

6.11 Ademption of legacies by portions

6.11.1 While the term ademption is used in situations where the subject matter of a gift by will has ceased to exist, or to conform to the description of it in the will, it is also used in the quite different sense of demonstrating the application of the maxim that "equity imputes an intention to fulfill an obligation."[102] The simplest example of the application of that maxim is where a testator who owes a debts dies without paying the debt, but leaves a legacy, equal to or greater in value than the debt to his creditor, in which case equity will presume that the legacy was given in satisfaction of the debt.[103]

6.11.2 The principle of satisfaction applies in a special way to the relationship which exists between a father and his child, to whom the father is deemed to owe a moral duty to make provision. If a father, or someone *in loco parentis*, undertakes to provide a portion[104] for a child and dies before providing such portion, but leaving a legacy to the child, the child will be unable to enforce the portion debt and claim the legacy, the legacy being presumed to be given in satisfaction of the obligation to provide a portion. Conversely, if the portion is paid prior to the execution of the will, no question of ademption can arise.[105]

6.11.3 The so-called rule against double portions[106] also applies where a father leaves a legacy to his child and, subsequent to the execution of the will gives a portion to that child. The legacy will be adeemed by the portion. Sullivan M.R. put it thus in *Curtin v Evans*:[107]

> "There is a presumption raised by the law against double portions; and accordingly, when a parent, or one standing *in loco parentis*, gives by will a sum of money to a child, and afterwards a like or greater sum is secured by a settlement on the marriage of that child, the law presumes the legacy to be adeemed. But this is only a presumption, and therefore it may be rebutted by evidence of intention to the contrary. The burden

---

[102] See generally Keane "Equity and the Law of Trusts in the Republic of Ireland" at pp. 309 *et seq.* and Wylie "Irish Land Law" at pp.134 *et seq.*

[103] See e.g. *Garner v Holmes* (1858) 8 Ir. Ch. R.469

[104] A portion is a financial provision of a significant kind such as would be needed to make permanent provision for a child on marriage, or setting him up in business. See *Taylor v Taylor* (1875) L.R.20 Eq. 155

[105] *Re Peacock's Estate* (1872) L.R. 14 Eq. 236; *Taylor v Cartwright* (1872) L.R. 14 Eq. 167

[106] See Monroe J.'s formulation of the rule in *Re Battersby's Estate* (1887) 19 L.R. Ir. 359 (Wylie "A Casebook on Equity and Trusts in Ireland" at p. 115) and that of Lord Greene M.R. in *Re Vaux* [1939] Ch. 465, 481

[107] (1872) I.R. 9 Eq. 553, 557–8 (Wylie "A Casebook on Equity and Trusts in Ireland" at p.117)

of proof of intention to countervail the presumption rests on the person claiming the double portion."

Sullivan M.R. went on to point out that parol evidence is admissible to rebut the presumption but warned that the court "ought to view and examine it with scrupulous care and great discrimination."[108]

6.11.4 It is easier to rebut the presumption of satisfaction of portion debts by legacies than it is to rebut the presumption of ademption of a legacy by a portion. Lord Cramworth gave reasons for this difference in *Lord Chichester* v *Coventry:*[109] when the will precedes the settlement it is only necessary to read the settlement as if the person making the provision had said, 'I mean this to be in lieu of what I have given by my will.,' But if the settlement precedes the will, the testator must be understood as saying, 'I give this in lieu of what I am already bound to give, if those to whom I am so bound will accept it.' It requires much less to rebut the latter than the former presumption.

6.11.5 A distinguished Irish author who has, in essence, paraphrased Lord Cramworth's observations in *Lord Chichester* v *Coventry* adds that

"to raise a presumption of satisfaction the two provisions must be *ejusdem generis* and that, provided the differences between the two gifts are not 'slight' the presumption will be rebutted. In the case of ademption, on the other hand, such differences may be regarded as insufficient"[110]

Be that as it may, both of the equitable presumptions are rebuttable by evidence of intrinsic differences between the portion and the legacy, or by extrinsic evidence of a testator's actual intention. While more substantial differences may be required to rebut the presumption of satisfaction of a debt by a legacy, each of the presumptions is rebuttable by evidence that the provisions are not *ejusdem generis*.[111]

6.11.6 Another important difference between satisfaction and ademption in this context touches on the question of election. In the case of a child who is owed a portion debt being left a legacy, the child is entitled to elect whether to take the portion debt or the legacy.[112] Where ademption of legacies by portions is concerned, however, there is no question of

---

[108] *Ibid.* See also *Kirk* v *Eddowes* (1844) 3 Hare 509

[109] (1867) L.R. 2 H.L. 71, 87

[110] Keane "Equity and the Law of Trusts in the Republic of Ireland" at p.314

[111] See *Re Jacques* [1903] 1 Ch. 267; *Re Georges W.T.* [1949] Ch. 154 and Parry and Clark "The Law of Succession" (8th ed. 1983) at pp. 437-8

[112] *Thyme* v *Earl of Glengall* (1848) 2 H.L.C. 131

[113] *Lord Chichester* v *Coventry* (1867) L.R. 2 H.L. 71

election; the child must take the portion and cannot claim the adeemed legacy. It is also the case that if a legacy is not wholly adeemed by a subsequent portion which is less in value than the legacy, the legacy will be adeemed *pro tanto*.[114]

6.11.7 Since the rule against double portions derives from the desire of courts of equity to achieve equality amongst the children of a testator the rule will not, generally, apply to gifts to strangers. Accordingly, a legatee who is neither a child of the testator, or someone to whom the testator stood *in loco parentis*, may claim both a legacy and a subsequent gift. There is, however, a circumstance in which a legacy given to a stranger may be adeemed by a subsequent gift. A presumption of ademption may arise where a legacy and later gift are both given for the same purpose.[115] Porter M.R. put it thus in *Griffith v Bourke*:[116]

> "where there is a gift in a will, of money and property, for an expressed object to which it is devoted by the testator, and there is afterwards a donation by the testator in his lifetime to the same object, the law presumes that he did not intend that both should take effect, but that the latter should be in substitution for the former gift. The object, however, must be clearly expressed, and it must clearly appear that what he did in his lifetime was done for the same object as that intended in his will – for the same identical object."

6.11.8 Porter M.R. held in *Griffith v Bourke* that a legacy of £1000 to the parish priest of Claremorris, to be laid out in the erection of a new church in Claremorris, was adeemed by a subsequent gift of £1000 to the Archbishop of Tuam for the same purpose. While the gift had not been given to the same person as the legacy, it had been given for the identical purpose which could, and would, be enforced by the court if the trustee were dead. Porter M.R. also referred to a peculiarity in the transaction which was that the testator had reserved to himself the interest on the subject matter of a gift during his life which made the gift correspond very closely in effect to a legacy.[117]

6.11.9 There is also some authority to the effect that a legacy may be adeemed by a subsequent gift if both are made for the purpose of fulfilling a specific moral obligation. Thus in the English case *Re Pollock*[118] a

---

[114] *Pym v Lockyer* (1841) 5 My. & Cr. 29; *Edgeworth v Johnston* (1877) I.R. 11 Eq. 326

[115] *Monck v Monck* (1810) 1 Ball. & B. 303; *Re Covett* [1903] 2 Ch. 326; *Re Jupp* [1922] 2 Ch. 359

[116] (1887) 20 L.R. Ir. 92 (Wylie "A Casebook on Equity and Trusts in Ireland" at p. 122)

[117] *Ibid*

[118] (1885) 28 Ch. D. 552

testatrix had left a legacy of £500 to her deceased husband's niece "according to the wish of my late beloved husband." She subsequently gave to the niece a gift of £300 which she referred to as a legacy from "Uncle John", the donor's late husband. It was held in these circumstances that the legacy was adeemed *pro tanto* by the subsequent gift.

6.11.10 There is an interesting divergence in the approaches of the Irish and English courts, and textwriters, to the question whether the rule against double portions can operate so as to confer benefits on strangers. While the rule against double portions is, as we have seen, intended to achieve equality among children, its application in particular circumstances could benefit strangers at the expense of the testator's children. If, for example, a testator leaves a legacy of £5,000 to his child, C, and his residuary estate to be divided equally between his child C and a stranger, S, and subsequently gives C a portion of £5,000, C's legacy is adeemed by the portion and passes into the residuary estate to the advantage of S.

6.11.11 That the English courts are prepared to exclude such an eventuality can be seen in the unequivocal statements by English textwriters to the effect that the presumptions of satisfaction and ademption which arise under the rule against double portions "must not be applied so as to benefit a stranger."[119] The approach of the English courts can be seen in *Meinertzagen* v *Walters*[120] in which it was held that where the testator's residuary estate was to be divided between his children and a stranger, albeit his widow, the application of the rule against double portions which followed the giving of a portion to a child, could not increase the stranger's share. James L.J. made the telling point that it would be monstrous if someone like the widow in the instant case, who would not herself be obliged to account for any advances given to her, could benefit because a child was obliged to account for any advances made to him.[121]

6.11.12 While doubts have been expressed in the Irish courts as to whether the presumption against double portions should operate to benefit strangers at the expense of children, a recent authoritative Irish textbook states "that the preponderance of authority is in favour of the view that it can."[122] The leading case, *Re Bannon*,[123] referred to in the latter work does not, however, unequivocally support the proposition that the

[119] See Parry and Clark "The Law of Succession" (8th ed. 1983) at p.437 and Mellows "The Law of Succession" (4th ed. 1983) at p. 404

[120] (1872) L.R. 7 Ch. App. 670; See also *Re Heather* [1906] 2 Ch. 230 and *Re Vaux* [1938] Ch. 581; [1939] Ch. 465

[121] (1872) L.R. 7 Ch. App. 670, Cf. *Mellish L.J.* at p.674

[122] Keane "Equity and the Law of Trusts in the Republic of Ireland" at p.315

[123] [1934] I.R. 701

presumption against double portions operates to benefit strangers. In that case a testator had left a legacy of £300 to a nephew J.D. and his residuary estate to another nephew. A marriage having been arranged between J.D. and a niece of the testator's wife, the testator contributed £225 of the purchase price of a business premises for the young couple. The Circuit Court judge held that the legacy of £300 had been adeemed *pro tanto* by the gift of £225, the testator being *in loco parentis* to J.D. The judges in the High Court were divided on the issue, Meredith J. being satisfied from the authorities, and on principle, that the presumption against double portions applied, even though the other nephew who would benefit from the operation of the presumption, was in effect a stranger. Johnston J., who expressed doubts as to whether this was the law, was able to hold that the presumption had, in any event, been rebutted on the facts. The High Court being evenly divided on the issue the decision of the Circuit Court stood, but was reversed on appeal by the Supreme Court.

6.11.13 Regrettably the Supreme Court did not have to consider directly whether the presumption against double portions should operate in favour of strangers, the majority (Kennedy C.J. and Fitzgibbon J.) holding that the facts proved did not support an inference that the testator was *in loco parentis* to J.D., and operation of the presumption did not arise. Murnaghan J., however, was of the same opinion as Meredith J. that the presumption would apply in a case where a stranger would benefit thereby. Indeed Murnaghan J. believed that a grave injustice "might be done if advancements are not taken into account except as between children."[124]

6.11.14 Murnaghan J.'s belief notwithstanding, the approach of the English courts is more consistent with the original purpose of the presumption against double portions, which was the achievement of equality among the children of the testator. Unfortunately the rule against double portions, like certain other equitable rules came to acquire a status and life of its own quite detached from it's original purpose, and was applied in circumstances where it manifestly did not give effect to the testator's intentions. In a celebrated and notorious passage in *Montagu v Earl of Sandwich*[125] Bowen L.J. said

> "Whatever may be the view to be taken of the rule against double portions it is a rule that exists; and there is nothing worse than frittering away an existing rule ... Feeling no confidence that in applying this doctrine of double portions in this particular case we are giving effect to the real intentions of the testator. I record my judgment accordingly in favour of the appeal as a sacrifice made upon the altar of authority."

[124] *Ibid* at p.734
[125] (1886) 32 Ch.D. 525, 544

If the rule against double portions is to play a meaningful role in the law of succession it must be made amenable to the test of the testator's intentions and in this respect a testator will rarely intend the rule to operate to the benefit of strangers.

6.12 Satisfaction of legacies by legacies

6.12.1 The question will arise when a testator gives two legacies in his will to the same person, whether the legacies are cumulative, the legatee can take both legacies or substitutional, the legatee can take only one of the legacies. Of course, if the testator has made it clear in his will that he intends the legacies to be either cumulative or substitutional, effect will be given to that intention.[126] Otherwise certain rules, which are in effect rules of construction, are applied to determine whether double legacies are cumulative or substitutional.

6.12.2 When legacies which are given in the same instrument (whether will or codicil) to the same person are of equal value there is an equitable presumption that they are substitutional, and the legatee can take only one of them.[127] Minor differences in the manner in which the legacies are payable will not rebut the presumption[128] but if the legacies are of different value then the contrary presumption will arise that they were intended to be cumulative.[129]

6.12.3. (ii) If a testator gives two legacies, albeit of the same value, to the same person by two different instruments (a will and a codicil are different for this purpose) then *prima facie* the legacies are cumulative, and the legatee takes both. Sullivan M.R. put it thus in *Quin* v *Armstrong:*[130]

"There is also a rule of law which has been established by the many cases which were relied on at the Bar, that where a testator by his will gives a benefit to a person, and by a codicil to his will gives a benefit to the same person, the presumption of law is that he means to give twice; and it lies on the party who disputes it, to show why that construction of them should not be adopted. That is a very sensible, and a very wise rule of law."

---

[126] *Re Silverston* [1949] Ch. 270

[127] *Garth v Meyrick* (1779) 1 Bro. C.C. 30; *Holford* v *Wood* (1798) 4 Ves. 76

[128] See e.g. *Holford* v *Wood* (1798) 4 Ves. 76 and Parry and Clark "The Law of Succession" (8th ed. 1983) at p.433

[129] *Brennan* v *Moran* (1857) 6 Ir. Ch. R. 126

[130] (1876) I.R. 11 Eq. 161 (Wylie "A Casebook on Equity and Trusts in Ireland" at p. 128); See also *Re Resch's W.T.* [1969] I.A.C. 514

6.12.4 If however, legacies of the same amount, given in two different instruments to the same person, are expressed to be given for the same motive, a presumption will arise that the legacies are substitutional, and the legatee is intended to take only one of them.[131] The English courts thus raise the presumption that legacies are substitutional if the double coincidence of the same amount and the same motive in each instrument is satisfied.[132] That the Irish courts might impose a slightly more exacting standard is suggested in the statement of an Irish textwriter to the effect, that

> "legacies will be regarded as substitutional only where the second instrument repeats the first in identical terms or where it makes it clear that it is revising or explaining the first."[133]

6.12.5 The courts lean in favour of legatees when applying these rules of construction, and where a presumption is raised that legacies are cumulative, parol evidence is inadmissible to rebut the presumption.[134] If however a presumption is raised that the legacies are substitutional parol evidence is admissible to rebut that presumption.[135]

6.13 Election

6.13.1 There is a long established principle of equity that a person who accepts a benefit under a transaction must also accept any burden in the same transaction.[136] It may happen, by accident or design, that a testator in his will purports to dispose of property which is not his to dispose of, and the will also confers a benefit on the owner of such property. The latter of course is not obliged to give up his property in such circumstances, but, if he wants to claim a benefit under the will, he must accept the will *in toto;* he cannot approbate and reprobate.[137]

---

[131] See *Hurst* v *Beach* (1821), 5 Madd. 351; *Re Royce's W.T.* [1959] Ch. 626

[132] See Parry and Clark "The Law of Succession" (8th ed. 1983) at p.433

[133] Wylie "Irish Land Law" (2nd ed. 1986) at p.138 citing *Re Armstrong* (1893) 31 L.R. Ir. 154 and *Bell* v *Park* [1914] 1 I.R. 158

[134] *Hall* v *Hill* (1841) 1 Dr. & War. 94, 132-3 (per Sugden L.C.) See also *Hurst* v *Beach* (1821) 5 Madd. 351

[135] See now the position in England under section 21 of the Administration of Justice Act 1982 (c.53).

[136] See Keane "Equity and the Law of Trusts in the Republic of Ireland" at pp. 303 *et seq.* and Hanbury and Maudsley "Modern Equity" (12th ed. by Jill E. Martin) at pp. 813 *et seq.*

[137] Lord Cairns said in *Codrington* v *Codrington* (1875) L.R. 7 H.L. 854 that "where a deed or will professes to make a general disposition of property for the benefit of the person named in it, such person cannot accept a benefit under the instrument without at the same time conforming to all its provisions and renouncing every right inconsistent with them." See also the observations of Ronan L.J. in *Re Sullivan* [1917] 1 I.R. 38, 42-3

6.13.2 The early basis of the doctrine was that it gave effect to the presumed intention of the testator, who had given the benefit in his will on the implied condition that the recipient would give his property to a third party.[138] The latter premise sat uneasily with the view that the doctrine applied whether or not the testator knew that the property he was disposing of was not his, and it came "to be associated more with cases where a testator has made a mistake than where he has made an eccentric or ineffective disposition."[139] It was made clear by the House of Lords in *Cooper* v *Cooper*[140] that the doctrine of election is not based on the testator's intention, either express or implied. Lord Hatherly pointed out that the only relevant intent, apart from the testator's intention to dispose of property not belonging to him, was the ordinary intent implied in the case of any man who makes a will that he intends that every part of it shall be effective.[141]

6.13.3 Intention however continues to play a role, albeit a negative one, in the application of the doctrine of election, since the doctrine will not apply where the testator has manifested a contrary intention in the will.

6.13.4 Although the doctrine still retains certain of the technical features which attached to it at various stages of its development, it is now perceived as a rule of equity which can be employed to achieve a just result in the circumstances of the particular case. This view of the modern doctrine is to be found in the judgment of Buckley L.J. in *Re Mengel's W.T.*[142] in which he said that it is

"a doctrine by which equity fastens on 'the conscience of the person who is put to his election, and refuses to allow him to take the benefit of a disposition contained in the will, the validity of which is not in question, except on certain conditions."

6.13.5 The elements of the modern doctrine of election were set out by Jenkins L.J. in an oft-quoted extract from his judgment in *Re Edwards:*[143]

"The essentials of election are that there should be an intention on the part of the testator or testatrix to dispose of certain property; secondly, that the property should not in fact be the testator's or testatrix's own

---

[138] See Mellows "The Law of Succession" (4th ed. 1983) at pp. 406 *et seq.*
[139] Hanbury and Maudsley "Modern Equity" at p.814. Buckley L.J. made the same point in *Re Mengel's W.T.* (1962) Ch. 791, 797 where he said: "In a great majority of cases to which the doctrine is applicable it applies because the testator has made a mistake."
[140] (1874) L.R. 7 H.L. 53
[141] *Ibid* at p.70
[142] (1962) Ch. 791,
[143] (1958) Ch. 168, 175

property; and, thirdly, that a benefit should be given by the will to the true owner of the property."

We will consider each of these elements.

6.13.6 The lay person might well be forgiven for assuming that the reference by Jenkins L.J. to an intention to dispose of "certain property", was to an intention to dispose of "certain property" belonging to someone other than the testator. But this is not so, since, as we have seen, a testator's mistake as to the ownership of the property he is purporting to dispose of in his will, does not preclude the doctrine of election.[144] Indeed Lord O'Hagan pointed out in *Cooper* v *Cooper*[145] that a testator does not generally know or understand anything about the doctrine of election, and the

> "intention that must be clearly demonstrated in evidence to the court, is an intention to do the particular thing – to give the property which the party has not a right to give, and to give a benefit to a person who has an interest in the property."

6.13.7 If it is evident from the will itself that the testator is purporting to dispose of property which belongs to someone else a case for election will arise if the true owner is given a benefit under the will. Likewise, the doctrine of election will apply, as we have seen, whether or not the testator is aware that he is disposing of another's property, if he gives the true owner a benefit under the will. It must be remembered however that in construing a will the courts operate on the assumption that a testator intends to dispose of his own property only, and the onus of proof lies on he who is claiming that a case of election has arisen.[146] Thus, if a testator has a limited interest in property the court will assume, in the absence of clear evidence to the contrary, that he intended only to dispose of his limited interest and a gift in general terms will be construed as relating only to the testator's property.[147]

6.13.8 The property belonging to another which a testator is purporting to dispose of must be susceptible of being transferred by the true owner to the person to whom the testator has bequeathed it, or an election will not arise. The point is illustrated by the facts in *Re Chesham*[148] where the testator left his own property to his eldest son, Lord Chesham, and certain

---

[144] See ante p.175

[145] (1874) L.R. 7 H.L. 53, 74-5

[146] See *Evans* v *Evans* (1863) 2 New Rep. 408 and Keane "Equity and the Law of Trusts" at p.305

[147] *Ibid*

[148] (1886) 3 1 Ch. D. 466

heirlooms which were held on trust to be enjoyed with settled land, to his younger sons. Chitty J. held that since Lord Chesham was unable to dispose of the heirlooms, in which he had only a life interest, he could keep both the heirlooms and the testator's residuary estate to which he was entitled under the will.

6.13.9 The doctrine of election is said to lead to compensation rather than forfeiture, in that the person whose property is being disposed of by a testator, and to whom the testator has given a benefit under his will, can keep his property *and* take a benefit under the will *but* must compensate the disappointed beneficiary.[149] Thus if A's house Greenlawn which is worth £40,000 is given to B, and A is left £50,000 in the same will, A can keep Greenlawn and claim £10,000 under the will but must compensate B to the tune of £40,000 the value of Greenham. The latter example is relatively straightforward and uncomplicated, but problems will arise if the person whose property is disposed of by the testator cannot use the property left to him in the will to compensate the disappointed beneficiary.

6.13.10 This was precisely the problem which arose in *Re Gordon's Will Trusts*[150] which has been described as the most significant decision in the field of election for many years.[151] The facts of that case were that T and A owned a property called the Old Rectory jointly. T by her will purported to leave it on trust for sale for the benefit of A and B in equal shares, the will also giving to A some furniture, £1,000 and a life interest on protective trusts in half of the residuary estate. A case of election having arisen, A elected against the will by selling the Old Rectory and keeping the proceeds. The furniture and the legacy of £1,000 being insufficient to compensate B, the question arose as to whether A's interest under the protective trust was subject to the doctrine of election, in which case it would terminate leaving nothing with which to compensate B. The Court of Appeal, reversing Goulding J.,[152] held that A's interest under the protective trust was inalienable and therefore not subject to the doctrine of election, whose essential feature was compensation, not forfeiture.[153] The

---

[149] Sir Thomas Plummer M.R. said of the principle of election in *Gretton* v *Howard* (1819) Swan 409, 423 that it "lays hold of the estate for the purpose of making satisfaction to the disappointed devisee. See Keane "Equity and the Law of Trusts" at p.304

[150] (1978) Ch. 145

[151] By Professor Maudsley in his preface to the 11th edition of Hanbury and Maudsley "Modern Equity" (1981)

[152] (1977) Ch. 27 See (1977) 93 Law Quarterly Review 65 (P.H. Pettit) and (1977) 41 Conveyancer (N.S.) 188 (T.G. Watkin)

[153] Sir John Pennycuick pointed out that "the doctrine does not require a beneficiary to surrender for the purpose of compensation an interest which would be destroyed by the very act of surrender, and thereby rendered unavailable to make compensation." ((1978) Ch. 145, 162) See Hanbury and Maudsley "Modern Equity" at p.822

essence of the Court of Appeal judgment was, therefore, that no case for election arose since the testator had left no property which could be used by the person put to his election for the purposes of compensation. It has been suggested by a distinguished Irish textwriter that in so far as the decision in *Re Saul's Trusts*[154] appears to suggest the contrary it was wrongly decided.[155]

6.13.11 In the latter case, a testator had bequeathed to his wife his residence and the contents thereof for her life or until her remarriage. After making certain other specific gifts he gave his residuary real and personal estate for the use and benefit of his wife and such of their children as may reside with her during her life or until her remarriage. By a codicil to his will he purported to bequeath to one of his sons certain leasehold premises, of which he and his wife were joint tenants, and which would pass on his death to his widow by right of survivorship. The widow, on the death of the testator, without electing, entered into enjoyment of the life estate of the residence conferred on her by the will, and also received the income which passed to her as surviving joint tenant until her death some eighteen years later. On her death the question arose as to whether her personal representatives could be called on to elect for or against the will and codicils.

6.13.12 Dixon J. held, that the widow's personal representatives could be called upon to elect for or against the will and codicils, and if against, the compensation, to be paid out of the estate of the widow to the disappointed legatee of the leasehold premises, should carry interest as from six years prior to the commencement of the proceedings and not from the testator's death. It is argued, by the aforementioned textwriter, that election at that stage was impossible since there was no property left to her by the will to which recourse could be had for compensation since her interest ceased on her death. Her personal representatives were, it is suggested, in no different position than the protected life tenant in *Re Gordon's Will Trusts*.[156] Be that as it may, Dixon J's decision in *Re Saul* was clearly equitable on the facts of that case and is consistent with the modern movement in equity jurisdiction from principles to pragmatism.[157] The learned judge was surely right in not allowing a technical requirement of the doctrine of election stand in the way of an equitable result.

---

[154] [1951] Ir. Jur. Rep. 34

[155] Keane "Equity and the Law of Trusts" at pp. 306 and 308

[156] Ibid

[157] See P.S. Atrijah "From Principles to Pragmatism" (Clarendon Press, Oxford, 1978)

6.13.13 A perfectly sensible technical requirement of the doctrine of election is, that the title of the true owner to the property which the testator is purporting to dispose, must arise independently of the will. The leading case is *Wollaston* v *King*[158] where James V.-C. said that the doctrine of election "is not to be applied as between one clause in a will and another clause in the same will."[159] In that case the testatrix had a power of appointment in favour of the children of her marriage, who were also entitled in default of appointment. The testatrix appointed part of the fund to her son for life with remainder to her daughters. The testatrix also gave some of her own property to her daughters. The appointment to the son being void as offending the rule against perpetuities, the daughters, as residuary objects of the fund, became entitled to his share. The question then arose as to whether the daughters were put to their election between the bequests given to them in the will of the testatrix's own property and the fund which came to them from the invalid exercise of the power of appointment. James V.-C. who had no doubt that an election did not arise put it bluntly:

"It would seem a very strange thing that in construing the same instrument the court, dealing with a clause in which a fund is expressed to be given partly to A., and partly to B., should hold that the gift to A., being void, the testator's intention is that B. should take the whole; and then, coming to another clause in which another fund is given to B., and no mention of A. at all, it should hold that there is an implied intention that he should take."[160]

6.13.14 Election may be expressed or implied. The circumstances which must attend a valid election however were set out by Chatterton V.-C. in *Sweetman* v *Sweetman*:[161]

"The requisites for holding a party bound by an election as concluded are, I think, these: first, he must have a knowledge of his rights, that is to say he must know that the property, which the testator attempted to give to another person, was not the testator's property, and that it would, upon the testator's decease, become, independently of the testator's will, the property of the person called upon to elect. It must be known by him, as a matter of fact, that the testator had not the power to give the property which he purported to devise and that it belongs, not by the will, but by an earlier title, to the person who is called upon to elect. Next, he must know the relative values of the properties between which

---

[158] (1869) L.R. 8 Eq. 165 Cf. *Re Macartney* [1918] 1 Ch. 300
[159] *Ibid* at p. 174
[160] *Ibid* See Mellows "The Law of Succession" (4th ed. 1983) at p. 548
[161] (1868) I.R. 2 Eq. 141, 152-3.

he is called upon to elect; and further, he must know, as a matter of fact, and not as a presumption of law that the rule of equity exists, that he cannot, under such circumstances, take both estates, but must make an election between the two, and further the court must be satisfied that he made a deliberate choice with the intention of making it."

6.14 The rule in *Lawes* v *Bennett*

6.14.1 The rule in *Lawes* v *Bennett*[162], like similar remnants of equity jurisdiction, defies rational explanation and is not easy to categorise, but, since its effect may be to deprive someone of a benefit he would otherwise take under a will, it is appropriate to consider it in a chapter dealing with failure of benefit. It is however unlike other rules governing failure of benefit, in that it involves no breach of condition or otherwise on the part of the person losing the benefit, and, the latter person is usually in no position to forestall or avoid his loss.

6.14.2 The rule in *Lawes* v *Bennett* involves an extension of the equitable doctrine of conversion to options to purchase. The more familiar application of the doctrine of conversion is to specifically enforceable contracts for the sale of land, where, on the basis of the maxim that equity treats that as done which ought to be done, the interest of the vendor is treated in equity as an interest in personalty and that of the purchaser as an interest in realty.[163] If the purchaser should die before completion his interest will pass to those entitled to his realty, subject of course to the obligation to pay the balance of the purchase price; if the vendor should die before completion the proceeds of sale will go to those entitled to his personalty.

6.14.3 The extension of the doctrine of conversion to options to purchase in *Lawes* v *Bennett* had the following result. If A who had leased Whiteacre to B had given B an option to purchase Whiteacre, which option was not exercised before A's death, then Whiteacre would pass to whomever would be entitled to A's realty. It would further be expected that should B exercise his option to buy Whiteacre after A's will has come into operation, the proceeds of sale would pass to the person who has been enjoying Whiteacre since A's estate was administered. The rule in *Lawes* v *Bennett* provides however, that when the option is exercised the proceeds of sale pass to whomever was entitled to A's personalty, the conversion relating back to the date of the agreement granting the option.[164]

---

[162] (1785) 1 Cox 167

[163] See generally Keane "Equity and the Law of Trusts in the Republic of Ireland" at pp. 197 *et seq.* Wylie "Irish Land Law" (2nd ed. 1986) at pp.125 *et seq.*

[164] Of course if the option is never exercised the property remains with the person who acquired it on the testator's death.

6.14.4 The rule would not apply, of course, if there was evidence of a contrary intention on the face of a will, and, perhaps not surprisingly in view of the arbitrary nature of the rule, the courts were anxious to find evidence of such contrary intention. Thus Palles C.B. pointed out in *Steele v Steele*[165] that when you find in a will made *after* a contract granting an option to purchase, the testator, knowing of the existence of the contract, and without referring to the contract in any way, devises the property which is the subject of the contract, that is a sufficient indication that he intends the devisee to take all the interest that he had in the property.

6.14.5 That the pendulum has not altogether swung against the rule in *Lawes* v *Bennett* can be seen in *Belshaw* v *Rollins*[166], where it was held that an option to purchase can be exercised by the personal representatives of a lessee to whom the option was given. Also the English Court of Appeal applied it to the case of an option to purchase shares given after the making of a will, which had the effect of taking the proceeds of sale from the specific legatees and adding it to residue.[167] The rule is generally perceived however as an interesting but indefensible curiosity, and the leading English textbook on equity points out that little can be said in defence of a rule which "makes the devolution of property depend upon events that occur subsequently to a testator's death."[168]

---

[165] [1913] 1 I.R. 292; Wylie "A Casebook on Equity and Trusts in Ireland" at p.88. Palles C.B. applied the principle set out by Lord Hatherby, then Vice-Chancellor Sir W. Page-Wood in *Weeding* v *Weeding* (1861) 1 J. & H. 424, 431.

[166] [1904] 1 I.R. 284

[167] *Re Carrington* [1932] 1 Ch. 1. See Hanbury and Maudsley "Modern Equity" at p.264

[168] *Ibid*. On the considerable volume of case law which arose in Ireland under the rule in *Lawes* v *Bennett* in relation to the Land Purchase Acts see Wylie "Irish Land Law" (2nd ed. 1986) at pp.127-8.

Chapter 7
FREEDOM OF TESTATION

7.1 Introduction

7.1.1 The principle of freedom of testation, which was an inseparable incident of the law of succession which we inherited from the English, meant in effect that a testator was free to dispose of his property as he saw fit.[1] As we have seen earlier, a consequence of that freedom was that a testator could be as arbitrary and capricious in his testamentary dispositions as he pleased, and if he was otherwise mentally competent, the court would admit his will to probate.[2] Other legal systems, more particularly the civilian systems of mainland Europe, placed limits on testamentary freedom by providing a fixed share of a deceased's estate for his surviving spouse and children and our legislators, who were impressed by the greater equity of the civilian systems, sought to replicate certain of those provisions in Part IX of the Succession Act.[3]

7.1.2 During the second stage reading of the Succession Bill the Minister for Justice argued, that the right to disinherit one's spouse and family was not a fundamental right inherent in property, and that there was no real basis, moral or historical, for the view that it was.[4] The Minister pointed out that in Roman law freedom of testation was considerably restricted by derived from a the Romans, the *legitima portio* existed in one form or

---

[1] It has been argued by some commentators that freedom of testation was less an immutable principle of English law than is commonly supposed. See Mellows (1963) 2 Soer. Qtrly. 109

[2] See *ante* p. 64

[3] See the Explanatory Memorandum with the Succession Bill at pp. 9 *et seq.*

[4] See the speech of the Minister for Justice during the second reading of the Succession Bill: Dail Debates Vol. 215, cols. 2016–2033

derived from a the Romans, the *legitima portio* existed in one form or other.[5] The Minister further argued that the principle of freedom of testation was a peculiarly English phenomenon which had been foisted on the Irish people with the enactment of the Irish Statute of Distributions in 1695.[6] Section 10 of the latter statute had abolished the so-called "Custom of Ireland" by which one third only of one's personal estate was disposable by will.[7]

7.1.3 The Minister referred to other compelling reasons for the diminution of the principle of freedom of testation not the least of which was the recognition in the Constitution of the family, as a "moral institution possessing inalienable and imprescriptible rights antecedent and superior to all positive law."[8] The Minister argued that in the context of this constitutional view of the family- freedom of testation was an indefensible paradox which was heightened by Article 41 of the Constitution, which recognises the support which a married woman gives to the state by her life within the home, without which the common good could not be achieved; the state for its part undertaking to ensure that mothers should not be obliged, by economic necessity, to engage in labour to the neglect of their duties in the home.[9] Such principle, it was argued, could not be reconciled with a system of law which allowed a man to disinherit his spouse and leave his property to strangers.

7.1.4 While there was general agreement on all sides in Dail Eireann on the need to place some restrictions on testamentary freedom, there was disagreement on the method to be employed, whether it should be one based on judicial discretion as in the English and Commonwealth systems, or one based on fixed shares in the deceased's estate as in the civil law systems.[10] In the event a compromise was effected between the competing systems in Part IX of the Succession Act, which gives to the surviving spouse a fixed share of the deceased's estate, and gives to a surviving child the right to apply to the court for a provision to be made out of the deceased's estate on the ground that he has failed to make proper provision for the applicant child in accordance with his means.[11]

[5] *Ibid*

[6] 7 Will 3 c. 6

[7] See the observations of Walsh J. in *Re Urquhart* [1974] I.R. 197, 208–209. See Wylie "A Casebook on Irish Land Law" at p. 516

[8] Article 41 1.1

[9] In *B.L.* v *M.L.*, unreported High Court judgement delivered 3rd October 1988, Barr J. invoked Article 41 to give a wife *qua* wife a beneficial interest in the matrimonial home. The case has gone on appeal to the Supreme Court.

[10] See Cooney "Succession and Judicial Discretion in Ireland" (1980) Irish Jurist (n.s.) 62

[11] See *post* p. 197

7.1.5 Part IX of the Succession Act, which includes sections 109 to 119, applies where a person dies wholly or partly testate, leaving a spouse or children or both spouse and children.[12] References to the estate of a testator in Part IX are to all estate to which he was beneficially entitled for an estate or interest not ceasing on his death and remaining after payment of all expenses, debts and liabilities, other than estate duty properly payable thereout.[13]

7.2 Legal right of surviving spouse

7.2.1 The right of the surviving spouse to a share in a testator's estate is contained in Section 111 which provides, that if the testator leaves a spouse and no children, the spouse shall have a right to one-half of the estate; if the testator leaves a spouse and children, the spouse shall have a right to one-third of the estate. The right of the surviving spouse, which is to be known as a legal right, is to have priority over devises, bequests, and shares on intestacy, and thus ranks in priority after the rights of creditors of the deceased.[14]

7.2.2 Kenny J. in *Re G.M: F.M.* v *T.A.M. and others*[15] contrasted the legal right given to a surviving spouse by section 111 of the Succession Act with comparable legislation in England, New Zealand and New South Wales, and pointed out that the concept underlying the legislation in the latter jurisdictions is, that a testator has a duty to make reasonable provision for the maintenance of his widow, whereas the concept underlying the Succession Act is not based on a duty to provide maintenance but rather on the idea that a testator has a duty to leave part of his estate to his widow.[16]

7.2.3 The legal right of a spouse may be renounced in an ante-nuptial contract in writing between the parties to an intended marriage, and it may also be renounced by a spouse in writing after marriage and during the lifetime of the testator.[17] There is no apparent advantage accruing to a spouse who renounces her legal right, rather the reverse it would seem, and in the absence of some consideration moving from the promisee such a contract would have to be under seal. If the contract is entered into prior to marriage the renunciation of the legal right might well be the other spouse's price for undertaking the marriage, but such condition would raise questions of public policy, not least those which undergird the existence of

---

[12] Section 109 (1)
[13] Section 109 (2)
[14] Section 112
[15] (1972) 106 I.L.T.R. 82
[16] *Ibid* at p. 86
[17] Section 113

a legal right in the surviving spouse.[18] An example of a benign circumstance in which a spouse would be asked to renounce his or her legal right is one where a couple, the female member of which is past the age of child-bearing, enter into a second marriage after the deaths of their former partners and intend the children of their first marriages to succeed to their respective estates.

7.2.4 It is also the case that the court will carefully scrutinise a contract where there is a social or economic imbalance between the parties where, for example, one of the parties is less well-educated than the others or is for some other reason unable to look after his or her interests.[19] While many spouses, and aspirant spouses, fall into one or other of the categories of vulnerable persons whom the court seeks to protect, it is arguable that a contract which renounces a spouse's legal right is one which should, without more, merit the closest scrutiny by the court.

7.2.5 There are at least four possible grounds on which such a contract might be impugned. Firstly, a spouse might claim that the contract was procured or induced by the undue influence of her husband.[20] Secondly-she might claim that she did not know, nor was she given an opportunity of understanding, the contents or the effect of the contract.[21] Thirdly,she might claim that she entered into the contract without the benefit of independent legal advice.[22] Lastly, a spouse might claim that the contract

---

[18] Which can be said to be that a surviving spouse will be properly provided for from the estate of a deceased person and not be dependent upon the goodwill or indulgence of the deceased.

[19] See generally Clark "Inequality of Bargaining Power" (1987)

[20] While no presumption of undue influence arises from the relationship of husband and wife the relationship would seem to be peculiarly amenable to the principle stated by Lord Chelmsford L.C. in *Tate* v *Williamson* (1886) L.R. 2 Ch. 55, 61, to the effect that wherever "two persons stand in such a relation that, while it continues, confidence is necessarily reposed by one, and the influence which naturally grows out of that confidence is possessed by the other, and this confidence is abused, or the influence is exerted to obtain an advantage at the expense of the confiding party, the person so availing himself of his position will not be permitted to retain the advantage, although the transaction could not have been impeached if no such confidential relation had existed."

[21] Most of the reported cases dealing with the principles affecting the husband and wife relationship have been concerned with the giving of security by a wife for a loan etc. made to her husband and her understanding of the nature of the loan. See *National Westminster Bank plc* v *Morgan* [1985] A.C. 686 and generally Keane "Equity and the Law of Trusts in the Republic of Ireland" at pp. 334 *et seq*.

[22] Lord Hailsham pointed out in *Inche Norian* v *Shain Allie Bin Omar* [1929] A.C. 127, 135 that the most obvious way to prove that a transaction was the result of the free exercise of an independent will was to establish that its nature and effect had been so fully explained to a donor by some independent and qualified person that the court was satisfied that he was acting independently of any influence from the donee and with full appreciation of what he was doing. See also *Gregg* v *Kidd* [1956] I.R. 183 and *Zamet* v *Hyman* [1961] 1 W.L.R. 1442 (engaged couple)

was an improvident one which the court should set aside in the exercise of its inherent equity jurisdiction.[23] This latter ground may be implicit in, or additional to, one of the other grounds and it has been pointed out that "the very improvidence of the bargain will produce intervention, regardless of the degree of advice present to the party who seeks relief."[24]

7.2.6 All the aforementioned grounds were considered by Keane J. in *J.H.* v *W.J.H.*[25], where the plaintiff, who was entitled to a legal right share in the estate of her deceased husband, had entered into a contract with her son by which she agreed to forego her legal right. Keane J. concluded that the evidence fell short of establishing that the plaintiff did not know or approve of the contents of the agreement, but it was none the less an improvident transaction which would normally be set aside by the court exercising its equitable jurisdiction. Keane J.'s observations on the contract before him would apply *a fortiori* to a contract between spouses. The plaintiff failed to have the contract set aside in the instant case because she had not acted with a promptitude which a court of is entitled to expect and had slept on her rights.[26]

7.2.7 It is an ironic fact that contracts in which spouses renounce their legal rights are most commonly encountered in practice as reciprocal parts of separation agreements when marriages have broken down. Such contracts would invariably be drawn up by professional legal advisers.

7.2.8 Where a devise or bequest is expressed in a will to be in addition to the share as a legal right of the surviving spouse, the testator is deemed to have made, by the will, a gift to the spouse consisting of, (a) a sum equal to the value of the share as a legal right of the spouse, and (b) the property so devised or bequeathed.[27] In the absence of such an express provision, a devise or bequest in a will to a spouse shall be deemed to have been intended by the testator to be in satisfaction of the share as a legal right of the spouse.[28]

---

[23] The equity jurisdiction had evolved to deal with cases involving expectant heirs but Lord Hatherly pointed out in *O'Rorke* v *Bolingbroke* (1877) 2 App. Cas. 814 that the principle being established the court "extended its aid to all cases in which the parties to a contract have not met on equal terms."

[24] See Clark "Inequality of Bargaining Power" at p. 150

[25] Unreported High Court judgement of Keane J. delivered 20th December 1979: 1977 No. 5831 P.

[26] *Ibid* at pp. 32–3. Keane J. referred to Snell's *Principles of Equity* (27th ed.) at p. 35 which defines laches as consisting essentially of a substantial lapse of time coupled with the existence of circumstances which make it inequitable to enforce a claim.

[27] Section 114 (1)

[28] Section 114 (2)

186

7.2.9 Of decreasing importance is section 116 which applies only to provisions made before the commencement of the act.[28a] That section provides, that where a testator has, during his lifetime, made permanent provision for his spouse, whether by contract or otherwise, all property which is the subject of such provision (other than periodical payments made for her maintenance during his lifetime) shall be taken as being given, in or towards satisfaction of, the share as a legal right of the surviving spouse.[28b] The value of such property is to be reckoned as at the date of the making of the provision, and if the value of the property is equal to, or greater than, the share of the spouse as a legal right, the spouse shall not be entitled to take any share as a legal right.[28c] If the value of the property is less than the share of the spouse as a legal right, the spouse is entitled to receive in satisfaction of such share so much only of the estate as when added to the value of the property is sufficient, as nearly as can be estimated, to make up the full amount of that share.[28d]

7.3. Election between legal right and rights under a will and on partial intestacy.

7.3.1 Where there is a devise or bequest to a spouse in the will of a deceased person who dies wholly testate such spouse may elect to take either that devise or bequest, or the share to which he or she is entitled as a legal right.[29] In default of election the spouse shall be entitled to take under the will and shall not be entitled to take any share as a legal right.[30] Likewise, where a person dies partly testate and partly intestate the surviving spouse may elect to take either (1) his or her share as a legal right, or (11) his or her share under the intestacy, together with any devise or bequest under the will of the deceased.[30] In default of election the surviving spouse shall be entitled to take his or her share under the intestacy, together with any devise or bequest under the will, and shall not be entitled to take any share as a legal right.[31]

[28a] The Succession Act commenced on 1st January 1970.

[28b] Section 116 (1)

[28c] Section 116 subsections (2) and (3)

[28d] Section 116 (4)

[29] Section 115 (1) (a)

[30] Section 115 (1) (b)

[30a] Section 115 (2) (a)

[31] Section 115 (2) (b)

7.3.2 A spouse, in electing to take his or her legal right share, may further elect to take any devise or bequest to him or her in the will which is less in value than the legal right share, in partial satisfaction thereof.[32]

7.3.3 The personal representatives of the deceased have a duty to notify the spouse, in writing, of the right of election conferred by section 115, which right shall not be exercisable after the expiration of six months from the receipt by the spouse of such notification, or one year from the first taking out of representation of the deceased's estate, whichever is the later.[33] This latter limitation period thus differs from that in respect of claims under section 111 which are governed by section 45 of the Statute of Limitations 1957, as amended by section 126 of the Succession Act, which provides that no action in respect of any claim to the estate of a deceased person, whether under a will, or intestacy, or under section 111 of the Succession Act, shall be brought after the expiration of six years from the date when the right to receive the share or interest accrued.[34]

7.3.4 Keane J. pointed out in *J.H.* v *W.J.H.*[35] that since, in default of election under section 115, the spouse may take only under the will, it follows that not merely is the right to enforce payment of the legal right postponed until a valid election is made, but also the right of the personal representative to transfer and the spouse to receive the share is also postponed. The legal right of a spouse under section 111 is thus entirely different from the interest of a legatee who is precluded from instituting proceedings for the payment of his legacy within the so-called executor's year, but otherwise his right to receive payment of his legacy dates from the death of the testator.[36]

7.3.5 There are other less obvious points about the operation of section 115 which emerged in *J.H.* v *W.J.H.*.. Although the limitation period in respect of election does not begin to run until the service of notice on the spouse by the personal representative, the spouse is not precluded from exercising the right of election before the service of such notice.[37] It is also the case

---

[32] Section 115 (3)

[33] Section 115 (4)

[34] See Brady and Kerr "The Limitation of Actions in the Republic of Ireland" at pp. 84 *et seq.*

[35] Unreported High Court judgement delivered 20th December 1979

[36] See *post* p. 289

[37] Keane J. pointed out that it is in no sense a necessary feature of the statutory scheme under s. 115 that the spouse should be precluded from exercising her right of election prior to the service of notice by the personal representatives under s. 115 (4). (See page 13 of the unreported judgement).

that the very act of a spouse in requesting or claiming payment of the legal right constitutes an election under section 115.[38] While the right of a spouse to receive payment must technically be preceded by an election to take the legal right, it could be difficult in practice to identify a preliminary act of election and such is clearly not necessary.[39]

7.3.6 It was argued in *J.H.* v *W.J.H.* that the aforementioned construction of sections 111 and 115 was anomalous in that it placed a spouse for whom provision was made in a will in a more favourable position than a spouse for whom no provision was made, since time would run against the former only when he or she received notice of the right of election. Keane J. pointed out that this would be so only if the personal representative failed in his express statutory duty of serving notice under section 115 and while he conceded that a personal representative might neglect to carry out his statutory duty he saw no reason why, in the case of a dilatory personal representative, the other beneficiaries affected should not be able to institute proceedings claiming administration of the estate and, if necessary, an order requiring the personal representative to fulfil his statutory duty.[40]

7.3.7 Whether a surviving spouse can be said to have acquired the legal right share under section 111 before he or she has elected to take it under section 115 also arose in the somewhat unusual circumstances of *Re Urquhart*.[41] There, a wife had bequeathed a legacy to her husband, on condition that he should survive her for at least one month.[42] The parties were involved in an automobile accident and the husband, who survived his wife for one day only, died without having regained consciousness. The husband thus died without having made an election pursuant to section 115 of the Succession Act, and in the events which happened his estate was benefitted neither by his legal right share in his wife's estate or the legacy in her will. Nevertheless, the Revenue Commissioners claimed that a one-half share in the wife's estate was property which the husband was competent to dispose of at the time of his death for the purposes of the Finance Act 1894.[43] Kenny J. having upheld the Revenue Commissioners' claim, the husband's executors appealed to the Supreme Court.

---

[38] See Brady and Kerr "The Limitation of Actions" at pp. 87–8

[39] Keane J. found in the instant case that the spouse had exercised her right of election in a letter from her solicitors to the defendant who was the sole executor and principal beneficiary of her late husband's will. (See p. 22 of Keane J.'s judgement).

[40] *Ibid* at pp. 25–26

[41] [1974] I.R. 197

[42] The husband made his will in similar terms.

[43] Section 2 (1) (a) of the 1894 Act provided that property passing on the death of a deceased person "shall be deemed to include the property following, that is to say:— (a) Property of which the deceased was at the time of his death competent to dispose."

7.3.8 The Supreme Court in a majority judgment (Fitzgerald C.J. and Walsh J., Henchy J. dissenting) allowed the appeal. The majority took the view that the husband could not be said to be in a position to dispose of a one-half in his wife's estate until he had made an election to take his legal right share. Walsh J. pointed out, that where there is no legacy or devise in a will, or where there is a legacy or devise expressed to be in addition to the legal right share of the surviving spouse, the legal right share vests upon the death of the testator. But, when a testator in his will makes a devise or bequest to a spouse which is not expressed to be in addition to the share as a legal right, then the spouse has a statutory right to take the legal right share, but such share does not vest until the spouse elects to take it. If the spouse does not so elect, then any legacy or devise under the will which vested in the spouse on the death of the testator will remain vested, without the spouse having to take any steps in relation to it.[44]

7.3.9 Fitzgerald C.J. felt fortified in his conclusion that the husband could not be deemed competent to dispose of his legal right share in his wife's estate without electing to take the share, by subsections 4 and 5 of section 115 which specifically provide for a case where the surviving spouse is of unsound mind and, consequently, not in a position to exercise the election himself. Section 115 (5) reads:

> "where the surviving spouse is a person of unsound mind, the right of election conferred by this section may, if there is a committee of the spouse's estate, be exercised on behalf of the spouse by the committee by leave of the court which has appointed the committee or, if there is no committee, be exercised by the High Court or, in a case within the jurisdiction of the Circuit Court, by that Court."[45]

7.3.10 Henchy J., in his dissenting judgment, could not accept that an election by the surviving spouse was a condition precedent to the existence of a competency to dispose of the legal right share, since he could see no reason why the election and the disposition could not coalesce in one legal act. Once the husband had the power to make the property his own, as he undoubtedly had, he also had the power to dispose of it, and all that stood between him and the exercise of that power was his state of health which, it was agreed, was an irrelevant consideration for the purposes of this case, Henchy J. admitted that his construction meant that the husband's estate was burdened with estate duty on property that was never part of the estate, but such an artificial basis for the incidence of estate duty has been part of our law since 1894.

[44] [1974] I.R. 197, 211
[45] *Ibid* at p. 204

7.3.11 It is difficult to find fault with Henchy J.'s reasoning and his conclusion, that it is for the legislature to introduce amending legislation to relieve against the wider incidence of estate duty resulting from the operation of Part IX of the Succession Act.

7.4 Right of surviving spouse to acquire family dwelling and household chattels

7.4.1 Given the constitutional rhetoric concerning the wife's place in the home which the Minister for Justice employed in defending the proposed diminution in the principle of freedom of testation, it was a modest and relatively uncontentious step to give the surviving spouse the right to acquire the family home in which she had served the public interest.[46]

7.4.2 Accordingly section 56 (1) of the Succession Act provides, that where the estate of a deceased person includes a dwelling in which, at the time of the deceased's death, the surviving spouse was ordinarily resident, the surviving spouse may require the personal representatives in writing to appropriate the dwelling under section 55 in or towards satisfaction of any share of the surviving spouse.[47] "Dwelling" here means an estate or interest in a building occupied as a separate dwelling or a part, so occupied, of any building and includes any garden or portion of ground attached to, and usually occupied with, the dwelling, or otherwise required for the amenity or convenience of the dwelling.[48]

7.4.3 The surviving spouse may also require the personal representatives in writing to appropriate any household chattels in or towards satisfaction of his or her share.[49] The term "household chattels" includes furniture, linen, china, glass, books, and other chattels of ordinary household use or market and consumable stores, garden effects and domestic animals but, does not include chattels used at the death of the deceased for business or professional purposes, or money, or security for money.[50]

7.4.4 The personal representatives of the deceased have a duty to notify the surviving spouse in writing of his or her rights under section 56, which rights must be exercised within six months from the receipt by the surviving spouse of the written notification or one year from the first taking out of representation, whichever is the later.[51] The rights to require appropriation under section 56 arise whether the deceased dies testate or intestate.

[46] See *ante* p. 183
[47] This provision is new to Irish law.
[48] Section 56 (14)
[49] Section 56 (2)
[50] Section 56 (14)
[51] Section 56 (4)

7.4.5 During the subsistence of rights to require appropriation by the surviving spouse the personal representatives shall not, without the written consent of the surviving spouse, or, in appropriate cases, the leave of the court, [52] sell or otherwise dispose of the dwelling or household chattels except in the course of administration owing to want of other assets. [53] The right of the surviving spouse to require the appropriation of the family home provides an interesting contrast with the rights of a non-owning spouse in the family home during the life of the other spouse. The Irish legislature has stopped short of giving a spouse *qua* spouse a proprietary interest in the so-called matrimonial home, being content merely to provide that the non-owning spouse must give his or her written consent to its transfer. [54]

7.4.6 Where the share of a surviving spouse is insufficient to enable the right to require appropriation to be exercised in respect of the family home, or household chattels, as the case may be, the right may also be exercised in relation to the share of any infant for whom the surviving spouse is a trustee under section 57 or otherwise. [55] Interestingly, the latter infant need not be a child of the deceased, but it could be said that limiting the right to share in the appropriation to children of the deceased would not have been calculated to assist in the primary purpose of section 56 which is to give to the surviving spouse the right to remain in the family home after the death of the deceased. In practical terms the infant whose share will be called in aid by the surviving spouse will be a child of the deceased or someone to whom the deceased stood in *loco parentis*.

7.4.7 If a surviving spouse is obliged to call in aid the share of any infant, it has been argued, that the surviving spouse should hold the family home on trust for herself, or himself, and the infant as tenants in common in proportion to their respective contributions. [56] Section 56 is silent on the matter, but it is also arguable that since the main thrust of the section is to secure the place of the surviving spouse in the family homehand such infant will invariably have succession rights to the estate of the surviving spouse, it is unnecessary to give such infant a share in the family home at the time of its appropriation under section 56.

7..4.8 If the family home and household chattels are worth more than the shares of the surviving spouse and any such infant, the surviving spouse

---

[52] Given on the refusal of an application under subsection (5) (b)

[53] Section 56 (8) (a) which subsection does not apply where the surviving spouse is a personal representative (see s. 56 (8) (b)).

[54] See the Family Home Protection Act, 1976, (No. 27)

[55] Section 56 (3)

[56] See McGuire and Pearce "The Succession Act, 1965: A Commentary" at p. 142

may settle up the balance in cash.[57] The court however may, if of opinion that in the special circumstances of the case hardship would otherwise be caused to the surviving spouse, or to the surviving spouse and any such infant, order that appropriation be made without the payment of such balance in cash, or with the payment of such amount as the court considers reasonable[58]

7.4.9 Where appropriation is ordered, the court may make such further order in relation to the administration of the deceased's estate as may appear to it to be just and equitable, having regard to all the circumstances. We are told in the Explanatory Memorandum that the purpose of this additional power is to enable the court not alone to appropriate the dwelling and household chattels, but also to deal with any consequential problems that may arise, thus avoiding the need for an administration suit where legacies to persons other than the spouse may have to abate in consequence of the appropriation.[59]

7.4.10 The question arose in *Re Hamilton, Hamilton* v *Armstrong*[60] whether, when a surviving spouse had claimed her right to require appropriation of the family home, and contents thereof, but died before appropriation was completed, her personal representatives could enforce her claim. There, the surviving spouse had elected to take her legal right share of her deceased husband's estate and applied to have the family home and contents appropriated in satisfaction of her claim. She died shortly after the institution of proceedings in which she asked the court to declare her entitlement to the family home and a five acre field attached to same, and these proceedings were reconstructed by substituting her acting executor as plaintiff in her place.

7.4.11 O'Hanlon J. held, that the widow's election in favour of her legal right constituted a claim against the husband's estate which could be enforced on behalf of her estate and, similarly, when she had applied for the appropriation of the family home in satisfaction of her claim an equity arose immediately in her favour which could be enforced by her personal representatives should she herself die before her husband's personal representatives has appropriated the dwelling in her favour.[61] This entitlement is subject to the obligation on the part of the surviving spouse, or his or her personal representatives as the case may be, to pay any balance that may be necessary to make up the difference in value between the share of

---

[57] Section 56 (9)
[58] Section 56 (10) (b)
[59] Explanatory Memorandum at para. 33 p. 5.
[60] (1984) I.L.R.M. 306
[61] *Ibid* at p. 310

the surviving spouse and the value of the dwelling which is to be appropriated. It seemed equitable to O'Hanlon, J. that the two valuations should be made with reference to the time when the request for appropriation was made.[62]

7.5 Limits on right to require appropriation

7.5.1 With respect to certain types of dwelling, the right to require appropriation is subject to the authorisation of a court, which must be satisfied, on application made by the personal representatives or the surviving spouse, that the exercise of that right is unlikely to diminish the value of the assets of the deceased other than the dwelling, or to make it more difficult to dispose of them in due course of administration.[63] Authorisation by the court must be sought where (a) the dwelling forms part of a building, and an estate or interest in the whole building forms part of the estate; (b) where the dwelling is held with agricultural land an estate or interest in which forms part of the estate; (c) where the whole or part of the dwelling was, at the time of the death, used as a hotel, guest house or boarding house; (d) where a part of the dwelling was, at the time of death, used for purposes other than domestic purposes.[64]

7.5.2 The limits on the right of a surviving spouse to require the appropriation of a dwelling which is located on agricultural land were considered in *H. v H.*[65] There a testator who died without issue leaving his widow, the plaintiff, surviving him, had left all his property which comprised some 113 acres and a dwelling, in which he had resided with the plaintiff, to Joseph H., the second named defendant, for his own benefit absolutely, subject to a right of the plaintiff to the exclusive use of a bedroom in the dwelling. The plaintiff, not surprisingly, elected under section 115 to exercise her legal right to one-half of the estate, and she required the first named defendant, as personal representative, to appropriate the dwelling and household chattels to her in satisfaction of her claim. Joseph H. objected to the appropriation of the dwelling to the plaintiff and the court had to determine if the appropriation was allowable under subsections (5) and (6) of section 56.

---

[62] *Ibid.* O'Hanlon J. also allowed the surviving spouse to appropriate with the dwelling a five acre field located immediately to the rear of the dwelling. O'Hanlon J. did not consider the field to be a "garden" within s. 56 (14), nor was it required for the amenity or convenience of the dwelling. It was however a portion of ground attached to the dwelling and the location on it of a septic tank which served the house and a well from which the house drew its supply of water led O'Hanlon J. to the conclusion that the widow was entitled to appropriate it as part of the dwelling.

[63] Section 56 (5) (b)

[64] Section 56 (b)

[65] [1978] I.R. 138. See Wylie "A Casebook on Irish Land Law" at p. 526.

7.5.3 Kenny J. held, in the High Court, that when the dwelling sought to be appropriated is held with agricultural land the onus of establishing to the satisfaction of the court that the exercise of the right of appropriation is unlikely to diminish the value of the assets other than the dwelling, and that it will not make it more difficult to dispose of them in due course of administration, is on the surviving spouse who wishes to exercise this right.

7.5.4 Kenny J. went on to address the question whether, when the surviving spouse, exercising her legal right, is entitled to one half the holding of land upon which the dwelling is located, does the value of the assets other than the dwelling mean all assets other than the dwelling, or the assets to which the other beneficiaries become entitled. If it meant the former Kenny J. believed, the right of appropriation could never be exercised when the dwelling is held with agricultural land for a residential holding, particularly a large one, is always more valuable than a non-residential one. But that seemed to the learned judge to be contrary to the purpose of section 56, for it would exclude all residential holdings from the right to appropriate and, that being so, it seemed to Kenny J. that the phrase "value of the assets other than the dwelling" in subsection (5)(b) means the value of the assets to which the beneficiaries other than the surviving spouse become entitled.[65a]

7.5.5 The Supreme Court (Parke J., Griffin J. and Henchy J.) affirmed Kenny J.'s finding that the onus of proof, in relation to the matters outlined in subsection (5)(b), lies upon the applicant spouse, but the court rejected the view, which was accepted by Kenny J., that the word "or" which separates the expressions "diminish the value of the assets of the deceased other than the dwelling" and "to make it more difficult to dispose of them in due course of administration" is disjunctive, and an applicant could discharge the onus of proof by establishing one or other of the requirements in subsection (5)(b).

7.5.6 The Supreme Court also rejected Kenny J.'s interpretation of the phrase "assets of the deceased other than the dwelling", holding that such assets included assets passing to a surviving spouse who has exercised her legal right to one-third or one-half of the deceased's estate, as the case may be. Parke J., who delivered the judgment of the court, did not agree with Kenny J. that it necessarily follows that a residential agricultural holding is more valuable than a non residential one. Parke J. believed that the common experience of the courts afforded many examples to the contrary, and he instanced the case of a large, old and dilapidated dwelling which will frequently diminish the value of the holding. He also referred to cases,

[65a] *Ibid* at p. 144

which he claimed were common enough nowadays, where there are two dwellings on a holding the exclusion of one of which will probably increase the value of what is left. These and other examples cited in argument reinforced Parke J.'s conclusion that it was not necessary to interfere with the clear wording of the legislation to avoid an irrational meaning or effect.[66]

7.5.7 With respect to Parke J., his ruminations on the circumstances which might attend the exercise of the right to require the appropriation of a dwelling on agricultural land are no less fanciful than those of Kenny J. Since the surviving spouse will ordinarily be seeking the appropriation of the dwelling in which she resided with the deceased such dwelling will not, in the usual case, be large, old and dilapidated. The first two adjectives might occasionally be relevant but the third rarely, if ever. It is also barely conceivable that of two dwellings on agricultural land the claimant spouse would have lived in, and be seeking to have appropriated, the less valuable and more ramshackle of the two.

7.5.8 It is arguably the case that the legislature and parliamentary draughtsmen simply failed to address the many ramifications of the right to require appropriation as it applies to dwellings on agricultural land. It is worth noting that during the second stage of the Succession Bill in the Seanad the Minister for Justice said, of section 56, that it would apply mainly to dwellings in urban areas.[67] Kenny J. felt obliged to point out in *H. v H.*[68] that it is a grave defect of the Succession Act that it does not provide any method by which lands may be divided between a widow, who is entitled to a one-third or one-half share, and the other beneficiaries and the only remedy, when agreement cannot be reached, is the expensive, cumbersome and dilatory action for partition.

7.5.9 The unsatisfactory and inconclusive nature of the provisions in section 56 is underlined by the fact that on the same day that Kenny J. gave judgment in her favour in *H. v H.* a second action was initiated by the plaintiff in the High Court, which was aimed primarily at getting an order under section 55 of the Succession Act allowing the first named defendant, as personal representative, to appropriate to her the part of the lands on which the dwelling stood in or towards satisfaction of her half share in the deceased's estate. McWilliam J. having made the order sought in the High Court, an appeal was taken to the Supreme Court.[69]

---

[66] *Ibid* at pp. 147, 148
[67] Dail Debates (Vol. 216 col. 155)
[68] [1978] I.R. 138, 141
[69] *H. v O.* [1978] I.R. 194. See Wylie "A Casebook on Irish Land Law" at p. 529

7.5.10 Henchy J., who delivered the judgment of the Supreme Court, pointed out that the right of appropriation given by section 55 is an enabling right, which may be exercised only by the personal representative, and a person entitled to a share in the estate is given no right to compel the personal representative to propose an appropriation under section 55. The personal representative had not chosen to operate the section so, strictly speaking, the plaintiff was misconceived in her efforts to compel him to do so. However in the High Court McWilliam J. had treated the personal representative as having served the notice of intended appropriation which is required by section 55 (3). Henchy J. did not think that this was correct, but, since counsel for the personal representative raised no objection to his being deemed to have served the necessary notice, and as all interested parties were before the court and none claimed to be prejudiced in any way by want of notice, the learned judge dealt with the matter on the footing that the personal representative was willing to operate section 55 and that the statutory preconditions as to notice had been complied with.[70]

7.5.11 Henchy J. wished to stress, that a beneficiary is not given any right to compel a personal representative to exercise a right of appropriation under section 55, and it was only because of the special circumstances in the instant case that the personal representative was being treated as having taken the necessary steps for an appropriation under section 55. Not the least of the special reasons for this eminently sound decision was the almost certain fact that a dismiss of this action would have the effect of burdening the estate with yet another High Court action.[71]

7.6 Rights of Children

7.6.1 With respect to the right of a child of the testator to claim a share of his estate, Part IX of the Succession Act, as we have seen, adopts the system of judicial discretion favoured in England and most Commonwealth countries rather than the fixed share system of the civil law jurisdictions.[72] Thus, it is provided in section 117(1) that, where on application by or on behalf of a child of a testator

"the court is of opinion that the testator has failed in his moral duty to make proper provision for the child in accordance with his means, whether by his will or otherwise, the court may order that such provision shall be made for the child out of the estate as the court thinks just."

7.6.2 The court must consider such application from the point of view of a prudent and just parent,

[70] *Ibid* at p. 205
[71] *Ibid*
[72] See *ante* p. 183

"taking into account the position of each of the children of the testator and any other circumstances which the court may consider of assistance in arriving at a decision that will be as fair as possible to the child to whom the application relates and to the other children."[73]

An order making provision for an applicant child may not, however, affect the legal right of a surviving spouse or, if the surviving spouse is the mother or father of the child, any devise or bequest to the spouse or any share to which the spouse is entitled on intestacy.[74]

7.6.3 It first fell to Kenny J. in *Re G.M.; F.M.* v. *T.A.M. and others*[75] to consider the scope and effect of section 117, and his formulation of the criteria which should govern the exercise of the court's discretion has been followed, with varying degrees of enthusiasm in subsequent cases. The facts of *Re G.M.* briefly were, that the testator who owned substantial property interests in the Republic of Ireland and England left all his property in the Republic of Ireland on trust for his wife for life, and, after her death, for his two nephews. There were no children of the marriage, but in 1941 the wife, with the testator's somewhat grudging consent, had informally adopted the plaintiff applicant, and the adoption had been formalised in 1952 when the Adoption Board made an order under the Adoption Act of that year.[76] The Succession Act provides in section 110 that an adopted child is in the same position as a child born of the marriage and, the testator having made no provision in his will for his adopted son, the latter made an application to the court under section 117.

7.6.4 The plaintiff, who was 32 years old at the time of the applications was a merchant seaman and married with two children of his own. He was therefore not dependent on the testator at the time of the testator's death but, Kenny J pointed out in the High Court, section 117 of the Succession Act, unlike comparable legislation in England and certain Commonwealth countries, is not limited in its application to dependent children.[77] His analysis of section 117 showed Kenny J. that the duty which it creates is not absolute, because it does not apply if the testator leaves all his property to his spouse, nor is it an obligation to each child to leave him something. Kenny J. went on:

"The obligation to make proper provision may be fulfilled by will or otherwise and so gifts or settlements made during the lifetime of the

[73] Section 117 (2)

[74] Section 117 (3)

[75] (1972) 106 I.L.T.R. 82

[76] There was no formal adoption in Ireland prior to the Adoption Act 1952, (No. 28)

[77] (1972) 106 I.L.T.R. 82, 86

testator in favour of a child or the provision of an expensive education for one child when the others have not received this may discharge the moral duty. It follows, I think, that the relationship of parent and child does not of itself and without regard to other circumstances create a moral duty to leave anything by will to the child. The duty is not to make adequate provision *but to make proper provision in accordance with the testator's means.*"[78] (emphasis added).

7.6.5 It seemed to Kenny J. that the existence of a moral duty to make proper provision for a child must be judged by the facts existing at the date of death, and must depend on (a) the amount left to the surviving spouse or to the value of the legal right if the survivor elects to take this, (b) the number of the testator's children, their ages and their positions in life at the date of the testator's death, (c) the means of the testator, (d) the age of the child whose case is being considered and his or her financial position and prospects in life, and, (e) whether the testator has already in his lifetime made proper provision for the child. Kenny J. added that the exercise of the duty must be judged by objective considerations, and the view of the testator that he did not owe a duty is not decisive.[79]

7.6.6 When he applied the foregoing criteria to the facts of the instant case, Kenny J. found that the testator had failed to make proper provision for the applicant in accordance with his means and, having so found, the learned judge then had to determine what provision should be made for the applicant out of the testator's estate, which was worth some £135,000. Kenny J. pointed out that the court

> "when deciding whether the moral duty has been fulfilled must take all the testator's property (including immoveable property outside the Republic of Ireland) into account, but if it decides that the duty has not been discharged, the provision for the child is to be made out of the estate excluding that immoveable property."[80]

Kenny J. accordingly held that a prudent and just parent would have given the plaintiff applicant one half of the testator's estate, excluding the immoveable property in England. Finlay C.J. delivering the judgment of the Supreme Court *nem. diss.* in *C. and Ch.* v *W.C. and T.C.*[80a] adopted and approved of Kenny J.'s statement in *Re G.M.*; *F.M.* v *T.A.M. and Others* of the principles applicable to applications under s. 117. Finlay C.J. added to it, however, further principles "which may to an extent be considered a qualification to it."[80b] The Chief Justice was satisfied that the

[78] *Ibid* at p. 87   [79] *Ibid*   [80] *Ibid*
[80a] Unreported Supreme Court Judgment delivered 24 July 1989
[80b] *Ibid* at p. 8

reference in s. 117(1) to a testator's failure in his moral duty to make proper provision for the child in accordance with his means, places a relatively high onus of proof on an applicant for relief under s. 117 and it would not be sufficient for such an applicant to establish that the provision made for him was not as great as it might have been, or appeared ungenerous compared with bequests to other children or beneficiaries in the will.

The court should not, Finlay C.J. considered, make an Order under s. 117 merely because it would on the facts proved have made different testamentary dispositions. The Chief Justice went on to say that a "positive failure in moral duty must be established."[80c] Finlay C.J. arguably added little to Kenny J.'s criteria by which failure of such moral duty is to be determined since under that criteria more generous provision in the will for other children or beneficiaries than the applicant would not, without more, be conclusive of the failure of moral duty. The court would also have to take cognisance of any *inter vivos* provisions made by the deceased for the applicant child. Interestingly Finlay C.J. laid great importance on the relationship between the applicant and the deceased during the latter's life and if that relationship was "one of caring and kindness" the court should "entertain some significant reluctance to vary the testator's disposition by will."[80d] On the other hand quite different considerations may apply where a marked hostility had been established to the satisfaction of the court, between the deceased and a particular child.

The most loving and caring of parents may well misconceive the extent of his moral duty to make proper provision for a particular child and however close the relationship between parent and child the court must determine, objectively, whether that duty has been fulfilled. It means to the present writer that Kenny in *Re G.M. F.M.* v *T.A.M. and Others* adequately established the objective criteria for the determination of the question whether that duty has been fulfilled.

Finlay C.J.'s emphasis on the heavy burden which lies on an applicant child under s. 117 may well stem the growing tide of s. 117 applications, but, it is to be hoped, that it will deter only the avaricious and frivolous and not the child who is genuinely "hard done by."

7.6.7 That the death of the testator is the crucial time in determining whether he has provided properly for an applicant child in accordance with his means is starkly underlined by the facts in *Re W.: W.* v *D.*[81] There the testator had made a will in 1962 which, because of altered circumstances, had become

---

[80c] *Ibid* at p. 9

[80d] *Ibid*

[81] Unreported High Court judgment of Parke J. delivered 28th May 1975

a "gross distortion" of his testamentary intentions by the time of his death in 1973. There were four applicants under section 117, the testator's eldest son and three daughters, one of whom had been born after the making of the will in 1962. The eldest son, who suffered from ill-health and was deemed unfit for a career in farming, had not been left any share in the testator's lands, which were left to his four brothers. The eldest son however had been given an expensive education which qualified him for a career in accounting.

7.6.8 The value of land in County Meath having increased dramatically in the period between the execution of the will and the testator's death, the eldest son and three daughters were in effect disinherited, the four other sons becoming entitled, after the surviving spouse claimed her legal right share, to an estate worth some £300,000. In these circumstances, Parke J. found, that although the testator had been blameworthy only in the sense that he had failed to make a new will, he had, nevertheless, failed to make proper provision for the applicants in accordance with his means. In deciding what provisions should be made for the applicant children, Parke J. was not prepared to take cognisance of actuarial evidence relating to the special needs of the three daughters, and held that the eight children of the testator should get approximately equal shares, with the eldest son getting a little more because of his ill-health.

7.6.9 It is not uncommon for testators, particularly testators in rural Ireland, as *Re W.: W.* v *D.* shows, to misconceive the extent of their moral duty to make proper provision for their daughters, and more particularly their married daughters. Thus, in *Re N.S.M. decd.*[82] Kenny J. pointed out, that married women are not a distinct class for the purposes of section 117, and in deciding whether a testator has fulfilled his moral duty the marriage of an applicant daughter is merely one of the factors to be taken into account by the court.[83] In that case the testator had excluded his two married daughters from his will since they were already well provided for from other funds. The evidence before Kenny J. disclosed that the married daughters were so provided for but, Kenny J. held, this did not relieve the testator of his moral duty to provide for his daughters in accordance with his means.[84] The fact that the applicant child is provided for from other sources is not conclusive is illustrated by another of Kenny J.'s decisions in *Re Michael Looney decd.*[85] in which he held that the statutory obligation of a county council to maintain a mentally retarded child in an institution did not relieve her father of his moral obligation to provide for her in accordance with his means.

[82] (1973) 107 I.L.T.R. 1
[83] *Ibid* at pp. 7, 8
[84] *Ibid*
[85] Unreported High Court judgement delivered 2nd November 1970, 1969 No. 126 Sp.

7.6.10 If the court finds that the testator has failed in his moral duty, it must then determine what provision should be made out of his estate for the applicant child, and at this point the facts before the court at the time of hearing may take precedence over those in existence at the time of the testator's death. The latter point is illustrated by certain of the facts in *Re N.S.M. decd.* where Kenny J. had to consider, not only the application under section 117 by the married daughter, but also that of the youngest son of the testator, who had been given a share of the testator's residuary estate. Because of the incidence of estate duty levied on the estate and legal costs incurred, including those of the instant proceedings, the residuary estate was depleted to the point that the youngest son would get nothing, and he was obliged to make an application under section 117.

7.6.11 Kenny J. pointed out, that in these circumstances it was no answer to say that the testator had tried to make provision for his youngest son and had failed because of the large amount of estate duty and legal costs payable out of the estate. Kenny J. went on:

"The court must attribute to the testator on the day before his death knowledge of the amount of estate duty which will be payable on his estate and a remarkable capacity to anticipate the costs of the litigation which will follow his death. I realise that this is unreal, that the amount of estate duty payable is usually mercifully hidden from most testators, and that it is impossible to anticipate what litigation will follow on death. I am convinced however that section 117 must be interpreted in this way."[86]

7.6.12 The causal link in section 117 between a testator's failure to fulfil his moral duty to make proper provision for his children, and the court's jurisdiction to do so, has obliged the courts, in cases like *Re N.S.M. decd.*, to attribute to the testator an anticipatory knowledge of events which occur after his death. Thus, a testator is expected to have taken cognisance not only of facts known to him, but also of foreseeable contingencies that will arise after his death. In determining the forseeability of certain contingencies the court might be obliged to indulge in intellectual gymnastics, but this is arguably an acceptable price to pay for a meaningful discretion under section 117. The alternative, which would be the exclusion of facts not in existence at the date of the testator's death, would be inconsistent with the main thrust of section 117, which is to ensure that parents provide properly for their children in accordance with their means.

7.6.13 There is always a risk, as the history of much equity jurisdiction shows, that the concretisation of criteria governing the exercise of judicial

[86] (1973) 107 I.L.T.R. 1, 6

discretion has the inevitable effect of impairing that discretion.[87] This has not been the case however, with Kenny J.'s judgment in *Re G.M.*, and both in relation to deciding if a testator's moral duty has been fulfilled and, if not, what provision should be made for an applicant child, judges have been prepared to exercise a robust discretion.[87a] This is nowhere more clearly evident than *M.L & A.W.* v *M.L.* in which Costello J. had to consider an application under section 117 brought by two children, aged 37 years and 33 years respectively, of the testator's first marriage. The testator had been divorced by the applicants' mother in England, and had then married the defendant, by whom he had two more children. He had made a will in 1951, in which he made certain limited provisions for the plaintiffs, but that will had been revoked by one made in 1960, in which no provision was made for his first wife or the children of his first marriage. Under the terms of the latter will the defendant became entitled to the entire of the deceased's estate.

7.6.14 It was contended for the applicant children, that the testator's English divorce was invalid in Irish law and, since the testator's second wife and their two children had no rights under the Succession Act, it followed that the second family should not be taken into account in considering the plaintiff's application under section 117.[89] Costello J. rejected the latter conclusion without having to consider the validity of the English divorce. The learned judge pointed out, that in considering whether or not a parent had acted justly and prudently within the terms of section 117, the court must weigh up carefully all his moral obligations, and these were not confined to his wife and children. He gave the example of a testator who may have aged and infirm parents who are dependent upon him and to whom he owes a moral duty; the court would have to bear in mind the testator's obligations to such parents in deciding whether he had acted justly and prudently towards his children. It followed that the court had to take cognisance of moral obligations of the testator other than those enforceable under the Succession Act and, within that category of obligations, Costello J. believed, were those owed by a testator to

---

[87] The contemporary revival of equity as an aneliorating jurisdiction owes much to the shift from principles to pragmatism in the administration of justice. See generally Atijah "From Principles to Pragmatism" (Oxford 1978)

[87a] See *H.L.* v *The Governor and Company of the Bank of Ireland* (1978 I.L.R.M. 160 where Costello J. created a discretionary trust in favour of an applicant child; *J.H. and C.D.H.* v *Allied Irish Banks Ltd. and Others* (1978) I.L.R.M. 203; *M.H. and N.McG.* v *N.M. and C.M.* (1983) I.L.R.M. 519 (where married female applicants were unsuccessful).

[88] [1978] I.R. 288

[89] The applicants claimed that the divorce had been procured by duress and, since neither party had been domiciled in England it was not valid in Irish law. See *Gaffrey* v *Gaffrey* [1975] I.R. 133.

illegitimate children.[90] That being so, the nature and extent of the testator's moral duty to the children of his second marriage could not be affected by a decision of the court that the second marriage should not be recognised in Irish law.

7.6.15 Costello J. went on to point out that, in deciding what provision should be made for an applicant child, in the event of the testator having failed to fulfill his moral duty to the child, the court must again have regard to moral obligations of the testator other than those enforceable under the Succession Act. However, since the children of the second marriage were not, in the events which happened, beneficiaries under the testator's will, nor were they claimants under section 117, Costello J. considered their position to be irrelevant to the consideration of what provision should be made for the plaintiff applicants. This aspect of Costello J.'s judgment is more problematic since there is no such limitation in section 117(2), which simply requires the court to arrive at a decision "that will be as fair as possible to the child to whom the application relates <u>and to the other children.</u>" (emphasis added). Indeed, an order in favour of the plaintiffs in the instant case would arguably affect the children of the second marriage since, it would reduce the interest of the defendant who, as their mother, was primarily responsible for their upkeep and general well-being.[91]

7.7 New rights of illegitimate children

7.7.1 Costello J.'s equation in *M.L. & A.W.* v *M.L.* of a testator's moral responsibility for his illegitimate child with that for an aged and infirm parent was a progressive piece of social thinking, but the learned judge was obliged to categorise both as unenforceable obligations under the Succession Act. The latter act was silent on the rights of illegitimate children, and words such as "child" or "issue" in wills, deeds, or other instruments, were construed as referring only to legitimate or legitimated children.[92]

7.7.2 The position of illegitimate children has now been radically altered by the Status of Children Act, 1987, which equalises the rights under the law of all children, whether born within or outside marriage.[93] Thus Part V of the Status of Children Act, which deals with property rights, applies to the Succession Act the general principle that relationships between persons are

---

[90] Costello J. found support for that view in *Re N.S.M. decd.* (1973) 107 I.L.T.R. 1.

[91] See Cooney "Succession and Judicial Discretion in Ireland" (1980) Irish Jurist. (n.s.) 62 at pp. 77 *et seq.*

[92] See *In the Goods of Walker decd.* (1985) I.L.R.M. 86

[93] See the Explanatory Memorandum with the Status of Children Bill 1986 at para. 1 p.1.

to be determined without regard to whether a person's parents are, or have been, married to each other.[94] Section 117 of the Succession Act has, accordingly, been amended by section 31 of the Act of 1987 so as to ensure that where a testator who was not married to the other parent of his or her child, dies after the commencement of Part V, the child will have a right to apply under section 117 for proper provision to be made out of the testator's estate <u>whether the will was made before or after the commencement date</u>. (emphasis added). Section 31 of the Act of 1987 does not, however, confer a right to make an application under section 117 in respect of the estate of a testator who dies before the commencement of Part V.

7.8 Discretion under section 117 and the acceptance of a substantial compliance doctrine

7.8.1 The wide discretion conferred on them by section 117 of the Succession Act should, arguably, make the Irish courts more amenable to the acceptance of a substantial compliance doctrine in relation to the statutory requirements governing the execution of wills.[95] It was no doubt often the unstated, but implicit fact, that the intestacy rules effected a fairer distribution of a deceased's estate, which led the courts to adopt an excessively technical interpretation of the statutory rules governing the execution of wills.[96] A parent might wilfully and inexplicably exclude one of his children from his will, the exclusion of which from probate would allow such child to acquire an interest under the intestacy rules.

7.8.2 The wheel may, however, have now turned full circle and, while the intestacy rules apply mathematically and inflexibly, the court can, in considering an application under section 117, take cognisance of the particular circumstances in the individual case. That being so, the court might be expected to lean against intestacy and, more particularly in a case where the need for the exercise of discretion is manifest. There is more than a hint of this approach in the decision of Carroll J. in *R.G.* v *P.S.G.* and *J.R.G.*[97] In that case, the deceased, the father of the plaintiff applicant under section 117, had made a will appointing his wife sole executrix and universal legatee and devisee. His wife, having predeceased the testator, his will was wholly inoperative, and his entire estate devolved as an intestacy. In these circumstances it was contended for the defendants that since section 109(1) of the Succession Act provides that Part IX, and

---

[94] See s. 3 of the Status of Children Act 1987.
[95] See generally Langbein "Substantial Compliance With the Wills Act" (1975) 88 Harvard Law Review, 489.
[96] *Ibid* at pp. 499 *et seq.*
[97] Unreported High Court judgement of Carroll J. delivered the 20th November 1980. See *post* p. 220

therefore section 117, can only apply to the estate of a person who dies wholly or partly testate, it did not apply in the instant case, since the deceased could not be said to have died wholly or partly testate. Carroll J. rejected that argument, pointing out, that the state of testacy does not depend on the effectiveness of a will, but rather on the effectiveness of the execution of the will and, if testacy is established, it follows that a person must die wholly or partly testate. Thus, the only way a testator, having executed a valid will, can cease to be a testator is by revoking the will in accordance with one of the means set out in section 85 of the Succession Act, other than by making a new will.

7.8.4 The plaintiff's application under section 117 in the instant case was, therefore, well founded, and Carroll J. went on to consider the merits of the application. There is no doubt that the facts disclosed that the plaintiff was eminently more entitled to the deceased's estate than those who would have shared it with him on an intestacy, and it is arguable that, although she did not say so explicitly, that factor weighed heavily with Carroll J. in deciding that the deceased died testate.[98]

7.9 Time limits to section 117 applications

7.9.1 An order under section 117 shall not be made except on an application made within twelve months from the first taking out of representation of the deceased's estate. Since applicants under section 117 would often, though not always, be infants, the question was bound to arise whether the status of infancy would have the effect of extending the time limit in section 117(6). It is provided in section 127 of the Succession Act that section 49 of the Statute of Limitations 1957

> "shall have effect in relation to an action in respect of a claim to the estate of a deceased person or to any share in such estate, whether under a will, on intestacy or as a legal right, as if the period of three years was substituted for the period of six years mentioned in sub-section (1) of that section."

7.9.2 The question accordingly arose, *inter alia*, in *M.P.D.* v *M.D.*[100] whether, section 127 applies to applications under section 117 so that in a case of disability, for example, infancy, the time limit fixed by section 117(6) is extended to a period of three years from when the disability ends. If it did not, Carroll J. pointed out, infants or other persons under a disability, would be unable to make an application under section 117 after one year from the

[98] The applicant child had remained at home with his parents to care for the family farm.
[99] Section 117 (6)
[100] (1981) I.L.R.M. 179

raising of representation, even if the appropriate person to bring such application on their behalf had a conflicting interest.[101] Such would be the case where the appropriate person to bring an action as "next friend" is the stepmother of the infant, whose share in the deceased's estate would be diminished by an order under section 117. Carroll J. also gave the example of a case where the father of a young family dies leaving a life estate in a farm or family business to his wife, with remainder to his eldest son. The surviving spouse may well be satisfied with that arrangement, knowing that she will look after all the children out of her life interest. However, if she dies more than a year after representation has been taken out and while the children are still infants, there will be no provision made in the father's will for any of the children other than the eldest son. Carroll J. was sure that there are many other examples which would show compelling reasons why the time limit set out in section 117(6) should be extended by the application of section 127 of the Succession Act, or in some other way.[102] The learned judge reluctantly concluded however, that the claims to which section 127 applies are limited to those specified in the section, and a claim under section 117 is excluded being a claim made independently of the will, not being a claim on intestacy and not being a legal right within section 3 of the Succession Act.

7.9.3 If our legislators had addressed the question of disability and applications under section 117, they would surely have included the latter in section 127, and their omission must rank as an oversight which cries out for amending legislation.[103] It has to be conceded of course that any extension of the time limit for applications under section 117 will create difficulties for personal representatives and not make it easier for them to administer estates promptly.[104] This is a reason, though not a compelling one, for refusing to extend the longer time limit in section 127 to applications under section 117, and amending legislation could be confined, if it is thought necessary, to hard cases of the type envisaged by Carroll J. in *M.P.D.* v *M.D.* Some guidance for amending legislation might be sought in the English Inheritance (Provision for Family and Dependents) Act, 1975, which contains a shorter ordinary time limit than the Succession Act viz. 6 months from the date when probate or letters of administration to the deceased's estate are first taken out. It is provided in section 4 of the English Act, that the period of six months can be extended "with the permission of the court." The Act is silent as to the grounds upon which the court will exercise this discretion but, as a general principle, the court will extent the time "if no hardship will ensue."[105]

---

[101] *Ibid* at p. 182

[102] *Ibid* at p. 163

[103] See the Law Reform Commission's proposals for an extension of the time limit for applications under s.117(b) contained in Report (LRC 30 1989) at pages 21–22

[104] See *Moynihan* v *Greensmyth* (1977) I.R. 55, 72

[105] See Mellows "The Law of Succession" (4th ed. 1983) at pp. 200 *et seq.*

7.9.4 Personal representatives of course might feel obliged to delay distribution of the deceased's estate because of the possibility that a child will avail of the longer time limit for applications under section 117. This problem could be met by affording personal representatives protection along the lines off section 20 of the English act which provides *inter alia,* that a personal representative shall not be liable for having distributed any part of the estate of the deceased after the expiry of six months from the first taking out of representation to the deceased's estate on the ground that he ought to have taken into account the possibility that the court might permit the making of an application under section 2 of the Act.[106]

7.9.5 All proceedings under Part X are to be heard in chambers[107], and applications under section 117 with the minimum of formality and expense. Accordingly, subsections (4) and (5) of section 117 require that Rules of Court shall provide for the conduct of proceedings under section 117 in a summary manner, and the costs of such proceedings to be at the discretion of the court.

7.10 Unworthiness to succeed and disinheritance

7.10.1 Part X of the Succession Act identifies persons who are deemed unworthy to succeed to the estate of a deceased person, and also renders ineffective dispositions made by a deceased within three years of his death for the purpose of disinheriting his spouse or children.

7.10.2 Thus section 120(1) provides, that any sane person who has been guilty of the murder, attempted murder or manslaughter of another, shall be precluded from taking any share in the estate of that other, except a share arising under a will made after the act constituting the offence, and shall not be entitled to make an application under section 117. This provision restates the long established rule of public policy which precludes a person from benefitting from his own crime.[108]

7.10.3 Section 120(2) provides, that a spouse against whom the deceased obtained a decree of divorce *a mensa et thoro,* a spouse who failed to comply with a decree of restitution of conjugal rights obtained by the deceased, and a spouse guilty of desertion for two years or more immediately prior to the deceased's death, shall be precluded from taking any share in the estate of the deceased on intestacy or as a legal right. A spouse who was guilty of conduct which justified the deceased in separating

---

[106] *Ibid* at p. 201–2
[107] Section 119
[108] See *ante* p. 158

and living apart from him or her shall be deemed to be guilty of desertion within the meaning of subsection (2).[109]

7.10.4 It is the case that relatively few decrees of divorce *a mensa et thoro*, are granted yearly in Ireland, and while formal separation agreements invariably contain reciprocal clauses by which the parties' renounce their rights under the Succession Act (many separations are informal and consensual, and the parties do not address the question of their rights under the Succession Act. Such parties may well believe that living apart for a number of years does affect their rights under the Succession Act, but, if one of the disabling grounds set out in subsections (2) and (3) of section 120 is not present, the fact of separation, without more, will not impair the right of a surviving spouse to claim a share in the deceased's estate.

7.10.5 It's a moot point which has not yet been decided by the Irish courts whether, if spouses are living apart informally and consensually, one of them makes an offer to resume cohabitation which is refused by the other party, such refusal constitutes constructive desertion. A person who has been found guilty of an offence against the deceased, or against the spouse or any child of the deceased, which is punishable by imprisonment for a maximum period of at least two years or by a more severe penalty, shall be precluded from taking any share in the estate of the deceased as a legal right, or from making an application under section 117.[110] "Child" in this context includes a child adopted under the Adoption Acts 1952 and 1964, and a person to whom the deceased was in *loco parentis* at the time of the offence, and presumably will now include an illegitimate child under the terms of the Status of Children Act 1987.[111]

7.10.6 Any share which a person is precluded from taking by section 120 is to be distributed as if such person had predeceased the testator.[112]

7.10.7 All subsections to section 120, other than subsection (1) are new to Irish law and, we are told in the Explanatory Memorandum, may be compared with provisions relating to unworthiness and disinheritance in the French, German and Swiss codes.[113]

7.10.8 Dispositions made by the deceased for the purpose of disinheriting his or her spouse or children are dealt with in section 121 which applies to a

[109] Section 120 (3)
[110] Section 120 (4)
[111] See *ante* p. 204
[112] Section 120 (5)
[113] Explanatory Memorandum at para. 75 p. 10

disposition of property, other than a testamentary disposition or a disposition to a purchaser, under which the beneficial ownership of the property vests in possession in the donee within three years before the death of the person who made it, or later.[114] If the court is satisfied that such disposition was made for the purpose of defeating or substantially diminishing the share of the disponer's spouse, whether as a legal right or on intestacy, or the intestate share of any of his children, or of leaving any of his children insufficiently provided for, then whether the disponer died testate or intestate, the court may order that such disposition, in whole or in part, be deemed to be a devise or bequest made by him by will.[115] Such dispositions shall be deemed, to the extent to which the court so orders, never to have had any effect and the donee of the property, or any person representing or claiming title under him, shall be a debtor of the estate for such amount as the court may direct.[116] The court is also empowered to make such further order as appears to be just and equitable having regard to the provisions and the spirit of the Act and to all the circumstances.[117]

7.10.9 The court may make an order under section 121, subject to subsections (6) and (7) of that section, (a) in the interest of a spouse on the application of the spouse or the personal representative of the deceased, made within one year from the first taking out of representation, (b) in the interest of a child, on an application under section 117.[118] The effect of the time limits in respect of applications under section 121 was considered, *inter alia*, by Carroll J. in *M.P.D.* v *M.D.*[119] There the testator was survived by his wife and four children and by the defendant with whom he had been living prior to his death and with whom he had two further children. During the lifetime of the testator and within three years of his death, the defendant had acquired a one-half share in his business, and had been named as joint tenant of the house in which she lived with the testator.

7.10.10 The defendant having been granted probate of the deceased's will, the plaintiff brought an application under section 117 as next friend of the children and, as we have seen, this application failed as being out of time.[120] The plaintiff also brought an application on her own behalf and on behalf of her four children under section 121. Carroll J. held that the wife

---

[114] Somewhat similar provisions are to be found in the French, German and Swiss Civil Codes. See the Explanatory Memorandum with the Succession Bill at para. 76 p. 11

[115] Section 121 (2)

[116] Section 121 (3)

[117] Section 121 (4)

[118] Section 121 (5)

[119] (1981) I.L.R.M. 179

[120] See *ante* p. 207

was barred from making an application under section 121 in her own interest, because it was not made within one year of the grant of probate as required by section 121(5)(a). Carroll J. rejected the argument of counsel for the widow,that her right under section 121 was dependent upon her having been served with notice of her right to elect under section 115. The learned judge held that the widow was entitled to make an application under section 12l independently of any other provision in the act.[121]

7.10.11 Carroll J. also rejected the argument made on behalf of the widow that because an application in the interest of the spouse may be made by the personal representative of the deceased, the defendant, as personal representative, having failed to make such application could not invoke the time limit laid down in section 121(5)(a). It appeared to Carroll J. that while a personal representative is empowered to make an application in the interest of the spouse there is no duty imposed on the personal representative to do so.[122] The defendant therefore was not estopped from pleading the time limit laid down in the section.

7.10.12 In so far as the application under section 121 was made in the interest of the children, it seemed to Carroll J. that section 121(5)(b) infers, that unless a claim lies under section 117 no application can be made on behalf of a child under section 121. It follows that where a child's interest is concerned the appropriate course is to make an application under section 117, and join with it a claim for an order under section 121. Thus only one application, one set of proceedings is necessary.[123] Carroll J. dismissed the apparent anomaly that where there is a claim by a child in respect of a diminished intestate share, which is allowed under section 121, an application can only be made under section 117 where the deceased died wholly or partly testate. Carroll J. pointed out that this is not really so "because, if the application under section 121 is successful, the disposition is deemed to be a devise or bequest made by the deceased by will, which would bring the child's claim within the ambit of section 117."[124]

7.10.13 The court will not be able to make an order under section 121 affecting a disposition made to the spouse of the disponer, except on the application by or on behalf of a child of the disponer who is not a child of the spouse. Nor may the court make an order under section 121 affecting a disposition made in favour of any child of the disponer if (a) the spouse of the disponer was dead when the disposition was made, or (b) the spouse

---

[121] (1981) I.L.R.M. 179, 181
[122] *Ibid*
[123] *Ibid*
[124] *Ibid* at pp. 181, 182

was alive when the disposition was made but was a person who, if the disponer had then died, would have been precluded under any of the provisions of section 120 from taking a share in his estate, or (c) the spouse was alive when the disposition was made and consented in writing to it.[125]

7.10.14 The latter provision is quite commonly used in parts of rural Ireland, where it is still the practice for a man to pass title in his holding, during his lifetime, to one of his children, usually the eldest son who has stayed behind to help work the farm which the others have left. It is not obvious however what, if any benefit will accrue to the spouse whose written consent is necessary to forestall a subsequent challenge to such transfer under section 121. Such consents would clearly be open to the same scrutiny in relation to undue influence, mistake and improvidence, as written agreements renouncing a spouse's legal right prior to, or during the subsistence of, the marriage.[126]

Chapter 8
INTESTACY

8.1 Introduction

8.1.1 A person may be said to have died intestate when, (i) he has failed to make a will disposing of his property on death, or, (ii) he has made a will which has not been properly executed, and fails to take effect.[1] It might reasonably be assumed by the lay person that if the will of a deceased person is wholly inoperative, for whatever reason, the deceased could be said to have died intestate. We have seen that this is not the case, however, and in *R.G.* v *P.S.G. and J.R.G.*[2] Carroll J. held, that the deceased had died testate, despite the fact that his wife, whom he had appointed sole executrix, and universal legatee and devisee had predeceased him. Carroll J. held, that the test of whether a person had died testate was not whether his will was effective to dispose of his property, but whether it had been validly executed.[3]

8.1.2 That the occurrence of events for which a testator has not provided in his will may lead to an intestacy, however, is illustrated by the decision in *Fitzpatrick* v *Collins and Collins*.[4] There, a testator had made provision in his will for what should happen to his property should his wife survive him, and then die within two months of his death. The property was to be sold and the proceeds of sale used for the purpose of having Masses said in

---

[1] "An intestate" is defined in s.3 (1) of the Succession Act as a person who leaves no will or leaves a will but leaves undisposed of some beneficial interest in his estate.

[2] Unreported High Court judgment of Carroll J. delivered the 20th Nov. 1980.

[3] See *ante* p. 205

[4] (1978) ILRM 244

public for the repose of the souls of the testator, his wife, and their respective parents. The testator's wife had predeceased him by some eight years, an eventuality for which the testator had made no provision in his will. The plaintiff, who was the administrator of the will, pointed out that the literal interpretation of the will would have the incongruous result that the testator had died intestate by failing to make provision for his wife predeceasing him, and he submitted that the court had power to transpose certain words within a clause or expression which is senseless or contradictory.[5] It was also submitted for the plaintiff that evidence from the solicitor who drew up the will should be admitted by the court under section 90 of the Succession Act.[6]

8.1.3 McWilliam J., in finding for an intestacy held, that the clause in the will dealing with the testator's wife surviving him, and dying within two months of his death, was neither senseless or contradictory, but had been put in deliberately by the testator, and was correctly phrased.[7] McWilliam J. pointed out that he was not entitled to make a will for the testator to cover circumstances which the testator had overlooked,[8] and he refused to admit extrinsic evidence under section 90 of the Succession Act because, while there was an inconsistency in the will, there was no ambiguity or contradiction, which is required for the admission of such evidence by the decision of the Supreme Court in *Rowe* v *Law*.[9]

8.1.4 The law governing the devolution and distribution of an intestate's property on death which has a long and complex history was greatly simplifed by the new rules introduced by the Succession Act 1965. One of the principle objectives of those rules was the assimilation of the laws governing the devolution and distribution of an intestate's realty and personalty.[10] The law governing devolution of a deceased's property determines to whom ownership or title to such property passes on death,[11] whereas the law on distribution determines how, and amongst whom, the deceased person's property is to be distributed.

---

[5] The clause in question was the one dealing with the case of the testator's wife surviving him and dying within two months of his death.

[6] See *ante* pp. 113 *et seq*

[7] McWilliam J. considered the judgment of Ungood-Thomas in *Macandrew's Will Trusts* [1963] 3 WLR 822, 834.

[8] [1978] ILRM 244, 247

[9] [1978] I.R. 55 See *ante* pp. 116 *et seq*

[10] See the Explanatory Memorandum with the Succession Act on p.1

[11] It reflects the common law's abhorrence of any *lacuna* in ownership. The deceased's property must vest in someone before it is distributed amongst those entitled to succeed him.

8.1.5 It is tempting for the textwriter to deal exclusively with the new simplifed rules governing intestate succession, but there are compelling reasons why cognisance must be taken of the old rules. Firstly, it is imperative for conveyancers to know the previous rules, more particularly the rules of inheritance governing the succession to real estate, which obtained prior to the coming into force of the Succession Act on the 1st January 1967. Secondly, the radical and innovative nature of many of the new rules can best be appreciated by juxtaposing them with the rules in force prior to the Succession Act. It is also appropriate to consider briefly, earlier legislative moves to assimilate the law of intestate succession in respect of realty and personality, but, otherwise it is not proposed to consider in any detail the long and complex history of the law governing intestate succession. That is now arguably the province of the legal historian.

8.1.6 The assimilation of the law in respect of the devolution of realty and personality had been in train towards the end of the 19th century and the Conveyancing Act, 1881,[12] had provided that trust and mortgage estates should devolve on the personal representatives of the deceased as if chattels real. A more significant step in the assimilation of the law on devolution in respect of realty and personality was taken with the Local Registration of Title (Ireland) Act, 1891,[13] which provided that all land purchased by tenant farmers under the Land Purchase Acts, after 1st January 1892, should continue to devolve on death and become vested in the personal representatives of the deceased as if chattels real. The personal representatives had the same duties and powers in respect of such property as they had in respect of the deceased's personality.[14] The Land Purchase Acts, which were perceived by virtually all British politicians as the answer to the otherwise intractable Irish land problem, were intended to allow the Irish tenant farmer to buy his way to the top of the pyramid of property interests affecting his property.[15] The success of the land purchase scheme meant that virtually all agricultural land in Ireland would pass to the personal representatives of a deceased landowner as chattels real under the provisions of the Local Registration of Title (Ireland) Act 1891.

8.1.7 The next step in the assimulation of the law on devolution of realty and personality came with the Administration of Estates Act, 1959,[16] which

---

[12] 44 & 45 Vict. c.4.1
[13] 54 & 55 Vict. c. 66
[14] See Wylie "Irish Land Law" (2nd ed. 1986) at p.751
[15] *Ibid* at pp. 24 *et seq.*
[16] No. 8 of 1959

provided that real estate to which a deceased person was entitled should devolve on, and become vested in, his personal representatives as if it was a chattel real.[17] The process of assimilation has now been completed by the Succession Act, section 10 (1) of which provides, that the real and personal estate of a deceased person shall on his death, notwithstanding any testamentary disposition, devolve on and become vested in his personal representatives. Such personal representatives for the time being of a deceased person are deemed in law his heirs and assigns within the meaning of all trusts and powers.[18]

8.2 Distribution on intestacy

8.2.1 Prior to the Succession Act, on a man's death intestate his realty and personalty descended differently. The rules governing the distribution of personalty were contained in the Intestate Estates Act 1954[19], which will later be compared with the new rules in the Succession Act.[20] Realty, however, descended according to the law of inheritance, a judge made law, which was given statutory recognition in the Inheritance Act 1833.[21]

8.2.2 The principal features of the law of inheritance which governed the descent of realty, other than entailed interests, were that the intestate's realty descended to his blood relations lineally, and his children and grandchildren were preferred to his parents and grandparents.[22] Males were preferred to females, and where there were two or more rules in an equal degree of relationship to the deceased, the principle of primogeniture ordained that the eldest should inherit. Thus the deceased's heir-at-law to whom his realty descended was generally his eldest son. If his eldest son predeceased the intestate it didn't follow that the next eldest son would inherit since the doctrine of representation provided, that the descendants of a deceased person who could have inherited stood in his place; thus the issue of an eldest son took in preference to a younger son and his issue.[23]

8.2.3 Women did less well than their male spouses in the pre-Succession Act scheme of intestate succession, but a widow was entitled to dower, which was the right to a life estate in one-third of the real estate of her deceased husband. This compared unfavourably with the surviving

---

[17] *Ibid* s. 6

[18] Section 10 (2)

[19] No. 12 of 1954 which rules replaced those in the Intestates Estates Act 1890 (53 & 54 Vict. c. 29)

[20] See *post* pp. 218 & 223

[21] 3 & 4 Will. 4 c.100. See Wylie "Irish Land Law" (2nd ed. 1986) at p.753.

[22] This preference for the younger relations is seen again in the Succession Act. see *post* p. 225

[23] See Wylie "Irish Land Law" (2nd ed. 1986) at pp. 753-4

husband's entitlement to curtesy, which was the right to a life estate in the whole of the real property of the deceased spouse.[24] Entitlement to either curtesy or dower could only arise however when the deceased husband or wife had held a freehold estate of inheritance, that is, a fee simple or fee tail during the marriage.[25] The conditions attaching to curtesy and dower favoured women in this respect, that a man lost his entitlement to curtesy if issue of the marriage capable of inheriting the land had not been born alive, but a woman did not lose her right to dower if no issue were born if it *had been possible* for heritable issue of the marriage to be born.[26]

8.2.4 The Succession Act has now abolished all existing rules, modes and canons of descent, including dower and tenancy by the curtesy, except in so far as they might apply to the descent of an estate tail.[27]

8.2.5 The assimilation of the law in respect of the distribution of an intestate's realty and personalty did not keep pace with the assimilation of the law in respect of the devolution of an intestates property, but both have now coincided in the Succession Act, Part VI of which contains the new rules governing the distribution of an intestate's estate. Those new rules apply to all property, both real and personal, in which the deceased person was entitle to an estate or interest not ceasing on his death. After payment of all expenses, debts and liabilities, and any legal right properly payable thereout, the intestate's estate is to be distributed in accordance with Part VI of the Act.[28] The rules contained in Part VI provide as follows:

8.3. Spouse and issue surviving

8.3.1 Where an intestate dies leaving a spouse and no issue, the spouse is entitled to the whole estate.[29] If spouse and issue survive the intestate, the spouse takes two-thirds of the estate and the remainder is to be distributed among the issue.[30] Distribution among the issue will be in equal shares if all are in equal degree of relationship to the deceased; otherwise it will be *per stirpes*.[31] If an intestate dies leaving issue and no spouse his entire estate will be divided among his issue, again in equal shares if all are in equal degree of relationship to the deceased, otherwise *per stirpes*.[32]

---

[24] Re dower and curtesy see Megarry and Wade "The Law of Real Property" (4th ed. 1975) at pp.514 *et seq.*

[25] *Ibid* See also Wylie "Irish Land Law" (2nd ed. 1986) at pp. 238 *et seq.*

[26] See Megarry and Wade "The Law of Real Property" at p.517

[27] Section 11

[28] Section 66

[29] Section 67 (1)

[30] Section 67 (2)

[31] Section 67 (4)

[32] Section 67 (3)

8.3.2 Where a deceased person's estate, or any share therein, is to be distributed *per stirpes* among his issue, "any issue more remote than a child of the deceased shall take through all degrees, according to their stocks, in equal shares if more than one, the share which the parent of such issue would have taken if living at the death of the deceased, and no issue of the deceased shall take if the parent of such issue is living at the death of the deceased and so capable of taking."[33] The operation of the *per stirpes* rule can be illustrated diagrammatically.

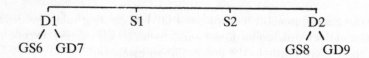

8.3.3 X had four children, two sons (S1 and S2) and two daughters (D1 and D2). X who dies intestate was predeceased by two of his children D1 and S2. D1 has left two children (GS6 and GD7), grandchildren of the intestate, but S2 dies unmarried and childless. Each of X's children who is alive or represented by issue at X's death form a stock of descent. In our diagram there are three such stocks, those of D1, S1 and D2. The intestate's estate will therefore be divided into three parts. The children of D1 will share their mothers one-third interest, each taking one-sixth of the deceased's estate but the children of D2 will take nothing, as their mother is still alive and entitled to her one-third share.

8.3.4 The new rules governing shares on intestacy have equalised the position between the sexes, and removed certain anomalies which determined the share of the surviving spouse according to gender. Thus, prior to the Succession Act, in the event of a husband's death leaving his wife and no issue, the wife took a first charge of £4,000 plus one-half of the remaining estate, the other half going to the deceased's next-of-kin in dual shares. If, however, a husband survived with no issue, he was entitled to his wife's entire estate.[34]

8.9 Illegitimate children

8.9.1 As we have seen, the term "issue" in the Succession Act did not include illegitimate children or other issue related through an illegitimate link.[35] A constitutional challenge was mounted in *O'B.* v *S* [36] to the

---

[33] Section 3 (3)

[34] See Appendix A of the Explanatory Memorandum with the Succession Act.

[35] See *ante* p. 204

[36] [1984] I.R. 316

apparent exclusion of illegitimate children from the provision in the Succession Act governing distribution on intestacy. The plaintiff, who was the sister of the deceased intestate, had applied for a grant of letters of administration to his estate which application was opposed by the defendant, the deceased's illegitimate daughter, who claimed to be issue of the deceased and lodged a caveat.

8.9.2 The plaintiff succeeded in the High Court, Darcy J. setting aside the caveat and giving her liberty to proceed with her application for a grant of letters of administration to her brother's estate.[37] The Supreme Court, disallowing the appeal from the judgment of Darcy J. held, *inter alia* that the meaning of the word "issue" in sections 67 and 69 of the Succession Act was governed by the context in which it appeared, being an act providing for succession to property on intestacy and providing expressly in section 110 for some succession rights of illegitimate children, without extending the meaning of the word issue to include such children. The court also held that the discrimination in favour of legitimate children effected by section 67 was justified by sections 1 and 3 of Article 41 of the Constitution, since sections 67 and 69 of the Succession Act form part of an act which is designed to strengthen the protection of the family in accordance with the provision of Article 41.[38]

8.9.3 However compelling and unavoidable the legal conclusions were in *O'B* v *S* equity was clearly not achieved in the circumstances of that case and public unease with such cases was one of the factors which led to the enactment of the Status of Children Act 1987.[39] As we have seen, the new section 4A being inserted into the Succession Act by section 29 of the 1987 Act provides, that in deducing any relationship for the purposes of the Succession Act the relationship between every person and his father and mother shall be determined without regard to the parents' marital status.[40] Section 4A (2) sets up a rebuttable presumption that a child, whose parents have not married each other and who dies intestate, is not survived by his father or by any person related to him through his father. This is an interesting and, some might say, poetic inversion of the gender distinction which obtained under the Legitimacy Act 1931,[41] section 9 (1) of which gave to an illegitimate child, or his issue, the right to succeed to the estate of his mother where she died wholly or partially intestate and was not survived by any legitimate children or issue.

---

[37] *Ibid* See the judgement of Darcy J. at pp. 320 *et seq.*
[38] See the judgement of Walsh J. at pp.335 *et seq.*
[39] No 26. of 1987
[40] See *ante* pp. 205 Section 4A (5) ensures that the provisions of the section will not retrospectively affect any rights under the intestacy of a person who died before the commencement of Part V.
[41] No. 13 of 1931

8.9.4 There is one important aspect of the new intestacy regime affecting issue of the deceased which provokes some critical comment. It is becoming increasingly anomalous that the discretion given to the courts under section 117 of the Succession Act to make proper provision for an applicant child in accordance with a testator's means, is not given to them when the deceased has died intestate.[42] The share of a child in the estate of an intestate parent will be determined arithmetically, and, as we have seen, if the deceased has left a spouse surviving, the child will be entitled to a share in one-third of the intestate's estate.[43]

8.9.5 It is an ironic fact that the courts' insistence on a literal compliance with the legislation governing wills was often explicable on the ground that the legislation governing intestacy effected a more equitable distribution of the deceased's estate. Thus, in the case of a will failing because of some formal defect, and the testator dying intestate, his estate will be distributed among those closest to him in terms of blood and marriage. An American commentator has said:

> "The backstopping effect of the intestate distribution statute may help explain why rigid enforcement of Wills Act formalities can take place, but it hardly justifies the phenomenon."[44]

8.9.6 Since the coming into effect of the Succession Act, the position in Ireland has changed and the equity pendulum has swung in favour of testacy. Thus, as we have seen, Carroll J. in *R.G.* v *P.S.G. and J.R.G.*[45] held, that the deceased had died testate despite the fact that his will was wholly inoperative and his estate had to be distributed according to the intestate rules. Finding so however allowed Carroll J. to consider an application under section 117 by a child of the deceased who, in the circumstances of that case, would have been badly served by the arithmatic distribution of his father's estate, which would have followed an intestacy.

8.9.7 Growing concern at the anomalous position of children whose parents die intestate was evident during the Dail Debates on the Status of Children Bill when Deputy Harney moved an amendment, the purpose of which was to enlarge the meaning of "testator" in section 117 of the Succession Act, notwithstanding anything in section 109 (1), to include any person who dies wholly intestate after the coming into force of Part V of

---

[42] See *ante* pp. 205 *et seq.*

[43] See *ante* p. 217

[44] Langbein "Substantial Compliance with The Wills Act" (1975) 88 Harvard Law Review, 489, 499

[45] See *ante* p. 205

the Status of Children Act 1987.[46] The Minister for Justice opposed the amendment on the ground, *inter alia* that it belonged in a general succession Bill and had nothing to do with equalising the rights of children, which was the essential purpose of the Status of Children Bill.[47] The Minister was also happy that, "the rules of distribution on intestacy guarantee a fair and suitable share to each child where no will has been made."[48]

8.9.8 It is precisely however because those rules may work an injustice in the particular case that the Minister's complacency is not widely shared. The typical instance where an injustice might arise is, where one of a number of children in a family gives up a career to stay at home and care for parents in the expectation that she, it is usually a daughter who finds herself in such a situation, will receive an inheritance on the death of the surviving parent. If such parent fails to make a will the other less dutiful children, who have left home, may return to claim their intestate shares. In this respect it is a sobering thought that statistics from the Probate Office reveal that the issue of letters of administration far exceeds the issue of grants of probate.[49] The daughter who eschews a career and stays at home to care for her parents may not be entirely without legal reddress, however, as recent developments in England in relation to the "new model" constructive trust and the principle of proprietary estoppel, show.[50] Be that as it may, it is not altogether surprising that the Law Reform Commission is recommending that section 117 of the Succession Act be extended to include applications on an intestacy.[51] Such a change would give the courts a more positive role in the distribution of an intestate's estate.

8.9.9 It must be conceded however, that the courts are not currently obliged to distribute an intestate's estate arithmetically and mechanically, and section 63 of the Succession Act provides, that any advancement made to the child of a deceased person during his lifetime shall, subject to a contrary intention being expressed by the deceased or appearing from the circumstances of the case, be taken into account in determining the child's share of the deceased's estate.[52] This provision which applies whether the deceased has left a will, or died intestate, also applies to an advancement made by the deceased to a person to whom he stands *in loco parentis*.[53]

---

[46] Dail Debates, 28th October 1987, Col. 1692

[47] *Ibid.* at Col. 1694

[48] *Ibid* at Col. 1695

[49] I am grateful to Mr. John Buckley of the Law Reform Commission for this information.

[50] See in particular *Re Basham* [1987] 1 All E.R. 405

[51].Report (LRC 30–1989) at p. 23

[52] Section 63 (1)

[53] Section 63 (10)

8.9.10 The concept of advancement which is a familiar one to equity lawyers,[54] is defined for the purposes of section 63 as meaning "a gift intended to make permanent provision for a child and includes advancement by way of portion or settlement, including any life or lesser interest and including property covenanted to be paid or settled. It also includes an advance or portion for the purpose of establishing a child in a profession, vocation, trade or business, a marriage portion and payments made for the education of a child to a standard higher than that provided by the deceased for any other or others of his children."[55]

8.9.11 An advancement shall, for the purposes of section 63 only, be reckoned as part of the estate of the deceased, and its value shall be reckoned as at the date of the advancement.[56] If the advancement is equal to, or greater than, the share which the child is entitled to receive under the will or on intestacy, the child, or the issue of the child, is precluded from any such share in the estate.[57] If, on the other hand, the advancement is less than such share, the child, or issue of the child is entitled to receive in satisfaction of such share so much only of the deceased's estate as, when added to the advancement, is sufficient, as nearly as can be estimated, to make up the full amount of that share.[58] In any event, it is also provided that nothing in section 63 shall prevent a child retaining the advancement and abandoning his right to a share under the will or on intestacy.[59]

8.9.12 The rationale of this so-called doctrine of "hotchpot" is the achievement of equality between the children of the deceased, by obliging any of them who have received substantial gifts by way of advancement from the deceased notionally to return such gifts to the deceased estate. The doctrine however works arbitrarily against the children of the deceased in that, a niece or nephew of the deceased is not obliged to account for any gifts by way of advancement while a son or daughter is so obliged. This arbitrariness has provoked judicial criticism and no less a

---

[54] See Hanbury and Maudsley "Modern Equity" at pp. 55 *et seq.* "Advancement" is used synonymously with "portion" as in *Taylor* v *Taylor* (1875) L.R. 20 Eq. 155, 157 (per Jessel M.R.). The term is also familiar to equity lawyers in the context of the presumption of advancement which negatives a resulting trust when a man buys property in the name of his wife. See *Heavey* v *Heavey* (1977) 111 I.L.T.R.I.

[55] Section 63 (6). Compare the criteria used by the courts in relation to applications under s.117 of the Succession Act at *ante* p. 198

[56] Section 63 (2)

[57] Section 63 (3)

[58] Section 63 (4)

[59] Section 63 (8)

personage than Lord Eldon spoke of its harshness.[60] A learned Irish author has written, rather resignedly, that despite "these (judicial) misgivings as to the desirability of the rule, it was expressly preserved in our law by section 63(9) of the Succession Act 1965."[61]

8.10 Parents surviving

8.10.1 If an intestate dies leaving neither spouse nor issue, but both parents surviving, his estate will be distributed equally between them; if only one parent survives the intestate, he or she will take the whole estate.[62]

8.10.2 This new provision removes an invidious piece of gender discrimination in the old rules which had provided, that when both parents survived an intestate the father took the whole estate.[63] Where an intestate's mother, and brothers and sisters survived him, all took in equal shares.[64]

8.10.3 Parents of a legitimated child have the same rights of succession to his estate as the parents of a legitimate child, if the child was legitimated at the time of his death.[65] Likewise, the adoptive parents of an adopted child have the same rights of succession to his estate as the parents of a child born in "lawful wedlock", from the making of the adoption order.[66]

Brothers and sisters surviving

8.11.1 If an intestate dies leaving neither spouse nor issue nor parent, his estate will be distributed among his brothers and sisters in equal shares, and, if any brother or sister of the intestate shall predecease him, the surviving children of such deceased brother or sister shall, where any other brother or sister of the intestate survives him, take in equal shares the share that their parent would have taken if he or she had survived the intestate.[67] If no brother or sister survives the intestate, is estate will be divided in equal shares among his nephews and nieces, if any such survive him.[68]

---

[60] *Ex. p. Pye* (1811) 18 Ves. 140, 151 and see *Montagu* v *Earl of Sandwich* (1886) 32 Ch. D. 525, 544 (per Bowen L.J.) and see Brady "Judicial Pragmatism and Justice Inter Partes" (1986) 21 Irish Jurist (N.S.) 47, 48.

[61] Keane "Equity and the Law of Trusts in the Republic of Ireland" at p.312

[62] Section 68

[63] See Appendix A of the Explanatory Memorandum with the Succession Act.

[64] *Ibid*

[65] Section 4 of the Legitimacy Act 1931

[66] Sections 24 and 26 of the Adoption Act 1952 (No. 25)

[67] Section 69 (1). Cf. the position in Northern Ireland under s.10 (1) of the Administration of Estates Act 1955 (c.24). See Wylie "Irish Land Law" (2nd ed. 1986) at p.758

[68] Section 69 (2)

8.11.2 As we have seen adopted and legitimated children are treated, from the making of an adoption order or the date of legitimation, as though they were born in lawful wedlock, and children of the family into which a child has been adopted or legitimated will have the usual rights of succession as brothers and sisters of a legitimate child.[69]

8.12 Next-of-kin surviving

8.12.1 If an intestate is survived by neither spouse, nor issue, nor parent, nor brothers and sisters nor children of same, his estate shall be divided in equal shares among his next-of-kin.[70] Representation, which means probate or administration,[71] of next-of-kin is not to be admitted amongst collaterals, except in the case of children of brothers and sisters of the intestate, where any other brother or sister of the intestate survives him.[72] Thus, if the deceased is survived only by nieces and nephews representation will be denied to them.

8.12.2 There may be valid policy reasons for not granting representation to collaterals, but the term collateral usually refers to descent from a common ancestor but by a different line and does not obviously enbrace children of a brother or sister of the deceased. Denial of representation to more remote issue of the deceased is understandable but not to nephews and nieces who, under section 69(2) are entitled to an equal distribution of the deceased's estate if no brother or sister survives him.

8.12.3 Subject to the rights of representation dealt with in section 70(2), the person or persons who, at the date of the death of the intestate, stand closest in blood relationship to him shall be taken to be his next-of-kin.[73] The rules for the ascertainment of next-of-kin are set out in section 71(2) as follows:

"Degrees of blood relationship of a direct lineal ancestor shall be computed by counting upwards from the intestate to that ancestor, and degrees of blood relationship of any other relative shall be ascertained by counting upwards from the intestate to the nearest ancestor common to the intestate and that relative, and then downwards from that ancestor to the relative; but, where a direct lineal ancestor and any other relative are so ascertained to be within the same degree of blood relationship to the intestate, the other relative shall be preferred to the exclusion of the direct lineal ancestor."

[69] See s.26 (1) of the Adoption Act 1952 and s.4 of the Legitimacy Act 1931
[70] Section 70 (1)
[71] See s.3 (3)
[72] Section 70 (2)
[73] Section 71 (1)

8.12.4 Applying these rules, where an intestate is survived by an uncle and grandfather, the grandfather, who is related in the second degree to the deceased, will take in preference to the uncle who is related to the deceased in the third degree. The uncle's degree of relationship to the deceased is calculated by counting upwards from the intestate to their nearest common ancestor, who is the intestate's grandfather, and then down to the uncle. If the intestate is survived by an uncle and great-grandfather each would be in the same third degree of relationship to the deceased, and in those circumstances the other relative, the uncle, is to be preferred to the direct lineal ancestor.[74]

8.12.5 The nature of the interests of next-of-kin in an intestate's estate was one of the questions which Barron J. recently had to consider in *M.H. and N.McG.* v *N.M. and C.M.*[75], which came before the court by way of application under section 117 of the Succession Act taken by two daughters of the testator. The testator had left his house and contents and all "my shares and interests in the business of licensed vinters carried on therin under the name of C.M. and Sons Limited" to his two sons N. and C., and the residue of his estate to his remaining four children. The testator's wife, who had predeceased the testator had held shares in the company which owned the licensed vintners business, and her estate remained unadministered at the testator's death. The question accordingly arose, as to whether the testator's proportion of the shares held by his wife in the company, which would have passed to him on completion of the administration of her estate, passed under the specific bequest in his will to his two sons, or, under the residuary bequest to his remaining children.

8.12.6 Barron J. cited *Cooper* v *Cooper*[76] as authority for the proposition that next-of-kin under an intestacy have the same interest in the estate of an intestate as a residuary legatee has in the residue of the testator's estate. In that case a testatrix, who had made an invalid appointment by will over assets which, in default of a valid appointment passed on an intestacy, also left benefits in her will to certain of those entitled as next-of-kin under such intestacy. It was held that the latter had to elect to take under the will or the intestacy.[77] Barron J. pointed out that *Cooper* v *Cooper* was followed specifically by the Irish Court of Appeal in *Tevlin* v *Gilsenan*[78], where the

---

[74] This preference for the younger relation has a long pedigree. See *Evelyn* v *Evelyn* (1754) 3 Atk. 762

[75] [1983] I.L.R.M. 519

[76] (1874) L.R. I.H.L. 53

[77] See Lord Cairns at p.67

[78] [1902] 1 I.R. 514

question was, whether the interest of one of the next-of-kin in a chattel real was of such a specific character as being capable of being the subject matter of a judgment mortgage under section 6 of the Judgment Mortgage (Ireland) Act, 1850. In holding that it was, Lord O'Brien L.C.J. said, that *Cooper* v *Cooper* showed, that "a next-of-kin takes a specific interest in each portion of the intestate's estate which he can assign or release."[79]

8.12.7 Barron J. added however, that this specific interest of a next-of-kin was not regarded as entitling him to claim an absolute interest in any particular asset such that the administrator had an obligation to hand it over in *in specie;*[80] nor was it of such a specific nature as to pass under a bequest of "my shares."[81] Barron J. did find guidance in the resolution of the problem before him in the decision in *Re Leigh's Will Trusts*[82], where it was held, that a bequest of "all shares which I hold and any other interest or assets which I may have" in a specified company, passed the interest which the testatrix had in shares which were part of the unadministered estate of her intestate husband. Buckley J. held, that she could transmit this right to require the administrator of her husband's estate to administer the estate in any manner she might require to her executor, coupled with a duty to exercise it in a particular manner."[83]

8.12.8 Applying those decisions to the problem before him Barron J. concluded, that the shares to which the testator would become entitled upon completion of the administration of his wife's estate, assuming that they did not have to be disposed of in due course of administration, did not become his shares but he did acquire a specific interest in them which passed to his executor. That being so, they would not have passed under a bequest of "my shares" but, the bequest being in the form it was, they did pass under the bequest of "all my interest in the business."[84]

8.12.9 It is provided in section 72 that relatives of the half-blood[85] shall be treated as, and shall succeed equally with, relatives of the whole blood and in the same degree. Thus half-brothers and half-sisters of a deceased intestate will share equally in the distribution of his estate with his brothers and sisters, and children of half-brothers and half-sisters will share equally with nephews and nieces of the intestate. This provision now equalises the positions of relatives of the whole blood and relatives of the half-blood in

---

[79] *Ibid* at p.521
[80] Barron J. referred to *Vanneck* v *Benham* [1917] 1 Ch. 60
[81] Barron J. referred to *Villiers* v *Holmes* [1917] 1 I.R. 165.
[82] [1969] 3 All E.R. 432
[83] *Ibid* at p. 346
[84] [1983] I.L.R.M. 519, 522
[85] Relatives of the half-blood share one parent or common ancestor.

the distribution of an intestate's estate since, under the previous law, relatives of the whole blood had preference as regards succession to real estate but ranked equally with relatives of the half-blood in the distribution of personalty.[86]

8.12.10 Distribution on intestacy is also affected by the provision in section 3 (2) that descendants and relatives of a deceased person, begotten before his death but born alive thereafter, shall be regarded as having been born in the lifetime of the deceased and as having survived him.[87]

8.13 Default of next-of-kin

8.13.1 It is provided in section 3 (1) that, in default of any person taking the estate of an intestate, whether under Part VI of the Succession Act or otherwise, the state shall take as ultimate intestate successor. This provision replaces the old rules of forfeit by way of escheat in respect of realty, and *bona vacantia* in respect of personalty.[88] This change making the state the ultimate intestate successor was apparently made because of the concern that foreign courts might treat the right of the state to *bona vacantia* as an aspect of public law, and not enforceable within the context of conflicts of law.[89]

8.13.2 The right of the State as ultimate intestate successor may be waived by the Minister for Finance, if he thinks it proper to do so, in whole or in part, and in favour of such person and upon such terms (whether including or not including the payment of money) as he thinks proper, having regard to all the circumstances of the case.[90] The Minister for Finance has a very wide discretion in waiving the right of the State, and, perhaps the only thing that one can be certain about in this age of fiscal rectitude and government parsimony is, that the Minister for Finance will rarely forego his right to claim money from an estate as one of the terms upon which the State waives its right. It is to be hoped that this right will in the main be restricted to recouping government costs and outlay.

8.13.3 There is little available evidence on the exercise by the Minister for Finance of his discretion to waive the State's right as ultimate intestate successor but it has apparently been exercised in favour of charities, where there was evidence that the deceased intended the charities to

---

[86] See the Explanatory Memorandum with the Succession Act at p.7

[87] See *ante* p. 153

[88] See Kenny J.'s consideration of the principle of *bona vacantia* in *Re Doherty* [1961] I.R. 219 and Wylie "A Casebook on Irish Land Law' (2nd ed. 1986) at p.52

[89] *Ibid* at p. 73

[90] Section 73(2)

benefit. It has also apparently been exercised in favour of a person with a moral claim on the deceased's bounty, who would otherwise have qualified as a next-of-kin and in favour of a particular beneficiary who was deprived of a benefit the deceased intended to give him because of the invalid execution of a will.[91]

8.13.4 The right of the State to disclaim certain land devolving by way of escheat or *bona vacantia* provided in section 32 of the State Property Act, 1954,[92] has been extended to include the grantee's interest under a fee farm grant and the lessee's interest under a lease, where the State has a right to such interest as ultimate intestate successor.[93]

8.13.5 The prerequisites for the exercise of the State's rights as ultimate intestate successor are straightforward in that the deceased must have died intestate, with no surviving next-of-kin, but that the establishment of these prerequisites might be problematical can be seen in *Re Doherty*[94] where Kenny J. had to consider an application made by the Minister for Finance in 1959 claiming that certain shares and accumulated dividends devolved on the State as *bona vacantia*. There, one James Doherty had, in 1919 instructed a firm of Dublin stockbrokers, to whom he was then unknown, to invest £30 in shares in Bolands Ltd. He further instructed the stockbrokers to retain the shares as he was going to Australia in the near future. The shares having been bought, the stockbrokers never heard from him again. Advertisements were published in Irish and Australian papers seeking information about him but none was obtained.

8.13.6 Kenny J. pointed out, that before he could hold the property as *bona vacantia* he must be satisfied that James Doherty was dead, that he died intestate and that he had no known next-of-kin.[95] Kenny J. referred to *McMahon* v *McElroy*[96] in which the Vice Chancellor had said of the circumstances in which the legal presumption of death arises: "The remaining question is whether, upon the evidence, I am to presume the death of Hugh Morgan the younger, and interfere at present with the actual possession of the defendant. Of his death there is not any positive evidence, and I am called upon to act entirely on the ordinary presumption as to which, and as to its operation, there can be no doubt – namely, that, as a general rule, a man's death will be presumed after an interval of seven

---

[91] These examples are taken from Maguire "The Succession Act 1965: A Commentary" (2nd ed. 1986 by Robert A Pearse) and were apparently provided by the Minister for Finance.
[92] No. 25 of 1954
[93] Section 73(3)
[94] [1961] I.R. 219
[95] *Ibid* at p. 221
[96] (1869) I.R. 5 Eq. 1

years since he was last heard of. But this is not an invariable rule, and it admits of exceptions; and indeed in any case the court in following the analogy of the statutes, on which analogy the rule depends, is bound to consider the circumstances of the particular case, in order to see whether the presumption is rebutted or rather whether it fairly arises."[97]

8.13.7 Kenny J. thought that the firm of stockbrokers who had purchased the shares for James Doherty could reasonably have expected to hear from him concerning the shares, over the forty years since they had been purchased, and, even if a false name had been given to the stockbrokers, Kenny J. could think of nobody more likely to hear from him than the firm of stockbrokers which had purchased the shares on his instructions.[98] In these circumstances, Kenny J. thought that this was a case in which the legal presumption of death arose, and he was prepared to presume that James Doherty was dead.[99]

8.13.8 It is difficult to see how Kenny J. could have arrived at any other conclusion on the facts of that case, but, the answer to the further question, whether Kenny J. could safely presume that James Doherty had died intestate, unmarried and without known next-of-kin was more problematic. A similar question had arisen in In *re Lavelle*[100] in which Patrick Lavelle had gone to the United States of America in 1910 and had not been heard of since, no replies being received to advertisements in papers in the United States. Gavan Duffy J. accordingly made an order presuming that Patrick Lavelle had died before 1927, but he refused to presume that he had died either intestate, or unmarried and childless.[101] In Kenny J.'s opinion, however, the court in that case would have been justified in presuming that Patrick Lavelle had died intestate and without issue.[102] Kenny J. pointed out that in *re Webb's Estate*[103] in which the Court of Appeal in Chancery held that a presumption that a person died without issue arose in somewhat similar circumstances to those in *In re Lavelle*, had not been cited to Gavan Duffy J.

8.13.9 That being so Kenny J. was not prepared to follow the decision in *In re Lavelle* in so far as it decided that on the facts of that case, the court would not have been justified in presuming that Patrick Lavelle died intestate, unmarried and childless. Kenny J. thought that he would be

[97] *Ibid.* at p.12
[98] (1961) I.R. 219
[99] *Ibid* at p. 222
[100] [1940] Ir. 3ur. Rep. 8
[101] *Ibid* at p. 9
[102] [1961] I.R. 219
[103] (1869) I.R. 5 Eq. 235

justified in the instant case in presuming that James Doherty had died intestate, unmarried and without known next-of-kin, and his property accordingly passed to the State as *bona vacantia.*[104]

8.13.10 Kenny J. considered whether he should direct an inquiry as to the next-of-kin of James Doherty, but was satisfied that the advertisements which would be directed for such an inquiry would be the same as those which had already been made and that no further information would be obtained.[105]

8.14 Partial intestacy

8.14.1 A partial intestacy occurs where a person leaves a will which effectively disposes of part only of the property in which he has a beneficial interest, in which case it is provided that "the remainder shall be distributed as if he had died intestate and left no other estate."[106] The test here is not whether a will has been validly executed, as it is in cases involving section 117 of the Succession Act,[107] but, whether the will effectively disposes of the testator's property.[108] The marginal note to section 74 refers simply to the Executors Act 1830[109] which makes it clear that section 74 is merely repeating the provision in that legislation that an executor was deemed to hold the undisposed of part of the deceased's estate for those entitled on his intestacy.

8.15 Construction of documents

8.15.1 References to any Statutes of Distribution in an *inter vivos* instrument, or in a will, coming into operation after the commencement of the Succession Act, are construed, unless a contrary intention appears, as references to Part VI of the Succession Act; references in such instrument or will to statutory next-of-kin are construed, unless the contrary appears, as referring to the persons who would succeed on an intestacy under Part VI.[110]

8.15.2 Where trusts were declared by reference to any Statutes of Distribution in an instrument made *inter vivos,* or will coming into

---

[104] [1961] I.R. 219

[105] *Ibid* at p.

[106] Section 74

[107] See *ante* p. 205

[108] See *Re Ford* [1902] 2 Ch. 605; *Re Skeats* [1936] Ch. 683 and Mellows "The Law of Succession" (4th ed. 1983) at pp. 222 *et seq.*

[109] 11 Geo. 4 & 1 Will. 4 c.40

[110] Section 75(1)

operation before the commencement of the Succession Act, such references are to be construed as referring to the enactments, other than the Intestates Estates Act 1954,[111] relating to the distribution of effects of intestates which were in force immediately prior to the commencement of the Succession Act.[112]

[111] No. 12 of 1954
[112] Section 75(2)

Chapter 9
THE ADMINISTRATION OF ESTATES

9.1 Introduction

9.1.1 The estate of a deceased person devolves on his death to his personal representatives, who are responsible for its administration, which involves, as we shall see, the payment of funeral, testamentary, and administration expenses, and the discharge of the deceased's debts and other liabilities, following which the estate is distributed among those entitled under the testator's will, or on his intestacy, as the case may be.

9.1.2 The personal representatives may be appointed by the testator in his will, in which case they are called executors, or they may be appointed by the court in cases of intestacy or where an executor has predeceased the testator, in which case they are called administrators.[1] The general term personal representatives is still used, though it reflects the fact that at one time only the personal estate of a deceased person passed to his personal representatives on death, his real estate passing directly to the devisee if there was a will, and to the heir-at-law on an intestacy.[2]

9.1.3 We have seen that the process of assimilation of realty and personalty for purposes of devolution was set in train by the Local Registration of Title (Irl.) Act, 1891, Part IV of which provided, that land purchased by tenant farmers under the Land Purchase Acts should continue to devolve to, and become vested in, the personal representatives of the deceased as chattel real property.[3] The personal representatives accordingly had the

[1] The female equivalents are executrix, or executrices, and administratrix, or administratices.

[2] See *ante* p. 216

[3] Sections 85 and 86 of the Local Registration of Title (Ireland) Act 1891. See generally Wylie "Irish Land Law" (2nd ed. 1986) at p.751

same powers in respect of such land as they had in respect of personalty. This process of assimilation was continued in the Administration of Estates Act, 1959,[4] and completed by the Succession Act which provides in section 10(1) that the real and personal estate of a deceased person shall on his death, notwithstanding any testamentary disposition, devolve on, and become vested in his personal representatives. The personal representatives for the time being of a deceased person are deemed in law to be his heirs and assigns within the meaning of all trusts and powers.[5]

9.1.4 Further assimilation of law respecting real and personal estates of deceased persons is contained in section 12(1) of the Succession Act which provides, that all enactments, including the Succession Act, and rules of law relating to certain specified matters, shall, so far as applicable, apply to real estate as if it were personal estate. The specified matters are (a) the effect of representation as respects personal estate, (b) the dealing with personal estate before representation, (c) the powers, rights, duties, and liabilities of personal representatives in respect of personal estate, (d) the payment of costs of administration, and (e) all other matters with respect to the administration of personal estate. It is also provided that a grant of representation shall, unless containing an express limitation to the contrary, have like effect over real as over personal estate.[6]

9.2 Vesting in the President of the High Court

9.2.1 While an executor derives his title and authority from the will, and the deceased's estate vests in him immediately upon death, an administrator derives his title and authority solely from the grant to him of letters of administration to the deceased's estate.[7] It is however a fundamental principle of our law of property that ownership should at all times lie in somebody and not *in vacuo,* and, to avoid a gap in ownership between the owner's death and the grant of letters of administration to his personal representatives, it is provided in section 13 of the Succession Act that where a person dies intestate, or dies testate but leaving no executor surviving him, "his real and personal estate, until administration is granted in respect thereof, shall vest in the President of the High Court who, for this purpose, shall be a corporation sole".[8]

---

[4] No. 8 of 1959

[5] Section 10(2). See s.30 of the Conveyancing Act 1881 (c.41) and ss.6, 7(1) and 15 of the Administration of Estates Act, 1959.

[6] Section 12(3)

[7] See *Chetty* v *Chetty* [1916] 1 A.C. 603, 608 (per Lord Parker of Waddington) and *Creed* v *Creed* [1913] 1 I.R. 48

[8] See s.15 of the Court of Probate (Ireland) Act, 1859, and s.13 of the Administration of Estates Act, 1959

9.2.2 The vesting of a deceased's estate in the President of the High Court has raised certain questions about the role of the President in the administration of an estate pending a grant of representation. Thus, in *Flack* v *President of the High Court and others*[9] it was sought to join the President of the High Court in an action taken by the executors of one Henry Holmes Flack, who were seeking orders that an account be taken of certain partnership dealings, that partnership assets be sold, and a receiver appointed. Henry Holmes Flack had been in partnership with his four brothers two of whom, including the last surviving partner, had died intestate and, when the plaintiffs started their action no representation had been taken out to the last surviving brother's estate. That being so, the plaintiffs sought to join the President of the High Court as a defendant, referring to section 13 of the Succession Act, and urging that it was because of the special difficulties in the instant case, including the urgency of the proceedings, that made it appropriate to join the President as the person in whom the estates of two of the deceased partners vested.

9.2.3 Costello J., however, thought it worthy of note that neither under the Court of Probate (Ireland) Act 1859, which vested the estate in the probate judge, nor under the Administration of Estates Act, 1959, which vested the estate in the President of the High Court, was the judge ever joined as a defendant in proceedings arising under the relevant vesting provision. The reason, Costello J. believed, was perfectly clear since in vesting personalty, and later both realty and personalty, in the President of the High Court, the legislature did not make him a trustee of the estate which vested in him, and he had no duty to perform and no obligation in respect of the estate.[10] Costello J. referred to *Re Deans*,[11] where it was held that the similar vesting provisions in section 9 of the English Administration of Estates Act, 1925, were "a mere matter of necessary convenience and protection";[12] the learned judge took the view that the position of the President of the High Court under section 13 of the Succession Act was exactly the same.

9.2.4 Costello J. did point out however that under the old law a plaintiff faced with similar difficulties to those which confronted the plaintiffs in the instant proceedings was not without a remedy, since he could apply for and obtain the appointment of an administrator *ad litem* and join him as a defendant in the suit; the court has a similar power under section 27 of the Succession Act to make a limited grant of administration.[13]

[9] Unreported High Court judgment of Costello J. delivered 29 November 1983; 1983 No. 2955P

[10] See now s.10(3) of the Succession Act

[11] [1954] 1 All E.R. 496

[12] *Ibid* at p.498

[13] See s.27 (4)

9.2.5 The proposition, that the vesting of a deceased's estate in the President of the High Court is essentially a matter of convenience, derives support from the well established practice in Ireland to the effect that where a tenant has died, and no legal representation has been raised to his estate, the landlord is not required to raise such representation or wait until it has been raised in order to determine the tenancy, but may serve the appropriate notice to quit on the person or persons who are found in possession of the demised premises.[14] Palles C.B. offered a simple and commonsense explanation of this practice when he said, in *Sweeney* v *Sweeney*,[15] that

"when by reason of a tenant not being in existence, or of any other circumstance, it is not reasonably possible to serve the tenant, either personally or through an agent, the landlord is entitled as against the original tenant and all claiming through him, to treat the person in possession as a person authorised to receive the notice."

A learned author has pointed out that it is a curious feature of *Sweeney* v *Sweeney* that section 15 of the Court of Probate (Irl.) Act 1859, which provided for vesting in the Probate Judge pending a grant of administration, was not, apparently cited to the court.[16] Be that as it may, *Sweeney* v *Sweeney* has been followed by the Supreme Court in *Hill* v *Carroll*,[17] which case underlines however the convenience reasons for, and limited scope of, the practice of serving a notice to quit on the person in possession of demised premises.

9.2.6 The Supreme Court held in *Hill* v *Carroll* that the service of such a notice did not make the person upon whom it was served a tenant of the premises for any intent or purpose save that of determining the tenancy, and did not vest in him the tenancy of the deceased tenant.[18] Accordingly, service of a notice to quit in the circumstances of that case did not confer on the recipient the status of a statutory tenant protected in his possession by the Rent Restrictions Acts, 1946 and 1949.[19]

9.2.7 That the practice of serving notice to quit on the occupier of demised premises survived the enactment of section 13 of the Succession Act was confirmed in *Dublin Corporation* v *Representatives of Patrick Sheridan*.[20] There the plaintiffs, in order to terminate an outstanding tenancy of a

[14] See *Hill* v *Carroll* [1953] I.R. 52, 58
[15] (1876) I.R 10 C.L. 375, 392. See also the judgment of Dowse B. at p.379
[16] Wylie "Irish Land Law" (2nd ed. 1986) at p.764 n. 7
[17] [1953] I.R. 52
[18]. *Ibid* at p.61 (per Lavery J.)
[19]. *Ibid* at pp. 61-63
[20] (1976) 111 I.L.T.R. 143

tenant who had died intestate, served notice to quit on his nephew who was in possession of the demised premises, and did not serve notice to quit on the President of the High Court. The notice to quit which was served on the nephew was addressed to "The Personal Representatives of and all persons claiming to represent Patrick Sheridan (deceased)".

9.2.8 It was contended for the defendant that the action should be dismissed as it was necessary, following section 13 of the Succession Act, that notice to quit should, in these circumstances, have been served on the President of the High Court. Counsel for the defendant argued that section 13 of the Succession Act is in substitution for the older method of termination by service on the party in posseession after the death intestate of the tenant. Counsel referred to *Fred Long and Sons Ltd* v *Burgess*[21] as showing, that service of a notice to quit on the President of the Probate, Divorce and Admiralty Division of the High Court was the only way in which termination could be effected under section 9 of the English Administration of Estates Act 1925.[22]

9.2.9 Judge Clark believed however, that he must take account of the long established practice and the Irish decisions thereon, and that it "would be too big a step to cast them aside and follow the English decisions".[23]

9.2.10 The quite different question arose in *Kelly* v *Tallon*[24] as to whether, where no representation had been raised to a tenant who had died intestate, his daughter who had lived with him on the demised premises, could claim to have derived title under section 2 of the Rent Restrictions Act 1946.[25] The court also had to consider the effect of section 9 of Deasy's Act[26] which provides, *inter alia*, that "in case the said estate or interest shall, on the death of the tenant, remain undisposed of and without any special occupant, it shall pass to the personal representative of the tenant as part of the personal estate of such tenant".

9.2.11 Judge Connolly held (1) that the person solely entitled to the beneficial interest and estate of a deceased tenant, by virtue of the operation of section 2 of the 1946 Act or section 9 of Deasy's Act, could not derive title under him unless he had raised representation to the personal estate of the deceased tenant, and (2) a notice to quit served on

[21] [1950] 1 K.B. 115. (See Bucknill L.J. at p.119)

[22] 15 Geo. 5 c. 23

[23] (1976) 111 I.L.T.R. 143, 144. See also *O'Sullivan Sons Ltd* v *O'Mahony* [1953] I.R. 125 and *O'Connor* v *Fitzgerald* (1959) 91 I.L.T.R. 32

[24] (1948) 84 I.L.T.R. 196

[25] No. 4 of 1946

[26] Landlord and Tenant Law Amendment Act (Ireland) 1860 (23 & 24 Vict. c.154)

such person as the representative of the deceased tenant determined the interest of the deceased tenant, even where the person beneficially entitled had lived with the tenant during the period of his tenancy and remained on in possession after the tenant's death. The second part of Judge Connolly's judgment was scarcely intended to throw any doubt on the long established practice that, in appropriate circumstances, service of a notice to quit on the person in possession of the demised premises will suffice.

9.3 The doctrine of "relation back"

9.3.1 In order to minimise the potentially harmful consequences for a deceased's estate of the postponement of the title and authority of administrators until the grant of administration, the courts have adopted the doctrine of "relation back". That doctrine means that, for certain limited purposes, a grant of administration will relate back to the death of the deceased.[27] The limits of the doctrine reflect its primary purpose of protecting the deceased's estate from wrongdoing in the interval between his death and a grant of representation. Thus Parke B. pointed out in *Foster* v *Bates*[28] that, although the title of an administrator does not exist until the grant of administration, it relates back to the time of death of an intestate "that he may recover against a wrongdoer who has seized or converted the goods of the intestate after his death, in an action of trespass or trover".

9.3.2 The limits of an administrator's authority prior to the grant of administration is illustrated by two English cases each of which had an Irish dimension. In *Finnegan* v *Cementation Co. Ltd*[29] an action was brought by a widow under the Fatal Accidents Act 1959 in respect of the death of her husband. The death had occurred in Ireland and the widow had taken out a grant here. It transpired however, that the head office of the company being located in England, the action should have been taken there. No grant of administration having been taken out in England, the writ was set aside.[30] In *Burns* v *Campbell*[31] a similar fate befell a writ issued by an administrator who had obtained a grant of administration in Northern Ireland but issued the writ in England before the resealing there of the Northern Ireland grant. It was held that the writ was defective, since a subsequent resealing did not have any retroactive effect.[32]

---

[27] See *Thorpe* v *Smallwood* (1843) 5 M. & Gr. 760 and *Re Pryse* [1904] P.301

[28] (1843) 12 M. & W. 226, 233

[29] [1953] 1 Q.B. 688. See Mellows "The Law of Succession" (4th ed. 1983) at p.318

[30] See also *Ingall* v *Moran* [1944] K.B. 160

[31] [1952] 1 K.B.15. See Mellows "The Law of Succession" at p.318

[32] Resealing of Northern Ireland grants is no longer necessary in England. See s.1(5) of the Administration of Estates Act 1971(c.31)

9.3.3 The doctrine of "relation back" cannot be invoked to revive an interest which has been validly terminated prior to the grant of administration.[33] Asquith L.J. put it graphically in *Fred Long & Son Ltd* v *Burgess;*[34] "The doctrine of 'relation back' cannot breathe new life into a corpse."

9.3.4 It has been suggested by a leading English textwriter that, although an administrator has no power whatever to execute an assent or conveyance prior to obtaining his grant of administration, where a recital of entitlement is contained in the assent or conveyance, the purchaser could in due course obtain the legal estate under the doctrine of "feeding" the estoppel."[35]

9.3.5 For the purposes of the provision of the Statute of Limitations 1957 relating to actions for the recovery of land, "an administrator of the estate of a deceased person shall be deemed to claim as if there had been no interval of time between the date of the death of the deceased person and the grant of letters of administration".[36]

9.4 Executors and administrators

9.4.1 Executors are, as we have seen, normally the persons appointed by a testator in his will to administer his estate. A testator may also in his will, or in an instrument executed in accordance with the formalities necessary for the execution of wills, confer on another person the power to appoint an executor or executors. The practice of conferring a power to appoint executors on others is uncommon, but among the persons on whom such power has been conferred are legatees under a will[37] and the survivor of two executors appointed by the will.[38] A testator may also nominate one or more persons who may be substituted for the executors appointed by the will on the occurrence of certain specified events, such as the death of an executor before that of the testator or the departure from the jurisdiction of someone appointed as executor.[39] In the absence of any contrary

[33] See *Long* v *Burgess* (1950) 1 K.B. 115

[34] *Ibid* at 121. See Parry and Clark "The Law of Succession" (8th ed. 1983) at p.163

[35] See Mellows "The Law of Succession at p.318 *referring to* Rawlin's Case (1587), Jenk. 254; *Mackley* v *Nutting* [1949] 2 K.B. 55; *Universal Permanent Building Society* v *Cooke* [1952] Ch. 95

[36] Section 23 of the 1957 Act.

[37] See e.g. *Re Kehoe* [1940] Ir. Jur. Rep. 35. See *In the Goods of Cringan* (1828) 1 Hagg. Ecc.548 and Parry and Clark "The Law of Succession" (8th ed. 1983) at p.136

[38] *In the Goods of Deichman* (1842) 3 Curt. 123; *In the Goods of Ryder* (1861) 2 Sw. & Tr. 127

[39] See e.g. *In the Goods of Lane* (1864) 33 L.J.P.M. & A. 185 and *In the Goods of Foster* (1871) L.R. 2 P. & D. 304

indication in the power, the donee of the power may substitute himself in place of an executor.[40]

9.4.2 The qualities required of an executor are similar in many respects to those required of a trustee and each is usually appointed because of his honesty, probity and business acumen. The office of executor is, accordingly, personal to the appointee and is non-assignable.[41] The personal nature of the office of executor was arguably not well served by the so-called chain of representation, which provided that the executor of the sole or last surviving executor of a testator was also the executor of that testator.[42] The chain of executorship rule was removed from Irish law by section 19 of the Succession Act which provides, in subsection (1), that where "the sole or last surviving executor of a testator dies after the commencement of this Act, the executor of such executor shall not be the executor of that testator". That section applies whether the testator died before or after the commencement of the Succession Act.[43]

9.4.3 A conveyancing sub-committee of the Law Reform Commission, of which the author is a member, has considered the desirability of restoring the chain of executorship rule to Irish law. While there was general agreement that such restoration would be particularly convenient for conveyancers, and avoid the necessity of taking out *de bonis non* grants, there was thought to be little logic in a rule which could result in a total stranger coming into control of a deceased's estate quite shortly after his death. The sub-committee was unimpressed by the oft-quoted reason for the rule that just as a testator has the utmost confidence in the executors he has chosen, he ought to have similar confidence in their choice of executors, a reason which an English textwriter has described as "specious".[44] It was accordingly decided not to recommend the restoration of the chain of executorship rule to Irish law.

9.5 Number of executors

9.5.1 There is no statutory limit to the number of executors whom a testator might appoint, but the Rules of the Superior Courts provide, that no grant of administration shall be made jointly to more than three persons

---

[40] See *In the Goods of Ryder* (1861) 2 Sw. & Tr. 127
[41] See e.g. *In the Goods of Galbraith* [1951] P.422 and *In the Estate of Skinner* [1958] 1 W.L.R. 1043
[42] See s.7(1) of the English Administration of Estates Act 1925 (15 Geo. 5 c.23)
[43] Section 19(2)
[44] Mellows "The Law of Succession" (4th ed. 1983) at p.219

unless the probate officer otherwise directs.[45] There is, likewise, no minimum number of executors to be appointed but, as with the appointment of trustees, prudence and convenience dictate the appointment of more than a single executor.

9.5.2 If only one or some of two or more executors named in a will take out probate then, whether or not power is reserved to the other or others to prove the will, all the powers which are conferred on personal representatives by the Succession Act, or otherwise conferred by law on personal representatives, are exercisable by the proving executor or executors or the survivor or survivors of them, and are as effectual as if all persons named as executors had concurred therein.[46] The foregoing provision applies whether a testator died before or after the commencement of the Succession Act.47

9.6 Capacity of executors

9.6.1 A testator is free to appoint whomever he pleases to be his executor, but problems arise if the appointee is an infant or suffers from some legal disability. Thus, it is provided, that where an infant is sole executor of a will, administration with the will annexed will be granted to his guardian, or to such other person as the High Court thinks fit, until the infant obtains the age of twenty-one years, and applies for, and obtains a grant of probate or letters of administration with the will annexed, and on his attaining that age, and not before, probate of the will may be granted to him.[48] It is also provided however in the Rules of the Superior Court that, unless the court or Probate Officer otherwise directs, a grant shall be given to a person not under a legal disability in preference to the committee or guardian of a person under a legal disability equally entitled, provided that in the case of an application by the committee of a person under a legal disability the court or Probate Officer shall, before a grant is given, consult the Registrar of Wards of Court.[49]

9.6.2 If a person who is appointed as an executor is suffering from a mental or physical infirmity which impairs his ability to manage his affairs he will be unable to act as executor while the disability continues.[50] If an executor

[45] Order 79 Rule 5(14). This new rule places limits, for the first time, on the number of persons who are entitled to take out a grant of probate, unless the probate officer otherwise directs.

[46] Section 20(10)

[47] Section 20(2)

[48] Section 32(1). The age of majority is now eighteen years.

[49] Order 79 Rule 5(9)(c)

[50] *Evans v Tyler* (1849) 2 Rob. 128

becomes unfit to act after a grant of administration to him, the grant may be revoked.[51] Under the Rules of the Superior Courts it is provided, that in the case of a person who, in the opinion of the court or the Probate Officer, is suffering from a severe continuing physical disability, administration, or administration with the will annexed, may be granted to his attorney, acting under a power of attorney.[52]

9.6.3 The Rules of the Superior Courts also provide that a grant of administration may be made to the committee of a person of unsound mind for such person's use and benefit.[53] Where a person of unsound mind does not have a committee appointed by the court, a grant may issue to such person as the Probate Officer may, by order, assign, with the consent of the Registrar of Wards of Court. Applications for such orders shall be grounded on an affidavit of the applicant showing the amount of the assets, the age and residence of the person of unsound mind, and his relationship to the applicant together with an affidavit of a medical practitioner dealing with the incapacity of such person.[54]

9.6.4 The Succession Act now provides for the issue of grants of representation to trust corporations.[55] Where a trust corporation is named in a will as executor, whether alone or jointly with another person, the High Court may grant probate to the corporation either solely or jointly with another person, as the case may require,[56] and, may grant administration to a trust corporation, either solely or jointly with another person.[57] A trust corporation is defined for the purposes of the Succession Act as meaning (a) a corporation appointed by the High Court in any particular case to be a trustee, and, (b) a company empowered by its constitution to undertake trust business, and having a place of business in the State, or in Northern Ireland, provided other criteria relating to the establishment of companies are met.[58] The definition also includes a corporation which satisfies the President of the High Court that it undertakes the administration of any charitable, ecclesiastical or public trust without remuneration, or that by its constitution it is required to apply the whole of its net income for such charitable, ecclesiastical or public purposes.[59]

---

[51] See *In the Goods of Ryan* [1927] I.R. 174; *In the Goods of Galbraith* [1951] P. 422

[52] Order 79 Rule 23 which also provide for the granting of administration to the attorney of a person residing out of, or about to leave the jurisdiction.

[53] Order 79 Rule 26

[54] Order 79 Rule 27

[55] Cf. the Bodies Corporate (Executors and Administrators) Act 1928 (No. 9)

[56] Section 30(1)(a)

[57] Section 30(1)(b)

[58] Section 30(4)

[59] Section 30(4)(c)

9.6.5 Where a body corporate, as defined by section 4 of the Bodies Corporate (Executors and Administrators) Act 1928, ceases to qualify for executorship under section 30(4) of the Succession Act, probate may still be granted to such body corporate if it was named as executor in a will executed before the commencement of the Succession Act on 1 January 1967.

9.7 Ways of appointing executors

9.7.1 A testator may appoint his executor or executors either expressly or by implication. If the appointment is made expressly there is usually no problem, and the person or persons who fit the names and description in the will are entitled to take out probate. An executor may also be designated by reference to an office, as in *In the Goods of Haynes*[60] where the executor was the Archbishop of Tuam for the time being; in such case a corporation sole may act as executor and take out probate in his own name.

9.7.2 If the identity of a person expressly appointed as executor is unclear or ambiguous, then extrinsic evidence is admissible to ascertain the testator's intention.[61] The benignity of the courts' approach in this respect is shown by the decision in *In re Woodroofe*[62] where a testatrix, who had two sons, specifically mentioned her son A.W. as her sole intended executor when giving instructions for the drawing up of her will. The person who drew up her will, the relevant part of which read "I appoint my son sole executor" omitted to insert A.W.'s name, (in the belief that such insertion was not necessary, since in the immediately preceding paragraph of the will the testatrix had devised and bequeathed all her property to the said A.W. and A.W. was the only son of the testatrix living with her when the will was drawn up. Haugh J., in making an order granting leave to A.W. to apply for a grant of probate, accepted the argument of counsel for the applicant that despite the omission of his name as executor of the will, it was abundantly clear from the wording thereof, as well as from the circumstances surrounding its execution that A.W. was the intended executor.

9.7.3 The courts made a distinction between a latent ambiguity in a will, in which case extrinsic evidence was admissible to resolve the ambiguity, and,

[60] (1842) 3 Curt. 75
[61] See e.g. *In the Goods of Twohill* (1879), 3 L.R. Ir. 21 (Application of the "armchair" principle and *Re Kehoe* [1940] Ir. Jur. Rep. 35
[62] [1953-54] Ir. Jur. Rep. 36

a patent ambiguity in which case extrinsic evidence was inadmissible.[63] This distinction must now be viewed, as we have seen, in the light of section 90 of the Succession Act which governs the admissibility of extrinsic evidence.[64]

9.8 Appointment by implication

9.8.1 If an executor is appointed by implication he is known as an "executor according to the tenor of the will". The testator must have intended such person to carry out the functions of an executor, and whether he had such an intention is essentially a matter of construction. The mere fact that a person is the universal legatee and devisee under a will will not entitle him to claim probate as an executor, unless the will manifests the testator's intention that he should act as executor.[65]

9.8.2 The description in a will of the office of an appointee as something other than that of executor will not necessarily prove fatal to his admission as an executor according to the tenor of the will. Thus, in *Re Gilpin*,[66] Hanna J. gave liberty to a person referred to in a will as the "administratrix" to apply for a grant of probate as executrix according to the tenor. Lord Penzance said, in *In the Goods of Baylis*,[67] of persons who were referred to in the will as trustees, that they "are to get in and receive the whole estate, to pay the debts and to divide the residue. Now that is the very office of an executor, and therefore it is clear that the trustees are executors according to the tenor".

9.8.3 The appointment of an executor may be absolute or contingent. Thus an appointment may be subject to a condition precedent, such as the refusal by another person to accept the office,[68] or a condition subsequent such as the departure from the jurisdiction of an executor, in which case his appointment will lapse and he will be substituted by another named person.[69]

---

[63] Compare *In the Goods of Blackwell* (1877) 2 P.D. 72 (case of patent ambiguity) with *In the Estate of Hubbock* [1905] P.129

[64] See *ante* pp. 113 *et seq.*

[65] See *In the Goods of Oliphant* (1860), 1 Sw. & Tr. 525; *In the Goods of Jones* (1861), 2 Sw. & Tr. 155 and *Re Pryse* [1904] P.301

[66] [1942] Ir. Jur. Rep. 52

[67] (1865) L.R. 1 P. & D. 21, 22. For other examples of appointment according to the tenor see *In the Goods of Brown* (1877) 2 P.D. 110; *In the Goods of Russell* [1892] P. 380; *In the Goods of Laird* [1892] P. 381 and *In the Estate of Fawcett* [1941] P. 85

[68] *In the Goods of Betts* (1861), 30 L.J.P.M. & A. 167. See *In the Goods of Langford* (1867) L.R. 1 P. & D. 458 where the condition precedent was the reaching of a certain age by the appointee

[69] *In the Goods of Lane* (1864) 33 L.J.P.M. & A. 185. See Mellows "The Law of Succession" (4th ed. 1983) at p.224

9.8.4 That the answer to the question whether the appointment of an executor is absolute or contingent is a matter of construction is shown by the decision in *In the Goods of Martin*.[70] There a testatrix, by her will, left all her property to her husband and, in the event of him predeceasing her, to her three children. The testatrix purported in the final clause in her will to appoint two of her children as executors and trustees giving them "all necessary powers for the purposes of distribution of same" and "full and ample discretion in dividing up my estate in whatever way they deem suitable or advisable".

9.8.5 Her husband having survived the testatrix, the probate office refused a grant of probate to the said executors on the ground that the entire of the final clause, including the appointment of executors, could be contingent on the failure of the prior gifts, which failure had not taken place. It was contended for the applicants, that they were entitled to a grant of probate as executors *simpliciter* since the testatrix intended to appoint her two children executors and trustees, and it was as such that they were to have the powers and discretion. Davitt P. granted the application sought, being satisfied that the appointment of the applicants as executors in the will was intended by the testatrix to be absolute and not contingent.[71]

9.9 Acceptance and renunciation

9.9.1 A person who is appointed executor in a will is not obliged to accept the office, which he is free to renounce even if he had agreed during the lifetime of the testator to act as his executor.[72] While an appointee may renounce the office of executor prior to taking out probate, the grant of probate fixes him with "duties and liabilities which he cannot afterwards shake off".[73] In this respect, it is the grant of probate and not the swearing of the executor's oath which is the crucial factor.[74]

9.9.2 The office of executor is accepted by taking out probate, but acceptance is also implied by the performance of acts by the appointee which are referrable to the functions of an executor.[75] As we shall see, acts of intermeddling with the estate of a testator by a person who has not been appointed an executor may constitute such person an executor *de son*

---

[70] [1955-56] Ir. Jur. Rep. 37

[71] *Ibid* at p. 38

[72] *Doyle* v *Blake* (1804), Sch. & Lef. 231, 239 (per Lord Redesdale); *In the Goods of Badenach* (1864) 3 Sw. & Tr. 465

[73] *In the Goods of Veiga* (1862) 32 L.J.P.M. & A. 9, 10.

[74] *McDonnell* v *Prendergast* (1830) 3 Hagg. Ecc. 212; See Miller "Irish Probate Practice" at p.209

[75] See *In the Goods of Hanlon* [1894] 1 I.R. 551

tort.[76] Acts of intermeddling which make a stranger an executor *de son tort* are similar to those which imply acceptance of the office by an executor named in the willf, and have been held to include the collection and release of debts owed to the testator.[77] Other examples of such acts are the publication of notices requesting claims to be brought against the deceased's estate by those entitled to such claims,[78] and the taking of possession of the goods of a testator, giving a power of attorney to sell a small part of such, which power was not in fact exercised.[79]

9.9.3 Whether an act amounts to intermeddling such as will constitute acceptance of the office of executor or make the actor an executor *de son tort* will depend upon the circumstances of the particular case. Accordingly, acts of necessity or charity such as burying the deceased,[80] or feeding his livestock,[81] will not, without more, constitute such acts of intermeddling.[82]

9.9.4 A person appointed executor has prior right to prove the will and, while he retains that right, no other person is usually entitled to a grant of administration. If, however, the person appointed executor fails to take any action, and another person wishes to apply for a grant of administration, such person may cite the executor to accept or refuse probate. The High Court has power to summon any person named as executor in a will to prove or renounce probate.[83] This power is exercised by the issue of a citation from the Probate Office and such citation shall not issue until an affidavit, in verification of the averments it contains, has been filed in the Probate Office.[84]

9.9.5 An appearance to a citation shall be entered in the Probate Office within fourteen days of the service thereof,[85] and, if a party who has been served with a citation fails to appear within the time limited by the citation, or if the time has been extended by the court or the Probate Officer, within such extended time, his non-appearance will be deemed and taken as a renunciation of his right to probate, and the party citing is entitled to

[76] See *post* p. 252
[77] .*Pytt* v *Fendall* (1754), 1 Lec 553; *Re Stevens* [1897] 1 Ch. 422
[78] *Long* v *Symes* (1832), 3 Hagg. Ecc. 771
[79] *Cummins* v *Cummins* (1845) 8 Ir. Eq. R. 723; *In the Goods of Hurley* (1871) 5 I.L.T.R. 64; *Carberry* v*Cody* (1867) I.R. 1 Eq. 76; *Ledwidge* v *Lynch* (1877) 11 I.L.T.R. 81
[80] *Camden* v *Fletcher* (1838) 4 M. & W. 378
[81] *Long* v *Symes* (1832) 3 Hagg. Ecc. 771
[82] See Miller "Irish Probate Practice" at p.209
[83] Section 16 of the Succession Act.
[84] R.S.C. 0.79 r.52
[85] R.S.C. 0.79 r. 56. The time for appearance may be considered to be extended until action or default has been taken under r.57

obtain from the Probate Officer a side-bar order to that effect.[86] A person cited to accept or refuse probate who wishes to accept probate shall so state on entering his appearance to the citation, and the party citing will be entitled to obtain from the Probate Officer a side-bar order which notes the acceptance and obliges the party cited to extract probate within fourteen days of the service of the order upon him, or such further time, if any, the court or Probate Officer allows, failing which the party cited will be deemed to have renounced his right to probate.[87]

9.9.6 The failure of a person appointed executor to appear to a citation to take out probate is one of three ways set out in section 17 of the Succession Act in which an executor's right to prove a will ceases.[88] Where a person appointed executor survives the testator but dies without having taken out probate the will is read as if such person had not been appointed executor.[89] Of course, since an executor derives his authority from the will and the grant of probate is confirmation of that authority, acts which an executor could perform prior to the grant are not invalidated by his death prior to the issue of a grant.[90]

9.9.7 If a person appointed executor renounces probate, his rights in respect of the executorship wholly cease and again representation to the testator, and the administration of his estate, devolve and are committed as if such person had not been appointed executor.[91] A renunciation must be in writing, signed by the person renouncing, witnessed, and filed in the Probate Office.[92] There is English authority to the effect that a renunciation becomes binding only on being recorded in the Probate Office, until which time it is ineffective and may be withdrawn at will.[93]

9.9.8 Be that as it may, a renunciation if final, having been filed and recorded in the Probate Office, may be withdrawn only with the leave of the court. The courts have been loath to allow the retraction of a formal renunciation and will do so only if satisfied that it is for the benefit of the estate or those entitled under the will.[94] It is provided, in section 18 of the

---

[86] R.S.C. 0.79 r. 57

[87] R.S.C. 0.79 r. 58

[88] Section 17(b)

[89] Section 17(a)

[90] See *Woolley* v *Clark* (1822), 5 B. & Ald. 744; *Re Stevens* [1897] 1 Ch. 422

[91] Section 17(c)

[92] The renunciation must be of the whole office. See Mellows at pp. 225–6

[93] *In the Goods of Morant* (1874), L.R. 3 P. & D. 151. See Mellows "The Law of Succession" (4th ed. 1983) at p.226

[94] See *In the Goods of Gill* (1873) L.R. 3 P. & D. 113; *In the Goods of Stiles* [1898] P.12; *In the Estate of Heathcote* [1913] P.42

Succession Act, that if an executor is permitted to retract his renunciation and prove the will, the probate shall take effect and be deemed always to have taken effect "without prejudice to the previous acts and dealings of and notices to any other personal representative who has previously taken out representation, and a memorandum of the subsequent probate shall be endorsed on the original grant,,.[95] This section applies whether the testator died before or after the commencement of the Succession Act.[96]

9.9.9 If a person renounces probate of a will or letters of administration of the estate of a deceased person in one character, he shall not be allowed to obtain representation to the same deceased in another character, unless the court shall otherwise order.[97]

9.9.10 A testator may appoint an executor for a limited purpose,[98] or for a limited time,[99] but otherwise an executor may not renounce part of his office and accept another part.[100] The Rules of the Superior Courts provide, that limited administration shall not be granted unless, every person entitled to the general grant has consented or renounced, or has been cited and failed to appear, unless the court or probate officer otherwise directs, and in this context the word "limited" means limited to part only of the assets or estate of the deceased.[101] It is also provided that no person entitled to a general grant of administration of the estate of a deceased person shall be permitted to take a limited grant, except by order of the court.[102]

9.9.11 When a grant of administration has been made in respect of the estate of a deceased person or any part of the estate it is provided in section 21 of the Succession Act, that "no person shall have power to bring any action or otherwise act as executor of the deceased person in respect of the estate comprised in or affected by the grant until the grant has been recalled or revoked or has expired". Thus, where a grant of administration has been made no person other than the grantee can act in relation to the estate while the administration is in force.[103]

---

[95] Section 18(1). This section applies whether permission to withdraw the renunciation was given before or after the commencement of the Succession Act.

[96] Section 18(2)

[97] R.S.C. 0.80 r. 43

[98] To deal e.g. only with the testator's personalty. See *In the Goods of Wallich* (1864), 3 Sw. & Tr. 423

[99] During the minority of a child or widowhood of a spouse for example. See Mellows "The Law of Succession" (4th ed. 1983) at p.224

[100] See *Brooke* v *Haymes* (1868), L.R. 6 Eq. 25, 30 (per Romilly M.R.)

[101] R.S.C. 0.80 r. 24

[102] R.S.C. 0.80 r. 25

[103] See Probates and Letters of Administration Act (Irl.) 1857 (20 & 21 Vict. c.79) s.80

9.10 Protection of persons acting on probate or administration.

9.10.1 It has been an essential feature of the law governing the administration of estates that a person dealing with the estate should be able to treat a grant of representation as conclusive, and the protection of persons acting on probate or administration is accordingly provided in section 22 of the Succession Act. That section provides in subsection (1) that every person making or permitting to be made any payment or disposition in good faith under a representation shall be indemnified and protected in so doing, notwithstanding any defect or circumstance whatsoever affecting the validity of the representation.[104] It is also provided that where a grant of representation is revoked, all payments and dispositions made in good faith to a personal representative under the representation before the revocation thereof are a valid discharge to the person making the same.[105] A personal representative who acted under the revoked representation may retain and reimburse himself in respect of any payments or dispositions made by him which the person to whom representation is afterwards granted might have properly made.[106]

9.10.2 There is an apparent inconsistency between subsections (1) and (2) of section 22 in that, the former provides an unqualified indemnity and protection for persons acting in good faith on probate or administration, while the latter, while providing the same indemnity and protection to persons making payments and dispositions to personal representatives, qualifies the protection afforded to the latter by limiting his right to reimburse himself in respect of payments, to those which a subsequent personal representative might have properly made. The reference in subsection (2) to a subsequent grant can scarcely have been intended to establish the need for such, the non-availability of which would deny a personal representative the right to reimbursement where, for example, a grant was revoked because the "deceased" was found to be alive. The better view of section 22 would be, that subsection (1) is the dominant subsection and personal representatives should be entitled to the protection of the section in respect of all payments and dispositions otherwise made in good faith.

9.10.3 Whether a personal representative has acted in good faith such as to entitle him to the protection and indemnity provided by section 22 would seem to depend on the circumstances of the individual case, and in particular whether he had notice of any claim which cast doubt on the

---

[104] *Ibid* s.82
[105] Section 22(2) (See s.83 of the 1857 Act)
[106] *Ibid*

validity of his grant.[107] If, despite having notice, and, without regard to such claim, a personal representative makes payments out of the deceased's estate, he may be liable to the estate if his grant is subsequently revoked. The point is illustrated by a New Zealand case which went on appeal to the Privy Council.[108] There, an executor who had paid certain pecuniary legacies to beneficiaries under the will, despite being aware that next-of-kin were contemplating an action to have the grant revoked on the grounds that the testatrix lacked testamentary capacity when she made her will, was held liable to the deceased's estate for the sums so paid, when the grant was revoked.

9.10.4 It has been argued, with some cogency, that an honest belief by an executor that the testatrix had testamentary capacity when she made her will and that an action for revocation would fail, should constitute good faith within section 27(1) of the English Administration of Estates Act 1925, which is couched in similar language to section 22 of the Succession Act.[109]

9.10.5 It was suggested, by an Irish commentator, that section 22 would apply only to voidable and not to void grants.[110] An example of the latter would be where a grant of administration issued in respect of the estate of a deceased person who was deemed to have died intestate, but whose will later turns up, in which case the estate would have vested on death in any executor appointed by the will, leaving nothing to vest in an administrator appointed by the court.[111] The grant to an administrator in such circumstances could be said to be void *ab initio* and it was this which prompted the distinction between void and voidable grants in the context of section 22.

9.10.6 The express language of section 22 makes no such distinction, however, and there is persuasive authority against making it.[112] It also sits uneasily with the purpose of section 22 which is stated, in its marginal note, to be the protection of persons acting on probate or administration. It is

---

[107] For a full treatment of the three kinds of notice (i) Actual, (ii) Constructure, and (iii) Imputed see *Bank of Ireland Finance* v *Rockfield Ltd* [1979] I.R.2 and *Somers* v *Weir* [1979] I.R. 94

[108] *Guardian Trust & Executors Company of New Zealand Ltd* v *Public Trustee of New Zealand* [1942] A.C. 115. See Parry and Clark "The Law of Succession" (8th ed. 1983) at p.200

[109] *Ibid*

[110] See W.J. McGuire "The Succession Act 1965, A Commentary" (I.L.S.I. 1968). This position has been resiled from by the editor of the 2nd ed. See now McGuire and Pearce "The Succession Act 1965" (1986) at p.57

[111] *In the Goods of Clarke* (1871), I.R. 6 Eq. 26. See the approach to this problem taken by Romer J. in *Re Bridgett & Hayes' Contract* [1928] Ch. 163

[112] See e.g. *Hewson* v *Shelley* [1914] 2 Ch. 13; *McParland* v *Conlon* [1930] N.I. 138

also the case that, apart from such statutory protection, a grant of probate or administration is an order of the court, and that being so, a person such as a debtor of the deceased who, in good faith, pays the personal representatives is entitled to regard such payment as a discharge of his debt.[113]

9.10.7 The protection afforded by section 22 does not extend to persons who have received payments under a grant which is subsequently revoked, and if a former personal representative has made such payment the usual remedies, particularly that of equitable tracing, will be available for its recovery to those properly entitled.[114]

9.10.8 Although no protection is afforded in the Succession Act to the recipients of payments or dispositions made under a grant which is subsequently revoked, the same is not true of purchasers who take conveyances from personal representatives under such grants. It is accordingly provided in section 25(1) of the Succession Act that all conveyances of any estate or interest in the estate of a deceased person made to a purchaser by a person to whom representation has been granted are valid, notwithstanding any subsequent revocation or variation of the grant.[115] Section 25 is wide in scope, and "conveyance" is defined in the Succession Act as including "a mortgage, charge, lease, assent, transfer, disclaimer, release and every other assurance of property by any instrument except a will".[116] "Purchaser" is defined as meaning, "a grantee, lessee, assignee, mortgagee, chargeant or other person who, in good faith acquires an estate or interest in property for valuable consideration."[117]

9.10.9 The language of section 25(1) excludes on its face dispositions of a deceased's property by his personal representatives which are not made by way of a conveyance. It is often the case however, that the transfer of the goods of a deceased to purchasers is effected by personal representatives without benefit of written instruments. Although such transfers would not qualify for the protection afforded to purchasers by section 25, such purchasers could rely on the general principle that title was acquired by them because they had purchased the goods in good faith.[118]

---

[113] See *Fitzpatrick* v *McGloyne* [1897] 2 I.R. 542

[114] See *Ministry of Health* v *Simpson* [1951] A.C. 251 and Keane "Equity and the Law of Trusts in the Republic of Ireland" at pp.279 *et seq.*

[115] Section 25(2) provides that the section takes effect without prejudice to any order of the court made before the commencement of the Succession Act, and applies whether the deceased died before or after the commencement of the Act.

[116] Section 3(1)

[117] *Ibid*

[118] *Ante* p. 248 Sec s.37 of the English Administration of Estates Act 1925 and the comments thereon in Parry and Clark "The Law of Succession" (8th ed. 1983) at p.198

9.11 Liability of personal representatives

9.11.1 The duties attached to the office of personal representative require him to preserve, protect, and administer properly the estate of the deceased.[119] Failure to do so will constitute a *devastavit*, literally a wasting of the assets of the deceased which will make him personally liable.

9.11.2 *Devastavit* may occur in a number of ways and, most obviously, where a personal representative improperly converts assets to his own use, such as the payment of his personal debts.[120] It may also occur when a personal representative fails to exercise due diligence in protecting the deceased's estate, as in failing to initiate action against a debtor of the deceased until the action is statute barred.[121] Another example of maladministration of the deceased's estate, constituting *devastavit*, occurs where a personal representative fails to pay off debts when he has assets to do so which leads to the estate being involved in additional expense when creditors sue.[122] When dealing with the duty of executors to pay the debts of the deceased with due diligence having regard to the assets available for that purpose, Uthwatt J. said in *Re Tankard*[123] in an oft-quoted judgment:

"The duty is owed not only to creditors, but also to beneficiaries, for the ultimate object of the administration of an estate is to place the beneficiaries in possession of their interest and that object cannot be fully achieved unless all debts are paid."

9.11.3 The liability of a personal representative for *devastavit* does not cease on his death but persists against his personal representatives. Thus section 24 of the Succession Act provides, that where

"a person as personal representative of a deceased person (including an executor in his own wrong) wastes or converts to his own use any part of the estate of the deceased, and dies, his personal representatives shall to the extent of the available assets of the defaulter be liable and chargeable in respect of such waste or conversion in the same manner as the defaulter would have been if living."

---

[119] See Mellows "The Law of Succession" (4th ed. 1983) at pp.275 *et seq.* and Parry and Clark "The Law of Succession" (8th ed. 1983) at pp.374 *et seq.*

[120] See e.g. *Re Morgan* (1881), 18 Ch. D. 93 and *Marsden* v *Regan* [1954] 1 W.L.R. 423

[121] *Hayward* v *Kinsey* (1701), 12 Mod. 573

[122] See Parry and Clark (8th ed. 1983) at pp.247 *et seq.*

[123] [1924] Ch. 69, 72

9.12 Liability of executor *de son tort*

9.12.1 As we have seen the expression executor *de son tort*, which literally means executor "in his own wrong", is most commonly used with reference to a person who acts in relation to the estate of a deceased person as though he were the duly appointed executor of that estate.[124] The liability of such person is dealt with in section 23 of the Succession Act which provides, in subsection (1), that if any person, to the defrauding of creditors or without full valuable consideration, obtains, receives or holds any part of the estate of a deceased person or effects the release of any debt or liability due to the estate of the deceased, he shall be charged as executor in his own wrong to the extent of the estate received or coming into his hands, or the debt or liability released.

9.12.2 An executor *de son tort* is permitted to offset two items against any such claim against him: (a) any debt for valuable consideration and without fraud due to him from the deceased person at the time of his death, and (b) any payment made by him which might properly be made by a personal representative. Subject to the foregoing deductions, an executor *de son tort* is liable to account for the assets which have come into his hands to creditors, beneficiaries and properly appointed personal representatives of the deceased.[125]

9.12.3 As we have seen the personal representative of the executor *de son tort* shall, to the extent of the available assets of the defaulter, be liable and chargeable in respect of waste or conversion of a deceased's assets in the same manner as the defaulter would have been if living.[126] The limits of an executor *de son tort's* personal liability were considered in *The Blackstaff Flax-Spinning and Weaving Company Ltd* v *Cameron*.[127] There, the defendant was sued by the Company to recover the amount of the calls due on foot of certain shares in the Company. The shares in question had been owned by the defendant's father who, before his death, had assigned by deed all his property, including the shares, to the defendant. The defendant admitted in evidence, that he had received and cashed dividend warrants drawn in favour of his father and that he had attended a meeting of shareholders. All of these acts constituted the defendant an executor *de son tort*, albeit a benign one, since the Company refused to register him as a shareholder, on the ground that the deed did not comply with the

---

[124] See *ante* p. 245

[125] See generally *Curtis* v *Vernon* (1790) 3 Term. Rep. 587; *Re Ryan* (1897) 1 I.R. 513; *New York Breweries Co. Ltd* v *A.G.* [1899] A.C.62; *Atthill* v *Woods* [1903] 2 I.R. 304

[126] Section 24 of the Succession Act. See *ante* p. 251

[127] [1899] 1 I.R. 252

Company's articles of association. In these circumstances the Vice-Chancellor held, that since the Company was aware that the defendant was not the registered owner of the shares and had themselves refused to register him as such, the defendant was not estopped by any conduct on his part from denying that he was a shareholder. In the absence of an estoppel the defendant could not be made personally liable for the payment of the calls, and, as executor *de son tort* he was not liable for such payments *de bonis propriis* but was only liable for the administration in due course of the assets that actually came to his hands.[128]

9.12.4 The expression "full valuable consideration", the giving of which will preclude a person being treated as an executor *de son tort* within section 23(1), is defined in subsection (2) as meaning, such valuable consideration as amounts or approximates to the value of "that for which it is given".[129] A similar provision in section 3(5) of the Family Home Protection Act 1976,[130] which states, that full value means "such value as amounts or approximates to the value of that for which it is given" has raised the question whether a mortgagee who lends only a proportion of the purchase price of mortgaged property can claim the protection afforded to a purchaser for full value.

9.12.5 It has been argued that it was not the intention of the legislature to discriminate against mortgagees, and that the phrase "that for which it is given" should be taken, in the case of a mortgage, as referring not to the total value of the property mortgaged but rather to its security value.[131] The question to be asked in the case of a mortgage, therefore, is whether the security given is so disproportionate to the amount of the loan given to the mortgagor that the mortgagee cannot be said to have given full value.[132]

9.12.6 The answer to that question should clearly depend on the circumstances of the particular case and, while the absence of predictability as to what constitutes full value may pose subsequent conveyancing problems in the context of the Family Home Protection Act, it is less objectionable in the context of section 23 which deals with the liability of persons who are guilty of intermeddling in the estate of a deceased person. The wages of such intermeddling such as to constitute one an executor *de son tort* should not be nicely calculable and there seems to be no pressing policy

---

[128] *Ibid* at p.258
[129] Cf. s.3 of the Succession Act which defines "valuable consideration" as consideration in money or money's worth.
[130] No. 27 of 1976
[131] See Wylie "Irish Conveyancing Law" (2nd ed. 1986) (1978) at p.206
[132] *Ibid*

reason, as there might well be in relation to the Family Homes Protection Act, for denying that a mortgagee has given "full valuable consideration" within section 23 because he has furnished only part of the purchase price of the property mortgaged. He has, arguably, given such consideration as measured by the value "of that for which it is given" which is the security for the loan provided by the mortgaged property. In any event, the extent of the mortgagee's interest in the mortgaged property is referable to the size of the loan together with interest and costs payable thereon.[133]

9.13 Personal representatives *qua* trustees

9.13.1 It is provided in the Succession Act that the personal representatives of a deceased person hold his real and personal estate as trustees for the persons by law entitled thereto.[134] Personal representatives are generally held liable as express trustees for the proper administration of the deceased's estate.[135] It is tempting for an Irish author to compare favourably this division of equitable and legal title to the deceased's estate during the period of administration with that obtaining in England, which has provoked academic criticism in that country.[136]

9.13.2 The position in England is, that although a personal representative is treated for many purposes as a trustee,[137] this does not mean that a beneficiary is regarded as having a beneficial interest during the period of administration.[138] During that time, legal title vests in the executor, who cannot however be said to have any beneficial interest, and the latter therefore must lie *in vacuo*. Certain lawyers' dismay at this somewhat disconcerting notion was dismissed by Lord Radcliffe, who said in *Stamp Duties Commissioner (Queensland)* v *Livingston*:[139]

"Where, it is asked, is the beneficial interest in those assets during the period of administration? It is not, *ex hypothesi*, in the executor: where else can it be but in the residuary legatee? This dilemma is founded on a fallacy, for it assumes mistakenly that for all purposes and at every moment of time the law requires the separate existence of two different kinds of estate or interest in property, the legal and the equitable. There is no need to make this assumption. When the whole right of property is

---

[133] See McGuire and Pearce "The Succession Act 1965: A Commentary" at p.60

[134] Section 10(3)

[135] For the duties of express trustees see generally Keane "Equity and the Law of Trusts in the Republic of Ireland" at pp.108 *et seq.* and Wylie "Irish Land Law" (2nd ed. 1986) at pp.533 *et seq.*

[136] See e.g. Mellows "The Law of Succession" (4th ed. 1983) at pp.367 *et seq.*

[137] See *Re Marsden* (1884), 26 Ch. D. 783, 789 (per Kay J.)

[138] See *Lall* v *Lall* [1965] 3 All E.R. 330 and *Barclay* v *Barclay* [1970] 2 Q.B. 677

[139] [1965] A.C. 694, 712

in a person, as it is in an executor, there is no need to distinguish between the legal and equitable interest in that property, any more than there is for the property of a full beneficial owner."

9.13.3 A textwriter who does not find Lord Radcliffe's argument convincing, draws attention to cases where the failure to regard the beneficiary as having any proprietary interest in the residuary estate worked to the disadvantage of the beneficiary.[140] The same textwriter goes on to point out, "the rather absurd result that although during the period of administration the beneficiary has no 'interest' in the assets, he nevertheless has rights in them which he can dispose of *inter vivos* or by will".[141]

9.13.4 It might reasonably have been presumed that the provision in the Succession Act that personal representatives hold the deceased's estate as trustees for those entitled at law thereto had clarified the position in Ireland, but this is apparently not so. A distinguished Irish textwriter, who happens also to be a High Court judge, has written that it is clear that

"until such time as the personal representative assents to the bequest or, in the case of the residue, until he has completed the administration of the estate by paying all debts and legacies, the beneficiaries have no interest, legal or equitable, in the property comprised in the estate. The entire ownership until that time is vested in the personal representatives and the only right of the beneficiaries is their right to require them to complete the administration of the estate in accordance with the law."[142]

9.13.5 The learned author concedes, that under section 10(3) of the Succession Act, the personal representatives hold as trustees, and he believes that "the words in the Act simply make clear the statutory obligation on the personal representative to apply the estate in the manner required by law".[143] If it is asked where the beneficial interest in the property lies during the course of the administration, the learned author believes that the authoritative answer is to be found in Lord Radcliffe's judgment in *Livingston*.[144]

9.13.6 This however is to treat the personal representative as like a trustee, rather than a trustee, and to revert to the English position articulated by

---

[140] Mellows "The Law of Succession" (4th ed. 1983) at p.368. See *Eastbourne Mutual Building Society* v *Hastings Corporation* [1965] 1 All E.R. 779 and *Lall* v *Lall* [1965] 3 All E.R. 330

[141] *Ibid* at p.371

[142] Keane "Equity and the Law of Trusts in the Republic of Ireland" at p.46 in which reference is made to *Lord Sudeley* v *A.-G.* [1897] A.C. 11; *Barnardo's Homes* v *Income Tax Special Comrs* [1921] A.C.1; *Moloney* v *Allied Irish Banks Ltd* [1986] I.R. 67

[143] *Ibid*

[144] *Supra* at p. 712

Kay J. when he said in *Re Marsden*,[145] that an "executor is personally liable in equity for all breaches of the ordinary trusts which in Courts of Equity are considered to arise from his office". If something along those lines had been intended surely the language of section 10(3) would have reflected that intention?

9.13.7 Of course there is an important sense in which it is unreal to speak of beneficiaries having interests in the deceased's estate prior to the completion of administration. They will only be entitled to their interests after the debts and liabilities of the deceased have been discharged and, if the estate is insolvent they will be entitled to nothing at all.[146] What a beneficiary is entitled to is a chose in action to ensure due administration of the estate, and it is this chose in action which is transmissible by the beneficiary prior to completion of administration.[147]

9.13.8 Be that as it may, the imposition of a trust on personal representatives by section 10(3) could perhaps best be accommodated by adopting the suggestion of an English textwriter, that the assets of the deceased could be treated as a present, though fluctuating, trust fund held for the benefit of those interested in the estate.[148]

9.13.9 An exception to the general rule that a personal representative is liable as express trustee, is the provision in the Succession Act that a personal representative is not a trustee for the purposes of the Statute of Limitations, 1957.[149]

9.13.10 Whether a personal representative could acquire a possessory title was a matter of considerable importance in rural Ireland, where it was not uncommon for a child who had stayed on the family farm, which the other children had left, to take out letters of administration to his deceased parent's estate. If such child remained on in possession of the farm the question would then arise as to whether he could acquire a possessory title.[150] Since virtually all land in rural Ireland was registered, the acquisition of possessory titles to such land by personal representatives depended on the courts' interpretation of section 86(1) of the Local Registration of Title (Irl.) Act 1891 which provided, that "the personal

---

[145] (1884), 26 Ch. D. 783, 789
[146] See Keane at p.102
[147] See *Re Leigh's Will Trusts* [1970] Ch. 277 and Parry and Clark "The Law of Succession" (8th ed. 1983) at p.357
[148] Mellows "The Law of Succession" (4th ed. 1983) at p. 368
[149] Section 123 of the Succession Act
[150] See Brady and Kerr "The Limitation of Actions in the Republic of Ireland" (1984) at pp.88-9

representatives of a deceased person shall hold such land as trustees for the persons by law beneficially entitled thereto".

9.13.11 The courts were to place different interpretations on the language of section 86(1). Maguire P. held in *Re Loughlin*,[151] that a personal representative being an express trustee of registered land vesting in him *qua* personal representative, could not claim the benefit of the statutes of limitation. The Supreme Court was to take a different view in *Vaughan* v *Cottingham*,[152] in holding that personal representatives though trustees under the law of devolution, were not *express* trustees, and so could acquire possessory titles against beneficiaries or intestate successors.[153]

9.13.12 The position of personal representatives had been clarified by the Statute of Limitations 1957 which provided in section 2(2)(d), that a personal representative in the capacity of personal representative should not, by reason only of section 1 of the Executors Act 1830, or section 86 of the Local Registration of Title Act 1891, be a trustee for the purposes of the Statute of Limitations – Section 2(2)(d) is now substituted by section 123 of the Succession Act which provides, in subsection (1), that a personal representative in the capacity of personal representative shall not, by reason only of section 10 of the Succession Act, be a trustee for the purposes of the Statute of Limitations 1957.

9.14 Grants of Representation

9.14.1 Jurisdiction to grant probate to one or more of the executors named in the will of a deceased person lies with the High Court, which may limit such grant in any way the court thinks fit.[1] The court also has the power to revoke, cancel or recall any grant of probate.[2]

9.14.2 The Circuit Court was given concurrent jurisdiction with the High Court in relation to the matters set out in section 6(2) of the Succession Act, which jurisdiction however was limited by section 6(3), unless the necessary parties to the proceedings consented in the proper form, by reference to the value of the deceased's personal estate and the rateable

---

[151] [1942] I.R.I5 Maguire P. followed the decision in the English case *Toates* v *Toates* [1926] 2 K.B. 30 Cf. *Owens* v *McGarry* [1948] I.R. 226

[152] [1961] I.R. 184

[153] Lavery J. preferred the reasoning of Stirling J. in *Re Lacy* (1899) 2 Ch. 149 to that of the court in *Toates* v *Toates* [1926] 2 K.B. 30 and he also referred approvingly to *McNeill* v *McNeill* [1957] N.I. 10

[1] Section 26(1) of the Succession Act

[2] Section 26(2)

valuation of his real estate.[3] That jurisdiction is now unlimited in respect of the monetary value of the deceased's personal estate and increased to £200 in respect of the rateable valuation of his real estate,[4] for proceedings commenced after 12 May 1982.[5]

9.14.3 Probate is generally granted to one or more of the executors appointed by a testator in his will, and, as we have seen such person may renounce his right to prove the will or lose that right by failing to appear to a citation to take or renounce probate.[6] We have also seen that the court may refuse probate to a person who lacks the capacity to act as an executor, and, may revoke a grant of probate where the grantee loses the capacity to act as executor after the grant has been made.[7]

9.14.4 A question which was not addressed earlier, but which merits attention, is that concerning the circumstances, other than physical or mental infirmity, in which a person appointed executor by a testator may be passed over by the court. It would seem obvious for example that a person who has been found guilty of the murder or manslaughter of a testator should be precluded from proving the will of the deceased just as he is precluded from taking any benefit under such will.[8] The classic English authority is *In the Estate of Crippen*[9] which concerned not the executorship of a will but a grant of representation to the estate of an intestate. There Crippen, the husband of the deceased intestate, had been convicted and executed for her murder and the court made a grant of representation to the next-of-kin of the wife, rather than the personal representatives of Crippen on whom the right to a grant would otherwise have devolved. *Crippen* was followed by Baker J. in *In the Estate of S.,*[10] where a woman who had been appointed by her husband sole executrix and beneficiary in his will was passed over following her conviction for her husband's manslaughter, and a grant was made to the deceased's daughter.

9.14.5 The wife's incarceration for her crime made it virtually impossible for her to act as executrix[11] and this fact as much as the crime itself seems to have led the court to pass her over as executrix. Thus an English

---

[3] The personal estate could not exceed £5,000 in value and the rateable valuation of the real estate could not exceed £100.

[4] Courts Act 1981 (No 11 of 1981) s.4

[5] *Ibid* s.33(3)

[6] See *ante* p. 244

[7] See *ante* p. 240

[8] See *ante* p. 158

[9] [1911] P.108

[10] [1968] P.302. See also *In the Estate of Drawsner* (1913) 108 L.T.732

[11] See [1968] P.302, 305

textwriter has written, that "Baker J. appeared to place equal weight on the fact of the wife's conviction and the fact that because she was serving a term of life imprisonment it was 'quite impossible' for her to act as executrix".[12]

9.14.6 It must surely surprise the lay person to learn that the murder of a testator by an executor does not automatically disqualify the latter from the executorship of the deceased's will,[13] but the case law suggests that this is the case, despite the fact that considerations of public policy would seem to dictate the contrary. The absence of automatic disqualification in a case of murder may not be of practical significance since the court may refuse probate to any person for lack of capacity and will invariably do so in such a case. As we have seen in a different, though related context, separate policy considerations apply in cases of manslaughter which has many shades of moral culpability, and the court should always have a discretion whether or not to grant probate in such a case.[14]

9.14.7 That the position in Ireland is not so very different to that obtaining in England is shown by the approach taken in the High Court to the somewhat unusual facts in *In the Estate of Glynn Decd.*[15] There one Kelly, who had been appointed executor by a testator in his will, was found guilty of the murder of the testator's sister and sentenced to a term of life imprisonment. Under the terms of the will the testator's sister was given a life interest in his farm with remainder to Kelly.

9.14.8 An application was made by counsel on behalf of Ireland and the Attorney General, for an order pursuant to section 27(4) of the Succession Act appointing the Chief State Solicitor as administrator of the Estate of the said Martin Glynn. It is provided in section 27(4) that, where by reason of any special circumstances it appears to the High Court, or to the Circuit Court in a case where the latter has jurisdiction, to be necessary or expedient to do so, the court may order that administration be granted to such person as it thinks fit.[16] The sole surviving next-of-kin of the deceased was one Michael Donoghue who was old and infirm and unwilling to assume the burdens of executorship.

9.14.9 There was evidence before the court that the deceased's lands were being abused by people who had no rights to them and to that extent it was in the interests of the deceased's estate that somebody take charge. In these circumstances Gannon J. made an order pursuant to section 27(4) of

[12] Mellows "The Law of Succession" (4th ed. 1983) at p. 229

[13] See Parry and Clark "The Law of Succession" (8th ed. 1983) at p.140 n.47

[14] See *ante* p. 160

[15] The Irish Times, 21 February 1989

[16] This jurisdiction would have suited admirably the facts of *In b. Walsh* (1923) 57 I.L.T.R. 78

the Succession Act that the Chief State Solicitor be at liberty to apply for a grant of letters of administration with the said will and a codicil thereto annexed. The said grant was limited to getting in the estate of the deceased and preserving them and further limited until Kelly, the sole executor named in the will, should be in a position to apply to the court for a grant of probate to the will and codicil.[17]

9.14.10 The court did not have to address the question whether Kelly's crime against the testator's sister disentitled him to any benefit under the will but, with respect to the separate but related question whether Kelly's crime against the testator's sister disqualified him from taking out probate, there is nothing in Gannon J.'s order which suggests that he would be so disqualified from seeking probate in the future. Since the court has a discretion whether or not to grant probate in a particular case, however, it would be a matter of considerable surprise if Mr Kelly was to prove successful in any future application for probate.[18]

9.15 Separate grants

9.15.1 Representation may be granted in respect of real estate together with personal estate, or separately in respect of real estate and personal estate, and may be granted in respect of either real estate or personal estate, although there is no property of the other kind.[19] Where the estate of a deceased person is known to be insolvent, however, a grant will not be severed except as regards an estate in respect of which the deceased was a trustee.[20]

9.15.2 As we have seen, probate may be granted of part only of a will where the court is not satisfied that the omitted part was included with the knowledge and approval of the testator.[21] It has to be remembered of course, that a clause inserted in a will with such knowledge and approval, will not be omitted from probate because the testator was mistaken as to its legal effect.[22] Parts of a will, the inclusion of which has been procured by a fraud on the testator,[23] or the commission of a forgery,[24] will be omitted from probate.

[17] Mr. John O'Donnell B.L., counsel for Mr. Kelly, kindly made available to me the papers of the case.

[18] For an English example of executors being deemed unsuitable on less obvious grounds than murder of the testator's sister see *In the Estate of Biggs* [1966] P.118

[19] Section 28(1) of the Succession Act. See Administration of Estates Act 1959, s.15

[20] Section 28(2)

[21] See *ante* p. 63

[22] See *ante* p. 109

[23] See *Allen* v *McPherson* (1847) 1 H.L.C. 191 and *In the Estate of Posner* [1953] P.277

[24] *Re Raphael* [1973] 1 W.L.R. 998

9.16 Grants where no estate in jurisdiction

9.16.1 Until comparatively recently the courts in Ireland had no juris-diction to make a grant of probate or letters of administration where a deceased person had left no property to be administered within the jurisdiction.[25] Thus, a will which disposed exclusively of property located abroad was inadmissible to probate, but, that it was otherwise with regard to a will which disposed of property some of which was located abroad and some in Ireland, is implicit in the judgment of Hanna J. in *Re Welland*[26] where the learned judge gave liberty to the applicant to prove a will which dealt with property in England and Ireland.[27]

9.16.2 The Irish courts were given jurisdiction to make grants of representation where the deceased left no estate within the jurisdiction by section 16 of the Administration of Estates Act 1959, which was replaced by section 29 of the Succession Act. The latter section provides that the High Court

"shall have jurisdiction to make a grant of representation in respect of a deceased person, notwithstanding that the deceased left no estate in the State, and to make a *de bonis non* or other form of grant in respect of unadministered estate of the deceased in the State."

9.16.3 The inclusion in section 29 of grants *de bonis non* and other forms of grant in respect of unadministered estate, reflects the fact that the exclusion of a grant of representation because the deceased had left no unadministered estate in the jurisdiction caused difficulties not only in relation to wills which purported to dispose of property located abroad. It might be necessary in a wholly domestic situation for someone to seek a grant of representation to a deceased person in order to make title to property which the deceased had failed to convey formally before his death. This might happen where a mortgage had been redeemed but the mortgagee had died before reconveying the property to the mortgagor, leaving no other estate. The lack of any unadministered estate of the

---

[25] See *In the Goods of Butson* (1882) 9 L.R. Ir. 21 where Warren J. refused to grant administration to an officer whose domicile was Ireland, but who died in India and whose only assets were some property in India and a sum of money in the hands of the Secretary for War. See *In the Goods of Tucker* (1864) 2 Sw. & Tr. 585

[26] [1940] Ir. Jur. Rep. 36

[27] The will in question was the second of two wills made by the textatrix the first of which dealing with her property in the Canary Islands had been given effect to by the Spanish courts and the High Court in England had granted probate of the second will dealing with her English and Irish property.

[28] No. 8 Of 1959

deceased within the jurisdiction is not now a bar to the making of a grant *de bonis non*, or other form of grant in respect of unadministered estate, as the particular case may require.

9.16.4 Comparable legislation in England,[29] permitting a grant of representation to be made where the deceased has left no estate within the jurisdiction, has led the English courts to insist that the circumstances of the particular case must reveal a good and sufficient reason for making such a grant.[30] The willingness of the English courts to exercise a robust discretion in this matter is shown in *Re Wayland*,[31] where Pearce J. admitted to probate not only the testator's English will dealing with his property in England, but also a will made in Belgium dealing exclusively with his Belgian property. The deceased's estate consisted of property to the value of about £3,000 in Belgium and to the value of about £64,000 in England. Pearce J. pointed out, that if the deceased's executors did not obtain a grant of the Belgian will in England, duty would be exigible under Belgian law on the whole of the estate including the English property. The practical effect of this would be that the executors would have to abandon the Belgian property since, if they tried to deal with it, the taxes would far exceed its value. Pearce J. believed that by virtue of section 2(1) of the Administration of Justice Act 1932, he was entitled to make a grant in respect of the Belgian will, and since the making of such a grant would obviate an injustice in respect of the Belgian property, it was proper that such a grant be made.[32]

9.16.5 It is hoped that the Irish courts will learn from the English experience and show an equal preparedness to assume a wide discretion in the exercise of the jurisdiction conferred on them by section 29 of the Succession Act.

9.17 Applications for grants of probate

9.17.1 An application for a grant or revocation of probate may be made to the Probate Office or to the District Probate Registry where the deceased, at the time of his death, had a fixed place of abode.[33] The application may be

---

[29] Section 2(1) of the Administration of Justice Act 1932, repealed, but substantially preserved in the Supreme Court Act 1981 (c.54)

[30] See *Aldrich* v *Att. Gen.* [1968] P.281

[31] [1951] 2 All E.R. 1041

[32] *Ibid* at p.1044. Pearce J. cited with approval the passage headed "Administration" in Dicey's "Conflict of Laws" 6th ed. at p.301

[33] Section 35(1) of the Succession Act replacing Probates and Letters of Administration Act (Ireland) 1857 (c.79) ss. 50, 63

made in person or through a solicitor.[34] Where an application is made to a District Registry the District Registrar, before he entertains such application, must ascertain whether the person had, at the time of his death a fixed place of abode in such district.[35]

9.17.2 The Rules of the Superior Courts may be said to discourage applications in person rather than through a solicitor by placing certain difficulties in the way of such applications. Thus, while an application for probate or letters of administration may be made at the probate office in all cases and such applications may be made through a solicitor or in person, they shall not be dealt with by letter.[36] An applicant attending in person may not be attended by another person acting, or appearing to act, as his adviser, unless the Probate Officer otherwise permits.[37] It is also provided that an application which, in the first instance, has been made through a solicitor, will not afterwards be treated as a personal application, unless the Probate Officer otherwise permits.[38] Also an application for a grant of probate or administration in a case which has already been before the court (on motion or otherwise) will not be entertained as a personal application, but must be made through a solicitor, unless the Probate Officer otherwise directs.[39]

9.17.3 The Probate Officer, or District registrar as the case may be, is not to allow probate or letters of administration until all the inquiries which he sees fit to institute have been answered to his satisfaction but is, notwithstanding, to afford as great facility for obtaining grants of probate or administration as is consistent with due regard to the prevention of error or fraud.[40] The same is true for District Registrars except that they are to be particularly vigilant when applications are made in person.[41]

9.17.4 The resolution of any contentious matter arising out of an application to the Probate Office is referrable to the High Court, but, where the High Court is satisfied that the Circuit Court has jurisdiction in the matter, it may remit the matter to the judge of the circuit where the deceased had a fixed place of abode at the time of his death, and the said

---

[34] Section 35(2)
[35] Rules of the Superior Courts, Ord. 80 r.2
[36] R.S.C. O. 79 r.3
[37] R.S.C. O. 79 r.76. The same rule applies to appearance at a District Registry O. 80 r.73
[38] R.S.C. O. 79 r.77 and O. 80 r.74
[39] R.S.C. O. 79 r.78 and O. 80 r.75
[40] R.S.C. O. 79 r.4
[41] R.S.C. O. 80 r.5

judge shall proceed in the matter as if the application had been made to the Circuit Court in the first instance.[42]

9.18 Grants in District Probate Registries

9.18.1 A grant may be made in common form[43] by a District Probate Registrar in the name of the High Court and under the seal of the registry where the deceased, at the time of his death, had a fixed place of abode within the district where the application for the grant is made.[44] No grant may be made by a District Probate Registrar in any contentious case until the contention is disposed of, or in any case in which it appears to him that a grant ought not to be made without the direction of the court.[45] In any case where it appears doubtful to a District Probate Registrar whether or not a grant should be made, or where any question arises in relation to a grant, the District Probate Registrar must send a statement of the matter to the probate office for the directions of the High Court judge, for the time being exercising probate jurisdiction. The judge may direct the registrar to proceed with the matter in accordance with such instructions as the judge thinks necessary, or he may forbid any further proceedings by the registrar, leaving the party applying for the grant to apply to the High Court or the Circuit Court, if the latter has jurisdiction.[46]

9.18.2 A District Probate Registrar must send to the Probate Office, a notice in the prescribed form of every application for a grant made in the Registry, and no grant may be made by him until he has received from the Probate Office a certificate that no other application appears to have been made in respect of the estate of the deceased.[47] All such notices transmitted from District Registries to the Probate Office are to be filed and kept in that office.[48] Where a notice is received from a District Probate Registry the Probate Officer must examine all notices of applications for grants received from the several other District Probate Registries, and all applications for grants at the Probate Office, to ascertain whether more than one application for a grant in respect of the estate of the same deceased person has been made.[49]

---

[42] Section 35(3) of the Succession Act
[43] See *post* p. 268
[44] Section 36(1) of the Succession Act
[45] Section 36(2)
[46] Section 36(3)
[47] Section 36(4)
[48] Section 36(6)
[49] Section 36(7)

9.18.3 District Probate Registrars are also bound to transmit to the Probate Office, twice in every month, a list of grants made and copies of the wills to which the grants relate, certified by the respective Registrar as being correct.[50]

9.19 Caveats

9.19.1 A caveat, which is a formal warning that nothing be done in relation to a grant of representation without prior notice being given to the person lodging the caveat, may be entered in the Probate Office or any District Probate Registry.[51] When a caveat is entered in a District Probate Registry, the District Probate Registrar must immediately send a copy thereof to the Probate Office to be entered among the caveats in that Office.[52] The District Probate Registrar must also send a copy of such caveat to the Registrar of any other District in which it is alleged that the deceased resided at the time of his death, or in which he is known to have had a fixed place of abode at such time.[53]

9.19.2 It is provided in the Rules of the Superior Courts that any person intending to oppose the issuing of a grant of probate or letters of administration may, either personally or by his solicitor, lodge a caveat in the Probate Office or in a District Registry.[54] Interestingly, the rules relating to District Probate Registries refer to the lodgment of a caveat in the "appropriate" District Registry.[55] The requirement that a caveat be lodged in the District Registry where the deceased had a fixed abode at the time of his death is so eminently sensible that its omission elsewhere in the Rules of the Superior Courts and in section 38(1) must rank as an oversight. This conclusion draws support from the fact that the Probate Officer must, immediately upon a caveat being lodged, send notice thereof to the District Registrar of the District in which it is alleged the deceased resided at the time of his death, or in which he is known to have had a fixed place of abode at the time of his death.[56]

9.19.3 A caveat remains in force for six months only, after which it expires and is of no effect, but caveats may be renewed from time to time.[57] Any

---

[50] Section 36(8)
[51] Section 38(1) of the Succession Act
[52] Section 38(2)
[53] R.S.C. Ord. 80 r.52
[54] R.S.C. Ord. 79 r.41
[55] R.S.C. Ord. 80 r.48
[56] R.S.C. Ord. 79 r.45
[57] R.S.C. Ord. 79 r.42 and Ord. 80 r.49

person who knowingly lodges, or causes to be lodged, in the Probate Office, a caveat in the name of a fictitious person, or with a false address of the person on whose behalf it purports to be lodged, shall be deemed guilty of a contempt of court.[58]

9.19.4 Every caveat must state the name and address of the person on whose behalf it is lodged, and the registered place of business of the solicitor lodging the same, or if there is no solicitor, an address for service, within the jurisdiction at which the caveat can be warned.[59] All caveats are warned from the Probate Office, and the warning is to be served by delivery of a copy thereof at the place mentioned in the caveat as the registered place of business of the solicitor, or address for service of the person who lodged the affidavit, as the case may be, within fourteen days of the date thereof.[60] In addition to the service of the warning the Probate Officer must, on the same day as the warning is signed by him, send by post a copy of it to the solicitor or person who lodged it and, on the same day, enter a memorandum of such posting in the book kept for that purpose.[61]

9.19.5 An appearance to a warning must be entered in the Probate Office within fourteen days of the service, provided that the time for appearance may be considered to be extended until action on default has been taken under rule 51.[62] The latter rule provides that in order to clear off a caveat, when no appearance has been entered to a warning duly served, an affidavit of the service of the warning in the prescribed manner, and a certificate of non-appearance must be filed.[63]

9.20 Second and subsequent grants

9.20.1 Second and subsequent grants are to be made in the Probate Office or District Probate Registry, as the case may be, from which the original grant issued.[64] The usual case in which a second or subsequent grant is necessary is where the sole or last surviving personal representative of a deceased person has died before administration of the estate is complete.

---

[58] R.S.C. Ord. 79 r.44 and Ord. 80 r.51
[59] R.S.C. Ord. 79 r.43
[60] R.S.C. Ord. 79 r.47
[61] R.S.C. Ord. 79 r.48
[62] R.S.C. Ord. 79 r.50
[63] R.S.C. Ord. 79 r.51
[64] Section 37 of the Succession Act

9.20.2 If such person is an executor and probate has been granted to one or some of two or more persons named as executors in the will, with power reserved to the others to prove, then a grant of unadministered probate may issue to the latter.[65] Otherwise a grant *de bonis non* may issue.[66]

9.21 Public inspection of wills

9.21.1 We have seen that on his death, a man's will assumes the status of a public document and this openness to public scrutiny helps to ensure that the testamentary wishes of the deceased are given effect to. A testator may disguise or hide the true objects of his bounty by employing a secret trust, but his will is otherwise open to public scrutiny and not least by the Revenue Commissioners. It is accordingly provided in the Succession Act that, subject to any arrangements which may from time to time be made between the President of the High Court and the Revenue Commissioners, the Probate Office and every District Probate Registry, will deliver to the Revenue Commissioners in the case of a probate, or of administration with a will annexe, the Inland Revenue affidavit and a copy of the will (if required).[67] The Inland Revenue affidavit, which must accompany every application for probate or letters of administration, should contain details of the deceased's property and the debts and expenses to be deducted therefrom in calculating the net estate on which inheritance tax is exigible.[68]

9.21.2 All original wills of which probate was granted in the Probate Office, copies of all wills transmitted from the District Probate Registries and such other documents as the President of the High Court may direct, are to be deposited and preserved in the Probate Office under the control of the President of the High Court and may be inspected in accordance with his directions. Such wills and other documents may be removed to the Public Records Office for safe-keeping pursuant to the provisions of the Public Records (Ireland) Act 1867.[69]

9.21.3 An official copy of the whole, or any part of a will, or of a grant of representation, may be obtained from the Probate Office or the relevant District Probate Registry.[70] Such copy will constitute sufficient evidence of

---

[65] See *ante* p. 240
[66] See Mongey "Probate Practice in a Nutshell" pp.46 *et seq.*
[67] Section 40(a)
[68] See Capital Acquisitions Tax Act, 1976 (No. 8), 1 Part VI
[69] 1867 c.70
[70] Section 43(1) of the Succession Act

the grant, whether the grant was made before or after the commencement of the Succession Act.[71]

9.21.4 The availability of wills for public inspection is further guaranteed and facilitated by the provision in the Succession Act that calendars of grants made in the Probate Office and in the several District Probate Registries are to be prepared from time to time.[72] Every such calendar is to contain a note of every probate or administration with the will annexed and of every other administration granted within the period specified in the calendar.[73] A copy of every calendar is to be sent to every District Probate Registry,[74] and such calendars and copies may be inspected in accordance with the directions of the President of the High Court.[75]

9.22 Proving a will

9.22.1 Usually a will is proved by the production of a testamentary instrument which has been duly executed in accordance with the statutory formalities, considered in an earlier chapter.[76] As we saw earlier, an applicant for probate or letters of administration must submit with his application an inland revenue affidavit.[77] It is also required of every applicant for a grant of probate or letters of administration that he produce a certificate of death or burial of the deceased, or give a satisfactory reason for the non-production thereof.[78]

9.22.2 A will may be proved in common form or in solemn form. Proof in common form occurs, where there is no contention touching the validity of the will and the testamentary instrument submitted to the appropriate registry has, on its face, been validly executed. As we saw earlier the inclusion in the will of a proper attestation clause will facilitate its admission to probate, which may be granted on the oath of the proving executor.[79] The Probate Officer may, if he deems it necessary, require proof in addition to the oath of the executor or administrator, of the identity of the deceased, or of the party applying for the grant.[80]

[71] Section 43(2)
[72] Section 39(1)
[73] Section 39(2)
[74] Section 39(3)
[75] Section 39(4)
[76] See *ante* pp. 30 *et seq.*
[77] See *ante* p. 267
[78] R.S.C. Ord. 79 r.81 and Ord. 80 r.83
[79] For attestation clauses see *ante* p. 49
[80] R.S.C. Ord. 79 r.36 and Ord. 80 r.41

9.22.3 If there is no attestation clause in a will presented for probate, or administration with the will annexed, or if the attestation clause is insufficient, the Probate Officer is to require an affidavit from at least one of the subscribing witnesses, if they or either of them be living, to prove that the will was duly executed.[81] If both subscribing witnesses are dead or an affidavit is otherwise unobtainable from either of them, resort may be had to any other person who may have been present at the execution of the will, but if no other person can be obtained, evidence on affidavit can be procured relating to the handwriting of the deceased and the subscribing witnesses, and any other circumstances which raise a presumption in favour of due execution.[82]

9.22.4 If it appears doubtful to the Probate Officer, having perused the affidavit or affidavits relating to the case, that the will was duly executed, he may require the parties to bring the matter before the court.[83] It is also provided in the Rules of the Superior Courts that in any case in which a will apparently duly executed has been produced for probate, or for administration with the will annexed, probate of any former will, or administration with any former will annexed, or administration to the deceased as having died intestate, must not be granted by a District Registrar without an order of the court, or the Probate Officer, showing that the last will is not entitled to probate.[84]

9.22.5 We have seen earlier that if the original will cannot be produced because it has been lost or accidentally destroyed, probate may be granted of a copy or draft of the will, provided that the authenticity of such draft or copy can otherwise be established.[85] It is provided in the Rules of the Superior Courts that if it can be shown on affidavit that a testamentary paper is in the possession, within the power, or under the control of any person, a *subpoena* for the production of the same may be issued by order of the Probate Officer.[86]

9.22.6 A grant of probate in common form may later be challenged in an action for revocation of the grant brought by an interested party.[87] Such party may seek to impugn the grant on grounds such as, that the testator

---

[81] R.S.C. Ord. 79 r.6 and Ord. 80 r.8

[82] R.S.C. Ord. 79 r.8 and Ord. 80 r.10. Affidavit evidence may also be required in respect of erasures obliterations and alterations in a will. See Ord. 79 r.12

[83] R.S.C. Ord. 79 r.9

[84] R.S.C. Ord. 80 r.11

[85] Which may be done by parol evidence. See *ante* p. 96

[86] R.S.C. Ord. 79 r.59

[87] Interested parties include persons entitled to a share of the deceased's estate on an intestacy or beneficiaries under a previous will or an executor under a previous will.

lacked testamentary capacity when the will was made or that the testator did not know or approve of the contents of the will.[88] The High Court, as we have seen, has the power to revoke, cancel or recall any grant of probate.[89]

9.22.7 The English courts have taken a liberal approach to actions by interested parties for the revocation of grants made in common form, and such a party has not been held to be barred from seeking revocation of a grant by his acquiesance in the making of the grant,[90] or by his acceptance of a legacy under the will which he is seeking to challenge.[91] This approach of the courts is no doubt a factor in the advice tendered by several English textwriters, that it is prudent for an executor to prove a will in solemn form if there is any doubt as to the validity of the will or any possibility of the will being challenged in the future.[92]

9.22.8 It is the case of course that persons acting under a grant in common form are protected in respect of acts done while the grant remains in force. We have seen that personal representatives are afforded protection with regard to payments made under a grant which is subsequently revoked,[93] as are purchasers who acquire property from such personal representatives.[94]

9.22.9 A will is proved in solemn form when a court has pronounced it to be a valid testamentary document following a probate action. A will so pronounced is *res judicata* and the order of the court is binding on the parties to the probate action. Such order is also binding on a party who was aware of the action and his own interest in the deceased's estate which would have entitled him to intervene in the proceedings.[95] A party will be bound by an order of the court if he could have opposed the issue of a grant but chose not to do so.[96] It is otherwise if a person, being aware of the probate action, is unaware of his own interest in the deceased's estate which would entitle him to intervene in the proceedings.[97]

---

[88] See *ante* p. 62
[89] Section 26(2) of the Succession Act
[90] *Goddard* v *Smith* (1873) L.R.3 P. & P. 7; *Re Jolley* (1964) P.262
[91] *Bell* v *Armstrong* (1822) 1 Add. 365; *Goddard* v *Norton* (1846) 5 N.C. 76 See Parry and Clark "The Law of Succession" (8th ed. 1983) at pp.159-160
[92] See e.g. Mellows "The Law of Succession" (4th ed. 1983) at pp. 261 and Parry and Clark "The Law of Succession" (8th ed. 1983) at p.159
[93] Section 22(1) of the Succession Act
[94] Section 25(1) of the Succession Act
[95] See *Young* v *Holloway* [1895] p.87; *In the Estate of Langton* [1964] P. 163
[96] See *Newell* v *Weeks* (1814) 2 Phill. 224; *Re Barraclough* [1967] P.1
[97] *Young* v *Holloway* [1895] P.87

9.22.10 A grant in solemn form is not inviolable however, and may be set aside on grounds which include evidence that the grant had been obtained by fraud,[98] or that a later will than the one propounded turned up.[99] A person who is not bound by an order of the court affecting the validity of a will, may re-open issues which have been adjudicated on in the action which preceded the grant.[100]

9.23 Grants of administration

9.23.1 We have seen that while an executor is appointed by the testator an administrator is appointed to his office by the court.[101] Grants of administration are made under two separate heads. Firstly, where the deceased leaves a will having failed to appoint an executor or no executor takes probate, in which case the court makes a grant of letters of administration with the will annexed. Secondly, where the deceased has died intestate and the court grants letters of administration, otherwise "simple" administration.

9.23.2 The High Court has power to grant administration, with or without will annexed, of the estate of a deceased person and such grant may be limited in any way the court thinks fit.[102] As with grants of probate the High Court has power to revoke, cancel or recall any grant of representation.[103]

9.23.3 The person or persons to whom administration is to be granted will be determined, subject to section 27(4) of the Succession Act,[104] in accordance with the rules of the Superior Courts.[105] Those rules provide, that the person or persons entitled to a grant of administration with will annexed are to be determined in accordance with the following order of priority:–[106]

(a) any residuary legatee or devisee holding in trust for any other person;

(b) any residuary legatee or devisee for life;

(c) any other residuary legatee or devisee or, subject to sub-rule (9)(b)

---

[98] *Birch* v *Birch* [1902] P.62

[99] *In b. O'Sullivan* [1960] Ir. Jur. Rep. 14

[100] See Parry and Clark "The Law of Succession" (8th ed. 1983) at p.161

[101] See *ante* p. 232

[102] Section 27(1) of the Succession Act

[103] Section 27(2)

[104] See *post* p. 274

[105] Section 27(3)

[106] R.S.C. Ord. 79 r.5(6) and Ord 80 r.6(1)

of rule 5, which provides that live interests be preferred to dead interests;[107]

(d) any residuary legatee or devisee for life jointly with any ultimate residuary legatee or devisee on the renunciation or consent of the remaining residuary legatees or devisees for life;

(e) where the residue is not in terms wholly disposed of, the Probate Officer may, if he is of opinion that the testator has nevertheless disposed of the whole or substantially the whole of the estate as ascertained at the time of the application for a grant, allow a grant to be made to any legatee or devisee entitled to, or to share in, the estate so disposed of, without regard to the person entitled to share in any residue not disposed of by the will;

(f) where the residue is not wholly disposed of by the will, any person (other than a creditor) entitled to a grant in the event of a total intestacy;

(g) any legatee or devisee or any creditor or, subject to sub-rule (9)(b), the personal representative of any such person.

9.23.4 Where a person dies wholly intestate and domiciled in Ireland, the persons having a beneficial interest in the estate of the deceased will be entitled to a grant of administration in the following order of priority:–

(a) the surviving spouse;

(b) the surviving spouse jointly with a child of the deceased nominated by the said spouse;

(c) the child or children of the deceased (including any person entitled by virtue of the Legitimacy Act, 1931, to succeed to the estate of the deceased);[108]

(d) the issue of any child who has died during the lifetime of the deceased;

(e) the father or mother of the deceased or, in the case of an illegitimate person who died without having been legitimated, the mother;[109]

(f) brothers and sisters of the deceased (whether of the whole or half-blood);

(g) where any brother or sister survived the deceased, the children of a predeceased brother or sister;

(h) nephews and nieces of the deceased (whether of the whole or half-blood);

(i) grandparents;

(j) uncles and aunts (whether of the whole or half-blood);

(k) great grandparents;

---

[107] A living member of a class is to be preferred to the personal representatives of a member of a class entitled to a grant who has died after the deceased.

[108] On the new position of "illegitimate" children see *ante* pp. 204 *et seq.*

[109] See *ante* p. 219

(l) other next-of-kin of nearest degree (whether of the whole or half blood) preferring collaterals to direct lineal ancestors;

(m) the nominee of the state.

9.23.5 The personal representative of any of the aforementioned named persons, other than the nominee of the State, has the same right to a grant as the person whom he represents, subject to the sub-rule which provides that live interests be preferred to dead interests.[110] If all the aforementioned persons entitled to a grant have been cleared off a grant may be made to a creditor of the deceased or, subject to sub-rule (9)(b) which prefers live interests to dead interests, the personal representative of a creditor.[111] Where the only person entitled to the estate of the deceased, whether under a will or on an intestacy, has assigned his whole interest in the estate the assignee replaces the assignor in the order of priority for a grant.[112]

9.23.6 Where a deceased person has died domiciled outside Ireland, since the commencement of the Succession Act, a grant of administration intestate or with will annexed of the moveable estate may be made by the Probate Officer as follows: (i) to the person entrusted with the administration of the moveable estate by the court with jurisdiction in the place where the deceased was domiciled at his death, and, (ii) to the person entitled to administer the moveable estate by the law of the place where the deceased was domiciled at his death.[113]

9.23.7 The Probate Officer may make a grant of administration intestate, or with will annexed, of the immoveable estate of a deceased person in accordance with the law which would have been applicable if the deceased had died domiciled in Ireland.[114] Nothing in this sub-rule is to be construed as prejudicially affecting any power which might otherwise be exercisable, if no executor was named in the will and if the will describes a named person in terms sufficient to make him an executor according to the tenor, in making a grant of probate to that person.[115]

9.23.8 While administration is ordinarily granted in accordance with the order of priority laid down by the Rules of the Superior Courts we have seen that, where by reason of any special circumstances it appears to the High Court, or to the Circuit Court in cases within the jurisdiction of that

---

[110] R.S.C. Ord. 79 r.5(2) and Ord. 80 r. 6(2)
[111] R.S.C. Ord. 79 r.5(4) and Ord. 80 r.6(4)
[112] R.S.C. Ord. 79 r.5(11) and Ord. 80 r.6(10)
[113] R.S.C. Ord. 79 r.5(8)(a)
[114] R.S.C. Ord. 79 r.5(8)(b)
[115] R.S.C. Ord. 79 r.5(8)(c)

court, to be necessary or expedient to do so, administration may be granted to such person as the court thinks fit.[116]

9.23.9 The provisions dealt with earlier in respect of grants of probate apply equally to grants of administration, where both types of grant are dealt with in the Succession Act under the umbrella term grants of representation. Thus the High Court may grant administration, as with probate, to a trust corporation either solely or jointly with another person.[117] We have seen, that where an infant is sole executor of a will, administration with the will annexed will be granted to his guardian, or to such other person as the High Court thinks fit, until the infant attains his majority and applies for and obtains a grant of probate or letters of administration with the will annexed.[118]

9.23.10 The Rules of the Superior Courts[119] provide where an infant does not have a testamentary guardian or a guardian appointed by the court, or by or under the provisions of the Guardianship of Infants Act 1964, a guardian will be assigned by order of the court or of the Probate Officer. The affidavit accompanying an application for such order must show, as nearly as possible, the amount of the assets, the age of the infant, with whom he resides, and that the proposed guardian is either the nearest relation of the infant or that, the nearest relation has renounced his right to guardianship or consents to the assignment of the proposed guardian. The court or Probate Officer must have regard to the expressed wishes of any infant over the age of twelve years.

9.23.11 A grant of administration made to a guardian of an infant is stated, in the Rules of the Superior Courts, to be made for the infant's use and it would seem to follow that an administrator *durante minore aetate* is accountable to the infant for his administration of the estate.[120] The grant of such an administrator will end when the infant attains majority and obtains a grant,[121] but otherwise such administrator has all the rights and duties of an ordinary administrator.[122]

[116] Section 27(4) of the Succession Act
[117] Section 30(1)(b) of the Succession Act
[118] Section 32(1)
[119] R.S.C. Ord. 79 r.25 and Ord. 80 r.29
[120] R.S.C. Ord.79 r.24 and Ord. 80 r.28. This is so even though the infant has no beneficial interest in the estate. See *Harvell* v *Foster* [1954] 2 Q.B. 367 and Mellows "The Law of Succession" (4th ed. 1983) at p. 257
[121] The position is different in England where administration is granted for the use and benefit of a minor until he attains the age of 18 years when the grant terminates automatically. See the Non Contentions Probate Rules 1954 r.31
[122] See *Re Cope* (1880) 16 Ch. D. 49, 52 (per Sir George Jessel M.R.)

9.23.12 Administration, like probate, may be granted separately in respect of real and personal estate,[123] but, as with a grant of probate, a grant of administration will not be severed where the estate of the deceased is known to be insolvent, except as regards a trust estate.[124]

9.23.13 The High Court may also make a grant of administration, as it can a grant of probate, where the deceased left no estate within the jurisdiction.[125] We have seen that this jurisdiction enables the Irish courts to facilitate the issue of foreign grants in respect of the estates of persons who were domiciled in Ireland and the foreign law requires that a grant be issued by the court of domicile.[126] We have also seen that the High Court may make a grant *de bonis non* in respect of an administered estate notwithstanding that there is no unadministered estate of the deceased in the jurisdiction. Since a grant *de bonis non* is normally made in respect of the unadministered part of a deceased's estate where a personal representative dies before administration is complete, some doubt has been expressed as to whether the aforementioned statutory powers allow an Irish court to grant letters of administration in respect of a deceased's estate which consists entirely of property which passes only outside the jurisdiction.[127] The language of the section[128] which confers this jurisdiction on the courts places no obvious fetters on the jurisdiction, and one can only repeat the suggestion made earlier that the Irish courts should only be prepared to exercise such jurisdiction when there is a compelling reason for doing so.[129]

9.24 Administration *pendente lite*

9.24.1 Where any legal proceedings are pending touching the validity of the will of a deceased person, or for obtaining, recalling or revoking any grant, the High Court may grant administration of the estate of the deceased pending such proceedings.[130] Proceedings will be considered as pending, for the purposes of such a grant, only when they have commenced with the issue of a writ, and the entry of a caveat will not suffice for this purpose.[131]

---

[123] Section 28(1) of the Succession Act.
[124] Section 28(2)
[125] Section 29
[126] See *ante* p. 261
[127] See Wylie "Irish Land Law" (2nd ed. 1986) at p.770
[128] Section 29 of the Succession Act
[129] See *ante* p. 262
[130] Section 27(7) of the Succession Act
[131] *Salter* v *Salter* [1896] p.291; *Re McCann* (1898) 33 I.L.T.R. 39

9.24.2 Such a grant, otherwise known as a grant *pendente lite*, is normally made to a person who is not a party to the action, and, more usually, to a professional person such as an accountant.[132] The grant will be limited to the duration of the proceedings and will end on the termination of the action, including any appeal therefrom.[133]

9.24.3 An administrator *pendente lite* will have all the rights and duties of a general administrator, other than the right to distribute the estate of the deceased, and will be subject to the immediate control of the court and act under its direction.[134] The court may, out of the estate of the deceased person, assign to an administrator *pendente lite* such reasonable remuneration as the court thinks fit.[135]

9.25 Grant *ad colligenda bona*

9.25.1 Where the assets of a deceased person require immediate attention because, for example, they are wasting or perishable, and no person has applied for a grant of probate or administration, a grant of administration *ad colligenda bona* may be obtained by some suitable person.[136]

9.25.2 An application may be made for an order of the court in the exercise of its jurisdiction to grant administration to such person as it thinks fit where, by reason of any special circumstances it appears to the court to be necessary or expedient to do so.[137] Such a grant is usually limited to the purpose of collecting and preserving the estate of the deceased, and distribution of the estate may not be done until a further grant of representation is made.

9.26 Special Administration

9.26.1 Where, after the expiration of twelve months from the death of the deceased, any personal representative to whom a grant was made is residing out of the jurisdiction, the High Court may, on the application of any creditor or person interested in the estate of the deceased person, grant to him in such form as the court thinks fit special administration of

---

[132] Cf. *Re Griffin* [1925] P.38 for circumstances in which a party to the action may be appointed.

[133] *Taylor* v *Taylor* (1881) 3 P.D. 29

[134] Section 27(7) of the Succession Act

[135] Section 27(8)

[136] See *In the Goods of Bolton* [1899] P. 186; *In the Goods of Roberts* [1898] P.149; *Re Cohen* [1975] V.R. 187; *Re Clore* [1982] 2 W.L.R. 314.

[137] Section 27(4) of the Succession Act

the estate of the deceased person.[138] The court may, for the purposes of any legal proceedings to which such special administrator is a party, order the transfer into court of any money or securities belonging to the estate of the deceased person.[139]

9.26.2 Where, however, a personal representative returns to the jurisdiction while any legal proceedings to which a special administrator is a party are pending, such personal representative must be made a party to the proceedings and the costs of, and incidental to, those proceedings and the special administration are to be paid by him and out of such fund as the court in which the proceedings are pending may direct.[140]

9.27 Administration Bond

9.27.1 Every person to whom a grant of administration is made must give a bond, a so-called administration bond, to the President of the High Court to inure for the benefit of the President of the High Court, for the time being and, if the High Court, the Probate Officer or District Probate Registrar so requires, with one or more surety or sureties conditioned for duly collecting, getting in, and administering the estate of the deceased.[141]

9.27.2 An administration bond is to be a penalty of double the amount at which the estate of the deceased is sworn unless the High Court, the Probate Officer or the District Probate Registrar, direct it to be reduced in any case.[142] The High Court, the Probate Officer or the District Probate Registrar may direct that more than one administration bond be given so as to limit the liability of any surety to such amount as the court, Probate Officer or District Probate Register thinks reasonable.[143]

9.27.3 An administration bond is not required in the case of the Chief State Solicitor or the Solicitor for the Attorney-General, in respect of administration for the use or benefit of the State[144] nor, are sureties to administration bonds required when the grant is made to a trust corporation.[145] The issue of an administration bond by a guarantee society

---

[138] Section 31(1) of the Succession Act. See *In b. Boyd* (1912) 46 I.L.T.R. 294; *In b. Walsh* (1923) 57 I.L.T.R. 78. See also *Re Walsh* [1931] I.R. 161
[139] Section 31(2)
[140] Section 31(3)
[141] Section 34(1). See *Hibernian Fire Insurance Co. v Dorgan* [1941] I.R. 514
[142] Section 34(2)(a)
[143] Sectioon 34(2)(b)
[144] Section 34(5)
[145] Section 34(6)

or insurance company approved by the President of the High Court is acceptable for these purposes, whether the application for the grant is made in person or by a solicitor.[146]

9.27.4 The Rules of the Superior Courts provide, that administration bonds must be attested by the Probate Officer or Assistant Probate Officer or by a District Registrar or by a Commissioner or other person authorised to take affidavits, but, in no case are they to be attested by the solicitor or agent of the party who executes them.[147] The Probate Officer and District Registrar are to take care as far as possible, that the sureties to administration bonds are responsible persons.[148]

9.27.5 Where the High Court is satisfied that the condition of an administration bond has been broken, it may order that the bond be assigned to such person as may be specified in the order, and such person will be entitled to sue in his own name as if it had originally been given to him rather than the President of the High Court, and to recover therefrom as trustee for all persons interested, the full amount recoverable in respect of the condition thereof.[149]

9.28 Status of administrator

9.28.1 Every person to whom administration is granted with or without the will annexed has, subject to any limitations contained in the grant, the same rights and liabilities and is accountable in the same manner as if he were the executor of the deceased.[150]

9.28.2 When administration is granted, no person is entitled without a grant to administer any estate to which such administration relates.[151]

[146] Section 34(7)
[147] R.S.C. Ord. 79 r.30 and Ord. 80 r.32
[148] R.S.C. Ord. 79 r.30 and Ord. 80 r.32
[149] Section 34(4)
[150] Section 27(6)
[151] Section 27(5)

Chapter 10
ADMINISTRATION OF ASSETS

10.1 Introduction

10.1.1 When a grant of representation, whether of probate or administration, has issued, it is the responsibility of the personal representatives to collect all the assets of the deceased person, and, having paid his funeral expenses and discharged his debts and other liabilities, to distribute the residue of his estate according to the terms of the will or the rules on intestacy, as the case may be. The distribution of any residue will depend of course upon whether or not the deceased's debts and other liabilities exceed his assets, and we shall see that a distinction is drawn between the rules governing the administration of solvent estates and those governing insolvent estates.[1]

10.1.2 The rules governing the administration of the assets of a deceased person are contained in Part V of the Succession Act, which continues the process of assimilation of the law relating to realty and personalty, by providing that real and personal estate will be administered in the same way.[2] It is accordingly provided that, without prejudice to the rights of incumbrances,[3] all the estate, whether legal or equitable, of a deceased person, and the estate of which he disposes by will in pursuance of any general power, are assets for payment of the funeral, testamentary and administration expenses, debts (whether by speciality or simple contract) and liabilities, and any legal right of a surviving spouse.[4] Any disposition

---

[1] See *post* p. 280
[2] See the Explanatory Memorandum with the Succession Act at p.4
[3] Section 45(2)
[4] Section 45(1)

by will which is inconsistent with the foregoing provision is void as against the creditors and anyone entitled to a legal right and the court will, if necessary, administer the property for the purpose of the payment of the expenses, debts and liabilities and any legal right.[5]

10.2 Insolvent estates

10.2.1 Where the estate of a deceased person is insolvent, which will be the case where the assets of such person are insufficient to pay the funeral, testamentary and administration expenses, and debts and liabilities of the deceased, it is to be administered in accordance with the rules set out in Part 1 of the First Schedule to the Succession Act.[6] These provide:

1. The funeral, testamentary and administration expenses have priority.
2. Subject as aforesaid, the same rules shall prevail and be observed as to the respective rights of secured and unsecured creditors, and as to debts and liabilities provable, and as to the valuation of annuities and future and contingent liabilities, respectively, and as to the priorities of debts and liabilities as may be in force for the time being under the law of bankruptcy with respect to the assets of persons adjudged bankrupt.
3. In the application of the said rules the date of death will be substituted for the date of adjudication in bankruptcy.

10.3 Funeral, testamentary and administration expenses

10.3.1 Funeral expenses, even in the case of insolvent estates, have long had first priority in the administration of a deceased's estate.[7] If such expenses are paid by someone other than the personal representative they may be recovered from the deceased's estate.[8] The funeral expenses incurred must be reasonable however, and such reasonableness is a question of fact to be determined in the light of the circumstances in the particular case.[9] The relevant circumstances include the deceased's position in life,[10] his religious beliefs and any wishes he may have expressed as to the conduct of his funeral. The pragmatic approach taken by the courts to this question is illustrated by cases involving the erection of a tombstone in memory of the deceased. Sometimes this is allowable but

[5] *Ibid*

[6] Section 46(1)

[7] See judicature (Irl.) Act 1877, s.28(1); *Moore* v *Smith* [1895] 1 I.R. 512; *McCausland* v *O'Callaghan* [1904] 1 I.R. 376 and Wylie "Irish Land Law" (2nd ed. 1986) at p.777

[8] See *Green* v *Salmon* (1838) 3 Ad. & E. 348

[9] See Parry and Clark "The Law of Succession" (8th ed. 1983) at pp. 245-6

[10] *Stag* v *Punter* (1744) 3 Atr. 119

[11] *Gammell* v *Wilson* [1982] A.C. 27

often it is condemned as an unjustifiable expense.[12]

10.3.2 If the estate is insolvent the test of reasonableness is less easily satisfied, and it has been held that only those funeral expenses which are absolutely necessary are payable out of the deceased's estate.[13] Such expenses were said by Lord Holt in *Shelly's Case*[14] to include the costs of the coffin, digging the grave, ringing the church bell and paying the parson clerk and undertaker.[15]

10.3.3 Testamentary and administration expenses are those expenses which are incidental to the duties of a personal representative and are properly incurred by him in the administration of the estate.[16] They include the expense incurred in obtaining a grant of representation, whether letters of administration or probate in common or solemn form, the cost of legal advice as to the administration of the estate and the costs incurred in realising and preserving the assets of the deceased.[17] The courts view with suspicion, however, any uncorroborated claims against the estate of a deceased person.[18]

10.3.4 When the funeral, testamentary and administration expenses have been discharged the personal representatives must apply the assets of the deceased in payment of his debts according to the rules laid down in the bankruptcy legislation.[19]

10.4 Secured creditors

10.4.1 A creditor who has security for his loan by way of mortgage, charge or lien is clearly in a more favourable position in relation to the administration of the estate. If the value of his security equals or exceeds the amount of the debt he is adequately covered, and if he is a mortgagee he can exercise his power of sale and repay himself in full. If the value of his security is less

---

[12] See *Re McIntyre* (1930) 64 I.L.T.R. 179; *Goldstein* v *Salvation Army Assurance Society* [1917] 2 K.B. 291; Cf. *Bridge* v *Brown* (1843), 2 Y. & C.C.C. 181; *Hart* v *Griffiths-Jones* [1948] 2 All E.R. 729

[13] See *Re Wester Wemyss* [1940] Ch. 1

[14] (1693) 1 Salk. 296

[15] See Mellows "The Law of Succession" (4th ed. 1983) at p. 322

[16] *Sharp* v *Lush* (1879) 10 Ch.D. 468; *Gilhooly* v *Plunkett* (1882) 9 L.R. Ir. 324; *Re Blake* [1955] I.R. 89; *Re Taylor's Estate* [1969] 2 Ch. 245

[17] *McFeely* v *Boyle* (1886) 17 L.R. Ir. 633 *Kelly* v *Kelly* (1888) 2 1 L.R. Ir. 243 *Re O'Kane* [1907] 1 I.R. 223

[18] See *Re Boak* (1881) 7 L.R. Ir. 322; *Somers* v *Erskine* (No. 2) [1944] I.R. 368 and Wylie "Irish Land Law" (2nd ed. 1986) at p.777

[19] Bankruptcy (Ir.) Amendment Act, 1872 (35 & 36 Vict. c.58) and Preferential Payments in Bankruptcy (Ir.) Act, 1889 (52 & 53) Vict. c.60

than the debt he can realise his security and prove for the balance of the debt.[20] A secured creditor could of course surrender his security and prove for the whole debt[21] but an English textwriter has written that it "is difficult to envisage anyone in his senses doing this."[22]

10.5 Preferential debts

10.5.1 An unsecured creditor runs the risk of getting nothing if the estate is insolvent, in which case the personal representatives must apply the assets of the deceased in payment of so-called "preferential" debts as laid down by the bankruptcy legislation.[23] These debts are (i) rates and taxes due at the testator's death;[24] (ii) wages or salary of a labourer or workman or clerk or servant in respect of services rendered within four months of the deceased's death;[25] (iii) sums due in respect of contributions payable by the deceased in the twelve months prior to death under the social welfare and national insurance legislation.[26]

10.6 Retainer and preference

10.6.1 A personal representative who was also a creditor of the estate could not sue himself, and there was the possibility of another creditor of equal standing getting priority by obtaining a judgment. In order to avoid this possibility the personal representative was given the right to retain debts due to him in preference to paying other creditors of equal standing with him.[27] The right of preference, as the name suggests, is the personal representative's right to pay one creditor in preference to others of the same class.[28]

10.6.2 The Succession Act now provides that the right of retainer of a personal representative, and his right to prefer creditors may be exercised in respect of all assets of the deceased, but the right of retainer shall only apply to debts owing to the personal representative in his own right

---

[20] *Re Love* (1863) 9 L.R. Ir. 6; *Re MacEntee* [1960] Ir. Jur. Rep. 55

[21] *Ex parte* Robinson (1886) 15 L.R. Ir. 496

[22] Mellows "The Law of Succession" at p. 329

[23] Preferential Payments in Bankruptcy (Ir.) Act, 1889

[24] *Re D.* [1927] I.R. 22 See Wylie "Irish Land Law" (2nd ed. 1986) at p.777

[25] *Re M.* [1956] N.I. 182, *Ibid*

[26] See e.g. Redundancy Payments Act, 1967 s.42(3) Health Contribution Act 1971 s. 11(3); Social Welfare Act, 1976, s.7

[27] See *Hanley* v *McDermott* (1874) I.R. 9 Eq. 35, *Taaffe* v *Taaffe* [1902] 1 I.R. 148; *Att.-Gen.*v *Jackson* [1932] A.C. 365. The right of retainer could also be invoked by an administrator subject to the terms of his administration bond. See *ante* p.277

[28] See *Re Rudd* [1942] Ch. 421

whether solely or jointly with another person, and shall not be exercisable where the estate is insolvent.[29] Subject to the foregoing provisions nothing in the Succession Act is to affect the right of retainer of a personal representative, or his right to prefer creditors.[30]

10.7 Solvent estates

10.7.1 Where the estate of a deceased person is solvent it will, subject to rules of court and the provisions as to charges on property of the deceased, and to the provisions if any in his will, be applicable towards the discharge of the funeral, testamentary and administration expenses debts and liabilities, and any legal right in the order mentioned in Part II of the First Schedule.[31] That order is as follows:

1. Property of the deceased undisposed of by will, subject to the retention thereout of a fund sufficient to meet any pecuniary legacies.
2. Property of the deceased not specifically devised or bequeathed but included (either by a specific or general description) in a residuary gift, subject to the retention out of such property of a fund sufficient to meet any pecuniary legacies, so far as not provided for as aforesaid.
3. Property of the deceased specifically appropriated or devised or bequeathed (either by a specific or general description) for the payment of debts.
4. Property of the deceased charged with, or devised or bequeathed (either by a specific or general description) subject to a charge for the payment of debts.
5. The fund, if any, retained to meet pecuniary legacies.
6. Property specifically devised or bequeathed, rateably according to value.
7. Property appointed by will under a general power, rateably according to value.

10.7.2 The foregoing order of application may be varied by the will of the deceased[32], and does not affect the liability of land to answer the death duty imposed thereon in exoneration of other assets.[33] Nor does that order of application affect the rights of any creditor of the deceased, or the legal right of a spouse.[34] A claim by a spouse to a share as a legal right or on

---

[29] Section 46(2)(a)

[30] Both rights have now been abolished in England and Northern Ireland. See Administration of Estates Act 1971, ss 10, 14(2) and Administration of Estates Act (N.I.) 1971 s.3(1)

[31] Section 46(3)

[32] 1st Schedule Part 11 para. 8(a)

[33] *Ibid* para. 8(b)

[34] Section 46(4)

intestacy in the estate of a deceased person, is a claim against the assets of the estate to a sum equal to the value of that share.[35] The lack of any clear guidelines in the Succession Act on how the personal representatives are to discharge a surviving spouses legal right to one-third or one-half of the deceased's estate led Henchy J. to say, in *H.* v *O.,*[36] that in the general context of the Act of 1965 "it must be assumed that the legislative intention was that the legal right (where elected for) is to be discharged in the same manner as if the one-half or one-third of the estate had been expressly given in the will in priority over all devises and bequests."

10.7.3 It is generally thought to be more prudent for personal representatives to distribute the assets among creditors on the basis that the estate is insolvent that is, to follow the statutory order for payment, until it becomes clear that the assets are sufficient to discharge all the debts and liabilities of the deceased.[37]

10.8 Marshalling

10.8.1 We have been dealing with the statutory order in which assets must be applied in the payment of debts and discharge of liabilities in respect of a solvent estate, which order may be varied by a testator.[38] If, however, the assets are applied out of the statutory order or that laid down by the testator the interests of beneficiaries under the will may be adversely affected.[39] Such beneficiary could invoke the equitable doctrine of marshalling, which permits him to have recourse to any of the deceased's property which should have been taken before his.[40]

10.8.2 The equitable doctrine of tracing has now been given statutory form in the Succession Act which provides, that where

"a creditor, a person entitled to a legal right or a personal representative applies an asset out of the order mentioned in Part II of the First Schedule, the persons entitled under the will or on intestacy shall have the right to have the assets marshalled so that a beneficiary whose estate or interest has been applied out of its order shall stand in the place of that creditor or person *pro tanto* as against any property that, in the said

[35] Section 46(6)
[36] [1978] I.R. 194, 204
[37] See e.g. Mellows "The Law of Succession" (4th ed. 1983) at p. 325
[38] See *ante* p. 283
[39] See *Aldrich* v *Cooper* (1803) 8 Ves. 382; Ellard v *Cooper* (1860) 11 Ir. Ch. R. 376; *Buckley* v *Buckley* (1887) 19 L.R. Ir. 561 See also *Re Matthews* W.T. [1961] 1 W.L.R. 1415, 1419 (per Pennycuick J.)
[40] See Keeton and Sheridan "Equity" (Belfast 1969) at pp. 438 *et seq.*

order, is liable before his own estate or interest."[41]

10.9 Charges on the deceased's property

10.9.1 It used to be the case that the devisee of land which was charged with a mortgage or other debt could require the debt to be discharged out of the personal estate of the deceased. That position was altered by the Real Estate Charges Act, 1854,[42] and amending acts of 1867[43] and 1877,[44] otherwise known at the Locke King's Acts. These Acts provided that the burden of discharging a mortgage or other debt generally descended with the property upon which the debt was charged.[45]

10.9.2 The provisions of the Real Estate Charges Act which, as the name indicates, were confined to realty, have now been extended by the Succession Act to all property, whether real or personal. It is accordingly provided, that when a person dies possessed of, or entitled to, or under a general power of appointment, by his will disposes of, an interest in property, which at the time of his death is charged with the payment of money, whether by way of legal or equitable mortgage or charge or otherwise, then, subject to a contrary intention in the will or otherwise, the interest so charged is, as between the different persons claiming through the deceased person, primarily liable for the payment of the charge.[46]

10.9.3 A contrary or other intention is not signified (a) by a general direction for the payment of debts of a testator out of his estate, or any part thereof, or (b) by a charge of debts upon any such estate, unless such intention is further signified by words expressly, or by necessary implication, referring to all or some part of the charge.[47]

10.9.4 The aforementioned provisions dealing with the payment of money charged on a deceased's property at the time of his death, do not affect the right of any person entitled to the charge to obtain payment or satisfaction thereof out of the estate or otherwise.[48] If a chargee obtains payment out of other assets of the deceased the doctrine of marshalling may be invoked

---

[41] Section 46(5)
[42] 17 & 18 Vict. c.113
[43] 30 & 31 Vict. c.69
[44] 40 & 41 Vict. c.34
[45] See *Dowdall* v *McCartan* (1881) 5 L.R. Ir. 642; *Nesbitt* v *Lawder* (1886) 17 L.R. Ir. 53: *Thompson* v *Bell* [1903] 1 I.R. 489. See Wylie "Irish Land Law" (2nd ed. 1986) at p. 781
[46] Section 47(1)
[47] Section 47(2)
[48] Section 47(3)

to ensure that the debt falls ultimately on the property charged with its repayment.[49]

10.9.5 As a consequence of the process of assimilation of the law on realty with that on personalty, the provisions relating to charges on a deceased's property at his death are not confined to charges on realty, though such charges are more common, but extend to charges on personalty as where a deceased's shares in a company were, under the articles of association, subject to an equitable charge for money owed by the deceased to the company at the time of his death.[50]

10.9.6 That the property interest in question must be an identifiable one to which the deceased was entitled at the time of his death, is illustrated by the decision in the English case *Re Coxen*.[51] There the court had to determine whether section 35 of the Administration of Estates Act 1925, which corresponds with section 47 of the Succession Act, was applicable in respect of a motor-car which the deceased had ordered prior to his death. Since no particular car had been appropriated to the deceased before his death, it was held, that section 35 had no application to the unpaid purchase price of a car which otherwise imposed a contractual liability on the deceased. It must also be clear, that the interest of the deceased in the property in question is charged with the payment of the debt at the deceased's death. The point is illustrated by the facts of *Re Birmingham*[52] where the deceased had entered a contract to buy a house paying part of the purchase price as a deposit. She died before completion of the sale but her estate included the equitable interest in the house, subject to a lien in favour of the vendor for the balance of the purchase money. In these circumstances it was held that the person entitled to the house under the deceased's will had to discharge the vendor's lien for the balance of the purchase money, but, the expenses incurred by the deceased's solicitors in completing the sale did not come within section 35(1) of the Administration of Estates Act, but were payable out of the deceased's residuary estate as an ordinary debt since the house was not charged with the payment of those expenses.[53]

10.9.7 It would seem from the case law that in order to pass with the property charged the charge must be specified, and an English textwriter has suggested that a general charge such as a banker's lien would not so

[49] See ante p. 284

[50] See *Re Turner* [1938] Ch. 593 and Parry and Clark "The Law of Succession" (8th ed. 1983) at p. 264

[51] [1948] 2 All E.R. 492

[52] [1959] Ch. 523. See Mellows (4th ed. 1983) at p. 434 and Parry and Clark (8th ed. 1983) at p.264

[53] *Ibid* at p. 265

pass.[54] Debts which pass with the property charged with their repayment include, however, payments due in respect of tax or duty exigible on property of the deceased and still outstanding on his death,[55] and, charges imposed by a court on the property of a judgment debtor.[56]

10.10 Contrary intention

10.10.1 We have seen that a contrary intention for the purposes of section 47(1) must be signified by words which expressly, or by necessary implication, refer to all or some part of the charge.[57] A contrary intention was found to arise, by implication, in the English case *Re Valpy*[58] where a direction to pay all the deceased's debts, except for a mortgage debt on a particular property, was held to show an intention that other mortgage debts should be paid out of the residuary estate.[59] If he intends that this should happen it is advisable for a testator to make absolutely clear in his will that a particular debt is to be paid out of the residuary estate.[60]

10.10.2 It might be expected that where the deceased had directed that debts should be paid out of a particular fund that would, without more, constitute a contrary intention within section 47(1). It has been held in England, however, that section 35(1) of the Administration of Estates Act is only excluded in such circumstances to the extent that the designated fund is adequate to satisfy the debts in question.[61]

10.11 Distribution of Assets

10.11.1 As we have seen, it is the duty of personal representatives to distribute the estate of the deceased amongst those entitled under his will or the rules on intestacy, after the payment of his debts and the discharge of all his other liabilities.[62] Before distributing the assets of the deceased the personal representatives are obliged, by section 49(1) of the Succession Act, to give such notices to creditors and others to send in their claims against the estate of the deceased as, in the opinion of the court in which the personal representatives are sought to be charged, would have been given by the court in an administration suit. At the expiration of the time

---

[54] See Mellows "The Law of Succession" (4th ed. 1983) at p.434
[55] See *Re Bowerman* [1908] 2 Ch. 340
[56] See *Re Anthony* [1892] I Ch. 450 and Parry and Clark at p.264
[57] Section 47(2). See *ante* p. 285
[58] [1906] 1 Ch. 531
[59] See Mellows at p.436
[60] *Ibid*
[61] See *Re Fegan* [1928] 1 Ch. 45
[62] See *ante* p. 279

named in the said notices, or the last of them, for sending in such claims, the personal representatives will be at liberty to distribute the assets of the deceased amongst the parties entitled thereto, having regard to the claims of which they then have notice.

10.11.2 A personal representative will not be liable to any person for the distribution of assets, or any part thereof, unless at the time of such distribution he had notice of that person's claim against the estate.[63] This provision in the Succession Act re-enacts section 29 of the Law of Property Amendment Act, 1859, otherwise Lord St Leonards Act.[64] Prior to that Act, personal representatives were under a strict obligation to pay the debts of the deceased and the absence of notice of any claim against the estate did not excuse them from satisfying the claim, if there were sufficient assets for that purpose. Section 29 of Lord St Leonards Act sought to mitigate this position by providing, that personal representatives when they had issued such notices to creditors as would be given by a court of competent jurisdiction in an administration suit, could distribute the deceased's assets without regard to any claims of which they had no notice.[65] The foregoing provision, however, did not apply in relation to real estate, an omission which has now been cured by section 49 of the Succession Act.

10.11.3 Nothing in section 49 is, however, to prejudice the right of any creditor or claimant to follow such assets into the hands of any person who may have received them.[66]

10.12 Time allowed for distribution

10.12.1 The personal representatives of a deceased person must distribute his estate as soon after his death as is reasonably practicable, having regard to the nature of the estate, the manner in which it is required to be distributed and all other relevant circumstances. Proceedings against personal representatives in respect of any failure to distribute the estate may not, without leave of the court, be brought within one year of the death of the deceased.[67] This is not to prejudice, however, the rights of creditors of a deceased person to bring proceedings against his personal representatives within one year of his death.[68]

10.12.2 The Succession Act thereby incorporates the long established rule

---

[63] Section 49(2)
[64] 22 & 23 Vict. c.35
[65] See the Explanatory Memorandum with the Succession Bill at p.4
[66] Section 49(3)
[67] Section 62 (1)
[68] Section 62 (2)

that personal representatives have one year from the death of the deceased in which to administer the estate and beneficiaries under a will may not initiate action against the executors until the end of the so-called executor's year.[69] There is nothing to prevent the personal representatives distributing the estate within the executor's year if they so choose and indeed failure to do so may leave them open to the charge that they have failed to administer the estate with due diligence. This is particularly the case with regard to payment of the deceased's debts, since failure to do will invariably mean that interest on the debt grows, and it may grow to a point where it threatens the interests of beneficiaries. Uthwatt J. pointed out in *Re Tankard*[70] that the duty of executors to pay debts of the deceased is owed not only to creditors "but also to beneficiaries, for the ultimate object of the administration of an estate is to place the beneficiaries in possession of their interest and that object cannot be fully achieved unless all debts are satisfied."[71] Uthwatt J. went on to say, that the circumstances of the particular case may justify a delay "but, if debts are not paid within the year, the onus is thrown on the executors to justify the delay."[72]

10.12.3 The court has jurisdiction to make an order directing the personal representatives to transfer land to the person entitled. Such jurisdiction may be exercised at any time after the expiration of one year from the death of an owner of land. If the personal representatives have failed to respond to the request of the person entitled, to transfer the land to such person, and the court, may if it thinks fit on the application of the person entitled, and after notice to the personal representatives make an order that such transfer be made.[73] If such order is not complied with within the time specified by the court the court may make a further order vesting the land in the person entitled as fully and effectually as might have been done by a transfer thereof by the personal representatives.[74]

10.12.4 Thus, a beneficiary who has failed to make the personal representatives transfer to him, by assent or otherwise, land to which he is entitled is not without legal redress on the expiry of one year from the death of the owner of the land. The quite separate question might arise however as to whether a beneficiary can institute proceedings against someone other than a personal representative to get in property to which he is entitled.

[69] See the Statute of Distributions (Ir.) 1695, s.4
[70] [1942] Ch. 69
[71] *Ibid* at p.72
[72] *Ibid* at p.73
[73] Section 52(4) of the Succession Act
[74] *Ibid*.

10.12.5 If an executor, after duly considering representations by a beneficiary under a will, declines to bring proceedings for the benefit of the estate which the beneficiary believes should be brought, does the beneficiary have *locus standi* to bring a suit in his own name? That very question recently came before Powell J. of the Equity Division of the Supreme Court of New South Wales in *Ramage* v *Waclaw*.[75] Powell J. was of the opinion that a beneficiary was entitled to sue in his own name only where the relief sought was within the equitable jurisdiction of the court, and then only when the circumstances were exceptional.[76] There is much to commend in the view taken by Powell J. and there is no reason to suppose that an Irish court would take a radically different one.

10.13 Assents

10.13.1 The usual way in which personal representatives transfer assets of a deceased person to those entitled under a will or on an intestacy is by a so-called "assent". As we shall see different rules apply to assents of realty and personality. Assents of personality are not affected by the general provisions governing assents and transfers by personal representatives which are contained in the Succession Act[77] and may, as before the Act, be made informally and without writing. Thus, an assent of personality may be made orally, or by the simple delivery or handing over of the property to the person entitled to it.[78] The personal representatives may make the assent expressly, by uttering some appropriate words when the property is handed over or, the assent may be implied from the conduct of the personal representatives. Whether or not an assent has been made in respect of personality is essentially a question of fact in each particular case.[79]

10.13.2 Assents of land, on the other hand, must be attended with rather more formality and made in accordance with the general provisions relating thereto in the Succession Act. Thus, an assent which is not in writing will not be effectual to pass any estate or interest in land.[80] The requirement of writing applies to assents of both legal and equitable interests in land, unlike the position obtaining in England, where a

---

[75] [1988] 12 N.S.W. L.R. 84

[76] See Starke in 1989 63 *Australian Law Journal* at pp. 51-52

[77] Secions 52-54

[78] See *Quinton* v *Frith* (1868) I.R. 2 Eq. 494; *Hunter* v *Hunter* (1870) I.R.3 C.L. 40; *McKinley* v *Kennedy* [1925] 1 I.R. 34 all noted in Wylie "Irish Land Law" (2nd ed. 1986) at p.783 n. 1

[79] See *Attenborough* v *Solomon* [1913] A.C. 76; *I.R.C.* v *Smith* [1930] 1 K.B. 713 and Parry and Clark "The Law of Succession" (8th ed. 1983) at p.359

[80] Section 52(5)

personal representative may assent orally or implicitly by conduct in the vesting of an equitable interest in land.[81]

10.13.3 Without prejudice to any other power conferred on them by the Succession Act in respect of any land of a deceased person, personal representatives may at any time after the death of the deceased execute an assent vesting any estate or interest in any such land in the person entitled thereto.[82]

10.13.4 The land of a deceased person in respect of which a personal representative may execute an assent is land to which such deceased person was entitled, or over which he exercised a general power of appointment by will.[83] A "person entitled" in relation to any estate or interest in land includes (i) the person or persons (including the personal representatives of the deceased or any of them) who (whether by devise, bequest, devolution or otherwise) may be beneficially entitled to that estate or interest, and (ii) the trustee or trustees or the personal representative or representatives of any such person or persons.[84]

10.13.5 An assent by the personal representatives vesting land in those entitled may be made subject to, or free from, a charge for the payment of any money which the personal representatives are liable to pay.[85] If an assent is made subject to such a charge all liabilities of the personal representatives in respect of the land shall cease, except as to any acts done or contracts entered into by them before the assent or transfer as the case may be.[86]

10.13.6 The statutory covenants which are implied where a person is expressed in a deed to convey as personal representative are also to be implied in any assent signed by a personal representative, unless the assent otherwise provides.[87] Various covenants are implied in different cases under section 7 of the Conveyancing Act 1881,[88] but it was necessary for the person in question to use the incorporating formula "as personal representative" since section 7 implied covenants according to the capacity

---

[81] See s.36(4) of the English Administration of Estates Act 1925 and *Re Edward W.T.* [1982] Ch. 30
[82] Section 52(2)
[83] Section 52(1) (a)
[84] Section 52(1) (b)
[85] Section 52(2)
[86] Section 52(3)
[87] Section 52(6)
[88] 44 & 45 Vict. c.41. See generally Wylie "Irish Conveyancing Law" (1978) at pp. 823 *et seq*

in which the grantor was expressed to convey the property.[89] There is now no need to employ such formula and, for example, a covenant for title is implied in any assent signed by a personal representative, unless the assent provides otherwise.[90]

10.13.7 Subject to section 20 of the Succession Act some or one only of several personal representatives cannot, without leave of the court, execute a valid assent or transfer of the deceased's land.[91] Section 20 provides, as we have seen, that where probate is granted to one or some of two or more persons named as executors, whether or not power is reserved to the other or others to prove, all the powers conferred on personal representatives may be exercised by the proving executor or executors and be as effectual as if all the persons named as executors had concurred therein.[92]

10.13.8 No stamp duty is payable in respect of an assent under section 52.[93]

10.13.9 The Succession Act contains special and separate provisions in respect of assents of unregistered and registered land.

10.14 Unregistered land

10.14.1 An assent to the vesting of any estate or interest in unregistered land of a deceased person in favour of the person entitled thereto must (a) be in writing, (b) be signed by the personal representatives, (c) be deemed, for the purposes of the Registration of Deeds Act, 1707, to be a conveyance of that estate or interest from the personal representatives to the person entitled, (d) operate, subject to the provisions of the Registration of Deeds Act, 1707, with respect to priorities, to vest that estate or interest in the person entitled subject to such charges and incumbrances, if any, as may be specified in the assent and as may otherwise affect that estate or interest, (e) subject to the provisions of the said Act of 1707, be deemed (unless a contrary intention appears therein) for all purposes necessary to establish the title of the person entitled to intervening rents and profits, to relate back to the death of the deceased but this is not to enable any person to establish a title inconsistent with the will of the deceased.[94]

---

[89] *Ibid* at p. 826

[90] *Ibid* at p. 828. Wylie points out that in any conveyance in which a person conveys, and is expressed to convey, "as personal representative" only one covenant is implied viz. a covenant against incumbrances. See "Irish Conveyancing Law" at pp. 827-8.

[91] Section 52(7)

[92] See *ante* p. 240

[93] Section 52(8)

[94] Section 53(1)

10.14.2 Any person in whose favour an assent or conveyance of any unregistered land is made by personal representatives may, at his own expense, require the personal representatives to register that assent or conveyance in the Registry of Deeds pursuant to the Registration of Deeds Act, 1707.[95] Registration of an assent under the act of 1707 is not compulsory but, as we have seen, an assent operates subject to the Act of 1707 with respect to priorities, and it is prudent for a person in whose favour an assent has been made to have it registered in order to protect its priority under the Act of 1707.

10.14.3 It is also now provided in the Succession Act, that an assent or conveyance of unregistered land by a personal representative will be conclusive evidence in favour of a purchaser, that the person in whose favour the assent or conveyance is made is the person who was entitled to have the estate or interest vested in him.[96] The foregoing provision will not otherwise prejudicially affect the claim of any person originally entitled to the estate or interest or to any mortgage or incumbrance thereon.[97]

10.14.4 A purchaser who buys land from a vendor who is a beneficiary is not therefore obliged to concern himself with the terms of the will or of the intestacy under which the vendor acquired the property, but need only see to it that the land was vested in the vendor by the personal representatives of the previous owner.[98] For that purpose the purchaser must inspect the relevant grant of representation and the vesting assent or transfer executed by the personal representatives.[99]

10.15 Registered land

10.15.1 It is provided in section 61(2) of the Registration of Title Act, 1964,[100] that on the death of a sole registered owner of land, or of the survivor of several registered full owners of land not being registered as tenants in common, the personal representatives of the deceased owner alone will be recognised by the Registrar as having any rights in respect of the land, and any registered dispositions by them shall have the same effect as if they were the registered owners of the land. Subsection (3) of section 61 of the Registration of Title Act is now substituted by section 54(2) of the Succession Act, which makes it clear that the will is no longer, in any

[95] Section 53(2)
[96] Section 53(3)
[97] *Ibid*
[98] See the Explanatory Memorandum with the Succession Bill at p.5 para. 31
[99] *Ibid*
[100] No. 16 of 1964

circumstances, a document of title to registered land, and that the Register of Titles has no responsibility for examining the will of a deceased owner in order to satisfy himself that its terms are being properly interpreted and implemented.[101] Production of an assent or transfer in the prescribed form suffices to enable the Registrar to register the person named in the assent or transfer as owner. The Registrar is not under any duty, nor shall he be entitled, to call for any information as to why any assent or transfer is, or was, made and is bound to assume that the personal representative is, or was, acting correctly and within his powers.[102]

10.16 Powers of sale by personal representatives

10.16.1 The personal representatives may sell the whole or any part of the estate of a deceased person for the purpose not only of paying debts, but also (whether or not there are debts) of distributing the estate among the persons entitled thereto. Before selling for the purposes of distribution the personal representatives shall, as far as practicable, give effect to the wishes of the persons of full age entitled to the property proposed to be sold or, in the case of dispute, of the majority (according to the value of their combined interests) of such persons.[103] However, a purchaser is not to be concerned to see that the personal representatives have complied with such wishes,[104] nor shall it be necessary, for any person entitled to such consultation, to concur in any such sale.[105]

10.16.2 As we have seen,[106] an executor derives his title from the will and can enter into a contract for sale on the death of the testator but cannot make title until probate is granted.[107] An administrator has no powers until a grant of representation has issued.[108]

10.16.3 As a general rule it shall not be lawful for some or one only of several personal representatives, without leave of the court, to exercise any power conferred by section 50, or section 60,[109] of the Succession Act. Again however this limitation is subject to section 20 which, as we have seen, allows proving executors to exercise their powers independently of named but non-proving executors.[110]

[101] See the Explanatory Memorandum with the Succession Act at p.5 para. 31
[102] 1964 Act s. 61(3) as substituted by s. 54(2) "(3) (c)" of the Succession Act.
[103] Section 50 (1) of the Succession Act
[104] Section 50 (1) (a)
[105] Section 50 (1) (b)
[106] See *ante* p. 233
[107] *Lynch* v *Harper* (1911) 43 I.L.T.R. 95
[108] See *ante* p. 233
[109] See *post* p. 305
[110] See *ante* p. 240

10.16.4 It is provided by section 50(3) of the Succession Act that, where land is settled by will and there are no trustees of the settlement, the personal representatives proving the will shall for all purposes be deemed to be trustees of the settlement until trustees of the settlement are appointed, but a sole personal representative shall not be deemed to be a trustee for the purposes of the Settled Land Acts, 1882 to 1890, until at least one other trustee is appointed. It has been argued, with respect to an identical provision in Northern Ireland legislation,[111] that it is apparent, especially from the phrase "for all purposes" that the personal representatives can make the appointment of trustees of the settlement, including appointment of themselves.[112]

10.16.5 A testator may of course give in his will, either expressly or by implication, much wider powers of sale to his personal representatives than those conferred on them by section 50 of the Succession Act. Indeed, a testator may impose a duty on his personal representatives to convert the property and, as we saw earlier, the equitable doctrine of conversion was evolved by the courts in order to ensure that effect was given to the testator's intention.[113]

10.17 Protection of purchases

10.17.1 A purchaser from the personal representatives of a deceased person of any property, being the whole or any part of the estate of the deceased, is entitled to hold that property freed and discharged from any debts or liabilities of the deceased, except such as are charged otherwise than by his will, and from all claims of persons entitled to shares in the estate, and such purchasers are not to be concerned to see to the application of the purchase money.[114]

10.17.2 Protection is also afforded to a person who buys property, other than property the ownership of which is registered under the Registration of Title Act 1964,[115] from a person to whom it has been transferred by the personal representatives of the deceased owner. Such a purchaser is entitled to hold the property freed and discharged from the claims of creditors of the deceased, and from any claims by persons entitled to shares

---

[111] See s.40(5) of the Administration of Estates Act (N.I.) 1955
[112] See Wylie "Irish Land Law" (2nd ed. 1986) at pp.429-30 and Leitch "Handbook on the Administration of Estates Act (N.I.) 1955" (1956) at p.123
[113] See *ante* p. 181 See also *Carlisle* v *Cooke* [1905] 1 I.R. 269; *Re Robinson* [1912] 1 I.R. 410; *Re Waldron* [1956] I.R. 315
[114] Section 51 (1)
[115] Section 51 (2)(a)

in the deceased's estate.[116] Such purchaser is therefore not under any obligation to satisfy himself that the person from whom he is buying the property is, in fact, the person who was entitled to receive it on the death of the previous owner.

10.17.3 It is to be remembered that "purchaser" is defined in the Succession Act to mean a person who acquires property in good faith and for "valuable consideration", which means consideration in money or money's worth.[117] Accordingly, if a purchaser colludes with the personal representatives to obtain property at an undervalue the sale will be set aside.[118]

10.17.4 As we have seen, a conveyance by personal representatives remains valid despite a subsequent revocation or variation of the grant of probate or letters of administration.[119] The protection given to purchasers by section 51 applies whether the deceased died before or after the commencement of the Succession Act.[120]

10.17.5 Despite the clear and unqualified language of section 51 a technical problem has re-emerged which threatens to undermine the protection afforded to purchasers by that section. Given that a personal representative's authority to sell derived from his duty to administer the estate of the deceased, a lot came to depend on whether a purchaser was justified in presuming that a sale to him by a personal representative was in due course of administration. The Irish and English courts were to take different views of the effect of the passage of time between the death of the owner and the sale by personal representatives on that presumption. The English courts took the view that a purchaser was entitled to presume that a sale was made in due course of administration, even if twenty years or more had elapsed since the death of the deceased.[121]

10.17.6 The Irish Court of Appeal, however, in *Molyneux* v *White*[122] held, that an executor could not give a good title to a purchaser without proof that there were unpaid debts, when thirty-seven years had elapsed between the date of death and the sale since, at the expiry of twenty years from the death of the deceased there was a presumption that all of the deceased's debts had been paid.

[116] Section 51 (2)(b)
[117] Section 3(1)
[118] *Boothman* v *Brown* (1901) 1 N.I.J.R. 41
[119] Sec. s. 25 of the Succession Act and *ante* p. 248
[120] Section 51(3)
[121] *Re Whistler* (1887) 35 Ch.D. 561; *Venn and Furze's Contract* [1894] 2 Ch. 101; Cf. *Verell's Contract* [1903] 1 Ch. 65
[122] (1894)13 L.R. Ir. 382

10.17.7 It might reasonably have been thought from the wide and unqualified language of section 51 that it was not intended by the legislators that the protection afforded to purchasers would be affected by the passage of time before the death and the sale. Indeed Kenny J. in *Shiels* v *Flynn*,[123] having pointed out that the correctness of the view in *Molyneux* v *White* was reinforced by the decision of Cusack Smith M.R. in *Bradley* v *Flood*,[124] went on to say that one of the effects of the Administration of Estates Act, 1959, and the Succession Act, 1965, is that in the case of persons who died on or after the 1st June, 1959, this is no longer the law.

10.17.8 The waters have been muddied however by the decision of Barron J. in *Crowley* v *Flynn*.[125] There the testatrix had died in May 1946 having bequeathed certain leasehold property to her executor and trustee on trust for sale. A grant of probate was obtained in July 1946. The executor died in August 1978 and letters of administration *de bonis non* were obtained by the testatrix's two daughters in March 1981. Following a contract for sale of the leasehold interest dated 7th August 1979, the purchaser refused to accept title from the administrices *de bonis non* submitting (i) that no power of sale had been shown to exist because no reason had been given for the exercise of such power by the personal representatives after a lapse of thirty three years, and (ii) that the delay had been such that an assent to the establishment of the will trust should be inferred.

10.17.9 The vendor replied that (i) an executor is always entitled to sell for the purposes of distribution of the assets among the beneficiaries, and (ii) that a purchaser would, in any event, be protected by section 51 of the Succession Act.

10.17.10 Barron J. in the course of his judgment referred to *Molyneux* v *White* as authority for the proposition that, where there has been a lapse of at least twenty years from the date of death, a purchaser is put on enquiry as to the reasons for the sale. The learned judge referred to *Somers* v *Weir*[126] in which the Supreme Court held the word "purchaser" in the Family Home Protection Act 1976, to mean somebody who acquired property in good faith, which puts such person on notice of all matters which would have come to the knowledge of the purchaser's solicitor if such enquiries had been made which ought reasonably to have been made. Barron J. pointed out that the word "purchaser" is defined in the same terms in the Succession Act and he could find nothing in section 51 nor in section 19 of the Administration of Estates Act 1959, which section 51

---

[123] [1975] I.R. 296. See Wylie "A Casebook on Irish Land Law" at p. 540
[124] (1864) 16 Ir. Ch. R. 236
[125] [1983] I.L.R.M. 513
[126] [1979] I.R. 94

replaces, which suggests that a purchaser is never to be put upon enquiry. It followed that

> "if more than twenty years had elapsed since the death of the testator, there is nothing in the section to negative the rule in *Molyneux* v *White*, so that a purchaser is still put on notice to enquire the reason for the sale, and if he fails to make such enquiry is bound with notice of what he would have discovered."[127]

10.17.11 With the greatest respect to Barron J. his interpretation is at odds with the rationale of section 51. It is interesting and revealing that Barron J. came to the conclusion that the instant sale was not to provide for the payment of debts of the deceased, nor in so far as it was for the distribution of the assets among the beneficiaries, was it something which the executor was required to do. His duty was to transfer the assets to the will trustee, albeit himself, and on this basis there was no ground for the exercise of a power of sale by the personal representatives.[128] Of course, these are all matters which the purchaser is spared the need to enquire into by the express language of section 51.

10.17.12 Barron J., rather surprisingly, made no reference to Kenny J.'s judgment in *Sheils* v *Flynn*, but a more serious omission is the absence of any reference to section 61 of the Succession Act which states, in blunt and unequivocal terms, that a "purchaser from personal representatives shall be entitled to assume that the personal representatives are acting correctly and within their powers".

10.17.3 A question arose as to whether it was reasonable or necessary to enquire into the position in relation to the Family Home Protection Act 1976 in respect of the occupation of a premises by non conveying beneficiaries on a sale by a personal representative. This question was considered by the Conveyancing Committee of the Incorporated Law Society which initially came to the conclusion that a purchaser from a personal representative *qua* personal representative should not be concerned with the Family Home Protection Act in relation to that particular assurance. It would be quite different however if an assent had been executed and the sale was by a beneficiary as beneficial owner.[128a]

10.17.4 This recommendation of the Conveyancing Committee did not apparently receive widespread acceptance, and the Committee became concerned that it was too simplistic, particularly where a personal

[127] [1983] I.L.R.M. 513, 515
[128] *Ibid*
[128a] See I.L.S.I. Gazette December 1980 at p. 233

representative was selling quite a number of years after a death. The Committee having taken Senior Counsel's advice was satisfied that only guidelines could be given and that each case must ultimately turn on its facts.[128b] Those guidelines indicate that where there is no evidence to suggest that the personal representative and his or her spouse have resided in the property no consent should be sought, though a Declaration confirming the non residency should be sought from the personal representatives.

10.17.5 Where there is some evidence that the personal representative and/or his or her spouse resided in the property for a short period for example while caring for the deceased during illness, but there is evidence to show that the personal representative's family home is elsewhere, again no consent should be sought, though a Declaration confirming the location of the personal representative's family home should be obtained.

10.17.6 Where the personal representative and his or her spouse have lived in the property and there is no evidence to suggest that their family home is elsewhere it would be reasonable to seek the consent of the spouse and this would apply particularly where the personal representative or his or her spouse are beneficially entitled under the will or intestacy to the property.

10.18 Appropriation

10.18.1 Personal representatives have wide powers under section 55 of the Succession Act to appropriate any part of the estate of a deceased person in its actual condition or state of investment at the time of appropriation in or towards satisfaction of any share in the estate, whether settled or not, according to the respective rights of the persons interested in the estate.[129]

10.18.2 An appropriation, other than one of the deceased's dwelling and household chattels for the surviving spouse under section 56,[130] may not be made where it would affect prejudicially any specific devise or bequest.[131] Nor may the personal representatives make an appropriation, with the exception of a case to which section 56 applies, unless notice of the intended appropriation has been served on all parties entitled to a share in the estate (other than persons who may come into existence after the time of the appropriation or who cannot, after reasonable enquiry, be found or ascertained at that time).[132]

[128b] See I.L.S.I. Gazette December 1980 at p. 71
[129] Section 55 (1)
[130] See *ante* p. 191
[131] Section 55 (2)
[132] Section 55 (3)

10.18.3 A party so notified may, within six weeks from the service of such notice, apply to the court to prohibit the appropriation.[133]

10.18.4 Consent to an appropriation must also be obtained from a person absolutely and beneficially entitled in possession to the property in question[134] and, when made in respect of any settled share, the consent of either the trustee thereof, if any (not being also the personal representative), or the person who may for the time being be entitled to the income.[135]

10.18.5 Unless the court, on an application by a person who, when notified of the appropriation seeks to prohibit it, otherwise directs, an appropriation binds all parties interested in the property of the deceased whose consent is not made requisite.[136] However, in making an appropriation the personal representatives must have regard to the rights of any person who may be born thereafter or who cannot, after reasonable enquiry, be found or ascertained at the time of appropriation, and, of any other person whose consent is not required by section 55.[137]

10.18.6 The intention of the testator remains paramount and he may confer wider powers of appropriation on his personal representatives in his will. Where an appropriation is made under section 55 in respect of a settled share, the property appropriated remains subject to all trusts for sale and powers of leasing, disposition and management which would have been applicable thereto had the appropriation not taken place.[138]

10.18.7 Any property which is duly appropriated under section 55 is to be treated thereafter as an authorised investment and may be retained or dealt with accordingly.[139] Where any property is appropriated under section 55 a conveyance thereof by the personal representatives to the person to whom it is appropriated shall not, by reason only that the property so conveyed is accepted by such person in or towards the satisfaction of a legacy or a share in residuary estate, be liable to any higher stamp duty than that payable on a transfer of personal property for the like purpose.[140]

---

[133] *Ibid*
[134] Section 55 (4)(a)
[135] Section 55 (4)(b)
[136] Section 55 (11)
[137] Section 55 (12)
[138] Section 55 (13)
[139] Section 55 (9)
[140] Section 55 (17) See McGuire and Pearce "The Succession Act 1965: A Commentary" at p.135

10.18.8 If, after property has been appropriated to a person under section 55, such person disposes of it or any interest therein, then, in favour of the purchaser from such person the appropriation is deemed to have been made in accordance with the requirements of section 55.[141]

10.18.9 The supervisory jurisdiction of the court in relation to the exercise by personal representatives of their power of appropriation under section 55 was considered by the Supreme Court in *H* v *O*.[142] We saw earlier that when the plaintiff's request for an order under section 56 was refused by the High Court in *H* v *H*[143] she commenced an action in the High Court, claiming the same division and conveyance by the executor in exercise of his general powers of appropriation under section 55 of the Succession Act.[144] McWilliam J. held that the provisions of section 55 empowered the personal representative of the testator's estate to divide the lands in the manner suggested by the plaintiff and to convey to her, in satisfaction *pro tanto* of her claims to the estate, the part of the lands desired by her. The case was taken on appeal to the Supreme Court.

10.18.10 Henchy J. pointed out that section 55 allows the personal representatives, subject to the provisions of the section, to appropriate any part of the estate in its actual condition at the time of appropriation in or towards satisfaction of a share. Henchy J. went on:

"While the right conferred by section 56 is a right conferred on a surviving spouse, the right conferred by section 55 is exercisable only by the personal representatives and is not confined to the share of a surviving spouse. When the plaintiff, as the surviving spouse who was entitled to a one-half share as her legal right, sought in the present action to get an order directing the first defendant to appropriate the part of the lands on which the dwelling is situate towards the satisfaction of her share, she was seeking to assert a right to which she was not entitled under section 55. The right of appropriation given by section 55 is an enabling right which may be exercised only by the personal representative. A person entitled to a share is given no right to compel the personal representative to propose an appropriation under section 55. The first defendant, as personal representative, has not chosen to operate the section so, strictly speaking, the plaintiff was misconceived in her efforts to compel him to do so."[145]

---

[141] Section 55 (4)
[142] [1978] I.R. 194. See Wylie "A Casebook on Irish Land Law" at p. 529
[143] [1978] I.R. 138. See Wylie "A Casebook on Irish Land Law" at p.526
[144] See *ante* p. 196
[145] [1978] I.R. 194, 205

10.18.11 The first defendant did not seem to Henchy J. to have served any document or delivered any pleadings which would be said to be a compliance with section 55(3), but, since counsel for the first defendant had raised no objection to his being deemed to have served the necessary notice, and as all the interested parties were before the court and had not claimed to be prejudiced in any way by want of notice, Henchy J. proposed to deal with the matter on the footing that the first defendant, as personal representative, was willing to operate section 55 and that the statutory preconditions as to notice had been complied with. The learned judge was prepared to do so particularly because no appeal had been taken by any party against the ruling of McWilliam J. in this respect, and also because a dismissal of the action on that ground would probably have the effect of burdening the estate with yet another High Court action.[146]

10.18.12 Henchy J. wished to stress however that a beneficiary is not given any right to compel a personal representative to exercise a power of appropriation under section 55, and it was only because of the special circumstances to which he had referred that the personal representatives in the instant case were being treated as having taken the necessary steps for an appropriation under section 55.[147]

10.18.13 Henchy J. went on to consider the nature of the court's jurisdiction in relation to the exercise by personal representatives of their power of appropriation, pointing out that such jurisdiction is only acquired by the court when a party, on being served with notice of an intended appropriation, applies within six weeks to the court to prohibit the appropriation.[148] Henchy J. went on:

> "The section is silent as to how the court is to exercise its jurisdiction, which is essentially supervisory and prohibitive. So it must be assumed, having regard to the tenor, the scope and the purpose of the section, that the court should prohibit an intended appropriation only (a) when the conditions in the section have not been complied with; or (b) when, notwithstanding such compliance, it would not be just or equitable to allow the appropriation to take place, having regard to the rights of all persons who are or will become entitled to an interest in the estate; or (c) when, apart from the section, the appropriation would not be legally permissible. Since the personal representatives hold the estate under section 10(3) as trustees for the persons by law entitled thereto, the exercise of the statutory discretion to appropriate must be viewed as an

---

[146] *Ibid*
[147] *Ibid*
[148] *Ibid* at pp. 206, 207

incident of the trusteeship, so that it is the court's duty to prohibit the appropriation if it is calculated to operate unjustly or inequitably by unduly benefitting one beneficiary at the expense of another. But otherwise, where the conditions of the section have been observed and the personal representatives have made a *bona fide* decision to appropriate, the exercise of their discretion to appropriate should not be interfered with unless for some reason unrelated to the terms of the section the appropriation would be legally unacceptable, for example, if it would amount to a sub-division prohibited by law."[149]

10.19 Infant's property

10.19.1 Where an infant is entitled to any share in the estate of a deceased person and there are no trustees of such share able and willing to act, the personal representatives of the deceased may appoint a trust corporation or any two or more persons (including any of the personal representatives or a trust corporation) to be trustees of such share and may vest the share in the trustees so appointed.[150] In default of appointment the personal representatives will be trustees of such share.[151]

10.19.2 When trustees are appointed and the property which is subject to the infant's share is vested in them, the personal representatives, as such, are discharged from all further liability in respect of the property vested in the trustees so appointed.[152] Property vested in such trustees may be retained in its existing condition or state of investment or may be re-invested in authorised securities with power, at the trustees' discretion, to change such investments for others so authorised.[153]

10.19.3 Where an infant becomes entitled to any estate or interest in land on intestacy and consequently there is no instrument under which the estate of the infant arises or is acquired, such estate or interest is deemed to be the subject of a settlement for the purposes of the Settled Land Acts 1882 to 1890, and the persons appointed trustees under section 57 are deemed to be trustees of that settlement.[153a] Trustees so appointed under section 57 are also deemed to be trustees for the purposes of sections 42 and 43 of the Conveyancing Act, 1881,[154] which confer wide powers of management on trustees during an infant's minority, including that to

[149] *Ibid* at pp. 206-7
[150] Section 57 (1)
[151] *Ibid*
[152] Section 57 (2)
[153] Section 58 (1)
[153a] Section 58 (2)
[154] 44 & 45 Vict. c. 41

apply income for the maintenance, education or benefit of the infant. Without prejudice to the powers under the aforementioned sections 42 and 43 trustees appointed under section 57 may, at any time, apply the capital of any share to which an infant is entitled for the advancement or benefit of the infant in any manner which the trustees, in their absolute discretion, think fit.[155] The trustees may, in particular, carry on any business in which the infant is entitled to a share.[156]

10.20 Powers to deal with estate

10.20.1 (a) Leases. A personal representative's power to grant leases was regarded by the courts as being incidental to, and dependant upon, his duty to administer the estate of a deceased person and a lessee would have to establish that his lease was granted for purposes of administration.[157] There were few cases where a lease could be granted by personal representatives other than for purposes of administration one of which was, where a lease was granted in pursuance of a contract which had been entered into by the deceased before his death.[158]

10.20.2 The powers of personal representatives to deal with the estates of deceased persons have been widened considerably by the Succession Act, section 60 of which provides, that the personal representatives of a deceased owner of land may make such leases of the land as may be reasonably necessary for the due administration of the estate of the deceased owner.[159] The courts have long accepted that due administration may require personal representatives to grant leases of business in order to protect the value of the business during the course of administration but, they have not favoured protracted involvement by personal representatives unless it had been expressly provided for by the testator.[160] The wishes of the testator remain paramount and the powers conferred on personal representatives by section 60 are to be exercised subject to any provisions in the will with respect to the disposal of the testator s estate.[161]

---

[155] Section 58 (5)

[156] *Ibid*

[157] *Drohan* v *Drohan* (1809) 1 Ba & B. 185; *Keating* v *Keating* (1835) Ll. & G. *temp* Sug. 113; *Hackett* v *Macnamara* (1836) Ll. & G. *temp.* Plunk. 203, and see Wylie "Irish Land Law" (2nd ed. 1986) at p. 789

[158] *Re O'Leary* [1961] Ir. Jur. Rep. 45. See now s.60(4) of the Succession Act

[159] Section 60 (1)(a)

[160] See *Perry* v *Perry* (1869) I.R. 3 Eq. 452; *Re Hodges* [1899] 1 I.R. 480; *Boylan* v *Fay* (1882) 8 L.R. Ir. 374; *Re Hickey* (1891) 27 L.R. Ir. 65 and *National Bank* v *Hamrock* (1928) 62 I.L.T.R. 165

[161] Section 60 (9)

10.20.3 Personal representatives may also, with the consent of the beneficiaries or the approval of the court, grant leases of the land for such term and on such conditions as they think proper.[162] Where the land of the deceased is already subject to a fee farm grant or a lease, the personal representatives may make, on such terms and conditions as they think proper, a sub-fee farm grant of the land, or a sub-lease thereof with a nominal reversion, where such sub-fee farm grant or sub-lease amounts in substance to a sale and the personal representatives have satisfied themselves that it is the most appropriate method of disposing of the land in the course of administering the estate.[163] Where personal representatives grant or lease any land in pursuance of the foregoing power they may sell any rent reserved on such grant or any reversion expectant upon the determination of any such lease.[164]

10.20.4 (b) Mortgages and charges. The personal representatives of a deceased person may from time to time raise money by way of mortgage or charge for the payment of expenses, debts and liabilities and any legal right of the surviving spouse.[165] They may also raise money with the approval of all the beneficiaries being *sui juris* or the court (but not otherwise) for the erection, repair, improvement or completion of buildings, or the improvement of lands forming part of the estate of the deceased.[166]

10.20.5 (c) Distress. The personal representatives of a deceased person may distrain upon land for arrears of rent due or accruing to the deceased, as the deceased might have done had he been living.[167] Such arrears may be distrained for after the termination of the lease or tenancy as if the term or interest had not determined if the distress is made (a) within six months after the termination of the lease or tenancy, or (b) during the continuance of the possession of the lessee or tenant from whom the arrears are due.[168]

---

[162] Section 60 (1)(b)

[163] Section 6) (1)(c). The making of a sub-lease or sub-grant which was in substance a sale was also an exception to the rule that a lease had to be made for purposes of administration. See *Re Braithwaite's Settled Estate* [1922] 1 I.R.71; *Re Clark's W.T.* [1920] 1 I.R. 47 and Wylie "Irish Land Law" (2nd ed. 1986) at pp. 445 *et seq.*

[164] Section 60 (1)

[165] See *ante* p 191

[166] Section 60 (3)

[167] Section 60 (5)

[168] Section 60 (6)

10.20.6 The Succession Act also includes a new provision to the effect that personal representatives may distrain for arrears of a rentcharge due, or accruing, to the defendant in his lifetime on the land affected or charged therewith as the deceased might have done had he been living, so long as the land remains in the possession of the person liable to pay the rentcharge or of persons deriving title under him.[169]

10.21 Settlement of claims

10.21.1 Personal representatives have now been given somewhat wider powers to settle claims and disputes concerning the estate of a deceased person than they had under section 21 of the Trustee Act, 1893.[170] In the exercise of these powers personal representatives may enter into such agreements or arrangements, and execute such documents as seem expedient without being personally liable for any loss occasioned by any act or thing so done by them in good faith.[171]

10.21.2 Such powers include, the payment or allowance of any debt or claim on any evidence the personal representative may reasonably deem sufficient,[172] the acceptance of any composition or security for any debt or property claimed,[173] or the allowance of time for the payment of any debt.[174] The personal representatives also have the power to compromise, compound, abandon, submit to arbitration, or otherwise settle, any debt, account, dispute, claim or other matter relating to the estate of the deceased.[175]

10.21.3 It is to be remembered that the personal representatives of a deceased person may sue and be sued in respect of all causes if action, which, by virtue of Part 11 of the Civil Liability Act, 1961,[176] survive for the benefit of, or against, the estate of the deceased.[177] The rule relating to the survival of actions on death is subject to the provisions of the Civil Liability Act which exclude from the operation of the rule certain actions such as those for breach of promise to marry, criminal conversation and action for defamation.[178] It is also provided in section 9(2) of the Civil

[169] Section 60 (7)
[170] c. 53
[171] Section 60 (8)
[172] Section 60 (8)(b)
[173] Section 60 (8)(c)
[174] Section 60 (8) (d)
[175] Section 60 (8)(e)
[176] No. 41 of 1961
[177] Section 48 of the Succession Act
[178] See s. 6 of the Civil Liability Act, 1961

Liability Act that no proceedings which have survived against the estate of a deceased person shall be maintainable unless proceedings were instituted within the relevant period fixed by the Statute of Limitations, 1957,[179] and were pending at the date of death, or were commenced within the relevant period of limitation or within two years after the death of the deceased, whichever period first expired.[180]

10.22 Right to follow property

10.22.1 The creditors of a deceased person may follow his property into the hands of beneficiaries to whom it has been distributed by the personal representatives. Thus it is provided by section 59(1) of the Succession Act that, so long as property which has been conveyed by personal representatives to any person, other than a purchaser, remains vested in such person, or any person claiming through him not being a purchaser, such property remains liable to answer the debts of the deceased, and any share in the estate to which it was liable when vested in the personal representatives.

10.22.2 Where a person to whom the personal representatives have conveyed property, not being a purchaser or anyone claiming through such person, sells or mortgages the property such seller or mortgagor continues to be personally liable for such debts and for any share in the estate to the extent to which the property was liable when vested in the personal representatives.[181]

10.22.3 We saw earlier that a creditor, legatee or next-of-kin of a deceased person who has not been paid is not limited to a claim against the personal representatives.[182] He can also invoke the remedy of tracing to recover money to which he is entitled from anyone who has been wrongly paid such money, and the House of Lords held in *Ministry of Health* v *Simpson*[183] that the right to recover was enforceable against a payee who was an innocent volunteer and to whom the payment had been made by a pesonal representative under a mistake of law.[184]

---

[179] No. 6 of 1957

[180] See *Moynihan v Greensmych* [1977] I.R. 55 where the constitutionality of s. 9 was upheld by the Supreme Court. See Brady and Kerr "The Limitation of Actions in the Republic of Ireland" (1984) at pp. 22 *et seq.*

[181] Section 59 (2)

[182] See *ante* p. 289

[183] [1951] A.C. 251

[184] See generally Keane "Equity" and the Law of Trusts in the Republic of Ireland" at pp. 279 *et seq.* and Hanbury and Maudsley "Modern Equity" (12 ed.) at pp. 636 *et seq.*

10.23 Personal Representatives and the Statute of Limitations

10.23.1 The period of limitation in respect of any claim to the personal estate of a deceased person, or to any share or interest in such estate was contained in section 45(1) of the Statute of Limitations, 1957, which provided that such claim had to be brought within twelve years from the accrual of the right to receive the share or interest. Section 45 was amended by section 126 of the Succession Act, which reduced the period of limitation from twelve years to six years.

10.23.2 McMahon J. was later to point out in *Drohan* v *Drohan*[185] that section 45(1), in neither its original nor amended form, had any application to an action *by* a personal representative to recover assets of the deceased from a person holding adversely to the estate but applied only to actions *against* personal representatives by those entitled to shares in the estate. The period of limitation in respect of an action by personal representatives to recover land belonging to the deceased was that in section 13(2) of the Statute of Limitations, 1957 viz. twelve years from the date of accrual of the action. McMahon J.'s observations in *Drohan* v *Drohan* on section 45(1) rank as *obiter dicta* but are perfectly consistent with the language of section 45(1), which refers to claims against the estate of a deceased person whether under a will or an intestacy.

10.23.3 The obvious question which is posed by McMahon J.'s obiter dicta is whether a personal representative who recovers land belonging to the deceased's estate within twelve years of the accrual of the right of action, but more than six years after the death of the deceased, can vest such land in those otherwise entitled but who are statute barred. The implications of such a course of action for the policy reasons undergirding the Statute of Limitations are serious, and particularly so when the facts of a case reveal that a personal representative is acting at the behest of next-of-kin of the deceased who are statute barred.

10.23.4 Such was the case in *Gleeson* v *Feehan* and *Gleeson* v *Purcell*[186] the facts of which, as agreed, revealed that the plaintiff had taken out letters of administration to the deceased's estate at the behest of next-of-kin of the deceased who lived in the United States. The fact that the personal representative was acting as attorney for next-of-kin, who were statute barred, led Judge Sheridan to the unavoidable conclusion that it would defeat the purpose of section 45(1), as amended, if the deceased's personal

---

[185] [1984] I.R. 311
[186] (1985) 3 I.L.T.R. 102

representative could acquire assets of the deceased and vest them in next-of-kin outside the six year limitation period.

10.23.5 Judge Sheridan sought to avoid that consequence by holding that McMahon J.'s *obiter dicta* in *Drohan* were referrable to the position prior to the Succession Act, and, "that by reason of the new section 45(1) as distinct from the old section which did not affect real property, the claims of the next-of- kin were barred after the lapse of six years from Edmund's death."[187] With respect to Judge Sheridan McMahon J.'s *obiter dicta* in *Drohan* is equally applicable to the new section 45(1) which, like the old section, refers only to *actions* in respect of claims to the estate of a deceased person whether under a will or intestacy. Judge Sheridan was on firmer ground however, when he cited the well established rule, that a subsequent issue of representation does not revive statute barred assets and the next-of-kin's entitlement to a grant, either by themselves or through their attorney, depended upon their entitlement to the assets which entitlement had ceased under section 45(1) at the time of the grant and certainly at the commencement of the instant proceedings.

10.23.6 If however the personal representative could recover the assets of the deceased under section 13(2) of the Statute of Limitations, it would, in Judge Sheridan's view, be defeating the scheme and purpose of section 45(1) if he could vest them in next-of-kin who were statute barred and oust the persons in possession. Judge Sheridan concluded that this result would be absurd and in his view the personal representative would acquire such title, if any, as quasi-trustee in favour of the persons in possession who had acquired the lands for value from one Jimmy Dwyer who had held the lands for six years so as to bar the next-of-kin.[188]

10.23.7 It is regrettable that judges are obliged to indulge in a form of intellectual gymnastics, such as the discovery of a quasi-trust, in order to achieve an equitable result in the circumstances of the particular case. McMahon J.'s *obiter dicta* in *Drohan* may well be defensible in the light of the language used in section 45(1) before and after its amendment by section 126 of the Succession Act, but they have far reaching ramifications which necessitate urgent amending legislation. The writer is aware that the Law Reform Commission has the matter under consideration.

---

[187] *Ibid* at p. 104
[188] *Ibid* See "A Limitations Conundrum" in I.L.S.I. Gazette Jan./Feb. 1986 at pp. 21-25

Index

313